CHARMAN · PETERSEN · GOVENDER

TOWNSHIP ECONOMY
PEOPLE, SPACES AND PRACTICES

Supported by:

UNIVERSITEIT VAN PRETORIA
UNIVERSITY OF PRETORIA
YUNIBESITHI YA PRETORIA

DST-NRF
Centre of Excellence
in Food Security

HSRC
PRESS

Published by HSRC Press
Private Bag X9182, Cape Town 8000, South Africa
www.hsrcpress.ac.za

First published 2020

ISBN (soft cover) 978-0-7969-2577-0
ISBN (pdf) 978-0-7969-2578-7

Copy-edited by Jacqueline Baumgardt
Typeset by Laura Brecher
Cover design by Riaan Wilmans
Printed by Novus Print , a division of Novus Holdings

Distributed in Africa by Blue Weaver
Tel: +27 (0) 21 701 4477 | Fax Local: +27 (0) 21 701 7302 | Fax International: 0927865242139
www.blueweaver.co.za

Distributed in Europe and the United Kingdom by Eurospan Distribution Services (EDS)
Tel: +44 (0) 17 6760 4972 | Fax: +44 (0) 17 6760 1640
www.eurospanbookstore.com

Distributed in United States, Canada and Asia except China, Lynne Rienner Publishers, Inc.
Tel: +1 303 444-6684 | Fax: +001 303 444-0824 | Email: cservice@rienner.com
www.rienner.com

Suggested citation: Charman A, Petersen L and Govender T (2020) *Township Economy: People,
Spaces and Practices*. Cape Town: HSRC Press

Township Economy Endorsements

This powerful and insightful book is a must-read for policy makers, researchers and anyone else seeking to understand township economies in South Africa. The book is rich in empirical detail collected using innovative approaches and research methods, and informed by cutting-edge theories. These enable key insights into complex and multi-layered realities not found in other research on the informal urban economy. The book provides a unique and nuanced analysis of the extraction of value from townships by powerful outsiders, including corporates, and explores the wider significance of these and other findings with admirable rigour. Its analysis of possible policy stances and interventions is exemplary in its subtlety, yet clarity. *A tour de force!*

Ben Cousins, DST/NRF Chair in Poverty, Land and Agrarian Studies and Senior Professor, School of Government, University of the Western Cape

Township Economy is written from the transdisciplinary perspectives of practitioners engaging in the micro-enterprises that make up much of the livelihoods in 'townships' in South Africa. This book is an utterly compelling labyrinth of ideas, images and mappings that evokes the complexity and vitality of economic life in peripheralised urban spaces. It is a must-read for planners, architects, policy makers, academics and students, and its rich visual format brings to life the miscellaneous nature of street transactions.

Suzanne Hall, Director of the Cities Programme, London School of Economics and Political Science

Township Economy is an extensive compilation of research on informal micro-enterprises. Townships were not designed to sustain independent economic life; and they are often now thought of as dormitory suburbs for the working poor. This book reveals their economic dynamism today. It documents the proliferating variety of its subjects. Businesses are located firmly in place, their main sectors (food, transport etc.) discussed separately and comparatively. Yet the authors also reach some striking general conclusions. Plentiful visual material and personal stories illuminate the denser empirical sections. This will be a standard work of reference for researchers and administrators – and an eye-opening read for anyone interested in South Africa's struggling democracy.

Keith Hart, Writer Paris

Our understanding of the economy is shaped very much but which part of the economy is seen in our models and which remains unseen. The informal economy is an important and growing part of our economies that remains largely unseen. This timely and thought provoking book brings into the purview of academics and policymakers a key part of the modern, capitalist economy. It takes an unusual approach which draws on area case studies, anecdotes of actual businesses, and a range of visual sources, including diagrams, drawings, enterprise maps and photographs. The analysis is firmly grounded in a spatial perspective. The authors show how different places, buildings and even objects shape opportunities for conducting business. Where much prior scholarship see informal businesses in passive terms, accepting market conditions, the book reveals the importance of power relations and local business strategies. *Township Economy* is likely to prove to be an indispensable contribution to comprehending South Africa's informal economy.

Imraan Valodia, Dean, Faculty of Commerce, Law & Management, University of the Witwatersrand

Contents

List of figures

List of tables

Acknowledgements

The authors acknowledge the support of numerous individuals in the preparation of the manuscript and publication of the book. We wish to thank the Sustainable Livelihoods Foundation for permitting us to draw upon and utilise the research data, visual material and other outputs produced in the course of a series of projects. In this respect, we recognise the important field research contributions of Rory Lieberman and Anthony Muteti. We thank the curious and dedicated members of our team, current and past, that have so generously added their unique contributions to this book. We are grateful to Justin Patrick for taking the studio photographs; Teresa Legg for conducting the geospatial analysis and producing the maps; and for Tova Lubinsky for the graphic design and developing the layout concept.

The framing of our arguments and presentation of the research findings benefited from two anonymous reviewers whose comments were very helpful. We thank Laurence Piper for his insightful, thorough and encouraging advice. At the HSRC, we gratefully appreciate the efforts of Mtunzi Nxawe and Jeremy Wightman in guiding and supporting us through the publication process from the initial concept to the publication stage.

We are especially grateful to our colleagues who afforded us the time, space and encouragement to write this book. Our biggest gratitude is to our families. Your patience, empathy and backing saw us through to the end.

Andrew, Leif and Thireshen, February 2020

Abbreviations and acronyms

ABInBev	Anheuser-Busch InBev
ANC	African National Congress
a.m.	morning hours before 12 noon
ATM	Automatic teller machine
B-BBEE	Broad-Based Black Economic Empowerment
BRT	Bus Rapid Transit
c	cents
CATA	Cape Amalgamated Taxi Association
CBD	Central Business District
CoCT	City of Cape Town
CODETA	Cape Organisation for Democratic Taxi Association
CoJ	City of Johannesburg
CoW	City of Windhoek
DA	Democratic Alliance
DBE	Department of Basic Education (National)
DSD	Department of Social Development (National)
DGH	Distell Group Holdings
DST	Digital story telling
DSTV	Digital satellite television
DSWD	Department of Social Welfare and Development
ECD	Early Childhood Development
ECDC	Early Childhood Development Centre
GIS	Geographic Information System
GPS	Geographic Positioning System
IPTA	Ivory Park Taxi Association
ISIC	International Standard Industrial Classification
JSE	Johannesburg Stock Exchange
LFS	Labour Force Survey
LSM	Living Standards Measure
MK	Umkhonto weSizwe
NBRBSA	National Building Regulations and Building Standards Act

n.d.	no date
NDoT	National Department of Transport
NGO	Non-governmental organisation
NPO	non-profit-organisation
NTA	National Taxi Alliance
pm	per month
p.m.	past midday
QLFS	Quarterly Labour Force Survey
RDP	Reconstruction and Development Programme
SA	South Africa
SAB	South African Breweries
SANCO	South African National Civics Organisation
SANTACO	South African National Taxi Council
SASSA	South African Social Security Agency
SMME	Small Medium and Micro-Enterprise
StatsSA	Statistics South Africa
ToD	Transit Oriented Development
US	United States
WCLA	Western Cape Liquor Act
ZCC	Zion Christian Church

1
INTRODUCTION

This book provides a unique insight into township informal businesses and entrepreneurship. The principal focus is on micro-enterprises, the business strategies of township entrepreneurs and the impact of autonomous informal economic activities on urban life.

CHAPTER 1

Introduction

This book provides a unique insight into township informal businesses and entrepreneurship. It is set in the post-apartheid period, in the third decade of South Africa's democracy and draws on evidence collected from 2010–2018 in 10 research sites, nine of which are in South Africa, and one in Namibia. The location of the sites is shown in Figure 1.1.

The principal focus is on micro-enterprises, the business strategies of township entrepreneurs and the impact of autonomous informal economic activities on urban life. This topic cannot be understood without taking cognisance of the dynamic of urbanism which has reshaped old townships and created new settlements at a speed that has outpaced the state's development strategies of urban planning, infrastructure installation and housing provision. Our focus has an intentional spatial and economic lens that considers livelihoods and entrepreneurship in order to analyse the urban fabric of townships of Southern African cities with similar histories of racial and spatial segregation. Within the place of the township, the book explores the precise spatial influences on business activities, from the area level of specific settlements and their neighbourhoods to the street and micro-context of individual actors. At these various gradients, we witness a profusion of entrepreneurship which responds to market impulses, activates social relationships, and profoundly disrupts the urban form desired by development planners. Our analysis of these processes has the objective of highlighting the significance of the township as not just a dormitory suburb for black South Africans (as was originally intended) but as an emerging sphere of economic activity, wherein micro-enterprise activities hold transformative potential. In this sense, the book provides an analysis of what constitutes the suitable conditions for maintaining and enhancing township enterprise potential, through identifying the influences that enable economic opportunities, and those that hinder, disturb and constrain them.

The businesses that constitute a central component of townships have been a neglected field of research. We shall refer to these businesses as micro-enterprises. The notion of a micro-enterprise is defined in terms of the South Africa's National Small Business Act (No. 26 of 2003) as an enterprise which employs fewer than five persons, having an annual turnover below R200 000 and assets worth less than R100 000. We do not use these criteria in a rigid manner as micro-enterprises have a highly malleable structure and close linkages to the household. Apart from their general smallness in employment absorption and financial turnover, micro-enterprises in our usage are informal businesses in that they operate outside the regulatory framework, possibly fulfilling some regulatory criteria but most are neither incorporated nor registered for taxation. While weak in linkages to formal institutions, which include laws, regulations, supporting state agencies and financial services, informal micro-enterprises have strong linkages to informal institutions, which include societal norms, values and cultural practices. This means that although most township micro-enterprises operate outside the framework of formality, and are hence illegal in some or all aspects, the businesses operate according to legitimate local practices and are largely considered legitimate endeavours within the township population. This point is necessary to draw a distinction between the subject of this book, legitimate informal micro-enterprises, and informal business activities that are illegal and seen as illegitimate. These include activities such as robberies, organised drug-selling by gangsters, the production of contraband and extortion by criminal syndicates. We restrict our consideration of such 'renegade' activities (Webb, Tihanyi, Ireland & Sirmon 2009) to situations where illegitimate practices directly impinge on legitimate business endeavours, though we recognise that the 'renegade economy' has an important influence on micro-entrepreneurship in the townships. For many enterprises featured in this book, economic informality is not necessarily a strategic choice. The literature draws a clear distinction between informal micro-entrepreneurs who engage in business on an involuntary basis, for reasons of poverty or structural constraints, and informal micro-entrepreneurs who voluntarily choose to pursue informal strategies, for example, to reduce the costs of regulation and compliance or to trade illegally and in illicit goods (Maloney 2004; Perry 2007). The latter avoid formal institutions through choice.

Knowledge foundation

Both the informality of the micro-enterprises and the opaqueness of their relationship to informal institutions present a challenge of data and research. The first challenge is that since informal micro-enterprises are not accessible and visible to state processes of enumeration or statistical capture, there is a paucity of quantitative and qualitative data on the scope and scale of these businesses and their internal workings. This has hindered research endeavours historically, especially among economists and scholars of business practice (Fourie 2018a). In 2000, Statistics South Africa (StatsSA) introduced a biannual Labour Force Survey (LFS) and subsequently, in 2008, a Quarterly Labour Force Survey (QLFS). The LFS and QLFS are the primary instruments of statistical surveys on employment and micro-enterprises. The LFS and QLFS data on micro-enterprise dynamics is of low granularity and the aggregation of the sample means that these instruments have limited potential to explain the behaviour of micro-entrepreneurs and their operation in geographically specific area contexts where the dataset is no longer statistically reliable.

In broad terms, research using LFS and QLFS data indicates that the South African informal sector (informal micro-enterprises and informal employees, paid or unpaid) provides employment to about 2.5 million persons (about 18% of the non-agricultural labour force). Worryingly, it has not expanded in size or share since 2008, whereas the total labour force has expanded by around 13% (Rogan & Skinner 2018). Seen against South Africa's unemployed population of around 6.655 million people (StatsSA 2019), the level of participation in the informal sector is low in absolute terms and also in comparison to similar middle-income developing countries. The unusual situation of high unemployment and low participation in the informal sector puts South Africa in the situation of an 'international outlier' (Yu 2012). In comparable countries in Asia and Latin America, the informal sector provides employment for more than half of all non-agricultural jobs (Chen 2018). The surprisingly small size of the South African informal sector has prompted labour economists to investigate why persons who are

FIGURE 1.1 Map of sites

otherwise unemployed do not initiate micro-enterprises. The answer to this remains unclear. There is evidence that the labour market is highly 'turbulent' as people move in and out of employment (formal and informal), while amongst those starting new businesses, around 40% are thought to 'exit' the enterprise within six months (Lloyd & Liebrandt 2018). Where these survive, there is evidence informal enterprises create jobs (Fourie 2018b) and reduce poverty (Cichello & Rogan 2018). For these reasons alone, the nurturing of informal businesses has been identified by development economists as important state strategy to reduce unemployment and create inclusive economic growth (see Fourie 2018a).

The second data challenge is that the relationship between informal micro-enterprises and the informal institutions that provide arrangements for undertaking business and reducing risks, is difficult to research using quantitative methodologies. Within the limits of national datasets, economists have postulated that the impediments to running an informal business include weakness in human capital (as a result of the apartheid legacy), the inadequacy of support services such as training and finance, high operational costs (especially transport) and the pervasiveness of crime (Kingdon & Knight 2004). There is also recognition that the nature of the business premises and its spatial location has a bearing on enterprise growth and employment creation, though the precise influence is unknown (Fourie 2018b). There is a substantial body of scholarship from a business management and social science perspective to examine socioeconomic contextual and sectoral influences on informal micro-enterprises. Much of this research uses qualitative research and shifts the methodological emphasis away from the sole reliance on quantitative data towards a mixed methods approach. The literature includes area studies, such as the World Bank supported research on Diepsloot Township (Mahajan 2014), and research on specific sectors such as grocery retailing, traditional healing, liquor trading and educational services. There has also been substantial research on street trading, though these studies are less influential to our enquiry as much of this literature focuses on the inner-city and municipal market contexts whose spatial characteristics are not reflective of the situation in township settings (Skinner 2008).

Sector studies are foundational to our understanding of the dynamics of informal micro-enterprises. While we draw upon these works in subsequent chapters, a note of caution is necessary as a result of the tendency for scholars to focus on a single sector, usually in a solitary site. This presents a double-edged challenge to the validity of the results; first, through focusing on a sector, the enquiry transposes business concepts and categorisation intended for formal businesses onto informal entities, thus ignoring the fluidity of the micro-enterprise in its relationship to home and income-generating opportunities. We will demonstrate that micro-enterprises should be understood as an explorative response, reacting in tentative ways to social and economic opportunities, rather than businesses which can be understood as fixed categories (such as a grocery retail shop) with common strategic elements. Second, single-sector research obscures the relationship between micro-enterprises in different sectors as well as the broader spatial influences that shape the conditions where, when and how people can run businesses legitimately.

Aside from noting these cautions, we learn from this research that informal micro-enterprises are indeed constrained as a result of limitations in human and financial capital (Woodward, Rolfe, Ligthelm & Guimarães 2011). Furthermore, we learn that crime is a challenge, particularly to cash businesses which account for virtually all township informal micro-enterprises (Mbonyane & Ladzani 2011). There is evidence that regulations do present an obstacle to businesses which seek to formalise, in other words register and comply with formal regulations, even though this finding is not reflected in quantitative studies or the earliest wave of informal business studies (Charman, Petersen & Piper 2013; Preston-Whyte & Rogerson 1991; Rogerson 1996). We see evidence that the encroachment of large formal businesses into township markets reduces opportunities for informal micro-enterprises which consequently struggle to compete in service or price (Ligthelm 2005). Phillip (2018) argues that the corporate dominance within the structure of the economy, as a consequence of an unusually high concentration in ownership and vertical integration in supply chains, imposes severe limits on market opportunities for small and micro-enterprises. In comparing different township businesses within sectors, there is evidence that while some businesses are on the trajectory of modernising, in other words becoming capital-intensive, utilising technologies, and expanding employment, the majority of informal business activities can best be described as livelihood strategies focused on supplementing needs (Mahajan 2014). It is argued that livelihood activities should not be seen through a lens focusing on profit or employment but understood in terms of the social context of mutual support and reciprocity (Neves & Du Toit 2012). As a collective, studies of township micro-enterprises reiterate rather than refute the concern that the informal sector has limited potential for growth in scope, scale and enterprise sophistication. The conclusion tends towards the argument that though less promising than formal businesses in development terms, informal micro-enterprises fulfil an important 'safety-net'-type function. The resulting policy implication, though subtle in articulation, is that the state should concentrate on stimulating growth in formal businesses which, it is hoped, will translate into employment opportunities.

In contrast to the conservative scenario of micro-enterprises as safety-nets, observers of the township are often struck by the vibrancy of entrepreneurship. In his dissection of the political economy of Diepsloot, the academic and journalist Anton Harber (2011) writes of a place intense in enterprise activity and resourcefulness. In his words:

> [t]he amount of business and trade is overwhelming. Everywhere I look, people are offering goods and services: large grocery or hardware stores rise next to shacks offering hair styles or internet cafes; roadside traders are selling anything you can think of from car and computer parts to clothing, caps and shoes, car wash and car repair; the flash of welding adds to the visual assault of the signs and advertising banners and prices lists that are hanging everywhere. (p. 29)

Observations such as his are less burdened with the weight of expectation from comparative perspectives across the global South and instead concentrate on the adaptations and innovations through which entrepreneurs make business. It was precisely with an eye to the possibilities of micro-enterprises, rather than to their (comparative) limitations, that the social anthropologist Keith Hart (1973) introduced the notion of an informal entrepreneurship. Writing about the urban poor in Accra, Hart described how, through informal economy activities, the unemployed acquired a means of generating an income and facilitating a redistribution of wealth from formal wage earners to themselves. In doing so, their strategies comprised both the provision of services and wealth transfers, some undertaken on terms of mutual agreement and some unjustly enforced. Just as Hart was enthusiastic over the inventiveness of actors in the informal economy, so too have market researchers found optimism in seeking out pathways for corporates to venture into frontier markets at the bottom of the pyramid. This term was proposed by Prahalad and Hart (2002) in advocating an approach to provide goods and services to the poorest people. In his book *KasiNomics*, which applies these ideas in the South African context, Alcock (2015) argues that although non-formal markets have enormous potential to generate wealth and create new opportunities, and do in fact achieve both objectives, to enter these markets requires a very different mindset. This is one that appreciates and understands the social relations and instructions which underpin enterprise strategies and institutional functions. In marketing to informal economies, he writes, 'we need to understand, recognise and open our eyes to the invisible matrix' (p. 172).

Our objective in this book is to help 'open our eyes' on hidden productive processes. We embark on this objective not because we believe a 'fortune' is obscured – quite the contrary – but to square the sincere concerns of the academic findings on the under-performance of township micro-enterprises with the ethnographic evidence of an environment in which business is vibrant, responsive and creative. Having spent eight years studying informal micro-enterprises across the Southern African region, we are certain that micro-enterprises are a means to uplift people from poverty and create wealth, though we recognise that much of this potential is structurally and politically constrained. So, our first objective is to provide a theoretical framing and evidence to advance our understanding of the constraints on township business and the local economy more broadly. A second objective is to highlight state and non-state actions that could unlock opportunities to sustain growth for existing businesses, accommodate new entrants within informal markets, and enable the more robust businesses to embark on a 'modernising' trajectory. A third objective is to take stock of the collective impact of township entrepreneurship on the place and space of townships, in order to highlight what are clearly sustainable but 'non-Western' forms of development. This ambition seeks to show how micro-enterprise activities continuously contribute towards the transformation of urban conditions, in ways that are anticipated and unanticipated, supportive and disruptive. Here we seek to stimulate an appreciation of what Pieterse and Simone (2013) refer to as rogue urbanism, or urban dynamics that are 'pregnant with possibility' (p. 12). The practices which give rise to such dynamics are central to the process of dismantling the apartheid urban form which, as geographers have argued (Pieterse 2009; Turok 2001), has hindered the emergence of commerce and restrained access to economic opportunities in marginalised geographies. Townships were intended to be devoid of commercial activities; thus, the rise of township micro-enterprises reveals an autonomous affront on the residential landscape, and the changing form and function of neighbourhoods.

In this book, we will illuminate the role of micro-enterprises in bringing the city to the township, carving out spaces for interactions, engagements and networking while provisioning goods and services in ways that are accessible, affordable and socio-culturally embedded. We will show that this development has taken place without – or indeed, in spite of – the modernist systems and institutions associated with orderliness and security. In embracing this perspective, we do not seek to make the argument that all informal entrepreneurship or 'rogue practices' (disruptive actions with unplanned outcomes) are necessarily good. We are acutely aware that informality, violence and political conflict (to name some of the everyday challenges of township life) can, in combination or separately, threaten the predictability and regularity on which economic and social development is premised. We have signposted warnings of these dangers throughout the book. But recognising the potential of entrepreneurial and disruptive processes, we believe, is a necessary first step towards developing appropriate strategies that can simultaneously harness the power of entrepreneurship while disrupting the spatial legacy of apartheid. The book will demonstrate, to use the notion of Roy (2009), that township informal micro-enterprises are 'examples of insurgence' (p. 85) within an economy structured around the requirements of corporate and large formal businesses. To this extent, we argue that the township economy remains a spatial entity from which surplus value is extracted. Under apartheid, the redirection of wealth was undertaken through the allocation of low-cost labour to urban industries and services, a subject that has been extensively theorised and researched (Legassick 1974; Morris 1976). In our time, the perpetuating situation of low-cost labour continues to aid the accumulation of wealth outside the township. Unlike the apartheid era, township-based businesses increasingly fulfil a complementary role in the process of surplus with profit extraction. We will show how both corporates and emerging businesses operate to extract profits from the township economy rather than investing in growing business, developing social capital or place making. Our focus, in respect to this process, is primarily on micro-enterprises; we only consider corporate actions in so far as these actions support particular business strategies. We argue that the state has enabled and afforded extractive businesses with institutional room to manoeuvre, in part through apartheid-inspired restrictions on where, when and how township residents are able to operate businesses, and in part through the state's inability and sometimes reluctance to intervene in certain business investments and practices. Throughout this book, we seek to unpack these contradictory logics (over-regulation versus under-regulation), in particular geographic spaces and places, sectors, role-players and timeframes.

Conceptual framework

We use a conceptual framework informed by an understanding of the relational and spatial dimensions on informal economic activities. Our insights draw from ethnographic and sociological research on enterprise activities, theorisation from urban geographers on processes of city-making and architectural studies of market spaces and infrastructure. In collecting data, a topic we address in Chapter 2, we were attuned to the social and reciprocal exchanges between micro-micro-enterprises and the extension of these relationships to clients (Neves & du Toit, 2012). There are spatial dimensions to these exchanges. Charman and Govender (2016), for example, document how township street traders negotiate the use of space, share access to utilities such as water and electricity and cooperate in providing surveillance in anticipation of state intervention and criminal threats. Socio-spatial relationships can also serve to create disadvantage, through for example, the gendered constraints on women who are often socially confined to home-based activities. Another dimension of these relationships pertains to the use of infrastructure, both physical (material) and non-physical (non-material). The use of business infrastructure offers a visual narrative of the strategies of entrepreneurship. Scholars of architecture have deciphered the spatial position of such infrastructure, the materials used and composition, the thresholds and lines of connectivity, to name some of the directions of inquiry (Mörtenböck & Mooshammer 2015). Yet an invisible infrastructure is also extant in informal economies. Simone (2004) gives the example from his research in inner-city Johannesburg of people as 'infrastructure' to draw attention to strategies of collaboration used to 'derive maximal outcomes from a minimal set of elements' (p. 11), while subverting state authority. In a similar vein, social networks provide a (hidden) infrastructure for cooperation and strategy. In their research on the township grocery retail market, Petersen, Thorogood, Charman and du Toit (2019) show how ethnic networks have enabled cooperative strategies to enhance competitiveness and thus dominate neighbourhood markets.

Our theoretical framing prioritises space/time considerations in different contexts and scales. Foregrounding of space and time enables us to shift between different research sites and from the area level of one site down to the micro-context of the street and person where we consider their particular sociological situations. The authors personally interviewed micro-entrepreneurs, spending time in each site to assemble evidence. The nine South African sites and their municipal locations, listed in the chronological order in which the research was undertaken, are: Delft South (City of Cape Town), Vrygrond (City of Cape Town), Sweet Home Farm (City of Cape Town), Browns Farm Philippi (City of Cape Town), Ivory Park (City of Johannesburg), Tembisa (City of Ekurhuleni), Imizamo Yethu (City Cape Town), KwaMashu (eThekwini Municipality) and Thabong (Matjhabeng Local Municipality). The Namibian site is situated in Goreangab settlement of the City of Windhoek. In Chapter 2, we describe our research methods in detail. The originality of our data, its breadth and scope, along with a substantial body of socio-spatial, ethnographic and visual evidence enables us to compare micro-enterprises in different sites and sector dynamics. There is no existing study of the topic that operates across such a wide diversity of scale or has access to the range of evidence on micro-enterprise trends across time.

In analysing township business dynamics, we differentiate between six levels of spatiality which we describe in descending orders of magnification. First, the comparative level wherein we assess multiple sites and compare quantitative data. Second, the city level wherein our research examines the relationship between specific settlements and their urban geography, including spatial situation and infrastructure connections. Third, the small-area level wherein the book relates to particular township sites, using a mixture of quantitative and qualitative sources to understand and compare entrepreneurial responses. Fourth, the neighbourhood level wherein we examine particular spatial dynamics such as a high-street or transport node. Fifth, the micro-context level wherein we discern intimate spatial and relational dynamics in particular sites or businesses. Finally, the sixth level of invisible infrastructure that constitutes the social relationships which secure and safeguard conditions for doing business. Through these six levels, our analysis transcends across space from making comparative arguments to the city-wide context wherein we consider township taxi routes, to the cadastral boundaries of individual properties, to settings in people's homes, or trader-stands on the high street or activities on open ground, and to the placement of objects in specific spaces for particular uses.

From a time perspective, our analysis operates in the context of past, present and future situations, but also embraces an understanding of the processes of change over time. We take cognisance of three different historical influences. First, the apartheid period of modernist town planning in which the urban segregated landscape was established in accordance with the mono-functional objective to house a labour supply while enabling state control. In this period, the state intentionally shut out opportunities for micro-entrepreneurship. Second, the post-apartheid period in which spatial adjustments and interventions have retained the core modernist preoccupation in spatial ordering and urban control, but where settlement establishment has been undertaken with expediency, to intensify the pace of building and density of residential houses. While the state has sought to provide core social and physical infrastructure, the support for township entrepreneurship has been peripheral. It is important to note that nearly all the business activities which we shall document in this book operate from market spaces which entrepreneurs have self-constructed. The burgeoning of informal settlements over the past three decades has shone a light on the inability of the state's development programmes to match urban demographic growth and demand for housing and economic opportunities. The pervasive reach of informality leads to our third situation, which is the unknown future, where we postulate imagined outcomes based on current trends and structural constraints. In respect to change over time, our conceptual framing takes consideration of seasonal change (from summer to winter, for example), episodic change in response to crises (such as the disruption of electricity supply or personal trauma), cyclical change over short-run cycles such as a shift in business activities from day to night, and transformative change such as institutional framework conditions.

In our consideration of the varying influence of space and time, we recognise two predominant intersecting influences that shape or determine livelihood opportunities and entrepreneurial responses. We characterise these as people-centred responses and power responses. Our analysis is preoccupied with two people-centred responses in particular. First, the livelihoods responses embedded in social and cultural mechanisms, including informal institutions, an understanding of which helps to explain why people trade particular products/services and the seemingly unusual spaces and places in which they conduct business. Second, the people-centred spatial responses, as expressed in vernacular architecture, building processes, and the use of space (with or without supporting physical infrastructure), an understanding of which helps to recognise the complexity of infrastructure forms in the township economy and the centrality of social relationships in choreographing the built environment.

Power responses are (sometimes) more self-evident where, for example, people are disallowed from trading in particular places, though it is important to recognise that power response are predicated on political processes and outcomes. With our focus on micro-entrepreneurship, we take into consideration power responses in diverse situations. One situation is the institutional power of the state across the three spheres of government. This is the power that derives from policy and is encountered in the execution of laws or the anticipation thereof. It is the power of law to restrict when, where, and how township residents can legally pursue economic opportunities. The absence of the state to fulfil these roles is also a matter of power, whereby state inaction such as the failure to uphold laws regulating business practice enables opportunities for the most powerful whose power enables them to dominate informal processes of regulation. Seen in the context of state power, our analysis seeks to identify the power of entrepreneurs and businesses to dominate markets and disadvantage other micro-enterprises. This form of power can advantage corporate retailers over township micro-enterprises through the substantial difference between their financial and institutional resources. Such power enables shopping-mall developers or corporates to comply with statutory processes which, in comparison, present insurmountable obstacles to micro-enterprises. Similarly, this is the power of bigger informal township enterprises to engage in business practices that challenge informal institutional rules and norms. Another situation is the power of organised groups to control and influence who should benefit from economic opportunities and under what arrangements. This is the power of community civic organisations to grant or deny permission to entrepreneurs to open business within the neighbourhood. A different example is the mobilisation of power through ethnicity or nationalism or race to influence de facto rights and opportunities. This power is witnessed, periodically, in xenophobic mobilisation against immigrant businesses.

At the local level, we recognise the power of personal politics, which includes patriarchy within homes and the gendered responsibilities of social reproduction which shape (and limit) opportunities for women. An important thread in our analysis is the contrasting gendered constraints and opportunities for women and men to operate businesses. These differences are seen in the involvement of women and men in specific sectors, with men dominant in mobility-related businesses and women often restricted to home through social pressures. Then, there is ideological power. This form of power can be embedded in cultural or religious practice that influences the way people pursue livelihoods, for example, restricting the charging of interest on the sale of particular products, or in a less benign manner, providing opportunities to use supernatural influences in pursuit of economic benefit. Finally, our analysis recognises the 'silent' power of resistance through which entrepreneurs push back against the powerful, selling products illegally (though the products themselves might be legally acquired), encroaching onto forbidden spaces, and mobilising informal institutions to sustain business. The collective weight of this power, in scale and persistence, has led political scientists to conclude that 'significant parts' of township life are 'ungoverned altogether' (Anciano & Piper, 2019 p. 15). While this might be true in specific spaces and moments of time, we agree with Du Toit and Neves (2014) in the argument that the poor 'live assertively' within the law, 'evading the law when they need to but insisting, when they can, on the rights and entitlements due to them as citizens' (p. 846).

Outlook

The book has been organised into 12 chapters. Each chapter concludes with a statement of outlook in which we seek to project the main message forward into time. Chapter 2 provides a detailed examination of the research methods through which we assembled the primary evidence upon which our analysis is founded. Since the originality of this book lies in the breadth and combination of mixed methods, it is necessary to explain the research processes and analytical approach in drawing upon quantitative data from surveys, qualitative evidence from interviews, ethnographic note-taking, participatory action research and visual representations, using geospatial maps, drawings, illustrations, photography and infographics. We do not repeat our explanation of the research methods in subsequent chapters. In Chapter 2, we include a description of the settlement characteristics and socio-demographic profile of the research sites, including maps to indicate their situation on the national and city-level scales. We explain the rationale for our research and acknowledge some of the limitations of our experiences, as non-township residents whose life histories are far removed from the subject matter, to interpret the domain of micro-enterprises and particular sensitivities of participants in this economy. In addition, we discuss the ethical considerations of undertaking research based on primary data, including knowledge sources which were co-produced with township residents and entrepreneurs.

We commence the evidence-centred content in Chapter 3, wherein we present an overview of the scope and scale of township micro-entrepreneurship in nine townships. In spatial terms, the analysis operates at the comparative and area levels specified above. Our dataset comprises the geospatial records of 10 842 micro-enterprises and firm surveys of 3 188 cases. The quantitative portion of the survey dataset is publicly accessible, though we include qualitative insights to bolster evidence at various points in the book. Having provided a macro-perspective of the different categories of business in the township economy and their respective significance, the book order follows a logic that begins with an analysis of formal and informal land use in Chapter 4, wherein we elucidate the institutional constraints and implications for entrepreneurship. Through case studies, we show that much current use of land for business is misaligned to formal frameworks with aspects of the land-use system presenting an obstacle to micro-enterprises that need or desire formalisation. In Chapter 5, we examine how micro-enterprises are spatially ordered and utilise infrastructure within the township in response to market opportunities. We describe the main spatial implications of the distribution of micro-enterprises at the area, neighbourhood and street levels. The concern with spatial ordering is advanced in Chapter 6, where we focus on the high street. Taking the analysis to Eveline Street in Namibia, we detail a case where development has been disruptive and transformative, reshaping the urban form and enabling a wave of entrepreneurial responses. We show how an intervention by the City of Windhoek to address one aspect of land-use system constraints resulted in the intensification and diversification of micro-enterprise activities over a period of eight years. Furthermore, we present evidence to illustrate spatial transformation in which the land potential has been unlocked through a combination of private investment, supportive micro-entrepreneurship, a nuanced approach to town planning and state actions to enhance public usability.

In Chapter 7, we consider the dual role of township transport services in the form of taxis, first, in connecting residents to the formal economy and second, in providing an internal network that connects homes to transport nodes. In spatial terms, the taxi sector includes evidence from the city-wide and neighbourhood levels. We argue that while minibus taxis are a relatively efficient mode of public transport, its collective operational system has negative externalities, one of which is the marginalisation of informal sedan taxis from fulfilling a role which could better enhance the township economy and activate spatial transformation. In Chapters 8 to 11, we provide an in-depth examination of the major sectoral components. In Chapter 8, we describe the struggle for grocery market capture, explaining why informal businesses that were bigger in scale than the micro-enterprises which historically operated in this segment were able to dominate the market, aided by their 'unconstrained' informality and state weakness to police the sector. We contrast this situation with the case of township businesses selling liquor products, in Chapter 9. This sector is the most heavily policed of all our categories and yet we show how micro-enterprises who are unable to acquire business licences chose to resist state pressure by conducting business illegally. As these businesses do not simply sell liquor products, but provide a social space, the chapter concentrates on informal drinking venues and examines the intimate micro-strategies through which business is conducted and the social space is managed to reduce risk. In Chapter 10, we examine businesses which retail food. Our core concern is with fast-food micro-enterprises. These micro-enterprises respond to consumer demand for accessible, affordable and culturally sensitive foods, though increasingly mirroring corporatised ideals. Unlike the drinking venues, township fast-food sellers do not directly support social engagements around the consumption of food. In Chapter 11, our analysis turns to the provision of personalised services. We focus on the common business strategies amongst hairdressers, childcare services and traditional healers. There are two strands that are common to these sectors: one is the centrality of social relationships in defining the relationship between the entrepreneurs and their clients; the other is the socio-spatial role of these micro-enterprises in place making.

The penultimate Chapter 12 examines some of the main informal institutions in the township economy. These institutions inform entrepreneurial strategies, enable micro-entrepreneurs to cope with risk and provide stability, predictability and integrity to the business environment. We show why successful township micro-entrepreneurs commonly seek to avoid raising their community profile through strategies such as fronting, divestment and building human and social capital within the family rather than the business itself. The conclusion, in Chapter 13, summarises our core arguments, restates the major themes and shows how our evidence and interpretation add value to the current understanding of the township economy. We end the book with a brief consideration of the kinds of actions which could enable productive responses and nurture transformative outcomes. These actions fall into three groups: entrepreneurial responses that ought to be protected; entrepreneurial responses that should be constrained; and entrepreneurial responses that would benefit from the disruption of prevailing systems of economic organisation, including power structures.

As we note above, the novelty of the book lies in the research approaches, the data itself, and our interpretation of micro-entrepreneurship through a spatial and ethnographic lens. Through embedding our research and engaging with hundreds of township entrepreneurs over years of field research, we have gained a rich understanding of business dynamics that simply cannot be learnt through quantitative surveys. One set of insights relates to the social and cultural context that frames responses to business opportunities. The use of photographs helps to show the intimate nature of socio-spatial relationships and the connections between actors, objects and specific localities, to name but some of the dynamics investigated. To explore complex spatial dynamics, we have documented the precise infrastructure configuration and spatial footprint of particular micro-enterprises using architectural drawings and sketches, thus allowing the reader to get as close as possible to the contextual situation. In the studies of land use, these drawings help distinguish between commercial and residential uses and show how actual land use deviates to property boundaries and building restrictions, a subject which may otherwise come across as abstract and distract the audience from complexities which entrepreneurs would need to navigate to align with formal land institutions.

Our analytical approaches include statistical examination of datasets, geospatial mapping of micro-enterprise distributions, and interpretation through diagrams, illustrations and image notation. To comprehend complex socio-cultural-entrepreneurial spaces, architectural sketches and annotated photographs are employed to understand the manner in which infrastructure has been configured to influence social outcomes, to differentiate businesses into niche segments, and maintain separation between public and private realms. In another instance, the use of sketches and photographs illuminates the relational dynamics of businesses, showing how micro-enterprises operate in symbiotic relationships and how vernacular infrastructure seeks to benefit from existing objects and structures (and space availability). Using architectural sketches, we are able to interpret the changes in high-street buildings in their spatial evolution to provide commercial space oriented towards the street (thus public realm) while simultaneously supporting the development of accommodation (in the private realm). Through using a combination of geospatial and planning data, we are able to identify the nodal characteristic of the high streets. Then using sketches, we are able to describe the relationships within these nodes and hence confirm the central role of small informal taxis in connecting people to businesses. Finally, through working with township entrepreneurs in the co-production of knowledge, we are able to draw on their personal accounts (through devices such as video stories and photographic narratives) in specific circumstances to comprehend the invisible, bolster evidence and substantiate our claims. We take full responsibility for the analysis. We trust that we have made wise use of some of the stories we have heard, while responding to the multiple concerns with enduring structural, socio-political and regulatory constraints in a manner which balances individual perspectives against broader collective interests, keeping our eye on our ultimate goal of contributing knowledge towards the cause of inclusive economic growth.

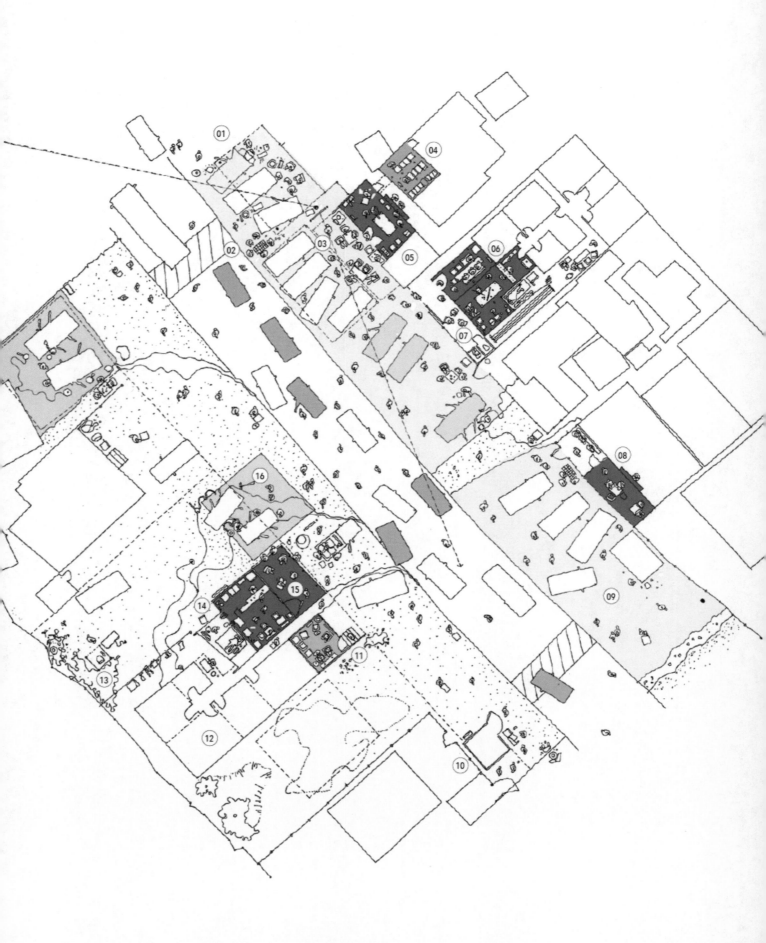

2
RESEARCHING OBJECTS, SPACES, PERSONS & PRACTICES

The analysis in the book is underpinned by original research which the authors conducted over seven years from 2010 to 2017 in nine townships in four South African provinces, and a township in Windhoek, Namibia.

CHAPTER 2

Researching objects, spaces, persons and practices

The analysis in the book is underpinned by original research which the authors conducted over seven years from 2010 to 2017 in nine townships in four South African provinces, and a township in Windhoek, Namibia. Some of this research was conducted under the auspices of the Sustainable Livelihoods Foundation (SLF), an organisation with whom the researchers worked. The authors acknowledge SLF for providing us with access to the data and authorisation to include particular research outcomes in this publication. Additional field research was undertaken to address identified knowledge gaps and to obtain a deeper understanding of certain issues. The authors conducted extensive desktop research to situate arguments within academic literature and gain insights from comparative perspectives. While it was not our intention to provide a comprehensive survey of academic writings on each topic, we have chosen to reference what we regard as the most relevant scholarship. We have drawn upon a range of secondary sources, including government reports, policy documents, legislation, media articles and material published on the internet. The authors are solely responsible for the interpretation of evidence and framing of arguments.

The cornerstone of our initial research was a small-area census of micro-enterprises through which we sought to measure the scope and scale of informal business activities in the Cape Town settlement of Delft South. Our initial focus on the micro-enterprise as the subject of investigation aimed to generate original insights on the types of micro-enterprises which existed and the places in which business was undertaken. Though useful as a tool of measurement, the quantitative approach of our business census could not provide deep insights into the social, political or spatial influences on business practices and opportunities. As such, to traverse the unknown and sometimes indiscernible logics of township businesses, we needed to refine our methodologies. We were particularly interested in engaging with the physical and spatial dimensions of the township economy which the literature, as well as our own observations, indicated bore influence on micro-enterprise opportunities. These dimensions extended from the invisible infrastructure of social relations; to the micro-context of the street where we engaged as researchers; to the settlement context as a particular place in which the micro-enterprises were strategically positioned; to the broader area of the township and city region beyond, including the geographical linkages of the township to the formal economy. At each of these levels, we set out to identify the extant micro-enterprise practices, examine business models and relationships, and describe the properties of the local economic and social environment. Finally, we needed our research methodologies to shed light on the development predicament of micro-enterprises themselves and implications for the broader township economy.

Through interviews, conversations and observations, we learnt that township businesses were embedded in social relationships, spatially restricted and subject to external influences, from the state, competitors and powerful individuals. These realisations fostered the embrace of research methods more suited to understanding socio-spatial phenomena, including people-object relationships and power dynamics. In expanding our methodological approach, we sought to respond to Simone's (2004) notion of 'people as infrastructure', not least to comprehend the combination of 'objects, spaces, persons and practices' (p. 408) through which informal actors seek out opportunities (in our sense, people-centred responses) and challenge those authorities (in our sense, power-centred responses) which seek to thwart their objectives. These lines of enquiry would provide original insights on why micro-enterprises did not appear to be growing in size and scale and why localised economies were under-performing.

Researcher reflexivity

In researching the topic, we acknowledge our individual limitations to understanding the mindsets and practices of micro-enterprise entrepreneurs. None of us grew up in a township. None have experience of running a micro-enterprise. We are all men. Two of us are South Africans. One has direct experience of the spatial and racial discrimination of apartheid. We write as observers, though also with a concern to contribute towards greater economic inclusion and the reduction of poverty in marginalised geographies.

With recognition of our socio-cultural, gendered, racial and economic positionalities, we spent extensive time in the field listening, probing and conversing with individuals in different business sectors at varying scales of operation. As part of our endeavour to elicit nuance, we were supported by research assistants with direct experience of the sites, of cultural practices and gendered priorities in running businesses, and of community dynamics, to address some of our concerns as 'outside' researchers. Our assistants included women, youth and migrants. We spent considerable time in discussion with these individuals, in the course of conducting research, wherein we interrogated assumptions and our own positionalities on issues. Through these discussions, some of our lines of enquiry were abandoned, such as asking people to explain the factors contributing to the 'success' of the business, and new directions were pursued, including probing personal histories and individual challenges. The authors personally interviewed many of the owners of the businesses on which we write. We traversed each street in the research sites, thus meeting countless individuals, explaining our objectives and learning through these informal conversations about a range of subjects outside the scope of the research. We spent long periods in the field, ranging between three weeks and two months within each site. Through immersion, we built relationships with individuals, earning their trust and ultimately being afforded access to people's homes where we sought to understand the thresholds between public (business) and private (family) lives. In many cases, the process to gain trust and acceptance required numerous engagements; in some instances, these relationships were built up over years.

An important part of our research approach, which we describe later in more detail, was the use of participatory methodologies, including visual methods. These research methods can afford participants a measure of autonomy as co-producers of knowledge, though the research process should strive to achieve inclusive decision making in each step (Black, Davies, Iskander & Chambers 2018). Through affording the participants a 'voice', participatory methods help to surface issues that might otherwise go unspoken, including insights of a very personal nature. Engaging with these methods, we were able to better understand the profound impact on a person's home life and business from traumatic experiences such as crime, violent police raids and unforeseen forms of business competition. Each of the participants faced their own vulnerabilities. The research could not happen without the researchers first investing time and effort to build trust and gain respect, taking small steps and affording them a role in collective decision making. Most first steps were simply intended for people to get to know one another. These processes took time: for example, we worked with street photographers for over two months and with shebeeners for four months, while each of the digital stories were co-produced in an intensive engagement over five days.

Our use of race terms follows the nomenclature applied by StatsSA. We have cautiously used the words 'migrant' to refer to persons who have relocated from one administrative region to another within South Africa, and 'immigrant' to refer to persons emanating from a foreign country and now living in South Africa.

The research sites

We used case sites as a means to develop a fine-grained comprehension of emergent entrepreneurial practices. As the nature and type of sites would influence our research outcomes, our selection took account of four major attributes. First, sites needed to be reflective of contemporary urban conditions of the township. Second, the sites needed to present different situations of economic opportunity (from deep poverty in informal shack settlements through to areas of rising economic status in formally settled and housed communities). Third, sites needed to exhibit contrasting spatial relationships to the inner city and employment centres. Fourth, sites needed to contain diverse social configurations, demographic particularities and administrative influences. We ultimately chose nine sites in South Africa and one in Namibia. In making our selection, we prioritised sites of different geographic localities as well as spatial positions within urban centres. Because two of the researchers are based in Cape Town, five of the nine South African sites were situated within this metropolitan area, with the additional four sites chosen to counterbalance this geographic bias.

Eight of the nine South African sites are situated in major metropolitan areas, a deliberate choice in recognition of the growing concentration of population within metropolitan areas. Our one exception was the township of Thabong that fringes the regional city of Welkom in the Free State. Because our focus was on urban townships, we excluded settlements in peri-urban situations where the urban form exists outside municipal management, on communal land, for example. The Eveline Street site in Goreangab, Windhoek was chosen to review the impacts of an innovative municipal government initiative to rezone a residential high street to allow for business activities.

The main demographic and settlement characteristics of the 10 research sites are described in the following paragraphs.

Browns Farm

The township of Browns Farm emerged in the late 1970s on the Cape Flats in the eastern part of Philippi. The Cape Flats is an expansive, low-lying area situated to the east of the Cape Town Central Business District (CBD) and the affluent residential areas of the southern suburbs. The site comprises a mixture of informal and formal housing (20% formal; 80% informal) (see Figure 2.1).

FIGURE 2.1 The research site of Browns Farm (incorporating Hazeldene), City of Cape Town

Browns Farm is situated between the two major transport routes of the N2 national freeway and the R300 regional artery. Our research site has a population of 41 895 (50% female) and density of 15 634 people/km² (StatsSA 2012). The unemployment rate (using the broad definition which includes discouraged work seekers) is 41%. The overwhelming majority of residents are ethnically Xhosa.

While we refer to Browns Farm, the research area collectively comprises the neighbourhoods of Browns Farm and Hazeldene Estate. Initially settled with informal dwellings, the area now comprises a mixture of settlement situations. Since the 1980s, the state has sought to institutionalise land use and provide housing. As with most townships, the urban form adheres to the apartheid land-use planning legacy with the formal residential settlements set out according to a cellular and mono-functional design, making no purposeful allowance for business activities. In these areas, most homeowners were afforded formal land titles with their state-built houses. Some homeowners have subsequently extended their properties, including constructing informal backyard dwellings. The residents of the informal areas, in contrast, have no legal land title and have self-constructed their dwellings ('shacks') using recycled and repurposed materials, including wood, cardboard and corrugated iron sheets.

Delft South

Delft South is a post-apartheid settlement established from 1989 with formally titled and zoned land use and housing (Figure 2.2).

FIGURE 2.2 The research site of Delft South (incorporating Eindhoven), City of Cape Town

It is situated on the Cape Flats east of Cape Town International Airport on the northern side of the N2 freeway. The settlement was planned as a neighbourhood community with streets set out in a 'garden city' layout and incorporating paved roads, pavements and traffic management devices such as circles. A high street bisects the site longitudinally. The formal housing was built in the period 1996–2000 as part of the post-apartheid government's Reconstruction and Development Programme (RDP) to provide residential accommodation for black and coloured families. Delft South has a population of 43 185 persons (51% are female) and a population density of 16 269 people/km^2 (StatsSA 2012). The unemployment rate (broad definition) is 46%.

In the national population census in 2011, all the residents were recorded as being formally housed. While the original settlers were afforded title deeds, some of the current residents do not hold land title as a result of acquiring the property informally. The case site collectively refers to the neighbourhoods of Delft South (a mixed demography of Xhosa and coloured ethnicities) and Eindhoven (a majority coloured settlement).

Imizamo Yethu

Meaning 'our efforts' in isiXhosa, Imizamo Yethu is a settlement of both informal and formal housing situated on a mountain slope amidst the affluent suburb of Hout Bay, about 20 km from the Cape Town CBD (Figure 2.3).

The township emerged in the 1980s through informal land occupation, becoming more established and densifying since the 1990s. Unlike most township settlements, Imizamo Yethu is spatially situated within a suburban neighbourhood. The population of the site is 15 537 (45% are female) with a population density of 26 682 people/km^2 (StatsSA 2012).

FIGURE 2.3 The research site of Imizamo Yethu, City of Cape Town

Imizamo Yethu comprises a mixture of formal (60%) and informal (39%) dwellings, though since the 2011 census, there has been a rapid increase in the informal component. The formal houses were established through the state's RDP programme and via private foundation investment. Much of the informal housing is situated on higher ground fringing the Table Mountain National Park and comprises densely settled shacks built from corrugated iron and repurposed timber. Most of these shacks are occupied by black African immigrants, predominantly men, hence the skewed gender distribution within the site. Due to the proximity of the site to formal businesses and work opportunities, unemployment is comparatively lower than the sites on the Cape Flats, with an unemployment rate (broad definition) of 35%. Approximately half of the population are of Xhosa ethnicity.

Ivory Park

Ivory Park was established in the late 1990s to accommodate people residing in informal settlements in Alexandra and Tembisa (Figure 2.4).

The township is located on the north-eastern rim of the City of Johannesburg (CoJ) municipality, close to Midrand. The research site comprises the neighbourhoods of Ivory Park called Sections 2 and 5. The site population is 45 435 (46% are female) and the population density is 28 065 people/km^2 (StatsSA 2012). The unemployment rate (broad definition) is 35%.

Ivory Park's proximity to the suburb of Midrand and access to both Johannesburg and Pretoria CBDs has meant that the site is a favoured destination for migrants seeking work and economic opportunities in the urban economy.

FIGURE 2.4 The research site of Ivory Park, City of Johannesburg

Although formally planned, the settlement has expanded rapidly with informal land use reshaping the layout. As such, present day land uses do not neatly conform to the cadastre plan: informal settlements occupy open spaces and residential homes have encroached across both public and private boundaries. The majority of residents are formally housed (87%) with the original houses built privately and through the state RDP programme. Although some of the homeowners have obtained title deeds, the process of issuing deeds has been irregular due to evolving inconsistencies in land-use status and ownership as settlement dynamics have changed. A sizeable portion of Ivory Park residents are housed in backyard dwellings which homeowners have built to provide an income stream from renting these out. The settlement has a heterogeneous mix of ethnicities with no dominant group and includes substantive immigrant communities from Mozambique and Zimbabwe, and many first-generation migrants from Limpopo Province.

KwaMashu

The township of KwaMashu, north of the city of Durban was named after Marshall Campbell who owned a sugar cane plantation on the original farm (Figure 2.5).

KwaMashu was established in the 1950s as a consequence of the apartheid Group Areas Act (No. 41 of 1950), accommodating persons forcibly relocated from the Durban informal settlement of Cato Manor. The KwaMashu research site includes both a portion of KwaMashu itself and the adjacent informal settlement of Bester. There are no roads in Bester and access to the shack dwellings is via pedestrian pathways in between households. The combined site thus comprises formal and informal settlements with 77% of the population formally housed. The site population is 74 037 (52% are female) with a population density of 11 391 people/km² (StatsSA 2012). The unemployment rate (broad definition) is 47%.

FIGURE 2.5 The research site of KwaMashu, Durban, City of eThekwini

The portion of KwaMashu under consideration was formally planned and most of the houses were originally established under the Bantustan council administration. A significant proportion of the property is under the ownership of eThekwini Municipality with the reported process of transferring property to private ownership being erratic. Where properties have been transferred to the residents there is evidence of considerable investment in these assets. KwaMashu is characterised by sprawling neighbourhoods separated by river valleys and greenbelts. State-established social facilities such as schools and churches have been clustered within the centre of the settlement, on raised ground, along with the now defunct municipal beer hall, although over time, additional social assets have been established in outlying areas. The overwhelming majority of the local population are of Zulu ethnicity.

Sweet Home Farm

Situated adjacent to Browns Farm on the Cape Flats, Sweet Home Farm is an informal settlement that emerged on unutilised farmland in the late 1970s, where the new residents expressed hope for a better life and hence 'sweet home' (Figure 2.6).

The site comprises two distinct areas: a compact informal settlement and the small formal settlement of Vukuzenzela comprising single- and double-storey brick houses. In the informal component, the predominant shack dwellings are made from corrugated iron and timber frames and, at the time of the initial survey, were not connected to water, sewerage or electricity. Access to water is via standpipes with communal toilet facilities laid out in blocks at accessible points for service vehicles. Three informal streets penetrate the settlement, though most houses are only accessible via narrow pedestrian pathways between shack structures.

FIGURE 2.6 The research site of Sweet Home Farm, City of Cape Town.
Credit: Justin Patrick

The residents have no direct access to educational and health facilities. Sweet Home Farm has a population of 7 836 people (46% female) with a population density of 21 117 people/km² (StatsSA 2012). The unemployment rate (broad definition) is 46%.

Despite its informal characteristics, Sweet Home Farm is considered by residents as a favourable location of opportunity due to its proximity to factories, retail outlets and farming operations. The majority of the population are of Xhosa ethnicity, in addition to a small coloured population. The Xhosa population includes a higher proportion of male migrants, hence the skewed gender distribution.

Tembisa

The township of Tembisa (meaning 'promise' in isiXhosa) was established in 1957, situated on the East Rand, north of Kempton Park (Figure 2.7) in the Ekurhuleni Metropolitan Municipality.

Tembisa is the second largest township in Gauteng after Soweto, thus the research focused on seven local neighbourhoods: Entshonalanga, Umnonjaneni, Moedi, Khatamping, Endayini, Umfuyaneni and Umthambeka. The site population is 41 673 persons (49% female) and population density is 15 959 people/ km² (StatsSA 2012). The unemployment rate (broad definition) is 38%.

The settlement of Tembisa was laid out in a grid pattern in accordance with apartheid ideas on township spatial planning. Within the site neighbourhoods, 96% of the population occupy privately owned formal housing reminiscent of the 'NE51/6' four room housing unit developed by Douglas Calderwood for the National Building Research Institute (SA History.org n.d.; Artefacts n.d).

FIGURE 2.7 The research site of Tembisa, Johannesburg, City of Ekurhuleni

As in parts of KwaMashu, there is evidence of a process of property improvement in Tembisa with owners investing to redevelop their properties, including complete home rebuilds. Unlike neighbouring Ivory Park, there is little evidence of backyard dwellings and the land area occupied by informal settlement is minimal. Tembisa's population comprises a heterogeneous mix of predominantly black South Africans.

Vrygrond

Vrygrond is situated near the coastal settlement of Muizenberg (Figure 2.8).

Before its formal establishment, Vrygrond (literally: 'free land') was one of Cape Town's oldest informal settlements occupied by subsistence fishermen and their families. The population of the research site is 25 197 (49% are female) with a population density of 16 190 people/km². The unemployment rate (broad definition) is 35%; a level that while relatively high is comparatively lower than other Cape Flats research areas. This is due to Vrygrond's greater proximity to formal labour markets and economic opportunities within nearby middle-class suburbs.

The Vrygrond research site comprises three adjacent but very different areas: a 1980s formal neighbourhood of semi-detached housing and flats named Seawinds, a formally planned settlement of freestanding and semi-detached brick dwellings called Capricorn established in the 2000s through a private-sector-led social housing development project; and, sandwiched between the two, an informal shack settlement on a proclaimed road reserve by the name of Overcome Heights, which originated in 2005. As an informal settlement, the residents access water and sewerage through communal facilities, though electricity is provided to individual dwellings.

FIGURE 2.8 The research site of Vrygrond, City of Cape Town

The collective Vrygrond research site has (increasingly) become heterogeneous in character and currently comprises Xhosa, coloured, and immigrants, notably from Malawi and Zimbabwe, although the neighbourhood of Seawinds to the north is predominantly a coloured neighbourhood.

Thabong

The name Thabong means 'place of happiness' in Southern Sotho (Figure 2.9). The apartheid-era township is situated on the periphery of the regional city of Welkom in the Matijhabeng Local Municipality of the Free State Province. The site population is 26 361 (49% are female).

Situated close to the goldfields, Thabong emerged as a settlement to accommodate (permanent) workers in local mines and ancillary industries. The majority of the population is formally housed in the portion of the township within our research site. As in most South African townships, the layout adheres to apartheid planning ideas with residential blocks set out in a grid pattern with no land provision for business activities. The houses are predominantly detached, four-room buildings that resemble the NE51/6 design. Although the homeowners are predominantly South Africans of Sotho and Xhosa ethnicities, immigrants from Lesotho, Zimbabwe and Mozambique have moved to Thabong in search of economic opportunities, including conducting informal gold mining as 'Zama-Zamas' (from the isiZulu word *ukuzama*, meaning to attempt to obtain something). Though once part of a thriving mining economy, the demise in gold mining has resulted in high (47%) unemployment (broad definition).

FIGURE 2.9 The research site of Thabong, Welkom, Matjhabeng Local Municipality

Eveline Street (Goreangab)

Eveline Street is a high street that bisects the township settlement of Goreangab, a north-western extension of Katutura established in 1991 (Figure 2.10).

FIGURE 2.10 The research site of Eveline Street, Goreangab, Windhoek

The settlement is situated on the periphery (approximately 20 km from the CBD) of the City of Windhoek (CoW), the capital of Namibia. The spatial dimensions of this research site comprise a two-kilometre stretch of high street as well as the housing and businesses situated along the road and informal trade. The site included a CoW managed market facility for informal traders.

In land use and settlement patterns, Goreangab (and Katutura more broadly) closely resembles the apartheid spatial system since the establishment of townships in Namibia was guided by the South African government's apartheid policy (Friedman 2000). Katutura, for example, was established through the forced relocation of people away from the town centre, thus acquiring a name which translates as 'a place where people don't want to live'. As in South African townships, Goreangab was set out for residential settlement in accordance with a mono-functional design principle, to provide residential accommodation with little provision for commercial activities outside supermarket precincts. High streets such as Eveline Street have since transformed into the commercial spine of these settlements, providing an epicentre for business activity and social interaction. Through focusing on the high street, the site brings into relief the influence of economic activities in providing alternative forms of infrastructure and contributing towards a more complex (and cohesive) social existence.

In the next section, we discuss the research methods used to study the township economy in the nine sites.

The small-area census method

In seeking to measure the scope and scale of micro-enterprise activities at the township scale, we developed a methodological approach with two central components applied concurrently: one, a census of all locatable business activities and two, a business survey of micro-enterprises. We have described this mixed qualitative and quantitative method as the small-area census approach (Charman, Petersen, Piper, Liedeman & Legg 2015) which was piloted in Delft South in 2010 and 2011. The approach required the researchers to traverse every street, pathway and passage within a predetermined neighbourhood area to record all business activities. Equipped with site maps and reports, notebooks, cameras and Geographic Positioning Systems (GPS) devices, the research team proceeded house by house and street by street, recording the spatial position and activity of each identified business, conducting surveys of specific businesses, taking photographs of business activities and contexts, gathering data from conversations, and collecting artefacts (such as flyers and posters). The team comprised expert social scientists and trained liaison persons who resided in the community and were thus conversant in local languages and had knowledge of the general informal business environment. In recognition of the authority embodied within research as a process, we chose a number of strategies to 'disempower' our status while cognisant of our position as outsiders. One such measure was to traverse the site on foot and using low specification bicycles (see Figure 2.11).

The use of bicycles, as opposed to motor vehicles, placed the researchers in a position to be more accessible for engagement with members of the community. We thus became a subject of inquiry ourselves, having to answer to unknown persons on questions such as 'what are you doing here?' or 'why are you in "our" community?' or 'how could I benefit from this research?'

The logic of the small-area census approach was to record all economic activities, regardless of type or situation, at the point of encounter across an area of roughly 10 000 households or geographic scope of up to 2 km^2.

FIGURE 2.11 The research team with their bicycles

The location and basic data for each micro-enterprise was electronically recorded. This data included sector categorisation, the longitude and latitude coordinates of the enterprise position, a photograph of the enterprise structure or signage, socio-demographic information and simple field notes. Our approach proved highly effective where micro-enterprises' activities were visually identifiable through observing the work of the entrepreneur or noting business-related infrastructure such as signage and equipment. Identifying home-based, hidden and out-of-working hours activities was more difficult, meaning that the researchers spent considerable time in each site talking with residents, passing pedestrians, community leaders and so forth to enquire as to the presence and whereabouts of businesses within the neighbourhood that might be less readily observed. These conversations were particularly useful in gaining community insights, listening to stories and obtaining alternative perspectives on particular businesses (including warnings that a business might be run by known criminals) or sector activities within the neighbourhood (Figure 2.12).

As the scope of our enquiry was inclusive of all micro-enterprise activities, we would often encounter residents requesting that a business which we had not initially identified be included in the research enquiry, presumably so as not to miss out on future opportunities or benefits. Despite our best endeavours, some business operations, including illegal and illegitimate activities (such as organised narcotics and drug-related activities and stolen vehicle 'chop-shops', among others), home-based activities (such as care of the elderly), sex work and mobile trading went under- or unrecorded in the census enumeration.

FIGURE 2.12 Conversations to gain community insights were had on a regular basis

After fieldwork, the data from the census process was checked for veracity and accuracy. The GPS devices generated a trail of the researchers' footsteps which helped to ensure that all spatial localities across a particular site were included in the census, while the photographic record and field notes were consulted in assessing the enterprise classification. Our method to classify the identified micro-enterprises into one of 36 categories is described in Chapter 3.

The geospatial data provides our core evidence of the scope and scale of different enterprise activities. The maps which underpin this evidence were produced using MapInfo Geographic Information System (GIS) software. In the maps, we have deliberately utilised a scale which disguises the precise spatial location, providing an ocular (not GPS accurate) perspective of enterprise distribution to aid our descriptions of spatial distributions and identifying patterns.

The business survey component was targeted at those sectors considered to be most significant in business size, scope and complexity of operations. From a size perspective, we focused on micro-enterprises with discernible business characteristics, including dedicated infrastructure (however modest, including a room in a house), a commercial identity (a name or signage), and evidence that the business was operational on a regular basis. From a scope perspective, we focused on the sectors of grocery retail (spaza shops), liquor retail (taverns and shebeens, the latter being unlicensed venues selling liquor and providing a space of socialisation), hair salons and businesses providing childcare (akin to Early Childhood Development Centres [ECDCs], known as educares – the term we use hereafter). In terms of the complexity of operations, taverns and educares are required to comply with complex regulatory requirements and their experiences in this regard provide an insightful analogy. The survey component allowed for a deeper level of inquiry into business practices. Interviews were undertaken with the use of a questionnaire (Figure 2.13).

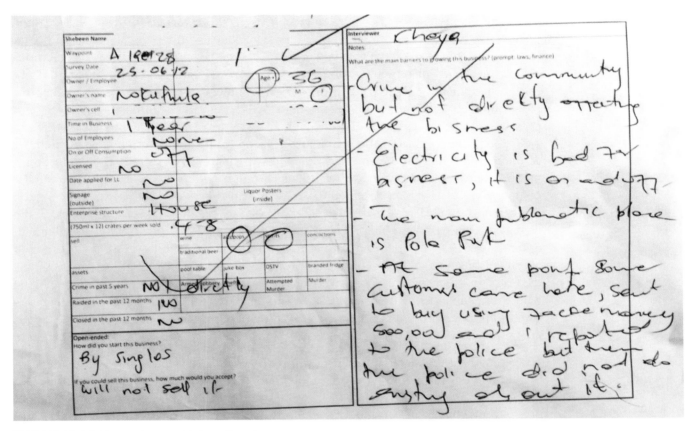

FIGURE 2.13 A field researcher completed questionnaire

We tailored the questionnaire tool for each sector; thus our inquiry into spaza shops included questions on grocery pricing; our inquiry into liquor retailing included questions on liquor products, entertainment facilities and issues of regulation; conversely our inquiry into educares included questions about costs, facilities offered and meal provision, and regulation, to highlight some of the differences. The data from the business survey were collated into a single dataset to permit comparison of business activities in similar sectors across the sites. In this book, we use both the quantitative data and qualitative notes, referencing the latter according to business category/unique survey number/gender/age. In terms of business category, code 1 refers to a tavern or shebeen; code 2 refers to a spaza shop; code 3 refers to an educare; code 4 refers to a hair-care business; code 5 refers to a traditional healer; code 6 refers to a person micro-manufacturing items; and code 7 refers to a street trader. The code 5/2714/F/54, for example, refers to a traditional healer, survey number 2714, a female person, of 54 years of age.

Having demonstrated the viability of the small-area census approach in the Delft South pilot, which enabled us to present original evidence on the emerged competition and conflict within the spaza shop sector (see Charman & Piper 2012; Charman, Petersen & Piper 2012), the method was then replicated with minor adjustments in the eight other sites. Further adjustments to the methodology were primarily made with respect to the enterprise survey component wherein we came to replace the paper-based tools with an electronic tablet system for enumeration and a cloud-based data management system for data storage and processing. We also extended the range of the sectors investigated to traditional healers in Vrygrond and micro-manufacturers in KwaMashu.

The initial objective of the small-area census method was to provide a 'snapshot' perspective of the scope and scale of business activities within particular sites. Although the method succeeded in providing a relatively accurate picture of micro-enterprise activity at a particular point in time and space, we recognised that the result did not reflect the dynamic nature of the business environment over time and space which we had witnessed from immersion in the field. To address this shortcoming, we revisited previous sites to access temporal changes. In 2015, five years after the first research in Delft South was conducted, the researchers resurveyed this site and found that the number of micro-enterprises in the site had doubled (Charman & Petersen 2017). Interestingly, many businesses had changed their spatial location within the site. In 2017, a similar comparative study (albeit confined to an investigation of spaza shops) was undertaken in Vrygrond, Ivory Park, Thabong and KwaMashu, whereupon we found considerable changes in the demographic profile of the shopkeepers (Petersen, Thorogood, Charman & du Toit 2019). In our Eveline Street research, we were able to access a government census of business activities aligned to properties situated along the high street. As this data was geospatially referenced, we were able to compare the historic situation in 2008 with the results of our own business census in 2016. A comparison of these datasets reveals important findings about the spatial growth of micro-enterprises and the changes in composition of enterprise categories over time. We detail these changes in Chapter 6.

The strength of the small-area census approach was the collection of both quantitative (including GPS data; enterprise data; price data and so forth) and qualitative data. The qualitative data included detailed answers to questions in the business survey, field notes from conversations and observations, photographs of business activities, and miscellaneous documents such as business flyers, advertisements and official records, including title deeds and fines (Figure 2.14).

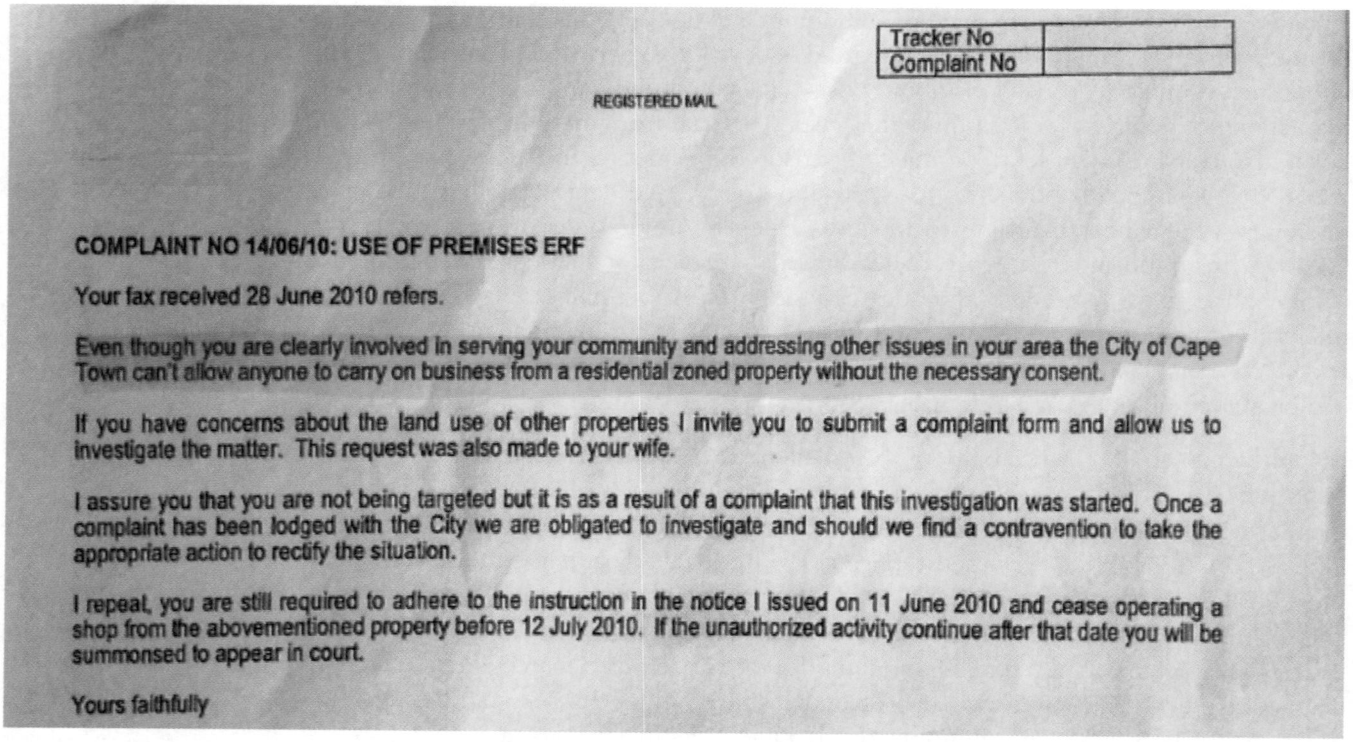

Tracker No	
Complaint No	

REGISTERED MAIL

COMPLAINT NO 14/06/10: USE OF PREMISES ERF

Your fax received 28 June 2010 refers.

Even though you are clearly involved in serving your community and addressing other issues in your area the City of Cape Town can't allow anyone to carry on business from a residential zoned property without the necessary consent.

If you have concerns about the land use of other properties I invite you to submit a complaint form and allow us to investigate the matter. This request was also made to your wife.

I assure you that you are not being targeted but it is as a result of a complaint that this investigation was started. Once a complaint has been lodged with the City we are obligated to investigate and should we find a contravention to take the appropriate action to rectify the situation.

I repeat, you are still required to adhere to the instruction in the notice I issued on 11 June 2010 and cease operating a shop from the abovementioned property before 12 July 2010. If the unauthorized activity continue after that date you will be summonsed to appear in court.

Yours faithfully

FIGURE 2.14 An official letter of sanction shown to the researchers by an enterprise owner
Note: refer to Chapter 4

Some of the qualitative findings were aligned to the quantitative data, thus allowing a convergence of methods and permitting a more complete understanding of the respondents' answers to questions on sector issues such as regulation or competition (see Creswell 2014, p. 219, on the importance of converging methods). Our qualitative data was especially valuable as it provided much of the substantive insight into the business practices of township micro-enterprises. In response to these insights, the researchers saw the need to better understand activities at various spatial levels as described in the Introduction, including the city-wide level and the neighbourhood level, down to the micro-context or the level of actual people and their relationship to space and objects.

Socio-spatial methods

To study the complexity of social-spatial dynamics and explore the relationships of power between actors, the researchers utilised an array of methods drawn from sociological, geographical and architectural traditions. These methods were used in both convergent and sequential research processes. Our starting point was usually with sociological methods wherein ethnography (and notably systematic observation), unstructured interviews and informal focus group discussions produced initial business insights. We would then examine particular geospatial or political dynamics through a sequential research process. In this second stage, we used methods which included mapping (both contextual and precise), architectural drawings and various forms of photography, while simultaneously probing subjects to greater depths through informal conversations, follow-up interviews and detailed observations. The purpose of using maps, drawings and photographs was to provide a metric for documenting the findings from the field to a level of detail that would be tangible and visually comprehensible, while illuminating strategic decisions in the use of space or relationships between actors (Figure 2.15).

FIGURE 2.15 Photographs were annotated to communicate site-specific relationships between people, objects, space, and infrastructure

An important criterion in this methodological approach was the need for scale-sensitivity to enable our analysis to calibrate between the extreme scales of urban geography (where townships connect to the inner city and centres of opportunities), neighbourhood dynamics and the micro-context of people, practices and objects such as tables in bars or trading stands along the street. In a subsequent (third) phase, the researchers used a further range of sociological methods to explore issues from a participant-centric perspective. These methods ranged from researcher-led engagements in workshops and focus group discussions, to 'citizen action'-led interventions that used the methods of photovoice, participatory mapping and digital story telling (DST). These processes provide a bottom-up perspective while empowering the subjects with an autonomous and independent 'voice'. We present some of these 'voices' in subsequent chapters. In all, 58 business persons partook in these research processes; 21 spaza shop operators were engaged in a series of focus group discussions; 14 shebeeners co-produced DSTs and developed a series of 'house rules' to influence patron behaviour; seven herbalists co-produced DSTs; a further nine business owners of educares, hair salons and taverns co-produced DSTs; and eight street photographers engaged a public audience through photovoice.

The combined findings from the small-area census approach and the socio-spatial research were exposed to public scrutiny through a number of exhibition events conducted during the research timeframe (Figure 2.16).

These exhibitions included our research on the spatial characteristics of shebeens in Sweet Home Farm; an examination of the importance of the street as a space of business in Ivory Park; a study of the rapidly changing characteristics and spatial distribution of micro-enterprises in Delft South; an engagement on the significance of informal food service businesses; and our research on the transformative potential of the high street

FIGURE 2.16 An in-situ street exhibition located within an empty trading structure
Notes: This was held by the researchers and hosted in Ivory Park

through the case of Eveline Street. Some of the material from these exhibits is showcased on the website: www.emergentcity.co.za. Apart from the Eveline Street research, the other exhibitions were conducted within the townships with the intention to stimulate dialogue between researchers, policy-makers and the entrepreneurs themselves. More than sharpening our focus, these public engagements helped to shine light on aspects of the township business environment and social processes that we had overlooked. This resulted in further inquiry to patch the gaps, while encouraging the researchers to contemplate higher order questions, such as the implications of the current state of the township micro-enterprises for the future development of the township economy and business growth.

In the next section, we detail the particular use of social-spatial methods to augment the evidence and arguments presented in this book.

Diagrams and drawings

Focusing on the way individual businesses utilise space, we used architectural methods to investigate the influence of layout, building structures, fixtures and objects. The findings of these explorations offer a unique perspective on the form and function of home-based township businesses. We used diagrams and drawings to show spatial arrangements, including the position of objects, openings and furniture; to provide an indication of size; and to describe the use of space between people and objects. In the same way we have used geospatial maps, our diagrams constitute a baseline reference against which the researchers have sought to indicate boundaries and thresholds subject to change. In documenting change, diagrams can fulfil an explanatory function, as we will describe in the Eveline Street case. To show how objects influence spatial and social situations, the researchers utilised ethnographic drawings. These drawings were produced *in situ* through observation. Ethnographic drawings are primarily descriptive in function, illustrating the actual as well as potential use of spaces. Their descriptive power helps to illuminate the interdependencies of people, objects and practices in particular contexts as well as their relative proximities, complementing textual narratives with a real-world perspective. In some of our diagrams and drawings, we have indicated ephemeral uses which, although inactive at the time of research, may have occurred in the past (as evident in building heritage) or are positioned to emerge in the future (as evident in a business set up to accommodate off-street parking).

In our study of land use (see Chapter 4), situational plan diagrams and three-dimensional axonometric diagrams enabled the researchers to identify and highlight commercial and residential uses of property and, importantly, indicate how actual land use deviates from legal property boundaries and building restrictions. As we argue in Chapter 4, these non-compliances impact on the ability of the entrepreneur to regularise her/his business. To document the spatial relationships between different uses of street space (see Chapter 5), including informal business, customers, vehicles and pedestrians, the researchers employed a combination of situational and ethnographic drawings and annotated photographs, triangulating these sources. The ethnographic drawings enabled us to isolate particular aspects of street life such as actor surveillance, and objects such as a sidewalk tree, to show the combinations of objects, spaces, persons and practices in the organisation and operation of informal street markets (see Figures 2.17 and 2.18).

To describe the changes in high-street buildings on Eveline Street (see Chapter 6), we used three-dimensional axonometric diagrams as an explanatory tool to describe the spatial evolution of residential property in two trajectories; to provide commercial space oriented towards the street (thus public realm) and to provide additional accommodation units (in a private realm). These drawings show how building functionality changed over time through piecing together evidence from aerial photographs and our physical inspection of the architectural heritage of buildings in diverse states of transformation. To research the complex socio-cultural-entrepreneurial space of shebeens (see Chapter 9), situational plan drawings, ethnographic sketches and annotated photographs enabled the researchers to understand the reciprocal manner in which infrastructure has been configured to influence social outcomes, differentiate businesses into niche segments, and maintain separation between public and private realms in a highly fluid context where the use of space has to be constantly managed to preserve home life while accommodating public patronage (see Figure 2.19).

FIGURE 2.17 Diagram illustrating the surveillance role of street traders

FIGURE 2.18 Diagram illustrating the use of an object (tree) for shade

SECURITY BARS
All windows are guarded with security bars to protect from theft. Windows that do not yet have glass are covered with sheeting from the outside, which can be tilted open for interaction with the porch.

BENCHES
Benches are made of scrap material placed on top of beer crates.

FRONT DOOR

POOL TABLE
The two pool tables in the shebeen attract a range of customers at different times in the day. In the afternoon, youth visit to play pool, though they are not permitted to drink. In the evenings there is a mix of young adults and middle-aged men and women. Although it gets very crowded in the evenings, pool playing continues.

TABLES
The three tables in Zwai's place facilitate relaxed socialising during the day, and large groups during the evening.

ASHTRAYS
Smoking is permitted in the shebeen.

SOAPY WATER
A bucket filled with soapy water props open the back door. Customers use it to clean their hands when returning from the urinal.

FIGURE 2.19 Annotated photograph of a shebeen interior, documenting relationships that influence the spatial use of the venue

In sum, our use of diagrams and drawings provides a narrative of the diverse ways that space is used and the multiple, complementary and contradictory demands for its use.

Our final use of drawings is in the form of infographics. This method is used to synthesise complex findings, while illustrating processes, systems and relationships of actors and transactions. To describe taxi routes in Delft South (see Chapter 7), infographics are used to show the spatial connection between this township and various destinations within the City of Cape Town (CoCT), the cost of fares, the scale of operations and the approximate distribution of revenue between the actors within the minibus taxi sector. Finally, we use graphics in a polemic manner, to communicate messages. This method was used in an action research intervention with shebeen businesses. Inspired by the deployment of graphics in instructive road traffic signs, we co-produced a series of signs to communicate 'dos and don'ts' of acceptable and unacceptable patron behaviour, which were then translated into house-rule signage to be prominently displayed within venues. This research process enabled us to understand the micro-control strategies that shebeen owners utilise to reduce the risks of harm in their venues, a subject we explore in Chapter 9.

Photography

A series of photographs is showcased in each chapter. Photographs were captured in all research sites, taken to record actual businesses and practices. We use photographs in four ways: firstly, as an observational introduction to the context or character of a place, space or micro-enterprise; secondly, as an analytical tool, supported with illustrations and annotations, to describe functional uses and people-object relationships; third, as a measure of the change in use through time; and fourth, as a polemic device. The first use is intended to connect the readers to the subject, enabling them to access the research in a more informed manner. The second use has been employed to detail specific relationships identified and researched through the qualitative investigation, such as the linkages between the positioning of objects (table, chairs, bar rails, lighting and so forth) within a business and its multiple users (see Chapter 9). Our third methodological use of photography was to document and communicate change. We employed time-lapse photography to record shifts in the use of space over time and show evidence of the differences in activities in the same locality from day to night. The polemical device of photographs, our fourth use, is applied to characterise the items costing less than R1.00 sold by survivalists (Chapter 3) and illustrates the widespread distribution of contraband, suspect and illicit products (Chapters 8, 9 and 11). These curated photographs convey powerful messages which, although substantiated in our qualitative research, invite the reader to contemplate the significance of the message in terms of the developmental implications (Figure 2.20).

Photographs underpin the narratives of the research to enrich our qualitative understanding. In Chapter 5, for example, we conducted an analysis of the street, using the photographic insights (including the photographer's framing of the images) from a photovoice research process undertaken by eight local street photographers who recorded photographs of street life in Ivory Park over the course of one month. Photographs were selected and uploaded by these photographers to a public Facebook page.

FIGURE 2.20 This image shows the range of food products that were purchased in the township of Delft South for the price of R1.00 or less
Credit: Justin Patrick

These daily postings and associated photographer musings were open for public engagement on the role of streets in socialisation and business, posts which in turn mobilised over 1 000 social media followers and highlighted the important role of informal businesses for township residents. Some of these images are reproduced in this book, with acknowledgement.

Personal stories

Throughout this book, we have sought to communicate the experiences of entrepreneurs through personal stories. Listening to local narratives was an important aspect of the small-area census research and our immersion in the field afforded an opportunity to learn from a diverse range of individuals, both entrepreneurs and community members. In the second research phase, the research specifically sought to understand entrepreneurship from an individual perspective. The resulting socio-spatial case studies focused on a narrower cohort of entrepreneurs with whom we investigated their business in depth. Some of the most interesting stories were obtained through unstructured interviews in which our informants spoke frankly about their challenges and were often surprisingly generous in sharing confidential information. Although most township entrepreneurs are cautious and apprehensive to engage with researchers, our experience was that roughly one individual in 10 would be accessible to tell their story with openness and in detail. Such individuals were wellsprings of insight and helped us to comprehend our collected evidence, and the unwritten rules and workings of informal institutions (Chapter 12). To contextualise individual voices into a broader context, we conducted a series of small-group focus discussions with spaza shopkeepers, liquor traders, waste collectors, taxi drivers, traditional medicine practitioners and entrepreneurs in food service and street trade.

Personal stories constituted the core evidence in the third phase of participatory visual action research, with the participants uninhibited by our research interests and free to focus on issues of significance in their personal lives and businesses. An important component of the story generating evidence were the DSTs. These were developed in action research with Rasta herbalists to understand their constraints in wild medicine harvesting; in a series of engagements with shebeen operators to document their experiences of informality and police action; in an engagement with street traders to understand their spatial vulnerability; and through research with educare owners to learn about their obstacles to formalisation and thus access to state subsidies.

While the personal stories we share in this book are subjective, we have sought to verify the evidence through triangulation to other data sources, including the business census and survey findings, diagrams and drawings, photographs and document artefacts. Personal stories were especially valuable in understanding both the social and cultural context of township entrepreneurs and the individual challenges of running a business. The researchers learnt through these stories, for example, about the personal experience of business failures as a result of external challenges, such as a sudden change in competition within the spaza sector (Chapter 8) or police raids on shebeens (Chapter 9). Personal stories gave us a more holistic understanding of the pressures on a micro-enterprise from within the household, with numerous individuals telling of their business struggles not from impersonal forces, as in the above examples, but individualised and idiosyncratic 'shocks' such as illness, a death in the family, or unscrupulous agents scamming them of their savings. As a collective, the various personal stories help to qualify and contextualise the abstract data sources which underpin our research. In each chapter, we use these stories in different ways (narration, quotations, and through visual products) to illustrate the nature of the various sectors within the township economy.

Ethical considerations

Undertaking research on the informal economy is challenging. Nearly all the businesses we identified were informal; many sold products illegally and some sold illicit products. Most businesses operated without municipal consent; thus, it was important to ensure that the identities of the research participants remained anonymous. Participation in the business survey was voluntary and no participants were paid for their insight. A minority of the identified business operators (typically the employees within the business who felt unauthorised to speak for the entity) refused to participate in the survey. Amongst the informants who voluntarily agreed to participate, some chose to withhold information on certain subjects whereupon the researchers did not press further on the matter. Prior to the survey commencement, the researchers explained that the research was not connected to government and respondent identities and other confidential information would not be shared. In the survey, the researcher recorded the information which was offered even when there was countervailing evidence (from observation, or stories that we had been told) to suggest a different answer. In conducting the research, the authors made no commitment to the participants to readdress their concerns or in any way alter their business situation. Some of the persons who participated in the research with the greatest enthusiasm took advantage of the opportunity to 'off-load' grievances, especially those directed at government.

The data obtained through these surveys were anonymised. The anonymised quantitative aspects of the dataset are publicly accessible to researchers and are available from the DataFirst (2016) portal (zaf-slf-tms-2010-2013-v1). In this dataset, we have not made the GPS coordinates of the businesses publicly accessible. Furthermore, the qualitative component has not been released since it includes information through which individual and specific businesses could be identifiable. As part of our effort to uphold confidentiality, we have removed facial recognition on all photographs through blurring. Similarly, we have sought to remove the names of the businesses in our case studies but have retained the names of those businesses whose location and enterprise dynamics are otherwise unreported. As discussed earlier, the enterprise distribution maps are illustrative and provide a general indication of the spatial position of businesses in particular areas. The relatively low granularity of these maps does not reveal the position of particular businesses at the property or micro-level. In our presentation of documents and artefacts, we have removed names and other confidential information, though we have retained this information in the case of billboards and flyers where these were intended for public use.

In participatory research, the methodologies require heightened sensitivity in respect of confidentially and consent. Black et al. (2018) have noted that the integrity of these methods lies in working with participants to make decisions about how to proceed with the research and securing agreement on 'if, where, when and how' (p. 23) the outputs can be used and shared. In our DST research processes and in the photovoice project the participants were afforded latitude to specify their terms of consent: some decided to make their stories publicly available, other specified restricted use. We have only included in this book visual materials and stories for which full consent was given. The business operators in our case studies of land use (Chapter 4 and Chapter 12) and shebeen venues (Chapter 9) all provided their consent for the research to be undertaken and materials to be used publicly. We have not revealed the business names or their precise locations. In sharing voices, we have referred to individuals by their first names, though some of these names are not their real names but the names by which they chose to be known.

In the course of the research, we endeavoured to share the research findings with the participants and afford them an opportunity to engage with the authors. This aim was difficult to fulfil in the business census and survey components, although by hosting exhibition events *in situ* some of the participants in certain sites are afforded access to the information. The translation of the research findings into visual outputs (such as maps, diagrams, signs, etc.) has helped to make aspects of our research accessible to people who might not be able to access academic text. The participatory research processes enabled the authors to share the research findings to a greater degree and collaborate in knowledge co-production. Our interaction with the participants would influence the way we thought about people-centred and power-centred responses, helping us to more fully recognise the personal struggles and achievements that underpin all township entrepreneurial endeavours. All participants were given printed (hard) copies and electronic (digital) copies of the outputs. It is our ambition to provide these individuals with a copy of this book.

Our research provided few concrete benefits to participants. Some individuals benefited from the chance to tell their 'story' to an attentive audience; some were able to speak about grievances; and some were able to express their development desires. A few of these 'voices' have found expression in this book. In the Conclusions (Chapter 13) we hold out little hope that our knowledge and understanding will influence policies, certainly not in the short-term. If it reshapes how other researchers, strategists and policy-shapers think about the township economy and micro-enterprises in particular, then we will feel satisfied that our job has been done. When policy traction towards these goals is finally achieved, we anticipate that the township business environment will have changed in shape and form. Many who shared information on which this book is based will, in all likelihood (see Chapter 3), not be operating their business from the same spaces and places or indeed even be running the same business in which we encountered them.

3
ENTREPRENEURS & SURVIVALISTS

The chapter examines the township economy in scope and scale. We provide an overview of business trends, microenterprise characteristics and the entrepreneurial strategies through which people pursue self-employment.

CHAPTER 3

Entrepreneurs and survivalists

The chapter examines the township economy in scope and scale. The evidence draws from our research using the small-area census approach. The chapter has three objectives. First, to describe the research results in terms of the relative number of micro-enterprises in each site and the range of business activities identified. Second, to draw broad comparisons across the studied sites and sectors to set the scene for subsequent chapters on specific sector and enterprise dynamics. Our spatial analysis is set at four gradients: one, on intra-site comparison; two, on-site specific business distribution; three, on the relative differences between high-street and residential settings; and four, the nuanced differences between formal settlements and informal settlements. The third objective is to provide an overview of business trends, micro-enterprise characteristics and the entrepreneurial strategies through which people pursue self-employment. Our focus is squarely on micro-enterprises, operating informally in the main, but including those businesses partly compliant with formal regulations. As such, the dataset includes a number of small-size wholesalers situated on the high street, though most operate on a semi-formal or wholly informal basis. We have not included medium size and large size formal businesses such as supermarkets and major retailers in our assessment of the township economy. Such formal businesses were only encountered in demarcated shopping centres and malls, most of which have been established on the periphery of township settlements, a subject we address in Chapter 8.

The micro-enterprise landscape is shaped in equal measure by historical legacies and current market conditions. In their original conceptualisation, townships were planned as residential settlements in which minimal provision was made for local business activities. In our ten sites, there is merely a handful of modest-sized council marketplaces though none of the scale found in inner city localities or common in developing countries (Mörtenböck & Mooshammer, 2015). The residential bias in township layout is an enduring feature of the state's land-use planning, perpetuating systems and policies that limit scope for entrepreneurship and business practice. In this way, the results of our business census provide an indication of the degree to which the apartheid legacy has been disrupted. Micro-enterprises represent a pioneering endeavour to respond to localised demand for goods and services which would otherwise have to be obtained outside the settlement. While some of these business activities constitute a sophisticated reading of cultural and social needs, providing goods and services in ways that are unique and appropriate to peoples' requirements, much township entrepreneurship is the outcome of struggle for survival. The situation of poverty imposes a framework of limitations on people-centred actions, influencing what business activities people seek to pursue and the conditions under which business is conducted. All responses are subject to the capacity of the actors for mobilising power; those with strong power, a minority, can more easily overcome these hurdles and sometimes turn them into an advantage. Most township micro-enterprises, in contrast, have weak power and thus should be considered as an emerging organic response to local economic opportunities within a constrained structural framework, rather than a final outcome, in other words, a business under construction. We are certain that the scope and scale we describe hereafter is rapidly changing, as people explore new business possibilities, micro-enterprises transition in form and function, and the actors deepen strategies to protect, constrain and disrupt the existing business environment. At the same time, powerful actors continue to profit at the expense of broad-based inclusion, monopolising opportunities and directing the extraction of surplus value out of the township economy. In this chapter, we introduce some of the major entrepreneurial role-players, including those whose power responses enable them to sustain their business interests at the disadvantage of persons struggling for survival.

The scope and scale of micro-enterprises

Across the nine townships, we identified and mapped 10 842 micro-enterprise activities. A micro-enterprise activity was understood as a specific economic endeavour, conforming to the system of classification we developed such as selling groceries or providing a business service. These activities were performed by 9 402 unique individuals with 13% of all micro-enterprise activities representing second or third 'businesses' for 730 persons (for example, individuals might cut hair but also separately provide financial services). We accounted for these activities separately in the dataset. To analyse the data, we developed 36 categories, grouping the 10 842 activities under the enterprise category that most accurately described the business. For each category, we developed an original icon to signify its meaning; these are used in the business distribution maps. Our system of classification substantially differs from the International Standard Industrial Classification (ISIC) and most existing studies on the informal sector in South Africa ((Rogan & Skinner 2018; Wills 2009). The reason for not following the ISIC classification is that it does not sufficiently disaggregate the diverse range of activities in the township that might otherwise be lumped within the broad ISIC classifications for 'retail trading'. For example, classification ISIC 6211 refers to 'retail trade in non-specialised stores with food, beverages and tobacco predominating' and ISIC 62190 refers to 'other retail trade in non-specialised stores'. Had we used the ISIC system, a large portion of the identified businesses would thus be classified under these two headings, which would conceal the nuances in our distinction between different forms of retail and business practice.

Some of our 36 categories are closely related, such as grocery retailing 'spaza shops' and 'house shops' or 'shebeens' (unlicensed liquor retailers) and 'taverns'. In these cases, we chose to employ separate categories to emphasise fundamental differences in business orientation and/or scale, as illustrated in Figure 3.1, Figure 3.2, Figure 3.3 and Figure 3.4.

Spaza shops could be distinguished from house shops in the range of products, assets available to the business such as soft drink fridges, business branding and signage, and in their operating hours. Similarly, taverns differ from shebeens by virtue of having a licence to sell liquor, which in turn enables the enterprise to benefit from upstream product branding and services. As illegal businesses, many shebeens operate in a covert manner and minimise investment in assets and infrastructure to obscure their activities from the police and reduce risks. We separated the street sellers of fresh and prepared food products into the categories of 'greengrocers', traders of 'meat, fish and poultry products' and businesses selling 'takeaway' meals.

FIGURE 3.1 A stand-alone spaza shop grocery retailer

FIGURE 3.2 A residential-based house shop with a limited range of products

FIGURE 3.3 Interior of an unlicensed shebeen liquor retailer

FIGURE 3.4 A licensed tavern liquor retailer

We applied the same logic to sellers of hardware (such as plumbing and electrical supplies) and homewares (such as buckets, plastic containers and ornamental items). The category 'hair salon' includes barber shops and hairdressers. We included various 'religious services' as a business category where these activities conformed to our definition of an informal micro-enterprise. This category does not include formal religious institutions. Those businesses categorised as 'street traders' sell a miscellaneous range of products, including and, most importantly, clothes and accessories such as handbags, caps, scarves and jewellery, snacks, cigarettes, newspapers and so forth. As the research had a predominantly urban focus, the category of 'agriculture' refers to persons rearing livestock or producing crops for home consumption, though these activities were generally small in scale and profoundly limited by the absence of open (and arable) land. We classified persons selling live chickens in the 'street trader' category (since they were not raising the chickens but obtaining supplies from other businesses), distinguishing these traders from those that sold prepared meat, poultry and fish products: activities are technically required to be registered in terms of the Businesses Act (No. 71 of 1991) (Schedule 1). In general, we avoided classifying micro-enterprises on the basis of their spatial location where the business activity could be more accurately reflected within a sector categorisation, such as greengrocer rather than street trader.

The total numbers and distribution of identified micro-enterprises categories in each site are shown in Table 3.1.

In numerical terms, the five most common micro-enterprises were the categories 'house shop' (1 612 businesses), 'shebeen' (1 493 businesses), 'grocery retail' (1 180 businesses), 'street trade' (775 businesses) and 'hair salon' (606 businesses). Together these top five categories equate to 52% of all micro-enterprises. Within the collective dataset, 56.4% of activities involved trade in groceries, food and beverages; 31.3% entail the provision of a service (such as hair care or mechanical repair); 8.9% are non-food retail activities; and 3.4% involve artisanal production or the micro-manufacturing of items, such as leather goods, tinsmithed basins, household furniture, welded bars and window frames, door frames and speaker-boxes. To permit the comparison of the data across the sites (given that the sites were of different geographic and demographic sizes), we analysed the data by population size using the variables of population and households. Our population-controlled variable is the number of businesses per 1 000 people. We selected this variable because it is likely to be more accurate than the corresponding variable for household numbers (businesses per 100 households), since household size is flexible as they may expand or contract in response to economic circumstances. To calculate a population-based variable we used StatsSA's 2011 National Population Census data, disaggregated by sub-place boundaries and aligned to our site boundaries. The ranking of all 36 enterprise categories across the nine South African sites, using a population-based variable, is presented in Figure 3.5.

At the top of the scale, the research identified 14.9 house shops for every 1 000 people and at the bottom of the scale 0.02 wholesalers per 1 000. Making up the top five, we identified 13.8 shebeens, 10.9 spaza shops, 7.1 street traders and 5.6 hair salons per 1 000 population respectively. Apart from the next most numerous micro-enterprise activities of takeaways (5.5 per 1 000) and recycling micro-enterprises (5.4 per 1 000), there are fewer than four enterprises per 1 000 people in all the remaining categories.

Across the different sites the ordering of the 36 categories varies slightly, though the variation indicates localised influences in particular categories with the general order and distribution consistent with the collective outcome. In Figure 3.6, we illustrate the different weighting with the aggregate top-five categories (overall) in each site.

TABLE 3.1 Total numbers and distribution of identified micro-enterprise categories in each site

	Browns Farm	Delft South	Imizamo Yethu	Ivory Park	KwaMashu	Sweet Home Farm	Tembisa	Thabong	Vrygrond	Total
Agriculture	10	7	0	8	57	5	23	6	10	**126**
Appliance repair	22	6	7	46	18	4	18	9	14	**144**
Arts and crafts	1	0	4	5	0	0	1	6	0	**17**
Building services	39	22	9	53	6	6	16	10	14	**175**
Business services	28	17	7	43	49	0	57	6	16	**223**
Car wash	22	6	5	17	11	1	27	6	3	**98**
Community service	6	8	0	3	2	0	2	8	3	**32**
Drug dealer	8	8	2	6	11	5	3	2	17	**62**
Educare	42	32	10	37	26	6	42	12	25	**232**
Entertainment service	9	30	7	18	13	7	11	0	10	**105**
Greengrocer	72	21	0	143	3	13	98	39	13	**402**
Grocery retail (spaza)	185	181	77	181	127	56	153	80	140	**1 180**
Hair care	133	63	44	141	39	12	97	48	29	**606**
Health services	49	5	23	39	32	12	25	9	15	**209**
Home maintenance services	0	0	0	0	52	0	0	2	0	**54**
House shop	229	131	47	429	156	37	449	85	49	**1 612**
Miscellaneous liquor sales	2	0	25	76	9	0	9	14	1	**136**
Meat, poultry and fish retail	56	17	4	29	3	9	11	22	14	**157**
Mechanical services	34	52	10	67	49	3	53	45	39	**352**
Micro-manufacturer	32	22	5	59	55	4	21	20	9	**227**
Personal services	0	0	12	4	0	2	6	4	1	**29**
Phones	35	10	4	49	29	4	39	0	4	**166**
Recycling	68	16	5	122	194	18	83	65	10	**581**
Religious services	65	38	13	24	42	11	27	38	35	**293**
Restaurants	3	5	6	2	1	2	10	2	1	**32**
Shoe repairs	15	4	2	32	6	3	21	10	1	**94**
Specialist stores	10	7	10	33	4	1	12	12	11	**100**
Shebeens	285	102	154	256	252	111	141	62	130	**1 493**
Street trade	51	17	30	313	122	36	118	77	11	**775**
Tailors	21	11	8	31	9	1	27	13	6	**127**
Takeaways	125	36	55	144	101	19	77	22	18	**597**
Taverns	7	18	1	21	21	0	29	32	1	**130**
Transport services	45	3	8	13	38	12	14	6	3	**142**
Tuck shops	0	0	1	62	21	0	0	19	0	**103**
Wholesalers	0	2	0	0	0	0	0	0	0	**2**
Wood and coal	0	4	0	14	2	1	0	2	6	**29**
Total	**1 709**	**901**	**595**	**2 508**	**1 556**	**401**	**1 720**	**793**	**659**	**10 842**

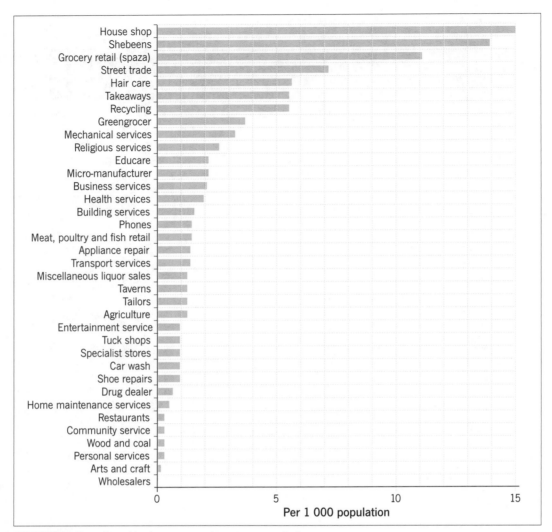

FIGURE 3.5 Proportion of businesses per category – across all sites

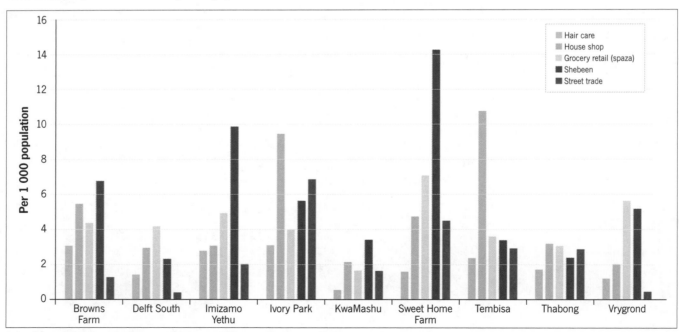

FIGURE 3.6 Top five categories (by business numbers) across all sites

Hair-care activities are relatively less frequent in KwaMashu, Vrygrond and Delft than in Browns Farm, Imizamo Yethu, Ivory Park and Tembisa for reasons that remain unclear, but might reflect either the comparative spatial distance of these latter settlements from inner-city informal markets where hair care is common. House shops were commonplace in Ivory Park and Tembisa, with some of these shops selling paraffin as a result of the then electricity crisis (the census was undertaken in 2012). Spaza shops were proportionately fewer in KwaMashu. This might reflect the influence of two retail malls within the site, though it could also reflect the relatively low penetration of migrant-operated businesses (and thus less competition) in this category in KwaMashu. This topic is discussed in Chapter 8. Street trade was especially important in Ivory Park and Sweet Home Farm. In the former, the result is attributable to the high number of immigrant traders from Mozambique and Zimbabwe for whom the trading space of the street has comparatively lower entry barriers than operating from business premises. We discuss this topic in Chapter 5. In the case of Sweet Home Farm, the high participation in street trade reflects two distinct spaces within the site in which an agglomeration of activities occur; in particular, the retail of live poultry and the recycling and sale of recycled bricks.

Businesses selling liquor and providing social spaces for leisure are common in all sites, though are particularly numerous in the informal settlements within the research site of Browns Farm, Sweet Home Farm, Imizamo Yethu and Vrygrond. The high number of on-consumption venues, as we explain in Chapter 9, reflects the demand for socially distinct environments where people connect around common (though divergent) social bonds. Such bonds include gender, culture, ethnicity and age, with venues responding to the desire for exclusiveness through spatial mechanisms and strategies to foster particular kinds of recreation. In Delft South, the initially low presence of liquor venues, we suspect, reflects their proportionate clandestine nature during what was a time of intense police action against unlicensed trading activities. A resurvey of the site four years later found that the number of located liquor retail outlets had increased by 32%, whereas spaza shops numerically decreased by 14% (Charman & Petersen 2017), thus indicating a degree of fluidity in the ordering of these categories over time.

Apart from hair care, which falls into the top-five group, the most numerous micro-enterprise activities providing services (in order of collective prevalence) were recycling, mechanical services for the repair of cars, equipment and machinery, educares, business services, health services (including traditional healers) and building services; see Figure 3.7 and Figure 3.8 for examples of some of these micro-enterprise categories.

Interestingly, the role of service businesses in the township economy varies considerably between sites. In Delft South, Thabong and Vrygrond, we identified a higher proportion of business activities providing mechanical repair services (such as panel beating or engine workshops) compared to other sites, notably informal settlements where poverty is more prevalent and people possess fewer assets such as cars that require maintenance. In contrast, we identified considerable numbers of health service micro-enterprises in the form of traditional healers in the informal settlements of Imizamo Yethu, Sweet Home Farm and Overcome Heights (part of Vrygrond). As a proportion of all identified activities, recycling of plastic and glass bottles was especially prominent in KwaMashu and Thabong where the collection is an activity driven by pensioners with support from upstream buy-back centres. Educares are present in equal measure across all sites, though a slightly higher proportion was noted in Vrygrond and Delft South where external religious organisations have established and support such businesses as part of their outreach programmes. The business services category incorporates a diverse range of micro-enterprises, including internet cafes, informal money lenders, street photographers, removal services, driving schools, sign writers, undertakers, recording studios and equipment hire, and businesses purchasing gold and jewellery to name some of the most notable activities identified. Within this category, we include phone shops, in other words, businesses which provide public payphones. Prior to the widespread availability of cell phones and low-cost increments of pay-as-you-go airtime such businesses were commonplace. As we subsequently learnt in Delft South, between 2010 and the resurvey in 2015, phone shops had completely vanished.

FIGURE 3.7 Waste recycling is an important livelihood activity for women pensioners

FIGURE 3.8 Automotive service businesses, such as car repairs, are largely male activities

Spatial patterns

A principal advantage of the small-area census approach is that it enabled us to map the spatial distribution of all businesses. Figures 3.9, Figure 3.10, Figure 3.11, Figure 3.12, Figure 3.13, Figure 3.14, Figure 3.15, Figure 3.16, and Figure 3.17 indicate the spatial distribution by category of the 10 842 micro-enterprises across the nine South African sites.

From an ocular perspective, one can readily discern a clustering of micro-enterprises in high streets and the relatively consistent spatial distribution of residential business in each of the localities. Within these sites, there is visual evidence of varying concentrations of businesses within particular sites (Browns Farm, Figure 3.9, top middle), contrasting with formally established neighbourhoods and informal settlements where incomes are comparatively lower and residents are more reliant on self-employment (Browns Farm, top middle). There are notable spatial patterns to the distribution of businesses. Across all nine South African sites, we noted a distinction between the kinds of businesses that gravitate towards the high street (defined as the main and secondary transport feeder routes utilised by minibus taxis) and those micro-enterprises situated within residential localities, operating either from private homes or on public land and serving localised neighbourhood markets. The contrasting situation can be seen in the comparison of the data showing the proportion of businesses in high streets (Figure 3.18) and residential locations (Figure 3.19).

In general, township high streets are the main destination for the activities of street trading and service-related activities such as hair care, specialist shops and greengrocers. Across all sites, 25% of business activities occur on high streets, though in respect to specific categories, the figure increases in the case of street trade (59%), appliance repair (54%), restaurants (53%), car washes (52%), and hair care (51%). The maps reveal how street-based micro-enterprises densify at sites of concentrated pedestrian activity in high streets, around transport nodes and retail hubs. We analyse the reasons for the gravitation of certain categories to street localities in Chapter 5. Conversely, within residential neighbourhoods, businesses are more evenly distributed: 90% of house shops, 90% of shebeens, 87% of entertainment services, 85% of tuck shops, 82% of businesses selling meat, poultry and fish, 81% of health services and 81% of spaza shops are situated in residential contexts. Most of these micro-enterprises operate from private landholdings, either from within the house/shack or from separate structures. Certain residential-based enterprises, including hair salons, grocery stores and food takeaways tend to operate from public pavements within residential areas, and commonly, rent utilities (such as electricity and water) from an adjacent property owner.

Focusing on the residential areas in these townships, one can discern a pattern of distribution which indicates the existence of markets that serve local neighbourhoods. This pattern can be clearly seen in the cases of grocery retailers and liquor retailers. The spatial distribution indicates that such businesses serve a neighbourhood niche, trading on their close proximity to people's homes to sell basic consumables on a regular 'as needed' basis. From discussions with residents, we learnt that in poor households, people limit the storage of consumables such as bread and liquor at home in order to proactively manage consumption demand from extended family members who may live in or have access to the house. In the case of spaza shops, the spatial distribution indicates that business competition is restricted to sub-neighbourhood markets that might comprise a small street section or an area of about 74 households (the average number of spaza shops per population unit across all nine South African sites).

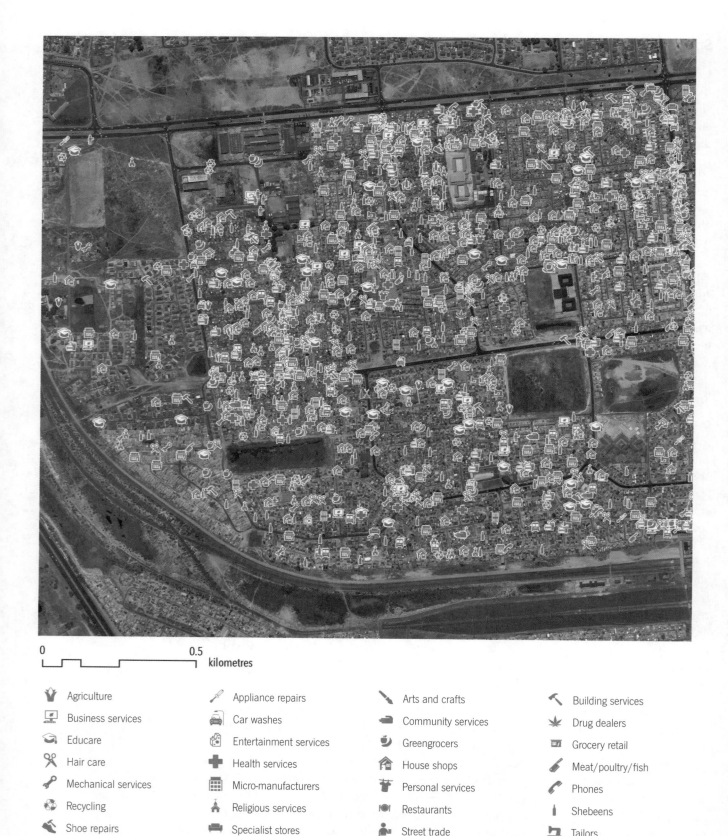

Agriculture

Business services

Educare

Hair care

Mechanical services

Recycling

Shoe repairs

Takeaways

Wood and coal

Appliance repairs

Car washes

Entertainment services

Health services

Micro-manufacturers

Religious services

Specialist stores

Taverns

Arts and crafts

Community services

Greengrocers

House shops

Personal services

Restaurants

Street trade

Transport services

Building services

Drug dealers

Grocery retail

Meat/poultry/fish

Phones

Shebeens

Tailors

Wholesalers

FIGURE 3.9 Distribution of micro-enterprises by enterprise category – Browns Farm and Hazeldene Estate, Philippi November 2011

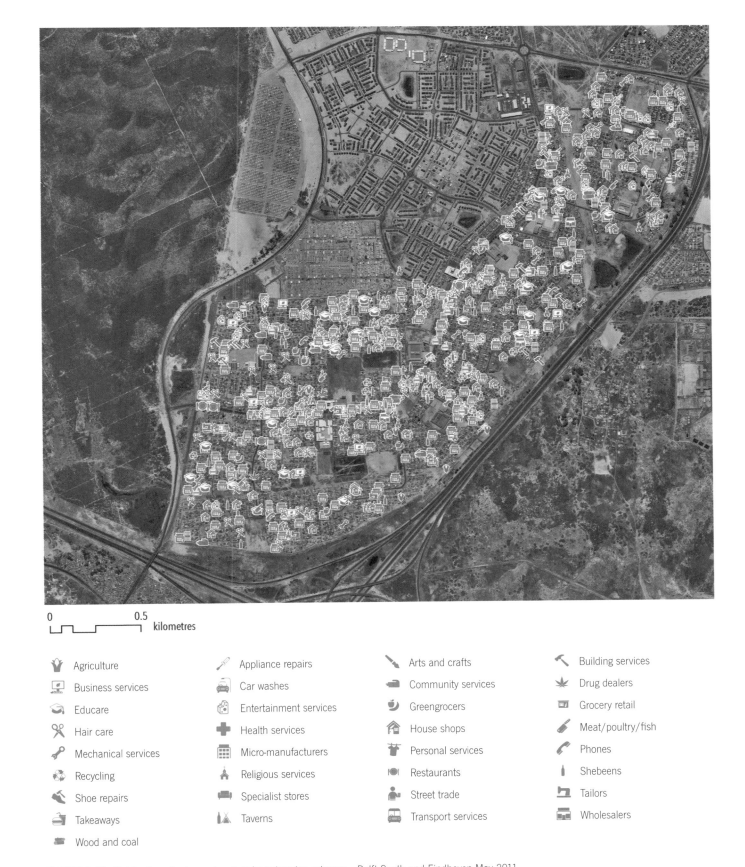

0   0.5
kilometres

🌱 Agriculture	🪛 Appliance repairs	🖌 Arts and crafts	🔨 Building services
💻 Business services	🚗 Car washes	🛋 Community services	🌿 Drug dealers
🛍 Educare	🎮 Entertainment services	🍴 Greengrocers	🛒 Grocery retail
✂ Hair care	➕ Health services	🏠 House shops	🔪 Meat/poultry/fish
🔧 Mechanical services	🗄 Micro-manufacturers	👕 Personal services	📞 Phones
♻ Recycling	⛪ Religious services	🍽 Restaurants	🍶 Shebeens
👟 Shoe repairs	🛋 Specialist stores	🧍 Street trade	🔨 Tailors
🥡 Takeaways	⛺ Taverns	🚌 Transport services	🗄 Wholesalers
🪵 Wood and coal			

FIGURE 3.10 Distribution of micro-enterprises by enterprise category – Delft South and Eindhoven May 2011

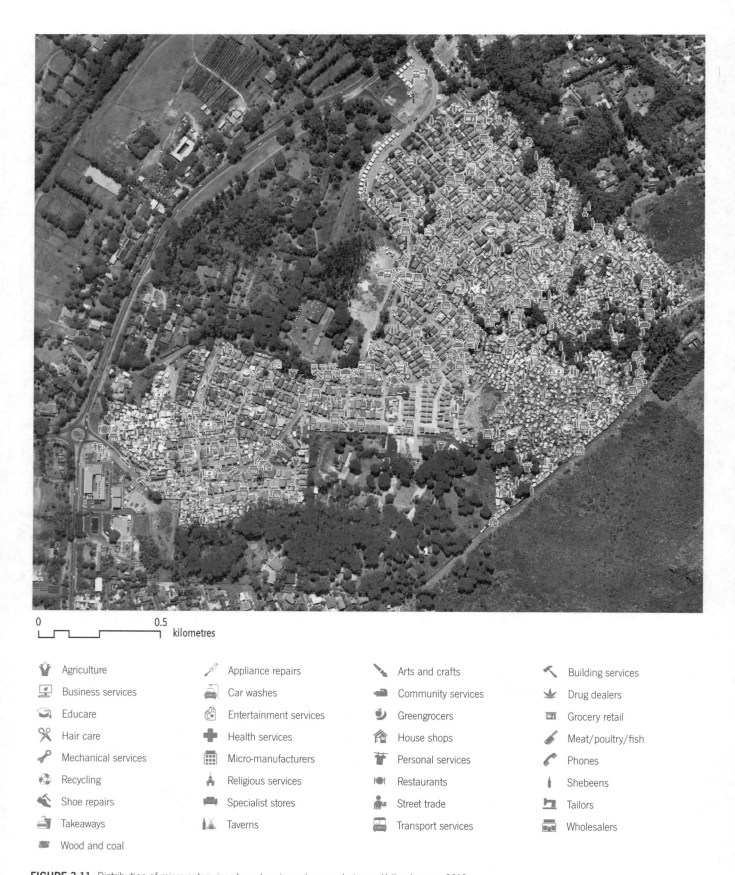

0			0.5	

kilometres

👑	Agriculture	🔧	Appliance repairs	🖌	Arts and crafts	🔨	Building services
💻	Business services	🚗	Car washes	🤝	Community services	🌿	Drug dealers
🎓	Educare	🎮	Entertainment services	🥕	Greengrocers	🛒	Grocery retail
✂	Hair care	➕	Health services	🏠	House shops	🔪	Meat/poultry/fish
🔑	Mechanical services	🏢	Micro-manufacturers	👕	Personal services	📞	Phones
♻	Recycling	⛪	Religious services	🍽	Restaurants	🍾	Shebeens
👟	Shoe repairs	🛋	Specialist stores	🧍	Street trade	🏪	Tailors
🍳	Takeaways	⛺	Taverns	🚌	Transport services	🏬	Wholesalers
🪵	Wood and coal						

FIGURE 3.11 Distribution of micro-enterprises by enterprise category – Imizamo Yethu January 2013

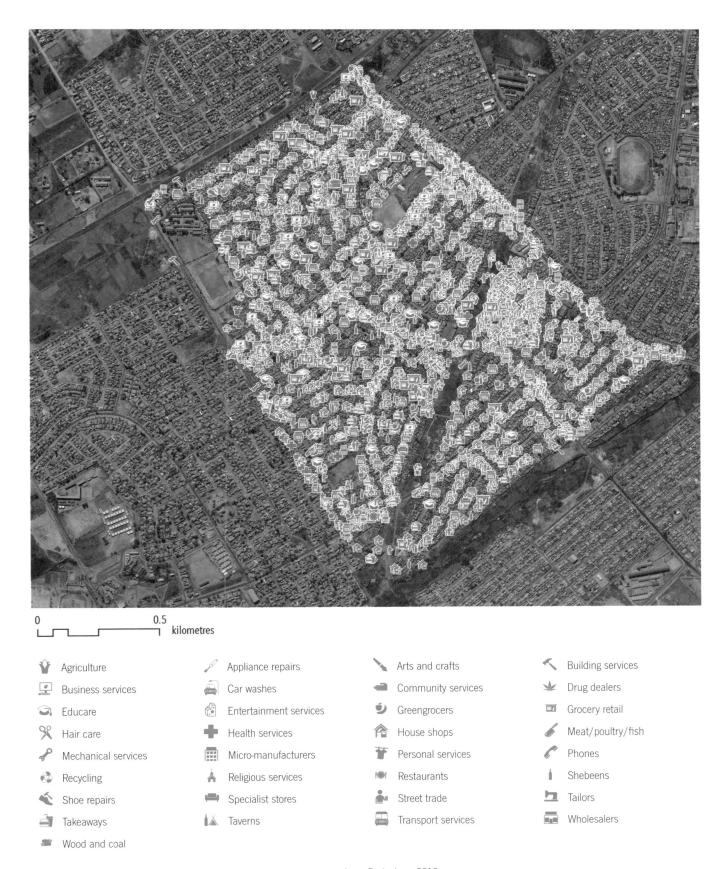

0   0.5
kilometres

Agriculture	Appliance repairs	Arts and crafts	Building services
Business services	Car washes	Community services	Drug dealers
Educare	Entertainment services	Greengrocers	Grocery retail
Hair care	Health services	House shops	Meat/poultry/fish
Mechanical services	Micro-manufacturers	Personal services	Phones
Recycling	Religious services	Restaurants	Shebeens
Shoe repairs	Specialist stores	Street trade	Tailors
Takeaways	Taverns	Transport services	Wholesalers
Wood and coal			

FIGURE 3.12 Distribution of micro-enterprises by enterprise category – Ivory Park, June 2012

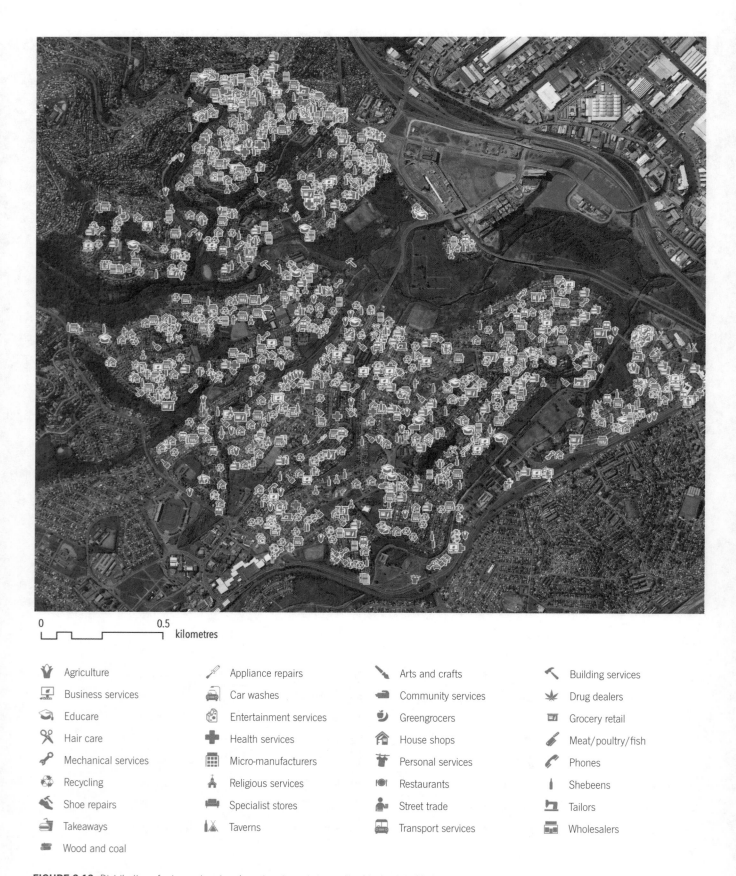

0   0.5   kilometres

	Agriculture		Appliance repairs		Arts and crafts		Building services
	Business services		Car washes		Community services		Drug dealers
	Educare		Entertainment services		Greengrocers		Grocery retail
	Hair care		Health services		House shops		Meat/poultry/fish
	Mechanical services		Micro-manufacturers		Personal services		Phones
	Recycling		Religious services		Restaurants		Shebeens
	Shoe repairs		Specialist stores		Street trade		Tailors
	Takeaways		Taverns		Transport services		Wholesalers
	Wood and coal						

FIGURE 3.13 Distribution of micro-enterprises by enterprise category – KwaMashu July 2013

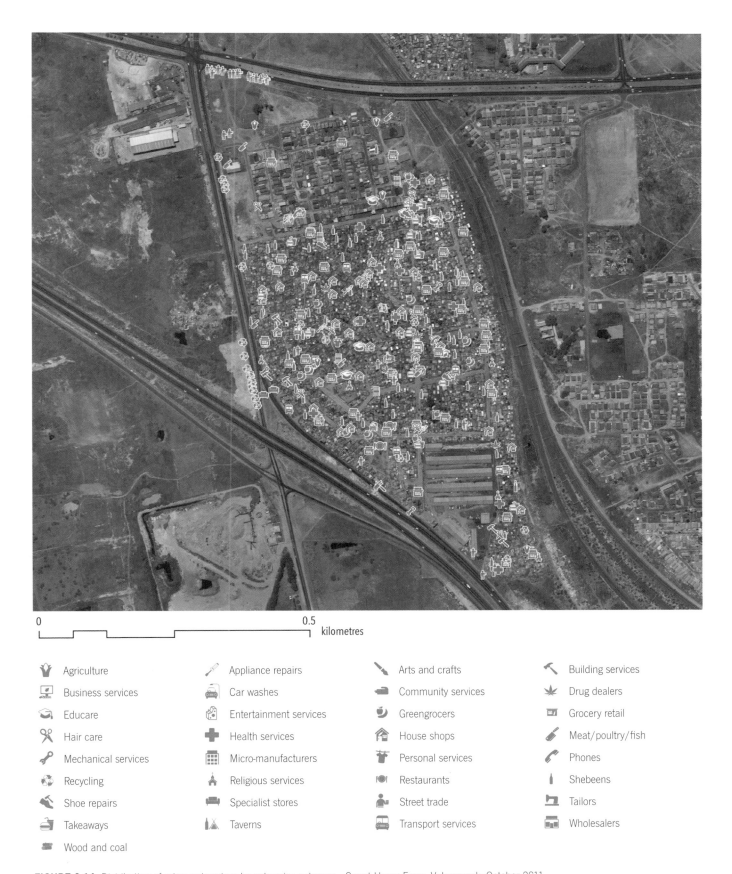

	Agriculture		Appliance repairs		Arts and crafts		Building services
	Business services		Car washes		Community services		Drug dealers
	Educare		Entertainment services		Greengrocers		Grocery retail
	Hair care		Health services		House shops		Meat/poultry/fish
	Mechanical services		Micro-manufacturers		Personal services		Phones
	Recycling		Religious services		Restaurants		Shebeens
	Shoe repairs		Specialist stores		Street trade		Tailors
	Takeaways		Taverns		Transport services		Wholesalers
	Wood and coal						

FIGURE 3.14 Distribution of micro-enterprises by enterprise category – Sweet Home Farm, Vukuzenzele October 2011

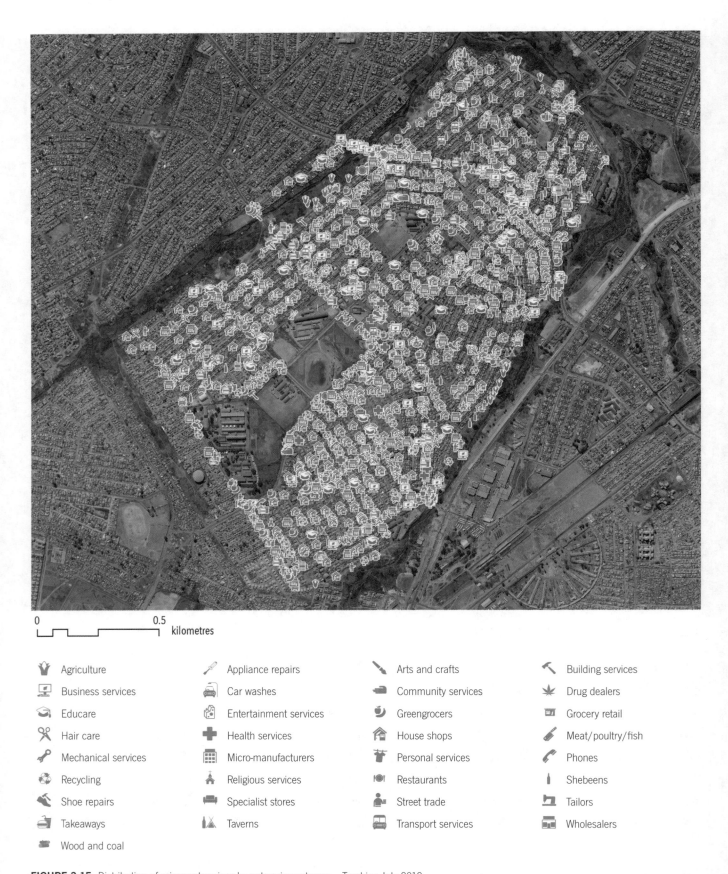

0   0.5
|___|___|___| kilometres

🜊 Agriculture	🔪 Appliance repairs	🜋 Arts and crafts	🔨 Building services
💻 Business services	🚗 Car washes	🖐 Community services	🌿 Drug dealers
🜍 Educare	🎮 Entertainment services	🜎 Greengrocers	🜏 Grocery retail
✂ Hair care	✚ Health services	🏠 House shops	🜐 Meat/poultry/fish
🔧 Mechanical services	▦ Micro-manufacturers	🜑 Personal services	📞 Phones
♻ Recycling	⛪ Religious services	🍽 Restaurants	🍾 Shebeens
👞 Shoe repairs	🛋 Specialist stores	🧍 Street trade	🜒 Tailors
🜓 Takeaways	🜔 Taverns	🚌 Transport services	🜕 Wholesalers
🪵 Wood and coal			

FIGURE 3.15 Distribution of micro-enterprises by enterprise category – Tembisa July 2012

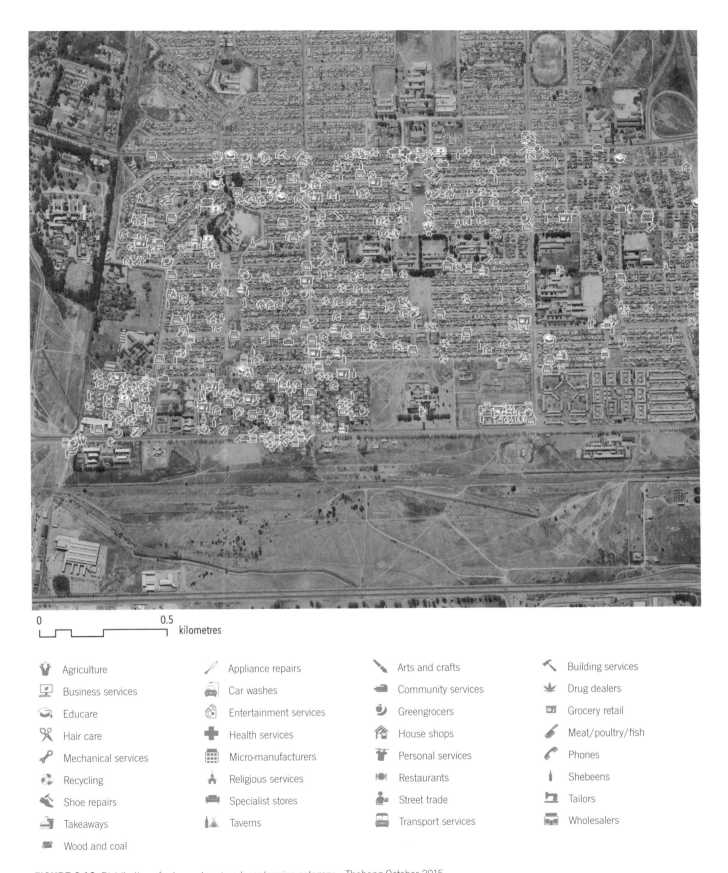

🌱 Agriculture	🔪 Appliance repairs	🗡 Arts and crafts	🔨 Building services
🖥 Business services	🚗 Car washes	Community services	🌿 Drug dealers
📬 Educare	🎲 Entertainment services	🍃 Greengrocers	Grocery retail
✂️ Hair care	➕ Health services	🏠 House shops	Meat/poultry/fish
🔧 Mechanical services	Micro-manufacturers	👕 Personal services	☎️ Phones
♻️ Recycling	⛪ Religious services	🍽 Restaurants	🍾 Shebeens
👞 Shoe repairs	🛋 Specialist stores	👤 Street trade	Tailors
🍴 Takeaways	🍸 Taverns	🚌 Transport services	Wholesalers
🔥 Wood and coal			

FIGURE 3.16 Distribution of micro-enterprises by enterprise category – Thabong October 2015

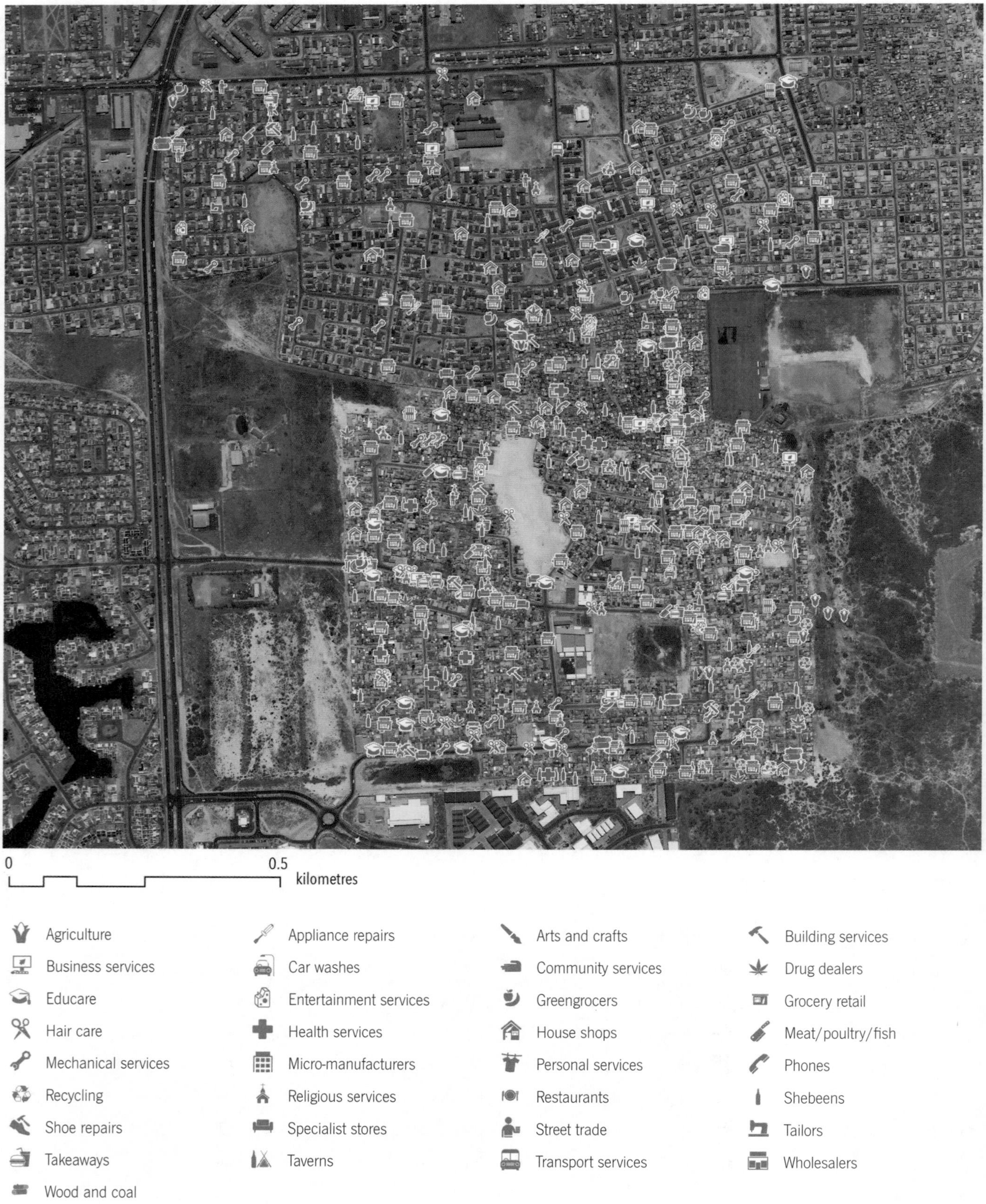

0
0.5
kilometres
Agriculture
Appliance repairs
Arts and crafts
Building services
Business services
Car washes
Community services
Drug dealers
Educare
Entertainment services
Greengrocers
Grocery retail
Hair care
Health services
House shops
Meat/poultry/fish
Mechanical services
Micro-manufacturers
Personal services
Phones
Recycling
Religious services
Restaurants
Shebeens
Shoe repairs
Specialist stores
Street trade
Tailors
Takeaways
Taverns
Transport services
Wholesalers
Wood and coal

FIGURE 3.17 Distribution of micro-enterprises by enterprise category – Vrygrond August 2011

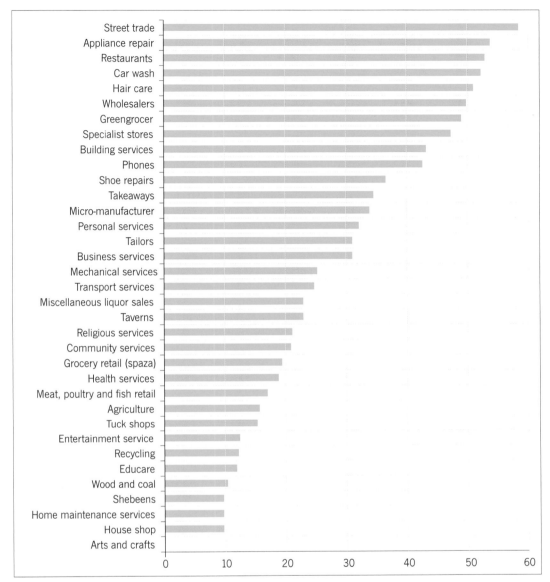

FIGURE 3.18 Proportion of micro-enterprises on high streets – by category (across all sites)

The availability of spaza shops ranges from one shop for every 131 households in KwaMashu to one shop for every 47 households in Vrygrond. For shebeens, the availability of businesses equates to one outlet for every 57 households on average but varies considerably across different sites. We found one venue for every 138 households in Thabong, whereas in the informal settlement of Sweet Home Farm there was one venue for every 29 households. In assessing the significance of the high frequency of shebeens, it should be noted that most of these micro-enterprises are extremely small, selling small quantities of liquor (such as single bottles of beer) to neighbours and operating as a proxy for home storage. While unlicensed shebeens occur in all sites, it must be recognised that within the townships there are relatively few licensed taverns with an average of one tavern for every 769 households. The sparsity of licensed venues is attributable to the policy prescriptions that seek to limit formal liquor trading in areas zoned for residential settlement, a subject addressed in Chapters 4 and 9.

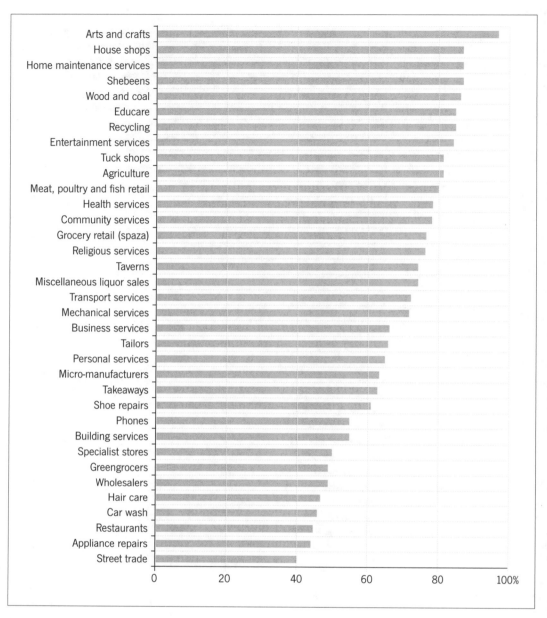

FIGURE 3.19 Proportion of micro-enterprises in residential areas – by category (across all sites)

Change and transition

Our picture of the township economy is far from static. In Delft South, as well as for Eveline Street in Windhoek, we acquired enterprise spatial data at two time points. The data permit an examination of the change in micro-enterprise activities over time. In Delft South, the dataset comprises our 2010/2011 small-area census which was repeated in 2015, while in Eveline Street, the dataset comprises a street survey conducted by the CoW in 2008 with our survey from 2016. The Eveline Street case is discussed in greater detail in Chapter 6.

The Delft South case (analysed in Charman & Petersen 2017; Hartnack & Liedeman, 2016) provides insights into the nature of change over time. Whereas the 2010/2011 census identified 879 micro-enterprises, the 2015 resurvey identified 1 798 micro-enterprises, representing a doubling in business activities. All categories apart from two (spazas shops and phone shops) recorded growth in numbers. Within the ranking of categories, takeaway businesses moved from 7th place in 2010/11 to 1st place in 2015 to become the most numerous enterprise category, spaza shops dropped to 2nd place, street trade moved from 13th place to 3rd place, liquor retail shifted down from 3rd to 4th place and house shops moved down from 2nd to 5th place. Despite these shifts, the resurvey showed the continued predominance of food, groceries and beverages in a retail-dominant economy.

In spatial terms, the research found that both high-street and residential areas experienced growth in micro-enterprise numbers as indicated in Figure 3.20 (and readily comparable to Figure 3.10).

In 2015, a noticeably greater proportion of all business activities took place in high streets (up from 25% to 46.2%), a result of the intensification of street trade around a retail hub and transport nodes. This result speaks to the Eveline Street findings where the number of business activities along the high street grew from 133 in 2008 to 270 in 2016, changing by 103%. The most notable change in the Eveline Street case was the shift in the business structure of the high street from a predominance of bars and carwashes in 2008 to a more diverse mix of businesses in 2016 that included vehicle repair businesses, hair care and business services and food sales.

These comparative sets of data give us an insight into the drivers of change. For example, although much of the Delft South township economy retained the same broad characteristics, new types of businesses had become established by the time of the revisit, including a law practice and micro-manufacturing businesses producing leather products and window frames. We noticed that some of the micro-entrepreneurs with whom we had previously engaged in 2011 had made important strides to grow their business, acquiring new assets and investing in business infrastructure. Yet the data reveals that the major growth in total enterprise activities happened as a consequence of new micro-enterprises commencing trade, most of which could best be described as 'survivalist' (see below for an analytical description of the term), the majority of which were engaged in selling food and beverages as house shops, shebeens and street traders.

The resurvey also revealed important gender dynamics: in Delft South in 2015, 91% of the takeaway outlets, 82% of house shops, 71% of the meat, poultry and fish sellers, and 65% of the liquor retailers were women, the majority of whom were between 40-49 years of age. Through our analysis of the data and interviews with entrepreneurs, we learnt that these female entrants were commonly unable to access employment in the formal sector and sought to utilise the opportunity to conduct business from their places of residence. Many said that they saw their business as a means to supplement overall household income, conducting the business while overseeing the care of their children or elderly parents and performing household duties. In contrast to the profile of food and beverage micro-entrepreneurs, service businesses such as appliance repair, building services, and mechanical services (including panel beating) were predominantly male-run activities. Both men and women are equally present in the hair-care category.

The changing characteristics of the Delft township economy has been influenced by demographic changes. Immigrant entrepreneurs have had altered businesses activities along the Delft high street in particular, where they have established a presence in a range of sectors, including hair care (48% of activities), appliance repair (46% of activities), micro-manufacturing (17% of activities), shoe repair (20% of activities) and specialist shops (50% of activities).

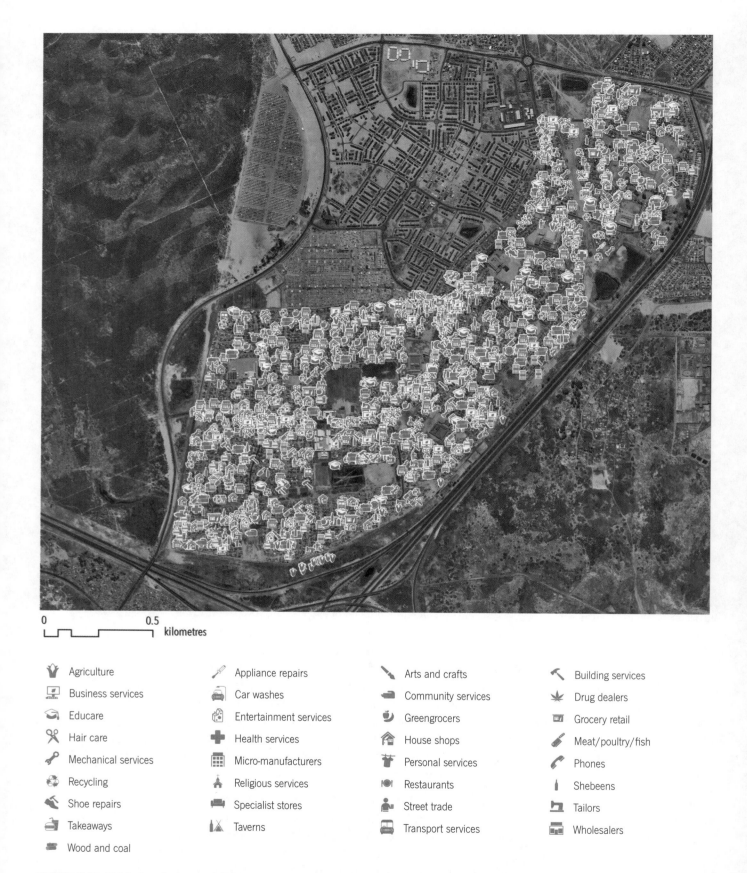

0   0.5   kilometres

🌱 Agriculture		✏️ Appliance repairs		🔨 Arts and crafts		⚒️ Building services
💻 Business services		🚗 Car washes		Community services		🌿 Drug dealers
Educare		🎲 Entertainment services		Greengrocers		Grocery retail
✂️ Hair care		➕ Health services		🏠 House shops		Meat/poultry/fish
🔧 Mechanical services		Micro-manufacturers		Personal services		✒️ Phones
♻️ Recycling		⛪ Religious services		🍽️ Restaurants		Shebeens
👟 Shoe repairs		🛋️ Specialist stores		🧍 Street trade		Tailors
Takeaways		Taverns		🚌 Transport services		Wholesalers
Wood and coal						

FIGURE 3.20 Distribution of micro-enterprises by enterprise category in site revisit – Delft South and Eindhoven September 2015

The research enabled us to inquire into enterprise longevity. Although there is inadequate scholarly evidence on this question, the prevailing view is that micro-enterprises are prone to business failure within the first year (Fatoki, 2014). The Delft South data suggest a slightly different outcome. Our research indicates that 65% of the micro-enterprises identified in 2010/2011 are still in business, a finding which suggests a much higher than anticipated rate of business survival than Fatoki's (2014) figure of 20–30%. Our analysis of the geospatial data found that only 288 micro-enterprises from 2010/2011 survey were still trading in precisely the same locality (within a 15-metre proximity) and conducting business in the same enterprise category. As such we deduce that a considerable number of these 576 long-standing businesses have (presumably) altered their business focus into new sectors and/or shifted their business location in a pivoting strategy (or abrupt shift). In terms of business closure, we noted (via observation and reports from local community members) 187 closed businesses, the bulk of which comprised spaza shops (36), house shops (41), and liquor traders (27), though the highest proportional rate of change was noted among phone shop and appliance repair businesses. Through a series of interviews with former business operators (as reported in Hartnack & Liedeman, 2016), we learnt that there are no simple causes behind business closure. Some micro-enterprises close in the face of substantive and changing business competition; others as a result of crises within the household; and others from changing family dynamics and work opportunities. An important finding was that the informants did not view business closure as a failure, not least because micro-enterprises are usually not reliant on large upfront investment, with respondents instead reflecting on the experience as one of building social capital, acquiring an income, and identifying a new business venture. For many, the experience of business failure had helped to engender 'grit', empowering the individual with a determination to continue their entrepreneurial endeavour though possibly changing the spatial dynamics in the business, changing its product focus and refining their strategies of social networking.

Pathways into business

Though the township economy demonstrates a vibrancy and diversity of micro-entrepreneurial activities, a considerable proportion of these activities are undertaken in pursuit of day-to-day economic survival rather than the longer-term accumulation of profit. This distinction might seem technical, but it highlights the difference in likely business trajectories. Whereas entrepreneurial businesses pursue strategies for firm growth (such as investing in assets, developing technical and business skills, utilising labour and enhancing property value), so-called 'survivalists' (as proposed by Mead & Liedholm 1988) tend to invest no further than maintaining an income stream through a simple trading activity or service offering. Such businesses generally have minimal stock, utilise existing skills, are owner-operated and make no investment in property-related assets. In using the term 'survivalist', we recognise that the notion does not simply reflect the entrepreneurial qualities of the business owner and their micro-enterprise but derives in equal measure from the framework conditions in which they find themselves. We shall examine some of these conditions, including the legacy of apartheid spatial planning; the dominance of large (and corporate) businesses in the food system; the limited skill sets and resources within micro-enterprises; insurmountable regulatory barriers; and institutional exclusion from the financial system. Framework conditions influence the ways in which survivalists conduct business as well as the strategies through which these individuals exercise power to defend or advance their interests. We broadly agree with the argument by Rolfe, Woodward, Ligthelm, and Guimarães (2010) that legal-structural impediments account, in large measure, for the under-capitalisation and resource constraints of township micro-enterprises. We would nevertheless add that framework conditions enable the transfer of wealth away from the township economy. As individuals with comparatively little power, survivalists are unable to redress this situation which reduces their opportunities for deriving a livelihood through self-employment.

Initiative, skills, investment and social capital

Our surveys with business owners indicate that there are four main pathways (or people-centred actions) through which micro-enterprises emerge. The first relates to what is sometimes referred to as 'make work jobs' (see Mukhopadhyay 2011): these usually start out as livelihood strategies through which persons that are unemployed seek to make 'ends meet' utilising whatever assets and resources are accessible and affordable. Potentially, two thirds of all micro-enterprises operate at this level. This is the main pathway for 'survivalist' businesses. Although businesses start out at a micro-scale, evidence indicates that some businesses can grow, sometimes in ways unimaginable at the outset. In this case, the notion that 'time helps', which we confirmed in the case of Delft South, is consistent with research in other African countries (Gulyani & Talukdar 2010; McPherson 1996), yet the literature also offers some important caveats to this reasoning. Gulyani and Talukdar (2010) emphasise that 'living conditions matter' (pp. 1711, 1722); in other words, the place at which people conduct business affects the formation of the enterprise as well as its performance. The authors argue that businesses which operate outside of resource-poor settlements (such as slums) are less likely to be poor. Another important consideration, as noted by McPherson (1996), is that human and social capital has a significant bearing on enterprise growth, such that persons with experience, education and training (and we would add social networks) are better able to grow their businesses than persons with few social resources or entitlements, using Sen's (1981) concept.

Most survivalists are women. This finding reflects the disadvantage women face in their scope for people-centred action and capabilities to mobilise power. Gender influences the space and places in which people conduct business. Women with home-based social responsibilities, such as childcare, are disadvantaged in conducting business activities distant from their residential homes. Care work substantially reduces the availability of time for doing business. Where women participate in business activities that respond to commuter cycles, such as selling takeaway meals in the early morning or early evening, their business has to simultaneously accommodate the social needs of children if there is no one to look after them at home or if the cost of educare is unaffordable. Where women run spaza business, the shop must either close or the operator must call upon someone to help out in the business during the times at which she has to collect children from school. The gender profile of business sectors (see the Delft South case above) reflects McPherson's argument on the role of human and social capital in enabling growth. Men dominate in sectors which require some vocational skills, business assets and specialist equipment, including repair work, micro-manufacturing, building services, transport and religious services. Women are most active in sectors where domestic skills are utilised, such as food preparation, care giving, traditional healing and the management of home-based social spaces for liquor consumption.

The second pathway we identified is based on the acquisition of skills, on-the-job experience and access to the market or customers through working in a business. Young entrepreneurs in the entertainment sector, such as disc jockeys, acquire their skills from their hobby of making and/or playing music which, in turn, can transition to self-employment as they come to master this domain and their service grows in reputation. The process of acquiring skills on the job is an important pathway for informal employees to acquire entrepreneurial skills. We found that the skills-led pathway to entrepreneurship is common in the educare and hair-care sectors. The hair-care business model is founded in the social relations between the hairdresser and client. Should the hairdresser decide to leave a business to set up independently, there is strong possibility that their clients will follow them into the new micro-enterprise. The importance of a customer base manifests in the varying marketing strategies in which hair salons seek to differentiate their brand and spatial position within the township economy, a subject we address in Chapter 11.

The third pathway into entrepreneurship is through strategic financial investment. In many cases, the investor is not involved in the day-to-day operations and instead, has a job or alternative business which provides the source of investment capital. Many of the immigrant-run spaza shops have been established by external investors, either through setting up new shops or buying out struggling businesses, a topic discussed in Chapter 8. Township spaza shops are increasingly being bought and sold as going concerns – a phenomenon not evident in other food and beverage trading sectors. These investors, through what we argue are 'informalist' tactics, aim to maximise business profits through extreme cost minimisation. Most of these investors have no social connection to the township. In contrast, people who grew up in the township and now in formal employment (usually outside the township) have family pressure to finance relatives to establish new micro-enterprises or boost existing businesses. In this alternative case the investment sums are modest, and the business tends to operate at a survivalist level. Businesses are supported with the aim of reducing family financial dependency on the investor, a demand colloquially known as the 'black tax'. Within this third pathway, we encountered several cases where financially 'successful' township entrepreneurs had established new businesses as part of a strategy to diversify their investments through spreading their risk across a range of sectors or operating multiple outlets in different localities. Some of the main risks which township entrepreneurs encounter are theft, state regulatory authorities and jealousy, a topic we examine in greater detail in Chapter 12. Strategies of divestment enable the entrepreneur to spread their risk across different sectors or localities and to reduce their appearance of wealth and its associated social critique.

A fourth pathway is observable where the business is passed on within the extended family from parents to children. This strategy is particularly evident where the business has secure trading rights or physical assets. We found evidence of this strategy in the case of tavern businesses, minibus taxis, and (successful) South African spaza shops.

The four pathways are subject to influences of power. Power is used in multiple ways to secure opportunities and defend markets. Women's exclusion from the taxi sector, as we argue in Chapter 7, reflects the hyper-masculinity of the drivers and patriarchal influence of male elites who control the organising taxi associations. Women are able to mobilise power through social networks, in a bottom-up perspective example, to provide reciprocal support, enable savings in *stokvels* (a subject we discuss in Chapter 12), manage the use of public space or agree on specific business-related protocols (such as informal rules). In these examples, power is mobilised in ways which shape the gendered characteristics of particular sectors.

Among non-survivalist micro-enterprises, we characterise three power-centred strategies to establish and grow profitable businesses: we associate these strategies with pioneers, informalists and violent thugs. The pioneers are individuals who 'trail blaze' the development of markets through, inter-alia, introducing original or uncommon business practices; or spatially positioning their businesses in particular sites to build synergies to other sectors; or investing in infrastructure to enhance the business environment. The central power-consideration to these investments is that the resulting disruption enhances opportunities for both the pioneer and other micro-enterprises. In the case of Eveline Street (Chapter 6), we examine how pioneer tavern investors operating licensed businesses have shaped a high-street economy which over time has expanded in scope and scale to accommodate more micro-enterprises and enable greater sector diversity. The informalists are persons (individuals and groupings) who purposefully operate their business on an informal basis and in contravention of regulatory frameworks, profiting from weaknesses in state enforcement and corruption. Unlike the survivalists, these entrepreneurs generate sufficient profit to theoretically enable legal compliance, but strategically remain informal as a strategy to maximise profits. In the spaza case, we show how informalists achieve this through employing unregistered labour (usually vulnerable persons), selling counterfeit and contraband products, ignoring municipal regulations and avoiding tax scrutiny. Spaza informalists reduce opportunities for survivalist micro-enterprises through selling items at much cheaper prices; this competitiveness is achieved through the scale of their networks and their freedom to operate the business informally. Violent thugs are persons (individuals and groups) that use coercion (both direct and indirect) to eliminate opposition and control markets. In the case of minibus taxi operators (Chapter 7), we describe how violent thugs control the sector via organised structures which allocate user rights on the demarcated routes. In this case, violence is used as an informal regulatory mechanism.

It is important to recognise that the power strategies of the pioneer, the informalist and the violent thug can be mutually inclusive. Pioneers might also use informality and violence to defend or advance their business. Similarly, informalists might have a pioneering impact and use violence. Thugs can be the operators of pioneer businesses and equally look to exploit informality to avoid regulatory compliance. We have used this categorisation of power responses to emphasise the major influence of these strategies, differentiating between actions which can engender wider opportunities and actions which enable profit extraction or restrict opportunities. Men predominate in sectors where informalists and violent thugs control the market.

Opportunity alignment

In service sectors and micro-manufacturing, technical skills training along with on-the-job work experience can provide an important resource for starting a business. Training alone is often insufficient to catalyse start-ups. Access to start-up capital is critical and local networks are important, to share equipment, collaborate on projects and build a base of clients. As we will argue throughout this book, space and infrastructure influences the ways in which the business operates, its risks and its market exposure. Starting-up the business is often not the main challenge; instead, managing income and expenditure and controlling for unforeseen risks are often the biggest obstacles. The relative weighting of these factors can be seen in the case of Mr Best's welding business. A board on a street pole outside a house in Philippi advertises 'Mr. Best: Welding. We do them all kind of work.' He has run his welding business for four years. When we interviewed him, Mr Best was in the process of manufacturing a security gate in the yard, which is his workplace. He works outdoors with an apprentice. Mr. Best has a welding mask but says he prefers to wear sunglasses and also does not wear gloves. '*We don't worry about gloves,*' he said. '*This is the township.*' Mr. Best completed a two-year welding course at

Northlink College and received a certificate, which he said he threw away because it was '*useless*'. After graduating from Northlink, he worked for a company but then decided he could make more money if he went into business for himself.

He had a car, but it was stolen, and now hires a car when he needs to transport material. He purchases his material – rods, steel, tubes – and buys when he has an order. Sometimes people come to sell him welding rods, which, he said, they have stolen from wholesalers. '*I'll buy from them. They also have to make money,*' he said. Burglar gates are the most popular products which he sells for between R750 and R850 each and makes about R250 profit. He also installs burglar bars on windows and manufactures and installs sliding gates. He said that customers pay a deposit, but his biggest challenge was getting customers to pay the balance after the work has been completed. He said work (and therefore income) was irregular and that some months he had no customers at all, but still made a '*good enough*' living from his business. Mr Best would not consider working for a company again. He said that on a good month he could make upwards of R8 000 (especially if he received an order for a couple of sliding gates), but this was balanced by some leaner months, where he earned between R2 000 or R3 000.

When he does not have business of his own, Mr. Best asks welders in his network if he can assist them on their projects. '*But if I have a big job, I will ask others to help me.*' He said there were '*a lot*' of metalworkers in the township and the competition for customers was tough but the welders co-operated with each other informally. '*We talk about where to get cheap material,*' he said. Mr Best used to promote his business at malls, handing out flyers, but now believes word-of-mouth is the best marketing. '*If people know you are the best, they will come to you. I'm Mr. Best – because I'm the best at whatever I do.*' He said the makeshift board on the pole outside his workplace was an effective marketing tool even though the cell phone numbers on it were incorrect.

Mr Best was content to operate from the residential location where he had access to water and electricity (a prepaid meter) in the house. He would not consider working outside on the street because he didn't want to be '*bothered*' by municipal officials. '*The government does nothing for us, so we want nothing to do with them – the best thing they can do is leave us alone.*' He informally transfers skills to young people who assist him when work requires, saying '*I teach young ones – they learn on the job and I pay them. If you don't pass your skill, it dies when you die – and that's useless.*' In subsequent chapters, we shall explore how municipal land-use systems impact to constrain entrepreneurs, preventing individuals such as Mr Best from situating their business in optimal spatial positions. We will also discuss the importance of invisible infrastructure such as social networks and reciprocity in enabling micro-enterprises such as his to maintain resilience and continue in business during a downturn in markets.

Outlook

Micro-enterprises provide township residents with a diverse (though not comprehensive) range of goods and services. Business opportunities lie in the provision of goods and services that are otherwise unobtainable; in operating shops in close spatial proximity to people's homes; aligning trading times to customer demand; providing affordable services (even though these might be inferior in quality) and flexible terms of payment, including credit; and preparing and presenting products in ways that are culturally anticipated and authentic. Through the comparative lens of our business surveys at nine South African sites, we are able to draw a clear picture of the scope of micro-enterprises and describe the patterns of their spatial distribution. Additionally, we have analysed business practices and can distil the common business strategies across the most prominent sectors. We unpack the sector-specific strategies in subsequent chapters. The financial scale of these businesses, however, is unknown. Though micro-enterprises are relatively numerous and provide a wide range of products and services, township residents are not solely dependent on these businesses. Township shoppers can obtain the bulk of their needs from formal business within shopping malls and from informal markets outside the township. Shopping malls also provide specialist products and services, including banking, medical services, pharmaceutical products, cell phone retailers, legitimately branded clothing and footwear, book shops and retailers of jewellery, to list some of the gaps. The absence of financial services outside the malls was noticeable throughout our sites. At the time of conducting our field research, there was only one automatic teller machine (ATM) for dispensing cash for the 45 000 residents of Ivory Park since the site does not contain a mall.

Anecdotal evidence and small-scale studies indicate that shopping malls, and informalist businesses and outside markets supply township residents with the bulk of their food as well as non-food requirements, certainly in value terms. We anticipate that the terms of trade will deteriorate for competing micro-enterprises in the future, through the combined competitiveness of these larger businesses. Whereas the corporates will continue to compete from the spatial isolation of shopping malls, informalist businesses will increasingly operate within the niche geographic markets of the township. While we do recognise opportunities for growth and diversification of micro-enterprises, barriers must be overcome. These barriers, in addition to the competition from bigger business, account at least in part for the reluctance among formally unemployed persons to embrace self-employment. In the next chapter, we examine land-related barriers such as the absence of suitable commercial land (on the high street) and land-use system rigidities which hinder enterprise growth and formalisation. Looming large on all micro-entrepreneurial ventures is the risk of crime, a challenge heightened by the necessity for virtually all transactions to be undertaken on a cash basis. Added to the crime obstacle is the risk of state power to restrict the spaces, places, times and products/services which informal micro-enterprises are permitted to conduct. In subsequent chapters, we will unpack these challenges in greater detail, while also shining a light on the opportunities through which survivalists and entrepreneurs seek to pursue business. Some micro-enterprises are fragile and unlikely to develop beyond a survivalist response intended to supplement income. But some micro-enterprises have deeper roots and offer prospects for sustainable income generation. Through focusing on specific entrepreneurial opportunities and constraints in particular sectors we aim to provide an insight to untangle the survivalists from the entrepreneurs and thus better comprehend these contrasting prospects. We will also demonstrate how some entrepreneurial actions, such as those of the pioneers, have potential to disrupt the trajectory we have outlined and generate new opportunities for emergent entrepreneurship.

CADASTRAL

BUILT INFRASTRUCTURE

GRASSROOTS CLAIMS

Erf 1320

Erf 2635

Erf 1321

Erf 1322

Erf 1338

APPROPRIATION

Erf 1339

4
THE RIGHT TO USE LAND

In this chapter we focus on the role that land and property fulfil in framing business opportunities and show that despite land reforms, apartheid mechanisms of spatial control still influence how land is utilised.

CHAPTER 4

The right to use land

The right to use land as well as restrictions on land use have been decisive in shaping South African cities both during and since the apartheid era of racial segregation. Urban planning established residential townships for black persons on the periphery of cities, often close to industrial centres though distant from white neighbourhoods and the CBD. Access to land as well as land use within townships was tightly restricted in order to strengthen the apartheid state's political control, prevent the encroachment of township settlements onto adjacent land and solidify a residential dormitory characteristic to these settlements. In this way, township residents were afforded access to certain urban labour markets (unskilled and low wage) but restricted from independently embracing entrepreneurship and operating businesses. Urban planning, Oranje (2014) has argued, was the 'handmaiden' of the apartheid state. The developmental consequences of this historical legacy in terms of spatial and income poverty has been extensively studied (including in works by Pieterse 2009; Sinclair-Smith & Turok 2012; Turok 2001), though there few studies that address the implications for entrepreneurship.

Since the rise of democracy, contemporary land-use management systems have been tasked with the challenge of addressing the historic burden of spatial injustice while being transformative and enabling economic opportunities. New laws have been crafted and old policies reformed with the intention to redress spatial injustice, enhance resilience and to streamline administrative processes. Yet the current institutions and systems of land use fall short of being meaningfully beneficial for the vast majority of (previously disadvantaged) urban residents, and specifically people running micro-enterprises. Over the past 20 years, the township economy has undergone significant organic change in terms of micro-enterprise activity, disrupting the land-use legacy from below. Businesses are now increasingly tolerated and permitted, although the institutional structure still poses considerable regulatory risks. Almost universally across South Africa, townships are isolated settlements, disconnected from commercial heartlands, while, within these settlements, people struggle to access land and utilise land rights. Places and spaces in which to conduct business are constrained as a result of the combined impact of the non-availability of greenfield sites, the under-provision of commercially zoned land, the dense residential layout within settlements and narrow streetscapes, as shown in Figure 4.1.

In this chapter, we focus on the role that land and property fulfil in framing business opportunities and show that despite land reforms, apartheid mechanisms of spatial control still influence how land is utilised. We also show how entrepreneurs and residents, to overcome disadvantage, have adopted practices and tactics which subvert, mitigate and circumnavigate these constraints.

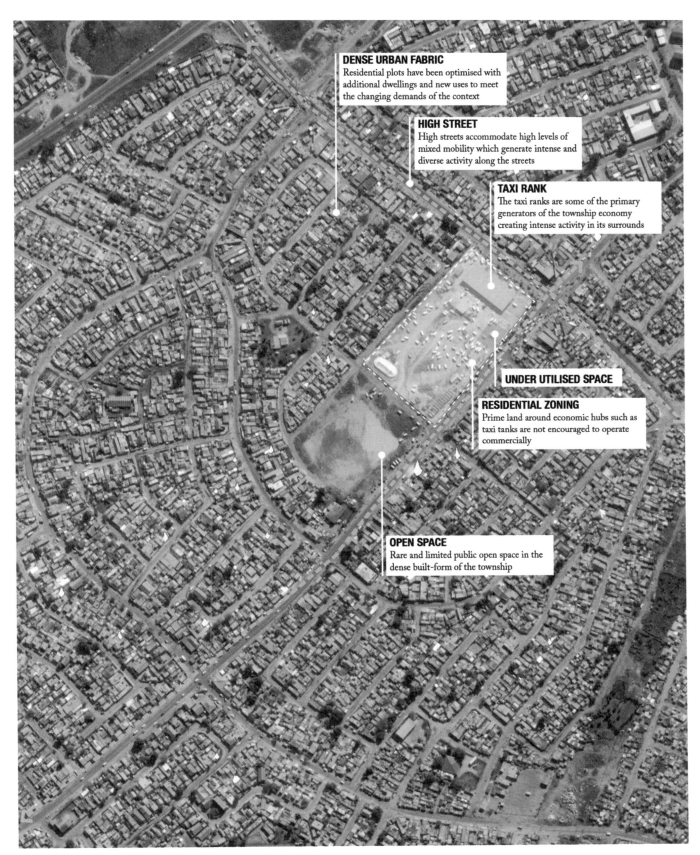

DENSE URBAN FABRIC
Residential plots have been optimised with additional dwellings and new uses to meet the changing demands of the context

HIGH STREET
High streets accommodate high levels of mixed mobility which generate intense and diverse activity along the streets

TAXI RANK
The taxi ranks are some of the primary generators of the township economy creating intense activity in its surrounds

UNDER UTILISED SPACE

RESIDENTIAL ZONING
Prime land around economic hubs such as taxi tanks are not encouraged to operate commercially

OPEN SPACE
Rare and limited public open space in the dense built-form of the township

FIGURE 4.1 The density of township settlements as illustrated in the case of Ivory Park
Note: A taxi rank is located at the intersection of two busy high streets. A portion of land immediately adjacent to the rank is largely underdeveloped and does not leverage off the spatial proximity to this bustling commuter site.

Municipal governments' land-use systems aim to provide a common set of guidelines to manage and reconcile the interests of business, the community and the environment, through measures such as specifying where, when and how entrepreneurs may conduct business. These systems can intentionally as well as unintentionally constrain business in those sectors that require land-related regulatory approval, including educares and liquor traders, grocery shops and street traders. In contrast, informal land use enables property owners to invest in land and develop property in response to market opportunities and to manage risks. We will argue that informal land use has paradoxical benefits in that, while it has enabled entrepreneurs to realise their 'rights' for residency and economic livelihoods, it has also entrenched informality. Beneficiation from land rights is influenced by the terms and conditions of both formal and informal land-use systems, which are subject to influences such as the form of land tenure, the strength of land claims and power of individuals to exert control over land.

Land-use systems

Land-use management centres on the notion of protecting people and the environment from the externalities of development (Nel 2016). It is central to strategic planning, enabling the state to ensure the sustainable provision of public utilities, transport infrastructure, housing and economic infrastructure to list some of the core functions. Land-use management also provides a key institutional framework to safeguard property values and thereby sustain the municipal tax base and private property investment. There is a complex web of legislation (which transverses the three tiers of government) through which the state aims to manage land, control building developments, and determine the places as well as forms in which people can use land to conduct business. Since 1994, land-use planning legislation has undergone a series of policy reforms to create a unified system and provide administrative mechanisms to redress the apartheid legacy of spatial injustice (on the history of these reforms, see Berrisford 2011). While the current policy framework, as set out in the Spatial Planning and Land Use Management Act (No. 16 of 2013), recognises the need for greater flexibility in land administration, the legislation nevertheless upholds the fundamental principles of a codified system, wherein land-use zones and spatial development plans determine the parameters of how land can be utilised. As such, when land is granted to an individual, two processes must have occurred. First, a surveyor must have recorded the dimensions of the land unit in question on a cadastre diagram. Secondly, a conveyancer must then draft the 'deed of grant', recording the beneficiary of the land to whom title is being given, which diagram or general plan depicts the land unit dimensions, and any restrictive conditions on the land or entitlements to which the owner is eligible. When a deed of grant or transfer is issued, the land unit comes with a 'bundle of rights' (Charman, Tonkin, Denoon-Stevens, Demeestére, 2017). These rights typically include the right to use the land for specified purposes such as to sell it or to build on it. The land-use management system is depicted in Figure 4.2.

Millions of eligible township residents have not received title deeds and therefore have not acquired the bundles of rights to develop their properties. According to Gordon, Nell, and Di Lollo (2011), an estimated 1.1 to 1.4 million housing subsidy beneficiaries (as of 2011) did not have a title deed. The same limitation applies to municipally owned residential properties issued to housing beneficiaries (on a rental basis) prior to the urban land reforms and housing programme after 1994, as happened in KwaMashu and Tembisa sites. In terms of legal entitlement, some of the titles transferred to homeowners in the apartheid period substantially differ from freehold title which constitutes the

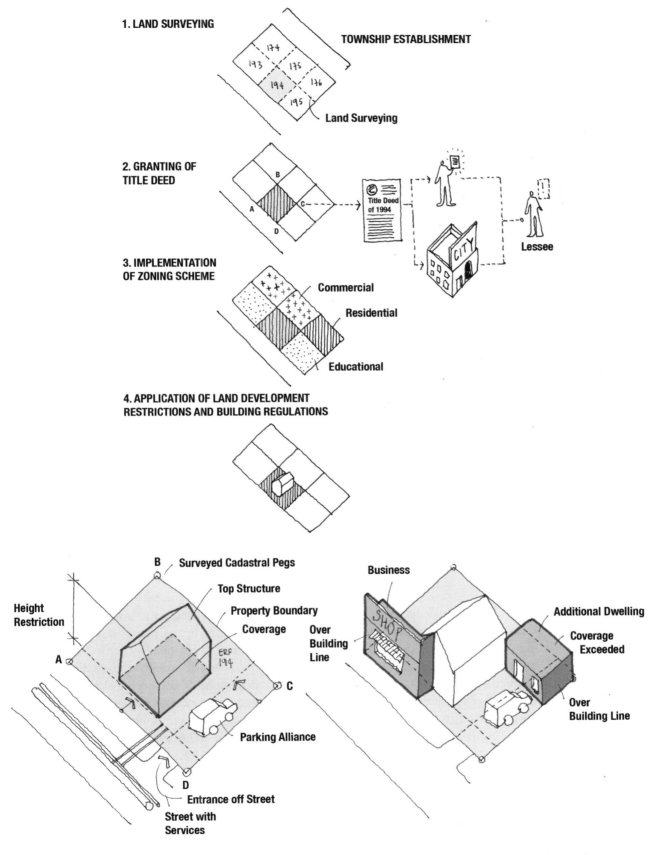

1. LAND SURVEYING

TOWNSHIP ESTABLISHMENT

174
193 175
194 176
195

Land Surveying

2. GRANTING OF TITLE DEED

B
A C
D

Title Deed of 1994

CITY

Lessee

3. IMPLEMENTATION OF ZONING SCHEME

Commercial

Residential

Educational

4. APPLICATION OF LAND DEVELOPMENT RESTRICTIONS AND BUILDING REGULATIONS

B   Surveyed Cadastral Pegs

Top Structure

Property Boundary

Coverage

Height Restriction

A

ERF 194

C

Parking Alliance

D

Entrance off Street

Street with Services

Business

SHOP

Over Building Line

Additional Dwelling

Coverage Exceeded

Over Building Line

FIGURE 4.2 Land-use management process illustrating the sequencing of steps for land to be available for development in the township

Note: The building controls attached to the land are intended to guide the nature of the top structures but are seldom adhered to.

foundations of wealth in property for white South Africans. Post-1994, the state issued RDP homeowners with title deeds containing a restrictive clause prohibiting their sale (an eight-year 'pre-emptive restriction') (Charman et al. 2017).

The South African land-use system aligns with modernist thinking and draws heavily on the development experience of European and North American countries, notably the UK and the US, where codifying systems were originally developed (Hirt 2007) for more established and predictable economic environments with a different profile of risks. A central mechanism in codified land-use management is the use of measures to control the density and/or intensity of land use in the belief that altering these variables would have a negative impact on people, the environment or wealth generation. One such mechanism is zoning schemes, applied to each land unit with the intention to facilitate 'appropriate' use (such as residential, industrial or commercial). Although there is merit to the delineation of different kinds of land use, the manner in which these schemes were implemented in the townships was inherently inflexible given that their reality approximates a 'mixed-use' scenario. Mixed-use means that residential and business premises are interwoven and do not necessarily conform to separate enclaves. Most townships wherein zoning has been instituted are simply classified for residential use, apart from those portions set aside for education and specific kinds of commercial use; the predominance of residential zoning can be seen in Figure 4.3.

Across all 10 sites, only isolated pockets of land have been afforded with business- or industrial-use rights. Such properties tend to be situated along high streets and near transport nodes. Each land-use scheme designates the permissible kinds of business activities, including the categories of acceptable enterprises and restrictive criteria on the kinds of commercial activities which can be undertaken on residential properties. For example, in the CoCT scheme for 'Single Residential 2' (incremental housing) (CoCT 2015), the properties can be used to operate a 'restaurant' or 'boarding house', but not a licensed tavern. Such inflexibility has led scholars to critique the application of land-use zoning in developing contexts such as townships as exclusionary, unjust and unsustainable (Watson, V 2009). Township settlements challenge normative ideas (i.e. social constructs that have become self-legitimising) about land use in residential areas since these settlements have had to accommodate 'non-appropriate' land uses (for a range of commercial activities and social functions) from the time of their first establishment as dormitory settlements.

When township settlements are planned, areas to be used as a public streets, roads, thoroughfares, squares or open commonage are demarcated as 'a public space' (Charman et al. 2017), with the consequence that the ownership automatically vests in the municipal authority. Land classified as a public space is entitled to special protection whereby municipal authorities can enact by-laws specifying rights of use and prohibitions, a topic we discuss in Chapter 5. Municipalities also have a wide range of controls (regulations and by-laws) over private land use, which includes building regulations with respect to the infrastructure development of the property. In a municipal land-use management scheme (town planning), the municipality assigns each land unit with a specific use category with parameters stipulating the kind of activities that can occur on the property, and setting building limits (e.g. maximum building height, setbacks from the boundaries, etc.). These parameters can only be changed through formal applications to the municipality which must then officially endorse any proposed land-use change. Municipalities furthermore enforce building standards in line with the National Building Regulations and Building Standards Act (NBRBSA) (No. 103 of 1977), as amended. NBRBSA regulations are similarly derived from modernist ideas of development which

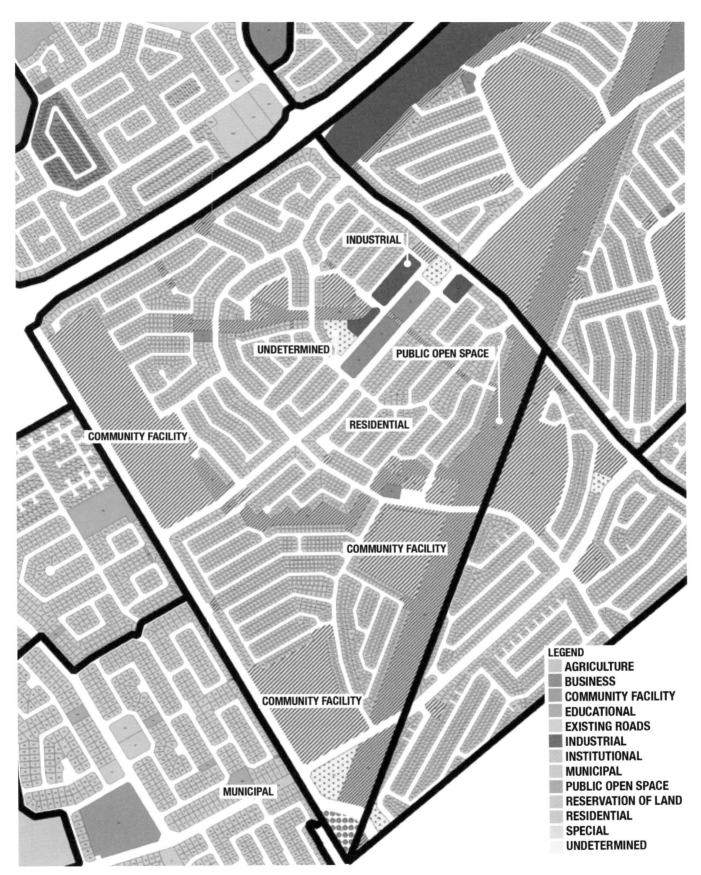

FIGURE 4.3 Municipal land-use plans are instituted to guide the nature of development in the township

Note: The plan makes little provision for the complexity of actual land uses.

LEGEND
- AGRICULTURE
- BUSINESS
- COMMUNITY FACILITY
- EDUCATIONAL
- EXISTING ROADS
- INDUSTRIAL
- INSTITUTIONAL
- MUNICIPAL
- PUBLIC OPEN SPACE
- RESERVATION OF LAND
- RESIDENTIAL
- SPECIAL
- UNDETERMINED

do not permit alternative, people-centred building techniques, materials and methods, as commonly used in informal settlements and backyard dwellings.

Realistically, compliance with land-management systems is almost impossible for most township micro-enterprises. The land-related processes which these entrepreneurs have to navigate to obtain business compliance are highly complex and, from the perspective of business owners, illogical. For example, to trade legally, home businesses must, firstly, comply with the zoning scheme (or have an approved departure); secondly, the proportion of the floor space dedicated to business should be less than the space allocated for residential use (or below a size threshold as specified in the scheme) while in certain sectors there needs to be a clear separation of space; thirdly, the building in which the micro-enterprise trades must have approved building plans; and fourthly, the business must adhere to a raft of municipal by-laws relating to environmental health, food safety and use of outdoor advertising signage. Street traders are also required to adhere to municipal 'informal trading' by-laws, which often restrict their activities to certain street localities and prohibit business activities such as cooking on an open fire, using mobile trolleys, and erecting trading structures. In addition, street traders must operate their businesses in compliance with the same municipal environmental health and food safety requirements applicable to residentially based businesses. Due to the technical and legal complexity of these measures as well as the costs attendant with compliance, most township entrepreneurs have no alternative than to trade illegally in terms of land use. We refer to this process as 'enforced informalisation' (Charman, Piper & Petersen 2013).

Opportunities and constraints

Our research found that around 60% of township micro-enterprises operate from residential properties. To enable business activities, these properties have undergone either purposeful conversions or temporary adaptations in response to their business needs. The adaptation of residential homes to create business premises is most notable in the case of educares, larger spaza shops, taverns/shebeens and other such business with significant space requirements such as micro-manufacturing entities and vehicle repair garages. The investment to create commercial space within homes tends to occur in a phased approach where the business commences from temporarily converting an existing residential room, with major investments undertaken only once the business has demonstrated its profitability and/or when regulatory risks require investment in separate infrastructure. The conversion of entire houses into a business, while less common, is evident along streets with a higher density and diversity of businesses. More often, property conversions entail two forms: the repurposing of a single room into a business unit; and the construction of a building often adjoining the original house.

To make sense of these land constraints, we examine the cases of two entrepreneurs operating businesses in Ivory Park. These cases were part of a research project which investigated 11 different situations (Charman, Govender, & De Villiers 2017). The first case concerns an educare and the second describes a spaza-takeaway-tavern. In both cases, the rigidity of the land-use system hinders the business from establishing itself within formal institutions. Both of the entrepreneurs conduct business informally, making investments to align their businesses with aspects of regulatory requirements and in incremental, affordable ways that are responsive to the risk environment and opportunities for returns.

Janes's educare in Ivory Park had been in business for nine years, operating informally. Jane is a pensioner who established the business in her retirement to provide quality education to local children, and like other entrepreneurs in this sector, drew on her work experiences as a domestic worker and caregiver to start the business. In 2012, when we conducted the initial business census, Jane's business was responsible for 32 children and had two employees. Her business operated out of two classroom blocks within a separate brick and mortar building, a sick bay/office, use of the home kitchen, an outdoor play area (furnished with a jungle-gym, swing and toys) and two toilets situated at the rear of the house, separate from the building; see Figure 4.4.

The classroom walls were adorned with posters and the children were provided with chairs and tables. Throughout the educare, there was a sense of compliance with societal norms and expectations, evident in the way in which the outside wall was painted with animal figures and names against a blue background, the paved tiles that line the side alley, and the ordering and furnishing of the classrooms. Janes took particular pride in the quality of the education, maintaining a structured programme and teaching the children in the English language. '*When my grade R go to primary school,*' she made a point of telling us, '*they always win academic* awards' (Business code 3 [educare]/survey number 2399/female/age unknown).

Jane reported in 2012 that the business made a profit (equivalent to a salary for the owner) of R4 000 per month. By 2017, when we resurveyed the business, the number of children had risen to 40, though this was reduced to 35 after the receipt of a municipal compliance order. The income from school fees was R8 750 and we estimate that Jane's salary had increased to around R5 000 pm. The business still employed two persons, each paid R1 200 pm. In the period between 2012 and 2017, the school fees rose from R230 pm to R250 pm. The business was registered as a non-profit organisation (NPO) but had been unsuccessful in registering with the Department of Social Welfare and Development (DSWD) to obtain the state subsidy for ECDCs. As Jane told us: '*Every time I go to hand in the papers, the tellers tell me that I haven't brought in the right information.*' Indeed, she had little knowledge of the precise requirements to formalise her business. The state subsidy of R330 per child exceeded the monthly fee Jane charged per child and would more than double her turnover should her business succeed in becoming registered.

Despite this incentive for formalisation, Jane was unable to register her business. Her main obstacles were land-system related. Jane acquired a lease to the site in the early 1990s from the municipality (Midrand Municipality prior to its incorporation into the CoJ). In terms of the lease agreement, Jane could utilise the site for residential purposes only, though she was entitled to build 'a prefabricated building on the site' subject to the submission of a building plan. She submitted the necessary plan and built a three-bedroomed brick and mortar residential house with the finance obtained from a retirement package of R42 000. The lease had not been converted to a title deed, for reasons that are unknown. As with many other Ivory Park residents, the municipal rates bill is simply addressed to 'The Occupier'. Because the property legally belongs to the CoJ, Jane as a leaseholder did not have consent to operate a business (in terms of the lease agreement), and in addition could not obtain the necessary land-use consent to run an educare (in other words, 'zoning consent use') and approval for building plans. The recent building changes are highlighted in Figure 4.5.

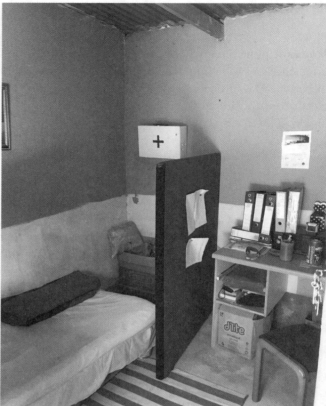

FIGURE 4.4 Photographs of the educare: the passage outside the classroom, the sick room and playground with equipment

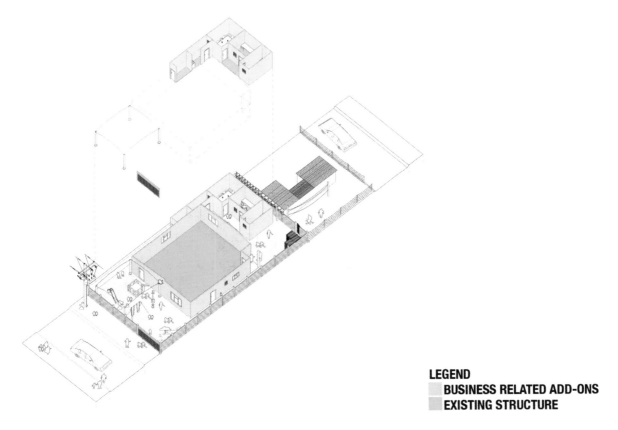

LEGEND
BUSINESS RELATED ADD-ONS
EXISTING STRUCTURE

FIGURE 4.5 Axonometric illustrating the investments made to the original structure over time

Her efforts to achieve compliance might result in an improved service for the benefit of the children, but in legal terms these actions would be meaningless under the current land-use system since she does not own the property and would be taxing on her financial resources, with little financial incentive. Furthermore, from Jane's perspective, these compliance-driven changes to the buildings might compromise any future use of the property should the educare be forced to close. In Chapter 11, we analyse similar strategies that could be considered 'ceremonial' acts of compliance within the educare sector. Should Jane submit building plans, it is likely that her application would be refused on the basis that the building structures are situated within a servitude and encroach onto neighbouring boundaries, as shown in Figure 4.6.

In January 2017, Jane's educare was inspected by an environmental official from the CoJ and issued with a compliance order. The order mandated the business to effect the following changes within 21 days: i) provide a kitchen for the day-care (separate from the household), ii) provide specialised toilet facilities (with small pans for children), iii) provide a separate sickbay and iv) reduce 'overcrowding'; a challenging demand for such a short timeframe. Jane had since endeavoured to address these issues: an additional block had been built (though it was still incomplete and not required given that she had adequate facilities within the house); she had also registered an NPO and had reduced the number of children.

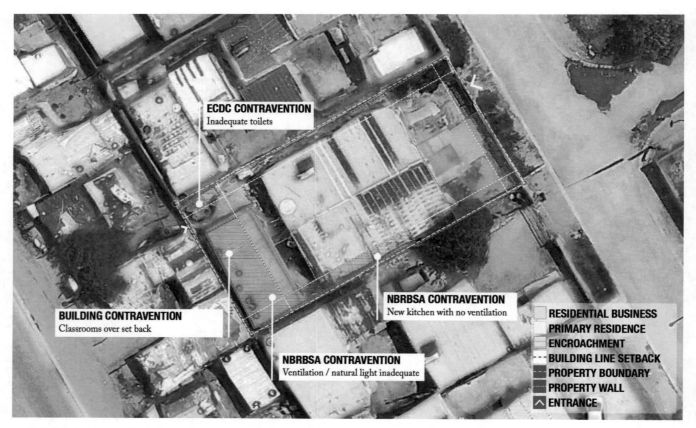

FIGURE 4.6 Aerial image illustrating the arrangement of infrastructure on the site and land-use contraventions

CASE STUDY: *Steve's spaza-takeaway-tavern; see Figure 4.7, Figure 4.8 and Figure 4.9.*

Steve commenced grocery trading in 2000 after he lost his job and fell on hard times. Working out of his mother's ±50 square-metre residential house situated on a minor high street in Ivory Park, Steve started selling popcorn to passing pedestrians. The small business returned about R70 per day in profit from an investment of about R9.50 in ingredients. He soon expanded the business to sell cool drinks, sweets and cigarettes. At that time, there were few competing spaza shops in Ivory Park. The cigarette component of his business thrived in the period 2001–2002 as a result of his linkages to a source of budget cigarette brands which competitors in Ivory Park were unable to access (note that this happened prior to the widespread availability of contraband tobacco, a topic we address in Chapter 8). Steve expanded his business in response to '*feedback from the street*': customers started to request bread, then beer, then entertainment facilities (arcade video games and pool or billiards). To accommodate the expanding business, Steve redeveloped the modest house and erf, expanding the walls sideward and frontward, thus converting all of the residential house and property into a commercial building, while internally removing walls so as to create four distinct spaces: an arcade game room; a serving area and pool-playing space; a spaza and kitchen for preparing takeaways; and a private office; the development of the property is shown in Figure 4.7. As Steve resided elsewhere, there was no need to retain a residential function to the original house, apart from a backyard dwelling to accommodate a security guard.

FIGURE 4.7 Photographs of the spaza-takeaway-tavern interior and street conditions

The story of how Steve acquired the property is familiar within the township. His father initially obtained the site at around the time Ivory Park was first settled through a process known colloquially as 'zabalising' (to struggle). Though residing in Daveyton, his father managed to acquire a stand upon which he settled a member of the family and erected a shack. Over time, his father built a brick and mortar dwelling and had the property registered with the municipal authorities in the name of his mother. In 2011, a formal title deed was issued in her name. Yet three years before the issuing of the title, Steve had informally acquired the property from his mother, paying a 'purchase' sum of R230 000. Since Steve's acquisition of the property was done through an informal exchange, the title deed had not been transferred from his mother's name into his name. As a residential property (like most properties in Ivory Park), the land parcel was subject to a 3 m servitude along the street boundary, a 2 m servitude along the rear boundary and a minimum 1 m along the side boundary.

We surveyed Steve's business in 2012. When we met, he said, '*We call this business a spaza shop, but the intention was to become the first black Ackermans here and run all the spaza shops off this informal settlement*' (Ackermans is a reference to the founder of the Pick n Pay supermarket group). It then employed three persons, though was in decline as a consequence of business competition from immigrant spaza entrepreneurs who had established shops in Ivory Park from around 2007. In response to this competitiveness challenge, Steve felt that the beer sales were the only way the shop could be '*salvaged*'. Back in 2012, he told us: '*I don't even know where to go for a liquor licence and when you hear people talking about their licences, it's like it will cost you an arm and a leg. And then it's not even guaranteed that you can actually end up getting a licence.*' He decided to commence liquor trading informally, though subsequently obtained a shebeen permit, thus affording Steve limited rights to trade. Since that time, he had expanded the liquor retail component and, in 2017, sold about 135 crates (12 × 750 ml) of beer per week in addition to other liquor products. His business carried about R150 000 in stock out of which liquor products comprise R90 000 in value. He received beer deliveries directly from the South African Breweries (SAB) and had a R50 000 line of credit with SAB which had to be reimbursed on a weekly basis. The spaza shop accounted for approximately 25% of the business turnover and the entertainment facilities generated an income of around R4 000 pm from the pool table and R1 000 pm from arcade games. The business layout can be seen from Figure 4.8.

While the business provided Steve with sufficient income, in theory, to meet the various costs of business compliance, the land-related obstacles made formalisation extremely complex and unattainable. His main incentive for regularising was the opportunity to legally trade in liquor products as shebeens were the most systematically regulated of all township businesses. Due to the insecurity of his land tenure and the stringency of other land-use requirements, Steve was unable to acquire a liquor licence. To formalise, he would need to acquire legal title in his own name, obtain building-plan approval and have the property rezoned from residential to business use. The buildings encroached onto the servitudes and overran onto a neighbouring property, as shown in Figure 4.9.

There were no public toilet facilities. A further obstacle was that the CoJ municipal land-use scheme required the entrepreneur to be a permanent resident on the site, while in respect to spaza shops, the scheme stipulated that 'no amusement machines of any kind shall be permitted on the premises' (City of Johannesburg 2017), which thus prevented him from running arcade games. As a strategy to circumscribe the obstacle of trading without a liquor licence, Steve had managed to obtain a shebeen permit to retail liquor

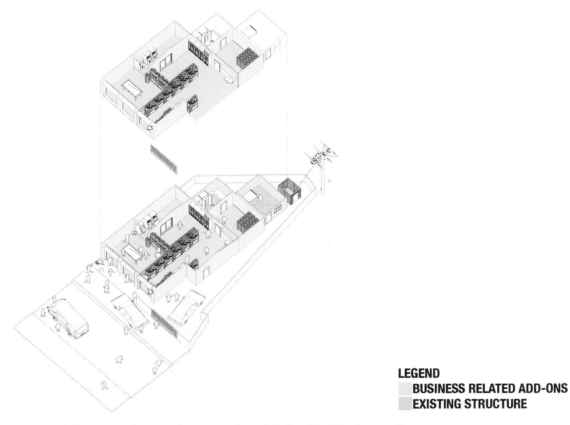

FIGURE 4.8 Axonometric illustrating the investments made to the original structure over time

ENCROACHMENT
Boundary wall over property boundary

BUILDING CONTRAVENTION
New tavern liquor storage area

BUILDING CONTRAVENTION
New games area over setbacks

BUILDING CONTRAVENTION
New bedroom addition sitting over setbacks

FIGURE 4.9 Aerial image illustrating the arrangement of infrastructure on the site and land-use contraventions

from his home in Daveyton (in the Ekurhuleni Municipality, though still within Gauteng province), entitling him to sell a maximum of 60 crates (12 × 750 ml) of beer a week. In 2012, he succeeded in transferring the permit to his property in Ivory Park, though the legality of the transfer was questionable. The permit was officially valid until 2013 but, in 2017, was still informally recognised as a consequence of a government impasse in liquor regulation in Gauteng province (for more on liquor licensing, see Chapter 9). Although Steve had a shebeen permit, he had not obtained a municipal permit for selling perishable goods and the use of the buildings was non-compliant with setbacks and building regulations.

Land transactions

These two cases illustrate how informal land use prevents the property owners from utilising constitutionally protected land rights. One consequence is that home entrepreneurs are unable to formalise their business. A second consequence is that informal homeowners are unable to transact their properties through formal markets, including mortgaging the property to financial institutions to raise capital. This scenario might arise from not having a title, as in Jane's case, or the non-compliance of the property with land use and building restrictions, as in both Jane and Steve's cases. A third consequence is that Jane and Steve had instead sought to minimise their investment risks, aiming to achieve a minimal level of functionality and regulatory compliance but holding back from investing to maximise beneficiation.

Despite the challenges of transacting property sales through formal institutions, people are able to buy and sell properties through informal markets. While national data on property retention amongst RDP beneficiaries is unavailable, smaller studies indicate that up to 40% of beneficiaries sell their properties to cash buyers (Centre for Affordable Housing Finance in Africa 2016). In the course of the field research, we encountered many examples of properties marketed informally on community notice boards and roadside signs. Internet trading sites including Gumtree, OLX and Property24 provide a virtual platform for transacting in property, formally or informally; in the case of Gumtree and OLX, most properties are sold to cash buyers. The subsequent transactions are not registered in the deeds office and the new property owners have no title and thus inherit the risks of economic and financial exclusion.

In all nine South African sites, property owners have succeeded in adding value to their investments. Table 4.1 provides an indication of the range in property prices.

Using low-price estimates obtained from the above open-source platforms, we calculate that the collective property market in the nine South African sites was worth a value in excess of R21 billion, with individual property marketed prices ranging between an average of R290 000 (low) and R369 000 (high). There are two important lessons from the township property market. First, informal transactions do not preclude the sale of property, nor the adding of value to property and second, possession of legal title does not indicate compliance with other aspects of the land-use system such as NBRBSA requirements and zoning. In our Ivory Park investigation, we found that the differences between the returns on property transacted in formal and informal markets were negligible. But transacting land informally passes on risks to the purchaser, while undermining the state's role in safeguarding land rights. We speculate that the informal township property market nevertheless benefits from aspects of the land-use system, in particular the cadastral grid-in setting out property boundaries vis-à-vis private and public land and through transferring an entitlement to the property holder to access municipal services. These aspects of entitlement are not present in informal settings.

TABLE 4.1 Real estate values in the nine South African sites based on open-access data

Site	Total HHs.	No. of formal houses	House price Low	House price High	Total value formal (low value)
Browns Farm	14 300	2 894	220 000	320 000	636 680 00
Delft South	11 322	11 322	150 000	460 000	1 698 300 000
Imizamo Yethu	6 015	2 375	400 000	–	950 042 479
Ivory Park	19 146	16 624	330 000	490 000	8 485 819 939
KwaMashu	16 683	12 855	420 000	790 000	5 399 305 345
Sweet Home Farm	3 210	0	–	–	–
Tembisa	10 467	10 016	400 000	650 000	4 006 259 132
Thabong	8 571	8 571	150 000	580 000	1 285 650 000
Vrygrond	6 627	5 239	250 000	500 000	1 309 777 364
Total	**96 396**	**60 040**	**290 000**	**3 690 000**	**20 771 824 250**
Grand total					**21 036 622 121**

Sources: OLX; Gumtree; Property24; Private Property. Accessed: 20 April 2018

Investment

Investment in property is an important strategy for township entrepreneurs to reduce risks (since property value is easier to protect than business assets), to strengthen family ties, to create a rental income stream, and for purposes of place making. These various strategies are influenced by investment returns and the land tenure situation. Where properties are used for commercial activities, homeowners have undertaken a range of micro-adjustments with functional objectives, such as the installation of lighting, advertising signage, paved pathways, carports, public toilets and washbasins, security bars on windows and doors, and closed circuit television (CCTV) monitoring. In situations where the business orientates towards the streetscape, adjustments have been effected to enhance public use, provide shelter and improve street surveillance. In our research on township property investments, we identified three notable strategies: land banking; investments to generate income through the provision of 'backyard' residential units; and investments of place making and value adding through gentrifying improvements.

Land banking

Wherever there are vacant land erven within the boundaries of a township, the land itself is often subject to contested claims. Such erven are characteristically located on high order streets, including high streets and arterial roads, and owned by the state who have set it aside for future commercial use or public infrastructure, as shown in Figure 4.1. Where the state has been unable or unwilling to utilise the land, individuals have laid subsequent claims over it and, in some situations, been afforded limited use rights. Unutilised commercial land sites have high potential for economic development, but often remain undeveloped in part due to conflicting ownership.

Harriet's land-banking case study

This exclusion from development can be seen in the case of Harriet's land holdings, which is visually evident in Figure 4.10 and Figure 4.11.

FIGURE 4.10 Photograph of the stand-alone container shop on Harriet's claimed site

CAR MECHANICAL OUTDOOR WORKSHOPS

TAXI PARKING

CHURCH

INFORMAL FOOD COURT

SPORTS FIELDS

COUNCIL STRUCTURE

BUSINESS PREMISES
PRIMARY RESIDENCE
ENCROACHMENT
BUILDING LINE SETBACK
PROPERTY BOUNDARY

FIGURE 4.11 Aerial image illustrating the arrangement of infrastructure on Harriet's site showing sub-optimal use

Harriet claimed ownership of three commercial sites in Ivory Park. She was one of the first settlers of the township. She 'acquired' these sites in the early 1990s through her family's political connections within the municipality, since her uncle was the first ward councillor and her husband was an Umkhonto weSizwe (MK) veteran and influential individual. One of the sites is situated next to the Emthonjeni taxi rank, occupying a corner stand and measuring 538 m². On the rear boundary there was a derelict park, while to the right of the property lay open ground which was also subject to similar claims. Her site was undeveloped apart from two shipping-container businesses which operated on the property, for which she obtained a monthly income of R3 700. The land was zoned for commercial use. In 2000, Harriet succeeded in having the site surveyed and its boundaries determined. She then obtained a lease agreement from CoJ in 2003, which was renewed several times. In about 2007, Harriet planted metal pegs to demarcate the boundaries of the land portion in anticipation that the CoJ would convert her lease into a title. While the lease was R85 per month, Harriet had an outstanding rates balance in excess of R10 000 suggesting that she had not paid for approximately nine years. As evidence of her continued authority to control activities on this land, in 2017, she requested that the CoJ Metro Police remove a container business that had opened up on the open ground site, which they actually did.

The case provides an example of land use which neither provides revenue to the municipality nor has an economic influence on the high-street and business activities. As Harriet does not have title to the land (and since the validity of the lease agreement is questionable), her land claim has no institutional support and thus the land is excluded from development.

Backyard dwellings

Backyard-dwelling investments were observed in all of the newer (post-1994) townships. In older settlements, such as Tembisa and KwaMashu, the phenomenon of backyard developments to generate income is less widely evident, though backyards are built on. These are a qualitatively different kind of investment and equate to an additional room or rooms for accommodating members of the extended household, rather than a business investment. By contrast, in newer settlements, property owners have sought to maximise income through utilising the greatest possible area within the property for independent accommodation units. The backyard rental strategy responds to the high demand for safe and affordable accommodation, especially from immigrants. The tenants who demand this accommodation are invariably single persons, though they may include couples and small families with young children. In places like Ivory Park, where the alternative accommodation possibilities in informal settlements are limited as a result of the geographical constraints, property owners have responded entrepreneurially to the high demand through creating a supply of single rooms on short-lease terms. To explore the dynamic of investment in backyard rental units, we now consider the case of an individual, Willi, who has established a portfolio of commercial units and accommodation units.

Willi's property portfolio

In the 1990s, when land became available in the emerging township of Ivory Park, Willi moved from Alexandra and, as one of the community leaders, succeeded in obtaining a corner plot. Initially, the stands were 'site-and-service' plots, measuring on average 180m² and containing an enclosed toilet structure, a stand-pipe for water and simple perimeter fencing of iron posts and three wires. Later, Willi received an RDP house which was situated in the centre of the stand and measured about 50 m². There remained

FIGURE 4.12 Photographs of the rental and business units, passages and yards that are made through the optimisation of the property for income generation

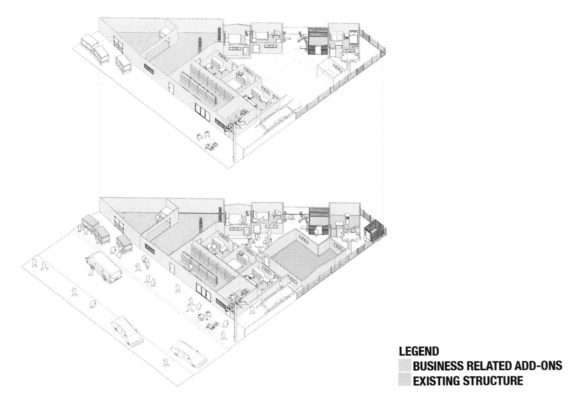

LEGEND
BUSINESS RELATED ADD-ONS
EXISTING STRUCTURE

FIGURE 4.13 Axonometric illustrating the investments made to the original structure over time

considerable space within his property for future development, allowing for both the expansion of the original home and construction of backyard units. How land holders like Willi have subsequently developed their site (see Figure 4.12) has been influenced by a number of considerations, including security of tenure, location of the plot with respect to high streets, and weighting between residential and commercial priorities.

Since obtaining a title deed certificate in 2012, Willi had substantially changed the use of the property, as shown in Figure 4.13 and Figure 4.14.

The property bordered a minor high street along which considerable informal trade had emerged, with micro-enterprises operating both from within properties and on the sidewalk. In the first phase of development, Willi permitted businesses to situate shipping containers on his property, oriented towards the street. In the backyard, Willi built two single-room residential units of rudimentary design constructed with mud, brick, timber and corrugated iron. He also used the site to operate a gym, known as 'Gym at Your Own Risk'. Since obtaining title, in a second phase of development, Willi had removed the containers and replaced them with three brick, mortar and cement buildings which were rented to shopkeepers. He expanded the number of accommodation units from two to four. The commercial units were leased on the basis of verbal agreements, with the largest unit leased for R4 000 per month. Half of the single rooms were leased on an in-kind basis and half on a commercial basis for R750 per month, the going rate for a basic single room. From this portfolio of property, Willi derived a monthly income of R9 200. Each unit had a separate electricity meter for the tenants' account. Both Willi and his tenants used a common toilet situated at the rear of the site. Passages and access points had been arranged to manage the sharing of resources. Buildings then comprised 83% of the property surface. Willi refused to pay municipal rates or comply with building regulations, saying '*I want to be free like Mandela*'.

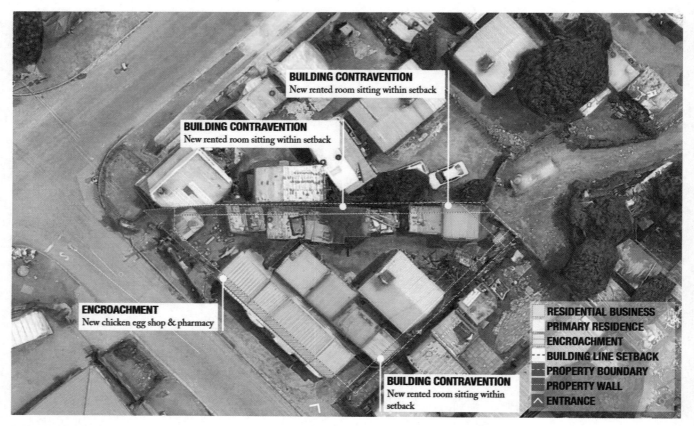

FIGURE 4.14 Aerial image illustrating the arrangement of infrastructure on the site and land-use contraventions

The financial returns from investing in backyard accommodation represent attractive, relatively passive incomes, often higher than the returns from running a micro-enterprise out of the property, which in addition carry greater land-use compliance risks.

Upgrades

Many property owners have made substantial investments to improve facilities and construct a 'modern' sense of place. In most instances, the decision to undertake these investments correlates with the security of tenure, the assessment of investment risk and income opportunities. The importance of tenure security is noticeable in the settlement of KwaMashu. All of the houses in this settlement were once council-owned. The municipality has begun to transfer ownership to home occupiers although the process has been slow and the majority of properties are still under municipal ownership. Upon receipt of the title, homeowners have commenced a process of investment, the scale and pace of which has correlated to the income of the household as well as their capacity to manage improvements. The sequencing of these investments follows a general pattern; first, perimeter walls are constructed to 'stop nonsense' between neighbours and enhance security; second, a driveway is constructed to enable a motor vehicle to access the property, usually upon which investments are made in the provision of a secure parking facility or a garage; third, the property is renovated to provide additional rooms and improvements to the kitchen and bathroom facilities; fourth, the significance of the property transition is underlined through the inclusion of a custom-built perimeter gate, a signature front door and, in KwaMashu, the replacement of original window frames with aluminium windows and doors; finally, aesthetic elements are added through tiling, paint work and plants. In some instances, the original properties are demolished and replaced with modern buildings by the residents.

Outlook

Land is a primary means to generate income, build wealth and secure livelihoods in the township economy. Through case studies, we have sought to show how people have utilised access to land to optimise economic benefit. One strategy to achieve this goal has been the repurposing of property for business, while other strategies have sought to derive rental income or simply enhance property value for future benefit. These investments are responsive to risks. Insecure land tenure and absence of land rights to conduct business heightens risks for persons operating businesses, particularly in sectors subject to regulatory oversight. While some township entrepreneurs do benefit from legal land rights and business licences, most operate within informal land-use systems that accommodate business flexibility and spatial fluidity. We have shown how the informality of land use enables entrepreneurs to spatially position their businesses in response to market impulses and best utilise available space and infrastructure. At the same time, informal land use may generate tension with the state through undermining its mandate to regulate land through systems designed to minimise and control unplanned uses. The emergent mixed land use of the township has disrupted apartheid land-use planning from below, refusing to conform to the proposed separation of different land uses in different zones. This insurgence has produced a complex set of social, spatial and economic outcomes, including transforming street and residential homes into multifunctional sites of economic activity and recreational spaces.

We have argued that formal land institutions are largely inaccessible to home businesses. This is because many homeowners do not have formal title deeds, while their businesses are often non-compliant with land-use systems and related business regulations. Such non-compliance is widespread, stunting business growth and justifying tentative and risk-averse investments. There is evidence to show that as the value of land rises, homeowners are willing to enhance their risk, repurposing the property to optimise a return on investment even though these developments might be unplanned, unauthorised in terms of land use and encroach boundaries. In a context within which informal land use is ubiquitous, the rigidity of the land system has compelled entrepreneurs to innovate the way buildings are set out and multiple functions accommodated. The capacity to utilise property in flexible ways, such as changing the function of rooms or modifying buildings, and without strictly complying with land-use restrictions and building standards, can be both highly beneficial and risky. The case of Jane's educare highlights the vulnerability of entrepreneurs who operate outside the regulatory system and in conflict with land use. These individuals are unable to realise the full bundle of land rights institutionalised within the land-use system. Their investments carry a high risk and they are vulnerable to state sanction, which may compel micro-enterprises to operate informally or indeed cease operations.

From a developmental perspective, it is unrealistic for the state to even consider remedying land-use deviations and illegal uses under its current systems. Alternative systems need to be developed since the current systems present a barrier to economic inclusion. We have sought to show the importance of enabling home-based businesses to attain regulatory compliance in land use through a more flexible system since many township entrepreneurs have demonstrated their capacity and willingness to invest in their properties to develop businesses and reduce land use externalities.

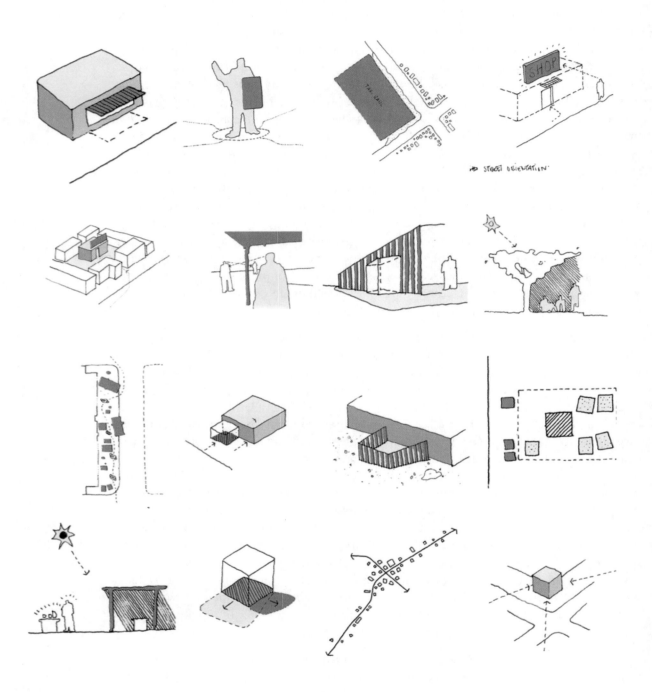

STREET ORIENTATION

5
SPATIAL ORDERING

In this chapter we examine the spatial ordering of the township economy. Our gradient of analysis operates at three levels: the neighbourhood, the microcontext, and the invisible infrastructure, especially in the context of street trading.

CHAPTER 5

Spatial ordering

This chapter examines the spatial ordering of the township economy. Our gradient of analysis operates at three levels: the neighbourhood, the micro-context, and the invisible infrastructure, especially in the context of street trading. We focus on the use of space; the infrastructure and architectural strategies which entrepreneurs use in response to market opportunities; the risk and pressures which influence businesses; and the unseen organisational logics as well as social processes through which people contest and cooperate to use geographic space. We argue that these contestations over space exert an organising dynamic within the neighbourhood economy, influencing where people conduct business and the spatial configuration of business activities.

Our analysis of the geospatial distribution of micro-enterprises in the 10 sites repeatedly shows the importance of different spaces in which business is conducted. These distributions highlight four main spatial situations for micro-enterprises: the home (including all property within a residential plot); non-residential buildings and structures established on streets, sometimes straddling property boundaries; the street environment (including sidewalks and the road reserve); and open spaces (under-utilised land and land servitudes). Whereas the space of the residential properties as well as buildings are situated within a private realm, activities on the street and open ground are conducted in a public context which necessitates negotiations with other users, various land claimants and authorities (both formal and informal).

In this chapter, we examine the spatial ordering at the neighbourhood level, shifting our analytical lens from individual properties towards the spatial-social relationships which connect micro-enterprises across the above spatial situations and in relation to informal markets. In the township context of significant spatial limitations, there are multiple contestations between different land claimants and land users. The ways in which people resolve these contestations, we will argue, help to foster relationship building, which in turn enables people to share resources and make informal claims to tenure.

The neighbourhood economy

The neighbourhood economy is spatially complex in enterprise distribution, organised around a multiplicity of logics, which are influenced by the product sold or service provided, the availability of infrastructure and or infrastructure requirements, the movement of people, the risks and threats of crime and state action, and the logic of neighbourhood accessibility (and social gathering). We have argued that the spatial dimensions of micro-enterprise activities are supported within a structure of social relationships (Charman & Govender 2016). Our geospatial maps of the distribution of micro-enterprises provides a tool to examine this complexity. To make sense of socio-spatial dynamics at a neighbourhood level, we consider three points within the Ivory Park enterprise distribution map introduced in Chapter 3. Figure 5.1 shows the spatial distribution of micro-enterprises within a 200-metre radius of points, A (on the site perimeter, hence incomplete data), B (along a high street), and C (a neighbourhood street).

The data in Table 5.1 compare the enterprise distribution for the top 10 categories on an Ivory Park high street (Site B) and neighbourhood street (Site C). The research identified 176 micro-enterprises in Site B and 231 in Site C.

Analysing the data, we can discern a shift in enterprise categories and intensity from the high street to the neighbourhood context: on the one hand, specialist services decrease within the neighbourhood along with a narrowing of enterprise activities (30 categories versus 26 categories), conversely, house-based retail activities as well as recreational offerings increase in Site C. Comparing the high street (Site B) to the neighbourhood street (Site C), we see that street traders decline in proportion to all identified businesses by 5%, educares by 4%, hair care by 3%, and micro-manufacturing and business services by 2%. In terms of their ranking within the top 10 categories, within the neighbourhood context, house-shop numbers grew (7% proportional change), as did shebeens (4%), greengrocers (3%), takeaways (4%), along with recycling and tuck shops. Hair care and building services declined in comparison.

The comparative data from Sites B and C show how the neighbourhood economy changes in composition as the role of streets (and high streets) and residential dwellings varies in influence. We found that residential localities are most likely to influence certain categories of businesses, especially micro-enterprises that sell liquor and provide a recreational environment (taverns and shebeens); provide childcare and educational services (educares); sell groceries and household consumables (spaza shops and tuck shops); store recyclables; provide personal services (such as clothes washing); and religious and medical services. These businesses utilise existing infrastructure or the scope afforded within private landholdings to develop functional and immobile infrastructure for business activities. The scale of financial investment in residential business structures is far greater than found amongst street-based businesses where tenure insecurity is greater.

TABLE 5.1 Enterprise distribution for the top 10 categories in high streets and neighbourhoods

Focal point B (200m)					Focal point C (200m)			
Rank	Category	No.	%		Rank	Category	No.	%
1	Street traders	22	13		1	House shops	43	19
2	House shops	20	11		2	Shebeens	36	16
3	Shebeens	20	11		3	Greengrocers	20	9
4	Hair care	15	9		4	Takeaways	19	8
5	Greengrocers	10	6		5	Street traders	18	8
6	Takeaways	7	4		6	Recycling	15	6
7	Misc liquor sales	7	4		7	Misc liquor sales	13	6
8	Micro-manufacturers	7	4		8	Hair care	8	3
9	Business services	7	4		9	Tuck shops	8	3
10	Educare	7	4		10	Building services	6	3

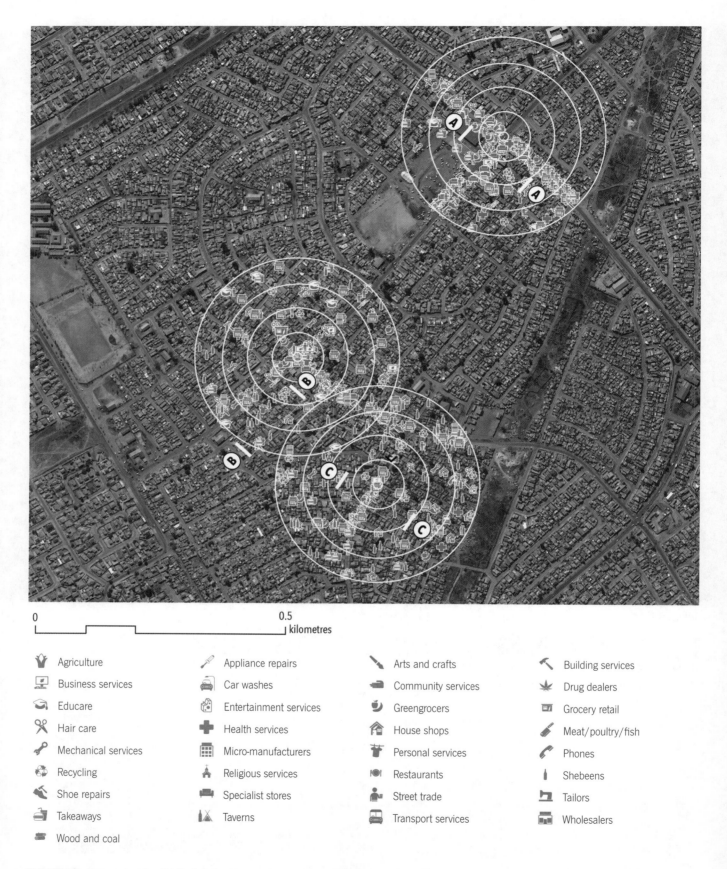

FIGURE 5.1 Micro-enterprise distribution, focusing on three distinct sites; A (at the taxi rank), B (high street), C (neighbourhood street)

Note: Micro-entrepreneurial activity within each site was mapped with a 200 m radii of the centre.

Legend:

- 🌱 Agriculture
- 🔧 Appliance repairs
- 🗡 Arts and crafts
- 🔨 Building services
- 💻 Business services
- 🚗 Car washes
- ➖ Community services
- 🌿 Drug dealers
- 🎓 Educare
- 🎮 Entertainment services
- 🥬 Greengrocers
- 🛒 Grocery retail
- ✂️ Hair care
- ➕ Health services
- 🏠 House shops
- 🔪 Meat/poultry/fish
- 🔧 Mechanical services
- 🏢 Micro-manufacturers
- 👕 Personal services
- 📞 Phones
- ♻️ Recycling
- ⛪ Religious services
- 🍴 Restaurants
- 🍾 Shebeens
- 👟 Shoe repairs
- 🛋 Specialist stores
- 👤 Street trade
- 🧵 Tailors
- 🍽 Takeaways
- 🏕 Taverns
- 🚐 Transport services
- 📦 Wholesalers
- 📚 Wood and coal

In addition, the architecture of residential structures is more heavily influenced by non-business priorities, including the need to manage private (home) and non-private (commercial) uses of the property as well as securing a long-term financial return on the investment. Women traders predominate in certain spaces within this neighbouring economy, often operating within clusters either on the high street selling fruit and vegetables, clothes and homeware, or within neighbourhood streets selling fresh meat, takeaway foods and products like jewellery or cosmetics.

Public open space and the street in particular (comprising both the sidewalk and road reserves) are key spaces for business. The street environment provides micro-enterprises with access to a market that is broader in its reach of customers and more flexible than residential homes, presents lower entry barriers and can benefit from enabling social-spatial arrangements. Many street-based micro-enterprises have emerged in response to the opportunities to utilise strategically beneficial positions on the street, such as a street corner or available infrastructure, and to position the business as close as possible to pedestrian traffic. High streets which serve as transport routes, connecting distant neighbourhoods, are especially dynamic spaces for undertaking service-oriented businesses as we showed in our analysis of census data in Chapter 3.

Micro-spatial influences

The businesses situated within public space function within a complex spatial system, subject to intricate ordering and nuanced positioning. This outcome reflects economic factors such as agglomeration and clustering, infrastructural synergies, the spatial morphology of the street, public infrastructure investments, social agreements and local power dynamics, to list some of the main influences. The complexity of these spatial arrangements can be seen through our analysis of three street cross-sections as shown in Figure 5.2, Figure 5.3 and Figure 5.4.

These sections correspond with the taxi rank (Site A; refer to Section A-A;), a high-street interchange that functions as an informal taxi rank (Site B; Section B-B) and a neighbourhood street (Site C; Section C-C). As we have seen, the business mixture shifts from the high street to the neighbourhood street in response to settlement dynamics and changing market forces. Through the sectional diagrams, we show how spatial influences within the streetscape refine this outcome.

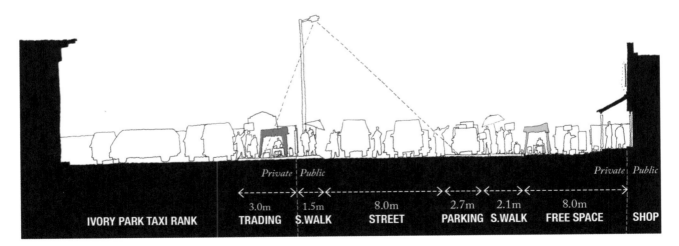

FIGURE 5.2 Section A-A, showing the street profile and activity directly adjacent to the taxi rank

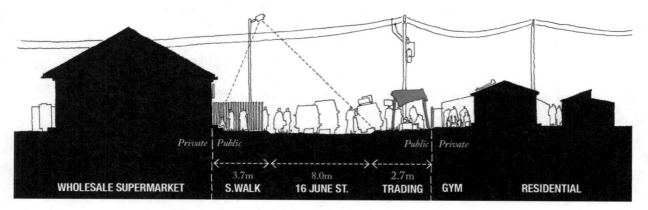

FIGURE 5.3 Section B-B, showing the street profile and activity at the intersection of a neighbourhood street and high street

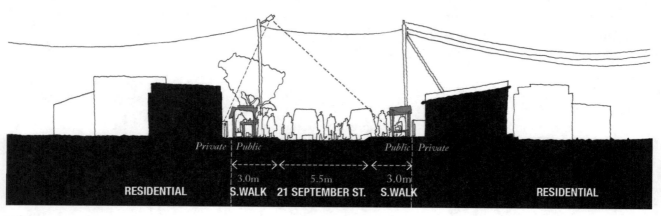

FIGURE 5.4 Section C-C, showing the street profile and activity along a neighbourhood street

Along the length of the entire high street (from Site A through to Site B), there is evidence of agglomerations and business synergies. As pedestrians emerge from the taxi rank, they encounter a series of clustered sectors, first the specialist shops and personal services such as the traditional healers (situated in buildings a distance away from the street frontage), then sellers of hardware products, and micro-manufacturers of cupboards and furniture. As they approach B-B Section, the clustering of stalls changes to those selling fruit and vegetables, retailers of fast-moving consumer goods and hair salons. The ordering is purposeful. Spatial proximity facilitates linkages between businesses that, for example, repair car engines, wash cars, install exhaust systems, train people in driving and prepare food for taxi drivers. Similarly, fruit and vegetable sellers cluster to provide shoppers with a wide selection of products with traders seeking to offer subtle variations in their range and style of presentation, selling loose or in pre-packed units. Along the high street, pedestrian movements follow multiple narrow channels, which permits an intensive use of the pavement, accommodating micro-enterprises of varying space requirements, from 1 m² (small) to 24 m² (large) units. The intersection of two high streets at Site B (Section B-B) provides a favourable location for the sale of live chickens, with the micro-enterprises able to market their goods to a wide range of customers in passing vehicles and pedestrians.

Street micro-enterprises are often reliant on adjacent private households. These properties provide access to services such as electricity and water, as indicated in Figure 5.5.

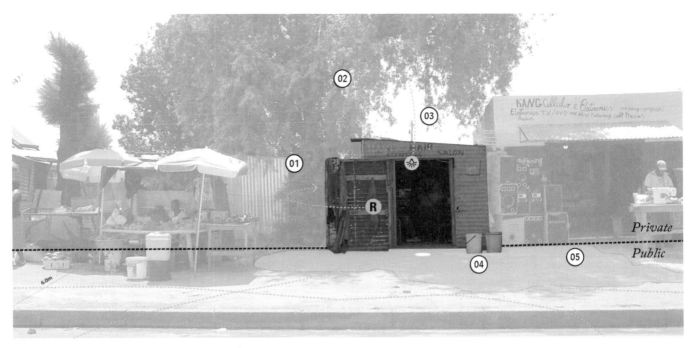

01 **Rental:** Located on private land and leased from owner
02 **Electricity:** Electricity from land owner as part of rental
03 **Advertising:** Signage addressing street traffic
04 **Water bucket:** Plastic buckets containing water from washing hair and cleaning (no running water available)
05 **Shade:** Shade in front of store allows for comfortable working space in summer. This creates an extension of the shop onto the street.

FIGURE 5.5 Trading structures create an active high street frontage and rely on the main residential dwelling for utilities and storage

In addition, property owners may permit traders to utilise residential infrastructure and space on their property while affording the trader with a degree of tenure security. We learnt from our discussion with traders that most homeowners claim 'ownership' of the pavements immediately outside of their properties. These claims are grounded in their capacity to mobilise law enforcement to remove traders from these positions, a 'right' which is embodied within most municipal by-laws on street trading which unintentionally permits homeowners the power to compel traders to 'rent' the space through transfers in cash or kind. While weighted in favour of the homeowner, the relationship does benefit traders as well. Apart from gaining access to water and electricity, services which are usually billed on a monthly basis, traders can secure agreements to store their stock overnight. We examined the spatial-property relationships of 34 micro-enterprises on the high-street at Site A. These businesses sold a variety of goods (from snacks, to homewares to furniture) from R5 to R5 000 and included business making furniture and providing services such as hair care and car washing. They made use of different infrastructures and configurations from simple tables to brick structures to containers. Half of these businesses reported paying 'rent', either to the homeowner or the structure owner where these differed. The rents ranged from R100 pm to R3 500 pm, with the average monthly rent equal to R50 per m^2. Separate costs for storing goods and acquiring electricity ranged from R200 pm to R1 000 pm. The revenue streams from street-based micro-enterprises which accrue to property owners create a common interest in sustaining street business.

We have argued that these mutual dependencies have strengthened cohesion between 'insiders' (property owners) and 'outsiders' (street traders), which, in the case of Ivory

Park, have softened ethnic or national tensions that have in other contexts resulted in violence towards informal businesses (Charman & Petersen 2015).

As the flow of pedestrian movement moves off the high street and enters the residential area, the spatial economy undergoes readjustment. Within residential areas, there are few permanent structures established within the streetscape. This is due to both the narrowing of the road reserve and the changing business opportunities of the residential context. As we have shown, the most demanded micro-enterprise activities relate to the sale of groceries, liquor and street food. This includes the provision of recreational facilities around food and liquor consumption. Spaza shops with their characteristic name signs directly interface with the street, either via serving hatches or doorways where in-store browsing is permitted (see Figure 5.6).

Shebeens, in contrast, are usually accessed via backyards through concealed entrances due to the risk of police detection as a result of their illegal operation. Though spatially oriented inward, shebeens serve a niche market and are known to neighbours and customers via word-of-mouth (see Figure 5.7).

On the street pavement, trading stalls have less permanence than those of the high street with most stands assembled from transportable materials for either the morning or later afternoon. Street businesses with the greatest frequency sell fast-food, snacks, fruit and vegetables or provide services with low infrastructure requirements such as hair braiding. These micro-enterprises appropriate the sidewalk with little or no space left for pedestrians who then walk in the street. The shift of pedestrians from the sidewalk to the street transforms the street into a space that people then control and cars surrender their dominance. Passing motor vehicles are obliged to slow down and 'negotiate' with the pedestrians for passage. The mountable kerbs permit vehicles to park on the sidewalk while the street itself now assumes the social function of the sidewalk. Through this spatial realignment, the street becomes a common social space where people congregate, children play games and cultural events are enacted wherein a large tent might be erected, for example, to cater for a major social event such as a wedding, funeral or unveiling.

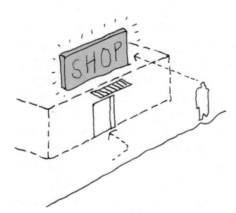

FIGURE 5.6 Spaza shops with characteristic name signs directly interface with the street

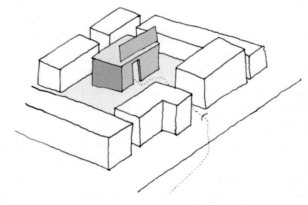

FIGURE 5.7 Shebeens are businesses that do not have a pronounced relationship to the street and are layered in their access

Infrastructure and architecture

The architecture of business infrastructure comprises an array of structures, materials and space usage. People establish business units using their own designs, though following the collective responses of existing forms. These forms are determined with varying degrees by the availability of space and its configuration. Additionally, the architecture is influenced by the strength of tenure security vis-à-vis external threats from the state (police), land holders as in the case above and community leadership structures like the taxi association and its control of businesses within the rank and adjacent street space (refer to Figure 5.2). Also important are factors of portability and mobility; opportunities for visibility and product display; the need to preserve commuter pathways; and exogenous risks to business from incidents such as rain and theft.

Permanent structures

We identified three types of permanent structures in public space: one, converted shipping containers; two, shops situated within private properties with forecourts that encroached onto the street; and three, shacks or small kiosks. Converted shipping containers (see Figure 5.8), are commonly utilised by micro-enterprises because they are moveable and yet cannot be easily dismantled and the components stolen.

The importance of mobile structures reflects the insecurity of tenure for street businesses. Containers offer a sizeable space (14 m^2 or 28 m^2) and are relatively secure, permitting the operator to lock her/his products inside overnight. Businesses that commonly operate from containers include spaza shops, hair salons, off-licence liquor sales (in Gauteng province), tyre-repair businesses and jewellery exchanges. Containers shops are easily identifiable (and can be branded) and importantly, enable the entrepreneur to attach property to their business, thus providing potential buyers (should they choose to sell their business) with a business in a box.

In properties along high streets, brick and mortar shops have been built to serve the passing pedestrians and benefit from the exposure to passing vehicles (see Figure 5.9).

In contrast to containers and other street-sited structures, these private property investments have a more secure legal position and risk profile. Indeed, throughout the township economy we noted that permanent infrastructures are established on properties with secure land rights (whether titled or not), while the more ephemeral structures occupy spaces where land tenure is insecure or contested. Most shops are small (30 m^2 or smaller) with customer access often restricted in certain retail businesses, including spaza shops, where instead trade is conducted through burglar-barred entrances or serving hatches. Shops utilised as hair salons, internet cafes, clothes stores or stores selling appliances keep their doors open to permit a fluid movement from the street into the store. In some instances, advertising boards are placed onto the street to extend the commercial reach of the business. The high-street shops tend to intrude onto the pavement and encroach on public space through the construction of an overhang or veranda. These structures offer shelter and permit the erection of signage and the display of goods. Some shopkeepers also rent forecourt space to other (non-competing) businesses. A retail shop along the stretch of Ivory Park high street within Site B, for example, rents space to a tailor to operate under the shelter of the overhang.

Our third type of permanent structure are small shacks (known as *zozo* huts in Gauteng) or prefabricated kiosks. These are either positioned in public space on the sidewalk or erected within the front yard of a private property and positioned along the street-facing boundary, sometimes encroaching onto the pavement. *Zozo* huts have an average size of 10 m² and are constructed from a timber frame and corrugated iron cladding. They can be bought new for prices ranging from R3 000–R6 000. Once erected at a suitable location, *zozo* units can be 'improved' through the installation of a concrete floor, access to electricity and business branding. *Zozo* structures are commonly utilised for hair salons, selling takeaways and operating service businesses repairing appliances or making clothes.

We would often encounter street-posted advertisements offering for sale a structure along with the contents of the business. The tradability of the enterprise structure and business contents occurs in all three infrastructure situations, with transactions conducted

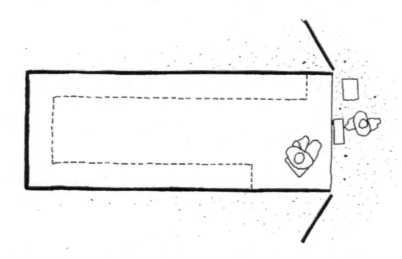

FIGURE 5.8 A shipping container as a business premises allows for quick establishment on site and is often not attached to any municipal services

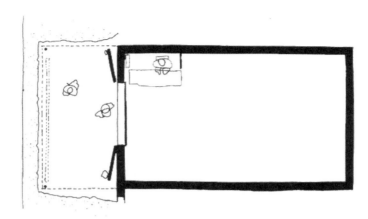

FIGURE 5.9 Small brick and mortar structure with customised signage and shopfront

without legal procedure or institutional oversight. Even in the case of shops established on private properties, entrepreneurs are able to purchase and sell businesses in their entirety, selling the lease agreements in situations where the structure itself is leased.

Temporary structures

Structures of non-permanence for conducting business are diverse in form. These range from the entrepreneurs that utilise no or minimal infrastructure, such as ambulatory traders, to businesses that operate from simple, portable stands to ones which operate from elaborate stalls which require substantial portaging of stand equipment. These are designed to provide overhead shelter, thus enabling the trader to endure rain or hot weather, as well as affording an infrastructure on which goods can be displayed (see Figure 5.10 and Figure 5.11).

FIGURE 5.10 Agglomeration of fruit trading from structures of varying degrees of investment and permanence

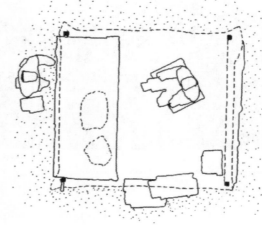

FIGURE 5.11 Trader table and a gazebo for marketing items and protection from the elements

Some of the micro-enterprises which utilise minimal or no infrastructure also have modest space requirements, allowing the trader to position their business in optimal spatial location close to likely customers. One of the clearest examples is the sellers of sweets, cigarettes and newspapers who operate within the street outside the taxi rank selling directly to customers seated within the taxis. An open patch of ground, or an infrastructural object such as street pole or concrete plinth provides an opportunity for traders to display their wares (using a tarpaulin as an under sheet) and maximise product exposure, coordinate colours and in some cases stack goods in elaborate ways to increase product exposure. Sellers of second-hand clothing or footwear effectively make use of this marketing strategy since their targets are not purposeful shoppers but impulse-buying pedestrians. This strategy is also effective for persons selling items of plastic homeware such as buckets and those trading second-hand goods, furniture and manufactured products like burglar bars. Pop-up activities use open space and concealed sites. Gamblers assemble in these localities, attracting the attention of pedestrians walking along the street, but discreetly positioned so as to minimise the risks of law enforcement or to allow for the settlement of disputes out of the public eye. Some micro-enterprises have extensive space needs. These include car mechanics and panel beaters, brick makers and furniture manufacturers. As a consequence of the spatial limitations within road reserves, such businesses tend to be situated on unutilised land portions, including vacant plots, open green space and utility servitudes. The insecurity of their spatial situation discourages the entrepreneur from investing in infrastructure to enhance the operation of the business. So, these micro-enterprises are highly susceptible to certain kinds of risk, including the effects of inclement weather and their forced removal for contravening municipal land-use restrictions or as a result of a change in land-use status if the property is sold.

The use of temporary structures is subject to considerations of transport. Most street-trading entrepreneurs are reliant on non-motorised transport to ferry their goods and stall infrastructure from home to market. We observed that traders commonly utilise either a wheelbarrow, shopping trolley or wheelie bin for this purpose. In consideration of transport factors, temporary infrastructure tends to be lightweight and compact when disassembled. For these reasons, traders utilise umbrellas, gazebos and simple tarpaulin and post structures. Structures made from tarpaulin and posts are probably the most common form of temporary infrastructure and are assembled to provide shade and a superstructure from which the trader can suspend goods, supplemented by tables to display wares at waist height. Traders can use innovative approaches to assemble these structures. In one example, a street trader in Tembisa had embedded plastic tubes into the ground wherein the corner posts of her structure could be dropped into place, thus enabling her to swiftly assemble and disassemble the stand. She transported the poles and tarpaulin to her trading stand using a wheelbarrow and had to make several trips to ferry the infrastructure, business equipment (for cooking food) and saleable goods.

The spatial flexibility afforded to temporary structures on streets, in addition to the market visibility and proximity to pedestrians from street localities, has been recognised by corporate business in its endeavour to penetrate the township market at low investment risk. We encountered several instances where formal businesses, such as bank agents and insurance sellers, make use of branded gazebos situated within the street to promote products and sign up new customers. Gazebos, stalls and umbrella stands are utilised to create pop-up shops, exploiting the opportunities of informality that are involuntarily afforded to micro-enterprises to conduct business in the neighbourhood economy on terms that would not be possible outside townships. Corporate-supported street traders operate with the understanding that the state policies on street trading are enforced on an inconsistent basis. Ordinary traders, who operate on a permanent basis, are often less fortunate. The group of traders with whom we engaged in Ivory Park to understand spatial politics reported that law enforcement officials would visit from time to time, requesting to see permits, asking to check identity documents, forcing them to relocate their stands and confiscating goods. Paton, a street photographer from Zimbabwe, with whom we collaborated (see Street Life Voices below), spoke on the vulnerability of street trade: '*Sometime the police officers ask us for permits. We don't have permits; we just operate informally. We are willing to get permits so we can operate formally [if this was possible]. I can't even bank my money, I put my money under a pillow which is very bad [because] my shack could burn down.*'

Mobility

Stationary trade constitutes only part of the street business and mobile micro-enterprises are common. On the high street, mobile traders are able to constantly shift their position in response to the availability of space and to get close to the market. In residential areas, mobility advantages the entrepreneur to serve a home-based clientele which would otherwise need to go to the high street for purchases. Mobilise traders are predominantly men. There are at least two reasons for this: first, mobile businesses operate away from the home; second, mobile traders are unable to rely on the kinds of social support afforded in clusters where female traders often look after one another's stores when they have to attend to social matters away from the business location.

The range of mobile traders in the township is diverse (Figure 5.12).

We encountered vehicles cruising the side streets using a loud hailer to promote their wares or purchase scrap materials; men pushing supermarket shopping trollies and

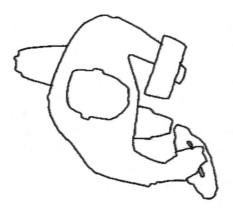

FIGURE 5.12 The human body affords a trading infrastructure, allowing for mobility of traders along the street

wheelbarrows and using distinctive whistle sounds and calls to alert residents and attract customers; ambulatory hawkers selling clothes, kitchen rags, brushes and broomsticks walking from house to house, some offering credit sales; horse-and-cart deliveries of coal; men ferrying crates of beer and cold drinks to taverns and spaza shops using wheelbarrows and wheelie bins; roving street photographers; and entrepreneurs providing home-maintenance services such as grass-cutting and pest control.

There are also cases of mobile businesses that operate on fixed arrangements, arriving at a particular place at a specified time to conduct their business. The 'Fafi' gambling circuit is one example (see Scott & Barr 2013). Players of Fafi are organised in informal groups which coalesce around a common meeting place at which bets are placed, the results recorded on a score board and winnings distributed (see Figure 5.13).

The game is simple. Each player has a purse into which they place their predictions and bet, recorded on a square sheet numbered from 201 to 236. A member of the group is responsible for collecting the bets. The purses are deposited into a bag and handed over to the Fafi (the gambling boss, so to speak) who operates from a vehicle with bullet proof armour; the Fafi never leaves the vehicle, whose engine runs constantly. Upon receiving the bag, the Fafi simultaneously hands over the bet results. They then open each purse to check the bets, placing the winning sum into those purses containing the successfully predicted number. The bag is returned to the group representative and the Fafi drives off to the next meeting place. The Fafi will return again at a designated time, often visiting a site several times per day in regular rounds.

Mobile services are important to a range of micro-enterprises. Spaza shops are reliant on daily deliveries for bread and milk supplies. We encountered a number of micro-laundry businesses that offered dry-cleaning services through an arrangement with a formal

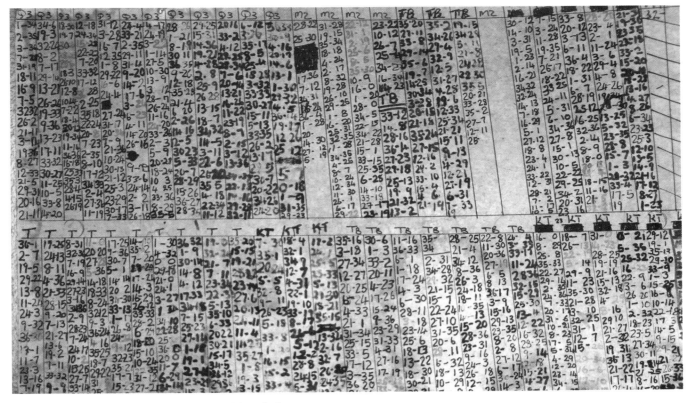

FIGURE 5.13 Fafi results are recorded on a board, Ivory Park

business, usually situated outside the township. In accordance with an agreed schedule, the formal business would collect clothes from the micro-enterprise in the evening and return the cleaned items early the following morning. Gold and coin exchanges operate on similar principles. These 'exchanges' purchase gold and jewellery and are often established in shipping-container structures situated along the high street. The business is operated by an employee whose sole function is to contact their superiors when an opportunity for an 'exchange' arises, since the buyers operate on a mobile basis and never work from the premises. This business model is also favoured by the dealers of narcotics, notably the 'merchants' of heroin derivatives, cocaine and crystal methamphetamine.

Street life voices

As part of our research on street businesses, we supported a group of street photographers to capture over 200 images of street life over a period of one month in 2012, using a photovoice participatory approach (Charman & Kotzen n.d). The photographs were used to spearhead an engagement with policy-makers on recognising the opportunities afforded by streets as a space of business, though simultaneously raising awareness of the vulnerability and resilience of street traders. Through the eyes of the eight street photographers, the subject of street life evoked a mix of reactions. These ranged from respect for entrepreneurship; the appreciation for the business diversity and vibrancy; the intimacy of the street as a social space; the hopes and aspirations for progress; to the frustrations and anger of street users directed towards the obstacles of selfish actions and state controls. While there is not space to address all these topics in detail, here we focus on two themes: firstly, the endeavours (indeed resilience) of the very poorest in seeking out a livelihood in the street environment, and secondly, the conceptualisation of the neighbourhood businesses as contributing towards the benefit of the community. The 'survivalist' struggles of businesses are illuminated in the photographs: 'woman frying fish' and 'beating all odds' (Figures 5.14 and 5.15).

FIGURE 5.14 'Woman frying fish': Trading stands are established temporarily to target the market for takeaway meals in the early evening
Credit: Patrick Manhica

FIGURE 5.15 'Beating all odds': The photograph highlights the influence of childcare responsibilities on livelihoods
Credit: Deweld Monyai

In both photographs, the subjects are each carrying a small child strapped to their back. For the woman selling takeaway food at a street location, her business comprises two plastic buckets and an iron drum on which she fries fish. Patrick Manhica (2013), the photographer, added this caption: 'The life she is living is not fit for a woman with a child, but she does not have a choice.' The man, in 'beating all odds', is collecting plastic, tin cans and bottles from the street verge. Develd Monyai (2013a), the photographer, writes: 'This man is recycling material with a baby on his back. It shows the beauty of caring for children and the environment,' a cross-reference to the idea that micro-enterprises benefit the broader community. Both photographs convey a sense of resilience, a tenacity to pursue a livelihood through reacting to demand and creating markets on the street where none previously existed (a concept of 'make-work jobs').

The idea of resilience also refers to the capacity to withstand and respond. The photographs 'trying' and 'the trolley' articulate this theme (Figure 5.16 and Figure 5.17).

In 'trying', a photograph of two police officers from the CoJ Municipal Police Department interrogating a street trader, Musa Ndlovu (2013), the photographer, wrote in his caption: 'we tried not to commit crime, but we always find ourselves against the law.' In 'the trolley', a photo sequence that tells the story of an agent (presumably working for a formal supermarket chain) apprehending a mobile fruit and vegetable hawker and then confiscating the (presumably stolen) trolley. The photographer, Develd Monyai (2013b) comments: 'A street vendor was using this trolley for business and the trolley owner came to collect it. The vendor lost his ease of mobility and his business changes, as he has to carry his goods.'

FIGURE 5.16 'Trying': Police officials engage a trader on the legality of their trading conditions
Credit: Bongumusa Ndlovu

FIGURE 5.17 'The trolley': The trolley which is used as a trading device is reclaimed by an agent of the original owners – the supermarket
Credit: Deweld Monyai

A significant theme in the photovoice narrative is that neighbourhood entrepreneurship has wider benefit. In their selection of subjects, the photographers sought to communicate the idea of businesses that serve in the 'community interest'. This speaks to Neves and Du Toit's (2012) observation of a 'relational economy of informality'. A photograph of men producing cement blocks on an open piece of ground, for example, is titled 'building the future' and subtitled 'local business makes a difference'. The business employs five men. A photograph of vegetable trolley venders, entitled 'mobile' (see Chapter 10, Figure 10.3), emphasises the innovativeness and benefit to the community. The photographer, IDTV Tivane (2013), explained in the caption: the vendors 'move around with the goods, selling from door-to-door. Children are not sent around in the evenings [to purchase fruit and vegetables], they are safe. This is a good service for the community.' The idea that entrepreneurship is to be admired is reflected in the photograph 'The businessman' (Figure 5.18).

The photograph shows a cobbler working from a simple street stand (table counter), head down in concentration, focusing on making original sandals using materials such as used tyres (for soles) and animal hides. Pairs of sandals are laid out neatly on display for passing customers. Paton Magonya (2013), the photographer, wrote this caption: 'This photo shows the beautiful art of manufacturing this man is doing. Showing his creativity turning animal skins into good use. The man is also empowering himself by selling this footwear to the community.'

FIGURE 5.18 'The businessman': A cobbler working from a temporary open structure alongside a sidewalk
Credit: Paton Magonya

Outlook

From our analysis of spatial ordering, three aspects should be highlighted. First, we note the flexible agility and responsiveness of micro-enterprises to space opportunities. Nearly every space within a township setting is utilised for business; some spaces are permanently used and others are used on a transitory and temporary basis in reaction to a particular time period or situation of market opportunity. There are also multiple users of particular spaces across time. One space might accommodate one set of traders in the early morning and another set of traders in the afternoon or evening. The case of mobile traders shows that businesses are able to respond to markets without micro-spatial commitments, including the need to secure land tenure rights and to establish infrastructure. Second, our research shows the unseen organisational logic that accommodates different business and non-business needs, including traders and pedestrians, small businesses and larger businesses, in spatial requirement. This can be seen in the contrasting situation of street traders on the high street and those operating on neighbourhood streets. Third, spatial utilisation is accompanied by social processes which support inclusivity. These range from surveillance, to the accommodation of potential competitive businesses in clusters of micro-enterprises selling the same products, to the sociability afforded by the publicness of interactions in spaces like the street.

The sociability of the township street economy has a similar role in producing social relations as has been recognised in marketplaces. In her research on a market in the UK, Watson, S (2009) found that markets were sites of social connections and places that memorialise the relationships between traders and shoppers, sometimes going back generations. Watson, S (2009) argues that these connections can include seemingly passive encounters which she conceptualised as 'rubbing along': 'recognition of different others through a glance or gaze, seeing and being seen, sharing embodied spaces, in talk and silence' (p. 1581). Hiebert, Rath and Vertovec (2015) explored the available literature in support of the notion that 'everyday interactions' within markets help people to develop 'methods of intercultural engagement' enabling them to acquire a 'repertoire of intercultural skills' that positively influence social relationships (across race, class and gender) (p. 6). The evidence indicates that such relationships enhance economic opportunities for diverse participants, a finding aligned to our interpretation of spatial reciprocity between businesses. Social interactions in public market spaces, including the township street, certainly enhance sociability. But some experiences may reinforce stereotypes, solidify divisions and uphold dominance, as might happen between 'insiders' and 'outsiders', the powerful and the weak, traders with large spatial requirements and those with fewer requirements, and not least between men and women. Some street businesses can have negative externalities on other kinds of businesses, such as the sellers of braai meat[1] whose businesses can generate considerable smoke. At night and in contexts where lighting is poor or non-existent, the street can become a dangerous place for traders and customers alike.

We have argued that the relationships between people, which are shaped through mutual use of space and responses to physical thresholds (the street, pavements, open space, private houses etc.), underpin a networked and 'relational economy' (Charman & Govender 2016, p. 312). While this relational outcome helps to accommodate different spatial demands and users, exactly how individuals benefit is subject to the dynamics of power. Power rests in diverse loci. The taxi association, in one situation, determines how space is utilised outside the rank, advancing their self-interests over those of traders

---

[1] Braai means barbecue

though still finding common ground to build relationships, such as policing against crime. Property owners, in another case, hold claim to the street space outside their homes and use their threat to mobilise the state to enforce by-laws as a means to extract tribute from traders. The street photographers recorded a case in which the police harassment of street traders who operate without licence or tenure highlights the arsenal of the state's 'spatial technologies of domination' (Rogerson 2016, p. 233) to shape and influence how micro-enterprises utilise space and the risks accompanying informality.

6
THE HIGH STREET & BUSINESS PIONEERS

In this chapter we argue that high streets are important to micro-enterprises and over time can emerge as economic spines which foster business development.

CHAPTER 6

The high street and business pioneers

In this chapter, we argue that high streets are important to micro-enterprises and over time can emerge as economic spines which foster business development. Yet, in many townships positive economic outcomes cannot be guaranteed because the use of high streets is hindered as a result of structural factors, such as rigid land-use systems, inappropriate spatial planning, non-supportive institutional infrastructure and inadequate public investment to enhance business as well as social use. Where high streets have begun to influence the business environment, they have generally benefited from a combination of policy design to enable business formalisation, flexible urban planning to accommodate multiple uses of the public sidewalk, strong linkages between transport services and businesses, and the presence of pioneering businesses that undertake significant property investments. Our consideration of high streets includes four spatial gradients: one, we consider the linkages between the high street and the wider city in terms of the role of public transport; two, we examine a case site at the small-area level, focusing on one street; three, at the neighbourhood level, we examine particular spatial relationships among clusters of businesses and their connection to the street; and four, in the micro-context, we describe the strategic use of objects and infrastructure which influence opportunities for micro-enterprises, pedestrians as well as social users.

High streets are the busy roads that bisect townships and along which public transport corridors operate, both formally and informally. It is from these corridors that minibus taxi ranks tend to commence their routes to inner-city destinations, which we found in Delft South, Browns Farm, Ivory Park and Tembisa. As reported in Chapters 3 and 5, service-oriented businesses as well as street-trading businesses selling hardware, homeware, clothes, and an array of traders selling cooked meat and other takeaway foods, are largely situated on high streets, often clustered together. High streets are furthermore the principal locality for furniture retailers, wholesalers and specialised retailers selling products such as electronics, fashion clothing and pharmaceuticals. In contrast, spaza shops and most liquor-selling and serving venues are situated in neighbourhood streets. In this chapter, we will show that absence of a leisure economy along high streets results from both the influence of structural hindrances and policy obstacles to the formalisation of these micro-enterprises. Where these constraints have been lessened (though, for example innovative policy reforms), a thriving high-street-centred leisure economy can fulfil a pioneering role in transforming the street environment in qualitative and quantitative terms.

Structural barriers

While township high streets commonly represent dynamic opportunities for micro-enterprises, their role as marketplaces and spatial evolution has been hampered through

124

intended and unintended outcomes of municipal authority spatial planning. In terms of allowable land use, most high-street properties are not zoned for business rights, but instead for residential use only. This restrictive zoning derives from the aims of apartheid spatial planning to create dormitory settlements and has remained largely unchanged into the present, apart from common concessions to permit a narrow range of permissible activities so long as the land use remains predominantly residential. In Browns Farm, as an indicative case in the South African situation, all properties along the high street have residential zoning. The high street nevertheless supports a dense and diverse range of micro-enterprises, though outside the station precinct, most business activities operate on the public sidewalk rather than from residential property, as shown in the aerial photograph and spatial distribution of micro-enterprises in Figure 6.1.

As a consequence, there has been little conversion of residential properties to support and amplify businesses along the high street. On the street itself, the layout – including the narrow road reserve and hard kerbs – reinforces the residential function. Most of the properties bordering the high street are accessible from side streets to which the buildings orientate, with the rear of these residential properties facing the busy pedestrian area. In this context, the spatial relationship of reciprocity between high-street businesses and adjoining properties tends to centre on backyard dwellings rather than the main building. The business dynamic on the Browns Farm high street is defined by the movement of pedestrian commuters up and down the pavement to and from the train station and taxi rank, with the street serving a retail function (see Figure 6.2 and Figure 6.3).

Once these commuters have returned home by early evening, most economic activity ceases as the high street closes for the night. There are almost no late-night businesses, including leisure activities which are generally positioned within the residential areas, closer to people's homes. This spatial outcome of micro-enterprise distribution presents both social benefits and disadvantages.

As we saw in Chapter 5, the position, architectural design and functionality of infrastructure to support businesses can influence entrepreneurial responses. Transport infrastructure, including bus stations, taxi ranks and train stations, presents favourable market opportunities, though these spaces are often subject to inflexible planning and actions to regulate trading. Where state authorities have sought to include traders within transport hubs, the spatial allocation for business activities has tended to be confined to peripheral areas in standardised and homogenous infrastructure, situated adrift from the pedestrian flow. Street traders have instead set up alternative and informal business structures in defiance of urban planning and municipal restrictions. Municipal by-laws render most street trading on high-street pavements illegal. Within the street pavement, by-laws manage street traders with the objectives of preserving space for the movement of pedestrians, providing access to emergency services (such as fire hydrants), maintaining access to residential properties, and minimising visual obstruction. The informal trading by-laws in CoCT and CoJ, drawing on the Businesses Act (No. 71 of 1991) (as amended), restrict or altogether ban street trading in a variety of locations, including outside religious buildings, public monuments, cash machines and police stations, within 5 m of any intersection or at any place likely to obstruct traffic, on a sidewalk which is less than 3 m wide, or on a sidewalk outside any formal business selling the same products – to list a few examples. In CoCT, these restrictions are further reinforced by the by-law Relating to Streets, Public Places and the Prevention of Noise Nuisances, 2007, which prohibits any person or vehicle from intentionally blocking or interfering in other ways with the 'safe or free passage of a pedestrian or motor vehicle'. In townships, these restrictions are not plausible because locations situated at busy intersections where taxis stop, along

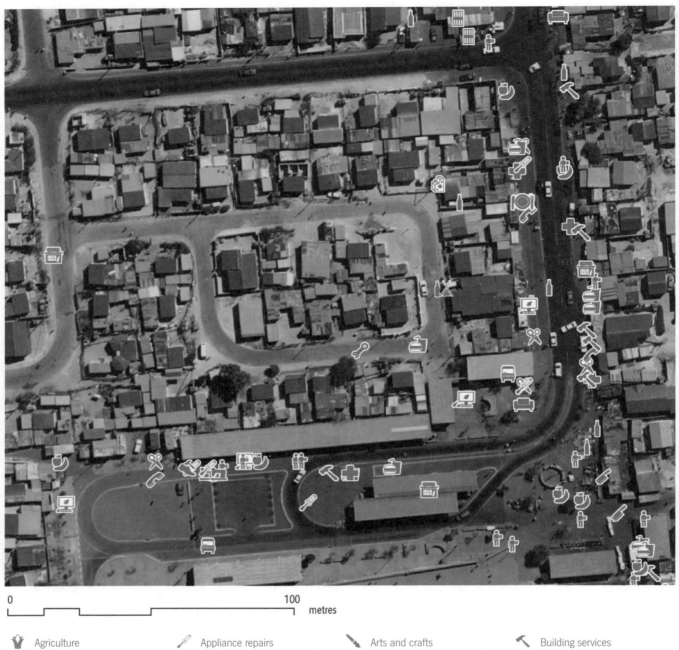

	Agriculture		Appliance repairs		Arts and crafts		Building services
	Business services		Car washes		Community services		Drug dealers
	Educare		Entertainment services		Greengrocers		Grocery retail
	Hair care		Health services		House shops		Meat/poultry/fish
	Mechanical services		Micro-manufacturers		Personal services		Phones
	Recycling		Religious services		Restaurants		Shebeens
	Shoe repairs		Specialist stores		Street trade		Tailors
	Takeaways		Taverns		Transport services		Wholesalers
	Wood and coal						

FIGURE 6.1 Distribution of micro-enterprises in Browns Farm illustrating the position of businesses relative to high street properties

Notes: Most businesses are situated on the sidewalks. The residential properties are not appropriately zoned or orientated to take advantage of the economic opportunities of either the high street or station.

FIGURE 6.2 Browns Farm high street businesses respond to the movement of pedestrian commuters along the pavement to transport nodes

FIGURE 6.3 High street businesses in Browns Farm encroach onto the sidewalk

pedestrian routes, and at sites outside of public buildings, to cite three examples, are the most profitable sites at which to conduct business. The net result is that most township high streets contain little supportive infrastructure suitable to micro-enterprise businesses, thus necessitating entrepreneurs to respond with disruption.

The morphology of township high streets is also misaligned to the dynamics of township micro-enterprises. Since townships were designed as residential settlements (without thought of the emergence of the high street), most high streets are narrow in width (both road surface and pedestrian pavement), with the road surface and street verge separated through the installation of a hard shoulder barrier kerb. This kerb has a dual intention, to channel rainwater towards the storm water drains and to prevent vehicles from embarking onto the pavement. The design intention is to encourage the movement of motor vehicles along the road as swiftly as possible, with traffic calming measures only implemented wherever deemed absolutely essential, such as outside schools or transport hubs. Investments in public infrastructure can both enable and disadvantage high-street markets. Streetlights and surveillance cameras lengthen the trading day and improve safety for entrepreneurs and pedestrians. The position, design and orientation (towards the street or otherwise) of community infrastructure such as libraries, clinics and schools can exert an influence to activate and intensify the business environment. Alternatively, the layout can dominate spaces and produce a negative influence on the broader street dynamic. On the high street in Delft South, for example, a community centre and library occupy a large section of high-street frontage adjacent to the epicentre of micro-enterprise activity, yet the building architecture of these facilities is oriented away from the high street. The design reinforces a spatial (and aesthetic) disconnection between the users of these facilities and traders on the street outside. At the suburb level, the Delft high street accommodates a range of community facilities (including two schools, a municipal clinic and two libraries, a community hall and a number of public parks), which collectively disrupt the growth of business activities and all of which are spatially disconnected from street activities. For these reasons, Isaacs and Silverman (2018) argue that these kinds of public investments should be conceptualised as the outcome of a 'city planning process' (p. 44) rather than a 'city building process' (p. 44) and as such, much public infrastructure undermines street vibrancy.

Eveline Street case

The structural disadvantages of many township high streets can be best illustrated through a contrasting case study. Our case comparison is Eveline Street, a high street within a Namibian township settlement in Windhoek, in which a series of spatial, policy and economic factors have conspired to produce a transformative outcome in the way the high street is utilised for businesses and has become the economic spine. Since land-use systems in Namibia are derived from apartheid systems and because micro-enterprises are similarly subject to complex regulatory requirements in which land-use restrictions can have a determining influence, the case is of direct relevance to South African townships. The notion of transformation is applied as a qualitative measure of the process through which an original settlement of a 'cellular, mono-functional, low-density' intention (Friedman 2000, p. 5) has altered its urban fabric, either in consort with urban planning or despite the intention of urban planners. At the heart of this proposition is the idea that aspects of spatial segregation can be undone from within the township.

In 2006, the CoW decided to establish business corridors on key township high streets. Their idea was to rezone the land along the corridor from residential to business and thus

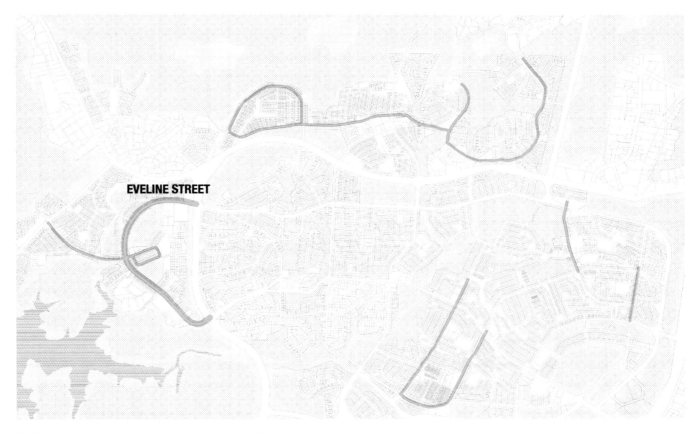

FIGURE 6.4 Map illustrating the Business Corridors of Katutura and its relationship to existing businesses

enable businesses to formalise. Nine such corridors were proposed, one of which was instituted in Eveline Street (see Figure 6.4 for the spatial position of the nine corridors).

Eveline Street is an important transport route in the Goreangab settlement, accommodating both public and private transport services, including public buses and private taxis. The street is not an ordinary high street but famed as a nightlife and leisure destination, home to bars, nightclubs and restaurants. Back in 2006, most of the bars on Eveline Street were unable to obtain licences as they were operating from residentially zoned properties. In order to sell liquor and operate venues, the bar and restaurant owners had to rezone their property from residential to commercial use. In addition, the operators had to obtain a business licence from the CoW, which entails multifaceted processes of compliance, including the payment of a property 'betterment fee', adherence to land-use restrictions and formal building regulations. Land rezoning is a complex process, as it is in South Africa, which requires the services of a conveyancer, the drafting of building plans, the attainment of public consent and technical approval from municipal planning officials. For these reasons less than 10 businesses had formalised their operations in Eveline Street at the time of introducing the business corridor intervention. To redress these obstacles the CoW facilitated a rezoning process which, although hamstrung with political obstacles and still not legally finalised (see SLF 2017a), nevertheless enabled businesses trading liquor products to formalise and obtain licences. By 2012 the number of formal businesses on Eveline Street had expanded from 10 in 2008 to 64; this latter figure included 34 licenced bars, 10 hair salons and five grocery shops (CoW 2012).

In 2016, we undertook a study of Eveline Street to analyse the impact of the business corridor intervention on the street environment and township business activities

(SLF & UrbanWorks 2017). Anticipating a shift in the legal status of businesses, we sought to understand the nature of social, spatial and economic changes which had occurred in the eight years following the corridor intervention. We found that the number of micro-enterprises had increased; the range and distribution of business categories had diversified; and the manner in which both private land and public space was utilised for economic and social activities had changed. Many of the bars for which the street had a famous/infamous reputation had benefited from capital investments to the properties, the business infrastructure, and expenditure on décor and public facilities to enhance their service offering. Throughout the street, there was evidence of investments which in turn supported a vibrant street culture for socialisation and business. At the heart of the functioning of the street economy, we identified a highly efficient transport system in which private sedan taxis fulfil the central role.

Economic growth, diversification and formalisation

Since 2008 and the corridor intervention, there has been a growth in micro-enterprises accompanied by a diversification of business activities. The number of micro-enterprises along the street doubled in eight years from 133 to 270 in 2016 (see Figure 6.5 and Figure 6.6).

The pioneer businesses were liquor retailing bars and clubs. Indeed, it was the very existence of such outlets along the street that prompted the CoW to establish the business corridor initiative. While some of this growth in enterprise numbers can be attributed to an increase in such outlets, whose number increased from 61 to 80, the proportion of bars in the total business mix along Eveline Street had decreased from 45% to 29% (see Figure 6.7).

In 2008, 74% of the businesses were either bars or car washes (with bar owners operating most of the car washes as an ancillary business), yet in 2016, the range of business categories had become considerably more diverse. Business types not present in 2008 such as hair salons, house shops, print shops, food takeaways and vehicle services, comprised a 37% share of the overall range of businesses by 2016. Furthermore, the growth in micro-enterprise activities was accompanied by an increase in the number of licensed (and thus formalised) businesses, increasing from 10 to 64. We also identified shifts in the pattern of business ownership with the pioneer bar owners becoming less dominant. In the case of hair salons, for example, merely 7% were subsidiaries of bars. New investors had set up businesses on Eveline Street to capitalise on the socio-spatial improvements and customers attracted by the leisure economy businesses.

🌱	Agriculture	🖌️	Appliance repairs	🖌️	Arts and crafts	⛏️ Building services
🖥️	Business services	🚗	Car washes	🛋️	Community services	🌿 Drug dealers
🎓	Educare	📸	Entertainment services	🥄	Greengrocers	🏧 Grocery retail
✂️	Hair care	➕	Health services	🏠	House shops	🖌️ Meat/poultry/fish
🔧	Mechanical services	▦	Micro-manufacturers	👕	Personal services	📞 Phones
♻️	Recycling	⛪	Religious services	🍴	Restaurants	▮ Shebeens
⛏️	Shoe repairs	🛋️	Specialist stores	👤	Street trade	🪡 Tailors
🥘	Takeaways	⛺	Taverns	🚐	Transport services	▭ Wholesalers
🪵	Wood and coal					

FIGURE 6.5 Micro-enterprise map of Eveline Street, Katutura 2008 at initiation of the Business Corridors initiative

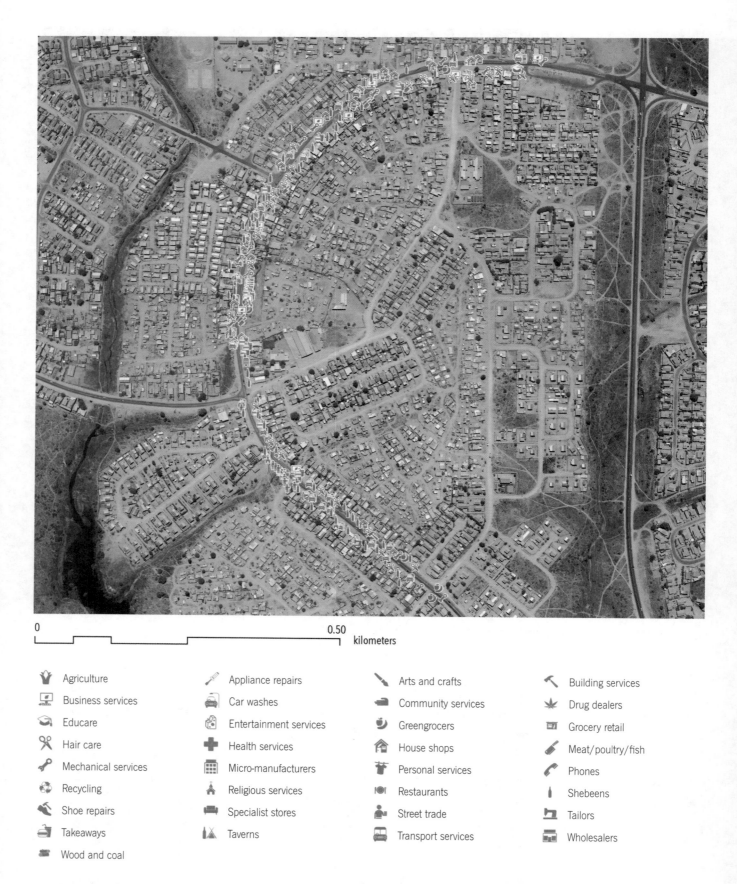

0   0.50
kilometers

Agriculture	Appliance repairs	Arts and crafts	Building services
Business services	Car washes	Community services	Drug dealers
Educare	Entertainment services	Greengrocers	Grocery retail
Hair care	Health services	House shops	Meat/poultry/fish
Mechanical services	Micro-manufacturers	Personal services	Phones
Recycling	Religious services	Restaurants	Shebeens
Shoe repairs	Specialist stores	Street trade	Tailors
Takeaways	Taverns	Transport services	Wholesalers
Wood and coal			

FIGURE 6.6 Micro-enterprise map of Eveline Street, Katutura 2016, eight years after the Business Corridors initiative

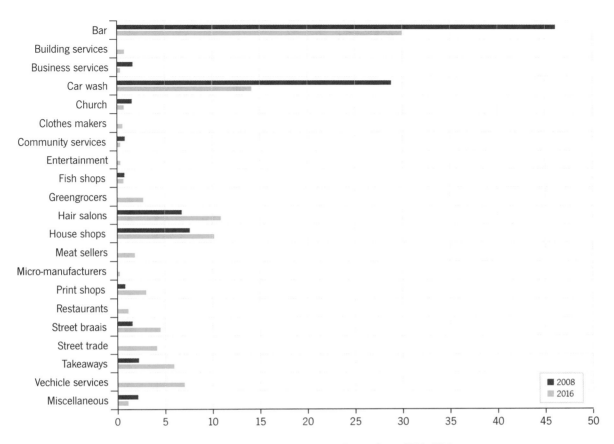

FIGURE 6.7 Change in business numbers and the enterprise categories in Eveline Street 2008–2016

Spatial transformations

There was evidence of change in the use of space. In outlets such as bars, nightclubs and restaurants, we observed building alterations (both horizontal and vertical); infrastructure adaptations (such as the use of now-paved and shaded sidewalks as al fresco seating areas for patrons); and investments to enhance the quality of customer experience, including separate gender toilets, a range of décor options to enable conversation and enjoyment of leisure activities, and business signage. The landholdings abutting the street were spatially integrated into the public space of the street, a transition which supported multiple economic uses both of the private landholding and public road reserve. On the private landholdings, business infrastructure had been positioned at the front of the plot, thus connecting with the street, whereas residential dwellings were established at the rear of the house through building extensions. This re-organisation of space to accommodate the logic of the street as a social and business space enabled a more integrated use of land than is evident in high streets in Delft and Browns Farm. The process of spatial transition is illustrated in Figure 6.8.

In Eveline Street, the road reserve accommodates a multitude of users, with the space shared (and contested) by pedestrians, parked vehicles, business activities and people socialising. On both private and public land, economic and social multipliers have been unlocked, allowing businesses to advance but simultaneously helping to improve the quality public space in terms of safety and accessibility.

Some of these spatial transitions benefited from particular preexisting conditions in respect to the layout of the street and residential properties. The original placement of

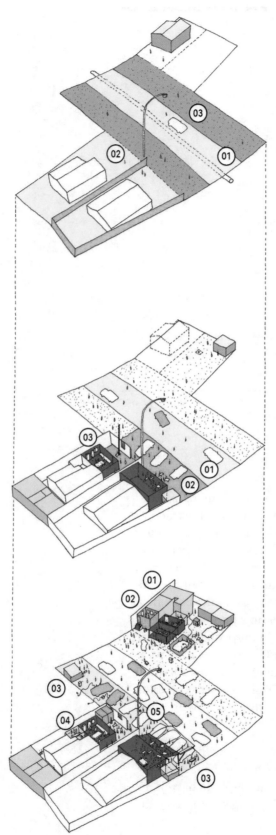

A. First fix

The accompanying diagram illustrates the original infrastructure that informed the properties along Eveline Street.

01 Serviced infrastructure including roads, sidewalks, drainage and lighting
02 Large street setback (±5,0 m)
03 Large sidewalk on both sides of street (±8,9 m)

B. Early transformations

Early responses to the original infrastructure sought to optimise and appropriate wherever possible.

01 The road increases in intensity and supports a public transport system (taxis).
02 Sidewalks are appropriated through the use of encroachments, objects and surface treatments. Mountable kerbs allow for cars to access the sidewalk with ease.
03 Additions are added to the front of original structures. In Eveline Street, leisure businesses were the first to utilise these property extensions.

C. Transformed streets

Over time, these small incremental changes result in a dramatic change to the street, creating a diversity of uses.

01 New top-structures are created to replace original houses that better suit the economic interests of owners.
02 Businesses have direct street relationships and are small in scale.
03 Smaller business opportunities such as car washing, kapano and car repairs are stimulated and accommodated along the sidewalk.
04 Services such as ablutions are provided by private enterprises for their patrons.
05 The sidewalk is highly appropriated to allow for circulation, socialisation, business and entertainment.

FIGURE 6.8 Diagram illustrating the spatial and economic transformations that occur over time along the high street and properties immediately adjacent to the high street

residential dwellings in the centre of the plot (in contrast to many South African township settlements where houses are built on the front building line) enabled the Eveline Street property owners to develop the land both in front of and behind the dwelling. On either side of Eveline Street, the road reserve is wide and symmetrical in width, providing equal opportunities for landholders on both sides to orientate businesses on their properties towards the public space of the street. At eight metres wide, the unusually spacious road reserve has permitted street businesses and activities of socialisation to migrate from private into public space. The road does not have a hard kerb boundary and vehicles can thus drive off the road onto the reserve. The breadth of the reserve allows visitors to the street to park their vehicles in a perpendicular manner, which in turn, supports destination-specific clusters (or nodes) within the street which relate to leisure businesses. To support street-based socialisation, bar owners have provided shaded forecourts, paved surfaces, street furniture and lighting. The CoW contributed towards this process of transformation through complementary investments in the provision of street lighting, the installation of CCTV to monitor street activities (and enable more effective policing of the streetscape), and traffic calming humps to reduce the speed of passing motor vehicles.

Nodal dynamic

Within the street itself, there is not a linear or mechanical flow of traffic and pedestrians in one direction, as often seen in South African townships. Instead, traffic flow is bidirectional and responsive to individual demands rather than institutionalised mass transport, provided by public buses and minibus taxis. Small sedan taxis as well as pedestrians move to and from particular destinations, responding to individualised demand, resulting in the dropping off of patrons or customers at a particular business. Sedan taxis enable destination-centred public transport through the flexibility of their operations and freedom to pick up and drop off passengers on demand. The micro-enterprises on Eveline Street are therefore not reliant on a linear flow for pedestrians from or to a transport hub, as is evidenced in the Browns Farm case. Micro-enterprises cluster in nodes, with the nodal dynamic reinforced as a result of the opportunity for off-street parking (outside venues) and access through sedan public transport. Clusters of interdependent social, spatial and economic nodes are clearly identifiable in the plan diagram (Figure 6.9).

Each node equates to concentrations of economic activities, comprising bars, restaurants, service businesses and car washes. The nodes expand and contract in intensity with time, oscillating from day to night when the leisure economy gears up and service economy gears down correspondingly.

At the very centre of Eveline Street's spine, there exists a portion of land which remains under municipal ownership and has yet to be subdivided into private land holdings. The adjacent residential land has been informally settled with shacks. On the one side of street, an informal marketplace has been established, comprising a single row of rudimentary timber frame structures. Most of the businesses in this node sell fruit and vegetables. On the opposite site, the CoW has established a formal trading market, comprising an open-sided linear market shelter and parking setback, enabling vehicle customers to park off the street. The influence of these nodes with respect to the street business environment is shown in Figure 6.10.

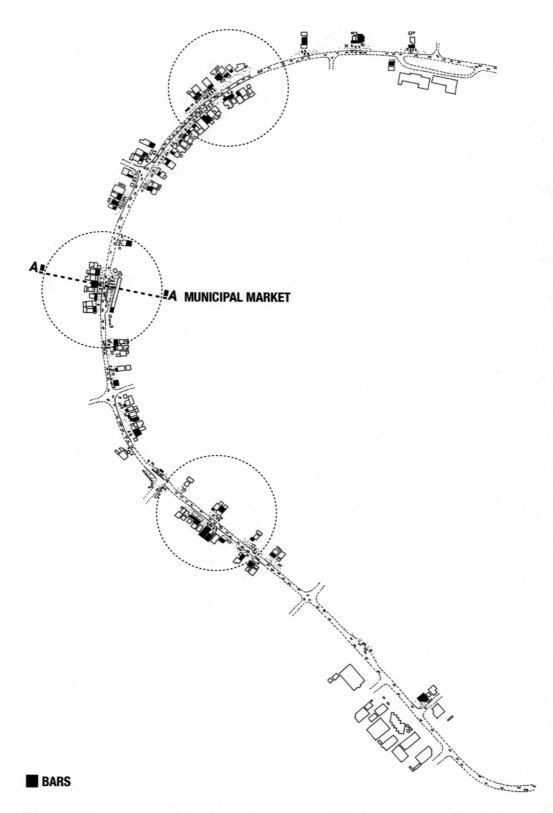

A ⟶ A MUNICIPAL MARKET

■ BARS

FIGURE 6.9 Diagram illustrating the nodal characteristics of the high street, wherein businesses cluster around leisure hubs and the municipal market

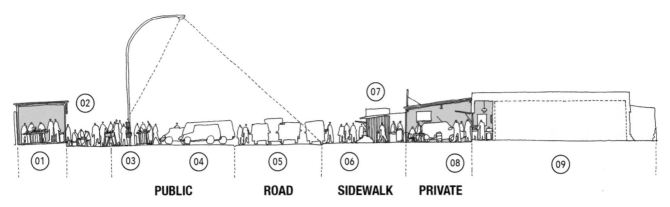

PUBLIC   **ROAD**   **SIDEWALK**   **PRIVATE**

Section A-A

Municipal Market generates a concentration of activity along and across the street.

01   Municipal structures for preparing meat

02   Demarcated space for cooking and selling meat

03   Space for purchasing and consuming meat (with washing and eating facilities)

04   Layby lane for off-street parking

05   Bidirectional vehicular traffic (including taxis)

06   Sidewalk for pedestrian movement

07   Encroachments of structures allowing for business with direct street frontage

08   Car wash and kiosk (extension of main dwelling)

FIGURE 6.10 Street section diagram illustrating the relationship of business to the street, sidewalk and municipal market

The municipal market accommodates a range of businesses selling fruit and vegetables, homeware and cooked meat. Meat braai businesses (*kapano* sellers) provide an anchor since this takeaway business attracts the majority of customers to the market, many via private cars and taxis. While the market is spatially disconnected from the various leisure nodes within the street, it complements the value of the street as a leisure 'destination' with the braaied meat sellers benefiting from a synergistic influence.

Public transport

Public transport services have played a role in facilitating the economic growth and spatial transformation of the street. Eveline Street is a transport corridor, where buses, taxis and private vehicles converge on their way to and from numerous points within the city. Amongst the range of public transport services, private sedan taxis are critical and provide a large portion of public transport service in the northern townships. As a reflection of the presence of sedan taxis, we measured the evening traffic over the weekend period and found that the sedan taxis represented over half of the vehicles traversing Eveline Street.

Sedan taxis support micro-enterprises in two ways. Firstly, they enable the nodal, bidirectional, irregular movement dynamic we see along the street. The taxis are relatively cheap to use (short-distance trips cost the equivalent of R10, while longer distance trips cost R20), and have no designated stopping and pick-up areas, thus allowing them to collect customers at will, and drop them off anywhere along the street. Sedan taxis also provide a key link between Eveline Street and the Windhoek CBD, particularly at night, when they ferry patrons back and forth from the city to their favoured destinations in Eveline Street. Secondly, the taxis create a range of spin-off businesses. Taxi vehicles are the main customers of the car-wash businesses. The taxi sector also provides a considerable source of revenue for print shops (where taxis obtain their compulsory signs) and for businesses providing wheel alignment, tyre repair, mechanical servicing and panel beating. The taxi drivers are also customers for hair salons, bars (where non-alcoholic drinks are commonly available), and the various street food sellers, in particular the *kapano* sellers at the municipal market.

The taxi-influenced nodes stand in contrast to the municipal bus-stops which are situated at distant points along the street. The bus-stop infrastructure comprises an off-road parking bay and modular shelter structure. We found no evidence of linkages between this infrastructure and local businesses, whether spatial connections or market synergies. The bus system passes through the Eveline Street corridor, collecting and dropping off passengers, having minimal impact on township micro-enterprise entrepreneurship and organic spatial change. Unlike the taxis, the buses do not support the vehicle service businesses and car washes. Yet the CoW has adopted a long-term transport policy to expand bus transport in general and establish a bus rapid transit (BRT) network (a topic we address in Chapter 7), thus introducing changes which would fundamentally change the role of sedan taxis (Ministry of Works and Transport & CoW 2013). The proposed 'integrated' public transport system would restrict the operational scope of sedan taxis with the aim of shifting dependence on what are perceived as costly, unsafe and environmentally harmful taxis to state-run buses and larger minibuses. This proposed policy shift ignores the localised positive social, spatial and economic contributions of taxi transport on township entrepreneurship. Indeed, the Transport Master Plan which outlines these changes argues that sedan taxis are 'the most uneconomic backbone one can think of' and their role should be limited to the 'distribution of passengers from bus lines in trunk roads' (Ministry of Works & City of Windhoek 2013, pp. 17, 122).

High-street bars

The bars on Eveline Street have a strong influence on the spatial ordering and temporality of activities within the street economy. The 80 bars are spatially distributed in nodes, and each bar is distinct in name and service offering. Bars target specific cultural or social niches, attracting custom through a combination of service offerings, proximity, familiarity and safety. Although corporate influences are discernible, noticeably in signage, décor and bar fridges, and reinforce corporate cultures of consumption, most venues have an independence of brand and identity. The business names provide insight into the cultural orientation and/or status-positioning of the owner. Some bars have vernacular names, some taken from the name of the proprietor, a person of significance or from geographic localities. A number of bars have names to convey an urban sophistication ('lounge' rather than simply 'bar'), connection with foreign places, or British football teams. Examples include: City Bar, Willy's Wine Bar, Tsunami.Com Bar, Long Street Bar, Old Trafford Bar and The Gunners Bar. Local sign writers are generally employed to paint this signage.

Each bar is differentiated in its leisure offering (in terms of amusements, entertainment, décor and facilities), service provision (in terms of operating times, range of liquor and non-liquor beverages, quality of service, entrance fee, etc.) and cultural orientation. Some of the notable strategies through which business owners have sought to influence the drinking occasion and thus differentiate the business are in seating arrangements to enable conversation (facilitated through the provision of chairs and tables); in the provision of music and entertainment, combining a spatial allocation for dancing and the availability of (loud) music or television watching (especially of sports matches, but also films and 'soap opera' shows, broadcast during the week); in the availability of gaming and gambling facilities; and of significance to street life, through the extension

FIGURE 6.11 Lighting, outdoor seating and entertainment project onto the street

of outdoor seating onto sidewalk. The spatial overlap between the bar, public social life and street business has the effect of facilitating multiple uses of space at the same time (leisure, movement, business and conversation). This combination of spatial users seldom occurs on South African high streets. The thresholds between these different uses of space are influenced by an array of devices such as shade, music, seating and entertainment. Nearly all the liquor outlets in Eveline Street have moveable chairs and tables, utilise the public space adjacent to their businesses, and sell a range of non-alcoholic beverages, including fruit juices. The sale of non-alcoholic drinks underlines the emergence of a comparatively sophisticated recreational and social culture that links to but also goes beyond the consumption of liquor. These elements are highlighted in Figure 6.11 and Figure 6.12.

There is a synergistic relationship between bars, car washes and hair salons. Car washes (and salons to a lesser degree) require access to water, electricity and space. Since water and electricity are accessed via property ownership, these individuals are favourably placed to also operate these businesses. Property owners have informally appropriated the public space in front of their land holdings, renting utility services to pop-up micro-enterprises which operate from the road reserve or running businesses in this space themselves. Car washes, hair salons and takeaways connect through the dynamic of the leisure economy, each micro-enterprise providing services that reinforce an economic interconnectedness. The spatial interdependence of businesses is illustrated in Figure 6.13.

FIGURE 6.12 Unlike in South African townships, Eveline Street bars utilise the public space adjacent to their businesses to create an amenable consumer environment

It is important to understand that the Eveline Street leisure economy does not simply comprise a strip or string of bars, but in itself constitutes a place where people 'go out'. For the participants, going out presents an opportunity for displaying a social statement of status and identity, which in turn influences where people drink, with whom they drink and what they drink. These variables combine with other signifiers of identity, such as vehicle ownership and make, clothing, attire and hair styles, for which the hair salons in the street fulfil an important role. As social spaces in their own right, hair salons also provide a meeting (and indeed drinking) place for persons, and women especially, to congregate before (and instead of) going out. It was thus unsurprising that we encountered the sale of liquor products in some hair salons, which in turn challenges our conceptualisation of drinking venues, a topic we explore in detail in Chapter 8.

Leisure businesses, especially bars, have the potential to generate social conflict, amplify the victimisation of vulnerable groups (including women) and result in harm to consumers (direct) and non-consumers (indirect). As in all leisure destinations, negative externalities do occur in Eveline Street. At both the level of the individual bar as well as the level of the street as a destination, measures have been instituted to reduce risks and manage conflicts when these occur. We have highlighted some of the spatial devices through which risks are tempered, such as the facilitation of seated socialisation and provision of separate gender toilets. We also noticed more overt strategies, such as the employment of bouncers to control patrons, the installation of surveillance cameras and regular police patrols. At the street level, the agglomeration of bars and their position in nodes (rather than within a linear strip) reduces the concentration effect, with most of the bars comparatively sparsely patronised in contrast to the South African township situation. Patrons do not tend to bar-hop but target specific venues.

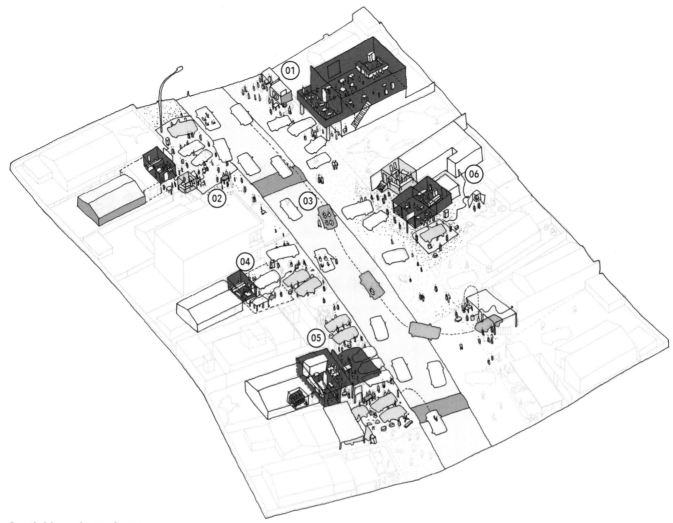

Spatial interdependence

01 Small structures encroach onto sidewalk to respond to pedestrian movement along high street

02 Related businesses such as car washing, hair salons, takeaways and *kapano* from an interdependent business and social network

03 Taxis move along the street collecting and dropping off customers at will

04 Business set back from the street allows for a yard and for additional space for cars to park, creating a dense layering of activity from street to original house

05 Bars with a direct relationship to the street and an allowance for expansion (through overhangs) allow for a dense concentration of socialising and business activity

06 Shared use of water

FIGURE 6.13 A series of pioneering businesses form unique clusters of interdependence along the high street
Note: This creates a diversity of uses and experiences along its length.

Property adaptations

We have argued that the road reserve on Eveline Street accommodates a fluid transition from the public sphere into the private. While street businesses influence the use of this space, the catalytic influence lies with the private land holders and their responses to their properties and opportunities of the street. While the property adaptations we document have been made in response to economic opportunities, the purpose of investments to create business facilities was enabled through the security of tenure (with land held under freehold title) and opportunities of land-use rights to conduct commercial activities as a result of the business corridor initiative.

FIGURE 6.14 Three properties in different stages of business development along Eveline Street; a hair salon (right), car wash (centre) and bar (left)

In the informal settlements adjacent to Eveline Street, property holders have also invested in their properties, but scope and scale of investments are qualitatively different in the objective to minimise risks. Investments in brick and mortar are not found where tenure is insecure and business rights are absent. The cumulative spatial adjustments of Eveline Street properties and street businesses, driven by individuals in pursuing livelihood opportunities, has transformed the street from a mono-functional purpose (transport corridor) to a multifunctional local economy. In response, many of the properties have been systematically rebuilt, shifting frontward and realigning towards the street and the public activities upon which these home businesses are reliant. The spatial transition from the original dwelling to double-story buildings is shown in Figure 6.14.

The economic and spatial changes have enabled the property owners to 'unlock' value through their investment in land. The net effect of spatial transformation is rising property values. High-street stands in Eveline Street are highly sought after, while properties with businesses sell for premium sums. One bar, for example, was put on the property market in January 2016 for the equivalent of R880 000. We heard anecdotal evidence that property values on the high street were, in 2017, selling for over R1 million, a sum virtually unheard of in our South African sites.

Street participants

Abraham and Eve's barber shop

Abraham was 35 years old and ran Abraham's Barber Shop. He worked in partnership with Eve, a close friend (see Figure 6.15).

He was unmarried and had no children. The business began operating on Eveline Street in 2012. He rented the business premises, a corrugated iron shack (*zozo*), from the plot owner. Abraham and Eve provided hairdressing for both men and women.

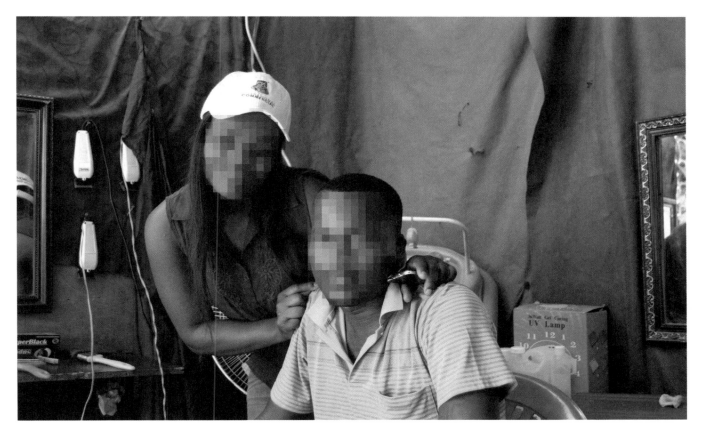

FIGURE 6.15 A hair salon partnership

They operated the business from 7.30 a.m. until 8.00 p.m. or later, especially on Saturdays and Sundays, sometimes employing an additional stylist. There was no music or television in the salon. On a regular day of trading, Abraham did about 20 haircuts, with prices ranging from R25–R45. The most popular cut for men was the 'English cut'. He liked Eveline Street for its 'busyness', saying that there was *always money to be made here*. But there were also challenges to the street, including theft. His ambition was to grow the business and open another salon in a different locality.

Hidipohamba's hair salon, bar and car repair

Hidipohamba was an Eveline Street pioneer (see Figure 6.16).

He was 41 years old. Hidipohamba originated from the Omusati Region in the far north of Namibia. He was married and had four children, and supported his four sisters from his businesses. He started his business as a hair salon in 1997. Through the profits of this micro-enterprise, in 2003, he opened a car wash, and then subsequently established a bar. His latest investment was a car maintenance shop, specialising in wheel alignment.

The hair salon did brisk trade from 1.00 p.m. until late in the evening. The weekends were the busiest, though. The business catered to a wide spectrum of customers, drawn from different areas (in other words, outside of the immediate area), professions and ethnic groups. On weekdays, he made between R2 000 and R3 500 per day. His monthly operational expenditure was around R13 000.

Hidipohamba felt that the main advantage of having a hair salon in Eveline Street was that the street was very busy, having a lot of foot traffic.

FIGURE 6.16 A pioneer businessman

'*People choose to come to the street*', he said, '*because they can find everything that they need.*' He did see some disadvantages as well. A particular concern was the limited space available to grow business. He also complained of the stiff competition between the different businesses. Hidipohamba expressed his concern with crime, saying that thugs capitalised on the busyness of the street: '*they grab bags, cell phones, tablets and other valuable goods, even inside the shop when it is too full.*'

Heini and Ndapanda's street-food kiosks

Heini worked in a kiosk, situated next to a bar (Figure 6.17).

She came to Windhoek in 2016 and stayed with her uncle in Eveline Street. She was unmarried and had no children, but still regularly sent money to her parents and siblings who lived in the north of Namibia. Part of her income was used to pay for her studies. The kiosk was owned by her uncle who owned the adjacent bar. She started work at 8.00 a.m. and finished at around 10.00 p.m., although she worked in shift with another woman. The kiosk sold prepared meals and made around R200 in profit per day.

Ndapanda was 23 years old. She was employed at a kiosk selling food takeaways (Figure 6.18).

She had worked in the business since 2015. She stayed with her husband elsewhere in Goreangab settlement; they did not have children. Ndapanda started work at 6.30 a.m. and ended at 5.30 p.m. when she closed the kiosk for the day. The shop sold chips, cool drinks and local cooked foods. The business was owned by the property owner of the erf on which the kiosk was situated. She earned a fixed salary of R1 500 per month, a portion of which was sent home to her family in the village.

FIGURE 6.17 A takeaway employee

FIGURE 6.18 A takeaway employee

Mathew's taxi business

Mathew was 21 years old and lived in Havana informal settlement. He operated a sedan taxi, using a Toyota Corolla (Figure 6.19).

Mathew started driving in 2013, working as an employee. Once he had gained experience, Mathew reached an agreement with this employer to enable him to gain ownership of the vehicle in return for generating a profit of R60 000. He surpassed this target and thus came to own the Corolla. His ambition was to raise R100 000 and purchase two (second-hand) vehicles from Japan. He frequented Eveline Street as this was a popular destination to obtain customers, especially at night when people went out socialising. We met Mathew in Eveline Street at a car wash which he supported on a regular basis to clean his taxi. He wore a shirt with the words: 'DESTINED FOR GREATNESS'.

FIGURE 6.19 A taxi driver entrepreneur

Outlook

The Eveline Street example highlights how through appropriate urban planning (thus reducing the obstacles of land zoning), a generously wide road reserve, and the provision of basic infrastructure investments (street lighting, utilities and CCTV), the state can contribute towards a more spatially inclusive development outcome. Part of this outcome is enabling businesses to formalise, which in turn reduces the risks of private sector and landowner investment. Although formalisation is not a requirement for business growth and diversity, the Eveline Street case shows that it can benefit businesses operating from private land holdings. The changes in infrastructure in response to the requirements for formalisation (including compliance with business registration, land use and building standards), indicate that the establishment of 'business corridors' wherein land-related regulatory barriers are reduced has good potential as a policy lever. While this intervention in Namibia was not finally concluded and some businesses continued to trade illegally, the more favourable policy environment which the initiative signalled had encouraged entrepreneurs to invest in land and business development. The evidence shows that businesses were formalising, with the street-oriented leisure businesses fulfilling a pioneering role. To establish bars, residential homes had been converted into mixed-use units and investments had been made on improving the adjacent public space for the benefit of both public and private users. The range of investments derived from a combination of regulatory pressure, economic opportunity and social conformity.

In South African township high streets where property driven investments have not taken place on such a scope or scale, a contrasting development outcome exists. Business owners who are uncertain or fearful of the illegality of their business are far less likely to invest in infrastructure and facilities to engender growth. Whereas bars are the pioneer business in Eveline Street, most South African township high streets have a limited leisure offering, lacking the agglomeration and synergies of a destination street. The service businesses such as hair salons and vehicle repairers and the fast-food retailers that dominate have less potential to build synergies and exert a cumulative growth effect on the business environment. Furthermore, most township high streets operate during a narrow timeframe, with businesses predominantly active during the early morning and late afternoon commuter transit. In Eveline Street, the bars that operate late into the night extend the trading hours to their nodal partners which, in turn, enables these micro-enterprises to attract bar customers. In the absence of leisure activities on South African high streets, there are few (if any) substitute enterprise pioneers that can both facilitate the development of spatial nodes and collectively facilitate spatial opportunities along the length and breadth of the street itself. These dual characteristics extend spatial opportunities (potentially along a street, on both sides) in a manner that cannot be attained through hub-based developments, such as transport nodes. In their current limited function, as transport corridors and street trader markets, the potential of high streets to assume a role in undoing apartheid spatial exclusion has not been realised.

While the planners of the business corridor idea sought to enable formalisation, the Eveline Street outcome shows how participants of the street economy seized opportunities for themselves in ways that were unintended. This people-centred transition was led by property owners and business investors. These individuals were comparatively well positioned in terms of human, social and financial capital to respond to the policy opportunity to formalise their enterprises in response to the business corridor intervention. Their actions, though self-focused, have extended economic opportunities to other micro-enterprises. The street is still a conglomerate of formal and informal activities, with the latter profiting from the former. The transformative land uses we describe were not foreseen; rather they were claimed by entrepreneurs who sought to disrupt the street for an alternative purpose, one that was to be more economically and socially vibrant. This process of disrupting spatial orders has elements of what Bayat (1997, p. 57) calls a 'quiet encroachment', though unlike informal settlements and street trader interventions, it demonstrates an opportunity for pioneer investors to provide organic direction and leadership.

KWAAL

7

TRANSPORT:
EFFICIENT BUT VIOLENT

In this chapter we examine the minibus and sedan taxi sectors. Whereas the minibus taxis sector is well capitalised, organised and reliable, we show that sedan taxis are highly responsive to emergent impulses and fulfil an important role in overcoming mobility constraints.

CHAPTER 7

Transport: efficient but violent

Taxi transport emerged as an organic entrepreneurial response to the spatial injustice of apartheid planning, providing a means of mobility to connect township residents to the centres of economic opportunity and resources situated within inner cities and suburbs, as well as connections to rural homes. In response to the inadequate services of state controlled public transport, trains and buses in particular, minibus taxis provided a complementary and ultimately competitive service. Since its origins in the late 1970s, the minibus taxi sector has become the most prominent example of autonomous black entrepreneurial achievement, providing a profitable business opportunity for thousands of township entrepreneurs (Fourie 2003). Today, formal (minibus) and informal (sedan) taxis provide a relatively efficient public transport service which helps to reduce the spatial injustices of township planning. In this chapter, we examine both the minibus and sedan components. Whereas the minibus taxi sector is well capitalised, organised and reliable (though possibly expensive), we will show that sedan taxis are highly responsive to emergent impulses and fulfil an important role in overcoming mobility constraints. We will argue that the mobility benefits from township transport need to be weighed against the interests of powerful groups whose control is underpinned by the use of violence. While the minibus sector is formally regulated, many of its operations are informal, illegal and criminal, with power vested in a mafia-styled business model that benefits the leaders, the fleet owners and a financial-industrial complex of corporate interests.

The state has a complex relationship with the township transport sector: on one hand, it supports the modernisation of the minibus sector and its continued monopolisation of intra-city minibus taxi transport; on the other hand, it seeks to reduce the high-risk driving and associated road accidents to which minibuses contribute. In contrast to its ambivalent stance towards the minibus sector, the state continues to 'enforce' the 'informalisation' (Charman, Petersen & Piper 2013) – in other words, to strategically confine businesses to the informal sector – of other segments of township taxi transport whose contribution to the local economy is potentially greater and whose negative impacts are similarly less. The power responses of both the state and violent entrepreneurs frame opportunities in the sector and constitute threats to new entrants and competing taxi operators. The alignment of powerful taxi business entities with regulatory institutions and corporate stakeholders, we argue, limits the scope of local beneficiation. Much of the surplus value from the minibus sector leaves the specific township (from which the taxi operates), and is accumulated by fleet owners and corporates, affording minimal benefit to service-oriented micro-enterprises.

In advancing this argument, our analysis is calibrated at three levels of spatial gradient: one, the city-wide level at which taxis connect particular settlements to CBD and economic destinations; two, the small-area level wherein we highlight the role of sedan taxis in connecting people to transport hubs and neighbouring suburbs; and three, the micro-contexts where we describe the organising influence of a taxi rank on surrounding street-trading activities. At the micro-level in addition, we describe how hand signs are used in communication between commuters and drivers, affording a legibility to the seemingly indiscernible logic of taxi routes.

The township transport sector

The transport sector is an important component of the township economy and comprises private vehicles, formal minibus taxis, informal sedan taxis, school transport, freight, and employee transport services. These modes of transport emerged as a people-centred response to the intersection of several challenges: the spatial location of townships on the urban periphery, the absence of private vehicles in the 1970s and 1980s, the inadequacy of state-funded public transport services within the townships, and the entrepreneurial impulse of local entrepreneurs. The result is a transport system which is highly adaptive (in parts, though not necessarily in totality), privately operated and commercially oriented, and tailored to localised needs for mobility on affordable terms. We should note that township taxi transport arose at a time of intense political resistance to apartheid injustice during the 1970s and 1980s, an era wherefrom it acquired an entrepreneurial culture imbued with ideas of resistance to the state, black power and violence as legitimate strategies.

Township transport competes with public bus transport and rail services. Unlike these services, which are reliant on operational subsidies, micro-enterprise transport businesses receive less than 1% of the direct public transport subsidy and this benefits only the minibus component (Kerr 2015; Lomme 2008). The apex township transport businesses are formally registered minibus taxis, which operate inter-suburban and regional routes. Minibuses provide transport to around 15 million persons per day and are the mainstay of a sector valued at some R90 billion per year (Tsele 2017). Minibus taxis are subject to state registration, and are regulated in terms of the particular vehicles that may be used, the routes along which they may operate, the licensing requirements (for the driver and use of the vehicle for public passengers), and the adherence of the moving vehicle to municipal traffic laws. In operational terms, the minibus business model has both formal and informal aspects. Formally, taxi operators require operating licences from the state, a function of provincial government, though simultaneously and informally, the operators are also beholden to organisational entities (associations) that control taxi routes and thus provide access to the route permits (Walters 2008).

At the neighbourhood level, public transport is provided by informal sedan taxis which operate largely within the township confines, though in some situations, they also ferry passengers to neighbouring suburbs. These taxis are prohibited from competing with the minibus taxis, with both state authorities and minibus taxi associations enforcing their exclusion. If the minibus taxis are the backbone of the township transport sector, the informal taxis are the arteries (akin to an informal 'Uber'), ferrying passengers from their home to shops and nearest transport nodes such as the taxi rank, train station or bus stop. Unlike the minibus taxis, informal taxis tend to be wholly informal, adhering neither to provincial public transport licensing requirements nor municipal by-laws.

From a macro-economic perspective, transport services stimulate opportunities via a multiplier effect for supporting micro-enterprises. Businesses which benefit include those that provide stickers and decals, car washes, driving schools, mechanics, panel beaters, suppliers of vehicle spare parts and micro-enterprises providing wheel repair services. Examples of these businesses are shown in Figure 7.1, Figure 7.2, Figure 7.3 and Figure 7.4.

FIGURE 7.1 Automotive service businesses such as panel beaters and tyre repairers share interdependence with the taxi sector

FIGURE 7.2 Car mechanics working on an informal taxi, Ivory Park

FIGURE 7.3 A business providing taxi signage, Eveline Street

FIGURE 7.4 Car wash businesses, Eveline Street
Note: Their main customers are sedan taxis.

The combination of the various transport services supports the functioning of micro-enterprises, providing the entrepreneurs with access to suppliers in the township and beyond as well as by bringing customers to their businesses. As in Eveline Street, taxis are an important component in the operation of the night-time economy and in nurturing nodal growth along the high street. In Browns Farm, Delft South and Ivory Park sites, the taxi hubs create markets to benefit a range of micro-enterprises, including street and stall-based traders and sellers of snacks, airtime, cigarettes and takeaway food. As points of convergence and connection between the township and wider economy, taxi ranks stimulate opportunities for adjacent businesses and contribute towards the vibrancy of the high street.

Apart from minibus and sedan taxis, the township economy sustains other forms of transport services. One such service is the provision of scholar transport, providing a door-to-door service for children to travel from their homes to schools within the township and beyond. School transport is provided by independent operators as well as taxi owners (both minibus and sedan) who return to collect passengers during school hours and in the late afternoon. Scholar transporters need to possess an operating licence and abide by regulations for the public transport of passengers, such as the requirement that vehicles are marked as 'scholar transport' and tested at a roadworthy centre every six months, though since there is little enforcement of these regulations, most operators trade informally with vehicles ranging from sedans to bakkies[1] (Western Cape Government, 2017).

The spatial economy of township transport

Minibus taxis

Minibuses are passenger vans that commonly carry up to 16 people. Taxi vehicles include the Toyota Quantum Ses'fikile (meaning 'we have arrived') and the older 14-seater Toyota HiAce Siyaya ('we are going'), Nissan Impendulo ('the answer') and newer models from Indian and Chinese manufacturers. The most modern vehicles have been purpose-built for the sector, designed to legally accommodate 16 seated persons, though some still illegally carry additional passengers. The collective fleet of township minibuses, which number in excess of 150 000 vehicles, are generally in a roadworthy condition, though vary in age and appearance, with some vehicles enhanced with sports mag wheels, spray designs, window tinting and the 'obligatory' on-board sound systems (Arrive Alive 2018; see http://autoraj-blog.tumblr.com/BIGBOSS on re-imagining taxi identity through art). Minibuses operate inter-suburban routes, usually departing from specific ranks established in the township and within the urban CBDs, connecting commuters in two daily waves of mobility. These occur in the morning to ferry commuters from the township to urban centres, and again at the end of the working day to ferry commuters in the reverse direction. Because the business model is based on operating a loaded vehicle on set routes, minibus taxis do not operate late at night when demand is reduced, nor do they offer customers a door-to-door transportation service.

Minibuses commence their activities from taxi ranks and only once fully laden with customers do the vehicles depart for their intended destinations, dropping-off and collecting passengers along the designated transport route. The operational system is subject to strict regulation, both formal and informal, which restricts the scope of adaptability. Taxi routes are controlled and overseen by the taxi associations, whose

---

1 Bakkies – light pickup trucks, generally open, but possibly fitted with a removable canopy or similar accessories, but distinct from a large truck and from a delivery van or similar small utility vehicle.

main function is to protect the market for its members in an industry which is considered overtraded and whose routes are subject to both competition and shifts in the urban form as a result of new settlements, demographic change and new transport routes (Lomme 2008). Taxi associations also manage the taxi ranks and monitor the vehicle drivers, with each departing vehicle subject to a small fee.

Passenger fees are determined by the taxi associations, applied on a route basis and are subject to change as a result of fluctuating costs and inflationary pressures. The division of income in the case of minibus taxis operating in Delft South, using 2015 data, is explained in the chart in Figure 7.5.

In this site, we made systematic observations of the organisational dynamics, counted the vehicles and passengers, and conducted interviews with commuters, drivers and owners. The Delft high street is the main taxi artery route connecting the township to various destinations within the metro region; the various routes are shown in Figure 7.6.

There are three ranks in Delft which accommodate about 450 minibus taxis; one is formally established and the other two are undeveloped and simply operate from open land sites. From our research in 2015, we have calculated that between 24 300–32 400 commuters travel by minibus from Delft South to various city destinations on a daily basis, generating an income for the Delft South taxi businesses of R11,5 million pm or R138,2 million per annum. As shown in Figure 7.5, the lion's share of this revenue (around 56%) accrues to the taxi owners, 27% is spent on fuel and miscellaneous operational costs, 15% goes to the driver and around 1% to the rank marshal. None of the drivers or owners with whom we spoke declared income for taxation purposes. As the majority of the Delft minibus fleet comprise the newer Quantum Ses'fikile models, a sizeable portion of the owner's share of turnover (up to R570 per day for finance over 60 months in 2018) is subtracted for vehicle repayments.

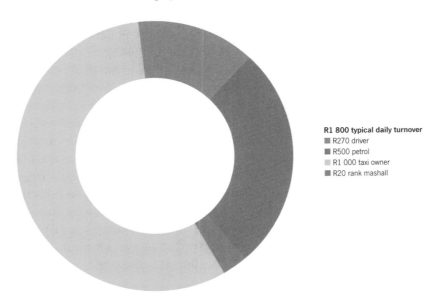

R1 800 typical daily turnover
- R270 driver
- R500 petrol
- R1 000 taxi owner
- R20 rank mashall

FIGURE 7.5 Diagram illustrating the division of earnings for a day's work in the minibus sector in Delft South, 2015

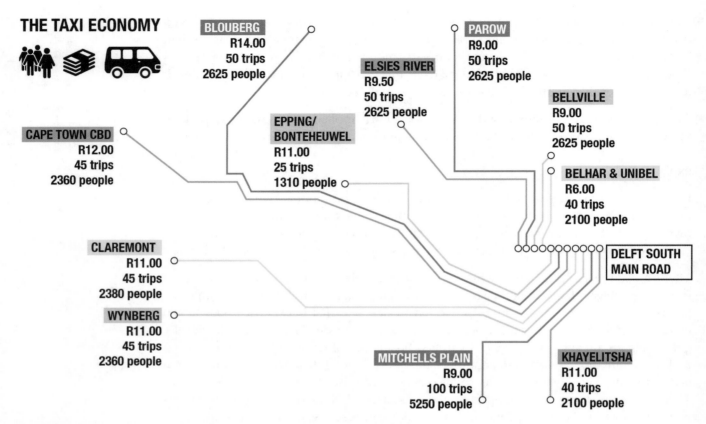

THE TAXI ECONOMY

BLOUBERG
R14.00
50 trips
2625 people

PAROW
R9.00
50 trips
2625 people

ELSIES RIVER
R9.50
50 trips
2625 people

BELLVILLE
R9.00
50 trips
2625 people

CAPE TOWN CBD
R12.00
45 trips
2360 people

EPPING/ BONTEHEUWEL
R11.00
25 trips
1310 people

BELHAR & UNIBEL
R6.00
40 trips
2100 people

CLAREMONT
R11.00
45 trips
2380 people

DELFT SOUTH MAIN ROAD

WYNBERG
R11.00
45 trips
2360 people

MITCHELLS PLAIN
R9.00
100 trips
5250 people

KHAYELITSHA
R11.00
40 trips
2100 people

FIGURE 7.6 Minibus routes and volume of traffic from Delft South to various Cape Town destinations

Minibus taxis are generally operated by hired drivers, the great majority of whom are men whose behaviour individually and collectively fosters a culture of hyper-masculinity (Gibbs 2014). This is evidenced through aggressive driving and behaviours, disdain for traffic rules, assertive collaborations on the road, and the fulfilment of the 'muscle' function in the association's rule of 'thugocracy' (see below). On routes with frequent stops and drops, the driver will be accompanied by an attendant (known as *gaatjie* in Cape Town) whose task is to tout for passengers and collect fares. The drivers (and attendants) 'work' for the taxi owner, engaged either as informal employees (paid a wage) or on a contractor basis in a target or commission system. As a sub-contractor, the driver is responsible for generating sufficient revenue to cover the 'fee' for the hire of the vehicle (under the target system), the costs of fuel, and the taxi rank charges (levied by the relevant associations). Any additional revenue is taken as income. In the commission system, the vehicle owner receives around 70% of the turnover from the day's operation. Taxi drivers play an important role in motivating for fare price increases as operating costs affect their daily target. Since the driver has to pay for petrol out of his wage, increases in petrol prices reduce his earnings unless these cost increases are offset through raising the fares.

In Ivory Park, the taxi rank serves around 200 minibuses. It is controlled by the Ivory Park Taxi Association (IPTA) who exerts authority over the routes connecting Ivory Park to Midrand and the CBDs. As an informal regulator, the IPTA employs marshals who dispatch the taxis and patrol the streets (from 'squad cars') to prevent route encroachment by informal taxi drivers or by minibus taxis from other associations. The marshals collect tributes from the unregistered informal taxis that ferry passengers to the rank, but which are prohibited from operating outside Ivory Park. Within the taxi rank itself, the IPTA controls trading activities, specifying the use of commercial space and imposing a daily levy on traders. Mobile traders are excluded from this levy and instead operate on the street outside the perimeter fence. The authority of the association is reinforced through the imposition of a rule code to which drivers must adhere. The code specifies rules and sanctions, some of which pertain to the state of vehicles (must be clean) and behaviour expected of drivers (abstinence from liquor consumption and dress code). The rules are posted on the wall of the association office, displayed adjacent to a pencil sketch of Eugène Terre'Blanche (former leader of the Afrikaner Weerstandsbeweging or AWB (Afrikaner Resistance Movement)), '*a strong South African leader*' according to the rank marshal. The poster reads as a symbolic gesture, underlying the patriarchal authority of the association and to indicate its distance from the 'unruliness' of comrade politics. Due to the power of the IPTA, the taxi rank and surrounding trading area is relatively safe from crime. Informal food service businesses are prevalent both inside and outside the rank and capitalise on the substantial commuter foot traffic this transport hub generates.

Surrounding the taxi rank there are three orders of spatial authority; these correspond to the street, the pedestrian pavement and open space of the street verge (see Figure 7.7).

The street itself is congested with minibus taxis jostling to enter the rank and informal taxis dropping off passengers: horns sound repeatedly as cars muscle through the congestion. Outside the rank, the sidewalks provide an open passage for commuters to access the taxis without hindrance, which in itself is evidence of the prioritisation of transport in the use of space.

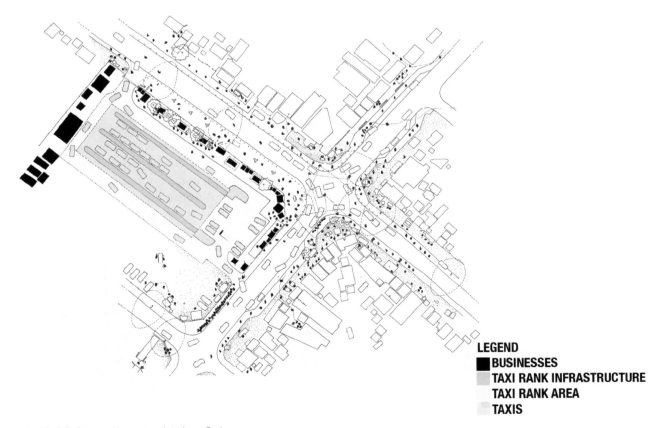

LEGEND

■ BUSINESSES

TAXI RANK INFRASTRUCTURE

TAXI RANK AREA

TAXIS

FIGURE 7.7 The minibus taxi rank in Ivory Park

Note: The taxi rank exerts spatial control over surrounding micro-enterprises, with taxi requirements dominant and traders largely confined to positions on the street outside the rank itself.

Where trading happens on the sidewalk, the stalls are small, minimising their consumption of sidewalk space. Most of the products sold address the needs of the taxi drivers and the commuters: cigarettes, airtime, newspapers, engine oil and fast food. Hawkers seek to capitalise on the market opportunities from the crowded and fast-paced spatial dynamic which encourages impulse purchases. On the opposite side of the street from the taxi rank, shops have encroached forward onto the street verge, though yield space to sidewalk traders who, in turn, yield to commuters. All role-players recognise that the extended node of activity is subject to the political authority of taxi bosses.

Once on the road, the authority of the IPTA wanes as the drivers gain autonomy over the vehicle and route, enabling them to make micro-adjustments to avoid traffic congestion or respond to commuter demands. Taxi drivers cooperate and collude in navigating traffic and congested roads. The demarcated route network is opaque; there are no maps, while route legibility and knowledge of fares is acquired through experiential learning. This system complexity restricts access for certain users, such as the disabled (including the blind), new and non-residents. An intricate language of hand signals has evolved between commuters and taxi drivers to communicate the destination to which commuters need to travel, thus enabling the drivers to stop only when required (Figure 7.8) (Woolf 2013).

An artist has sought to translate taxi signals into braille signs to enhance access for blind persons, though her suggestion has not been translated from a speculative art intervention to sector adoption. Though the drivers are tightly networked within the association, to the outside world their attitude is unsympathetic or 'kwaal', township slang meaning a closed heart (in a jealous sense) towards success or achievements (see graphic on the Chapter cover).

The minibus taxi system has both benefits and disadvantages for its participants. As part of the business, risk is transferred to the driver, as owner-entrepreneurs have oversupplied the market with vehicles. Because the drivers need to fulfil daily targets, they are incentivised to conduct as many journeys as possible with the maximum number of passengers in a given workday. Under pressure to fulfil targets, drivers drive as fast as possible, rat-race through side roads to avoid traffic jams and collect and drop off passengers at any point along the route in response to demand. Some drivers have sought to increase the vehicle carrying capacity through adding 'laptop' seats, positioned in the seating aisle. The more passengers that drivers can collect outside of the taxi ranks along the route, the more profitable the business return to the driver.

Johannesburg   Alexandra   Sandton

FIGURE 7.8 Hand signs are used by awaiting commuters to communicate to taxi drivers their desired destinations out of Ivory Park

Though the conduct of taxi drivers has negative externalities in terms of road accidents or poor commuter experiences, from a business perspective the minibus system is seen as comparatively safe and efficient (Lomme 2008). Indeed, survey data indicates that taxi passengers are considered safer than passengers on other modes of public transport, notably trains, while the frenetic driving of taxi operators (to shorten the trip) needs to be seen in the context of the long commute times for township residents travelling to work of between 68–94 minutes per day on average (Kerr 2015).

Sedan taxis

In townships across South Africa, informal taxis sometimes known as '*amaphela*' (meaning 'cockroach') and '*amahoender*' (meaning 'chicken') or '*jikeleza*' (meaning 'turn-around'), provide short-distance transport services. These names accurately describe the scurrying of these taxis. The vehicles used as informal taxis reflect the challenging operating conditions (such as poor roads) and the high mileages that such vehicles travel in the course of business. Some of the most durable vehicles in service are 1980s sedans, including Toyota Cressidas, and to a lesser extent, older model Nissan sedans and Mazda hatchbacks. Most informal taxis show signs of considerable fatigue, having undergone numerous repairs and panel beating; many would not fulfil roadworthy requirements. Yet these taxis remain operational through the services of other township micro-enterprises and the frequent requirement for repairs is a boon to mechanics and panel beaters. Over the past decade, Toyota Avanza vehicles have become used as informal taxis due to their high fuel economy and carrying capacity of seven passengers. Relative to the minibus sector, a higher proportion of the drivers of informal taxis are owner-operators, although the arrival of the Avanza presents a shift towards non-driver ownership and investment of taxi owners in the informal segment.

In Browns Farm, Cressida taxis provide a niche transport service for shoppers utilising local supermarkets (see Figure 7.9).

FIGURE 7.9 Cressida sedan taxis await customers at a rank at the rear of the shopping mall, Philippi township

These taxis ferry people and their possessions as a door-to-door service and are also commonly used to transport goods for local businesses, collecting supplies from wholesalers for street braaier businesses or spaza shops, for example. In these cases, the drivers can even assist in loading and unloading procedures. For passenger travel, the fees are charged on a distance basis. Similarly to the minibus taxi sector, the fees are centrally determined and vary according to distance travelled. Price discounting to outcompete other operators does not occur. Informal *amaphela* do not adhere to specific routes; instead, the drivers respond to demand situations and customer needs. The informal taxi system is emergent in that it is able to quickly absorb information on customer preferences and respond through minor changes to routes and drop-off points. In the Imizamo Yethu site, the *amaphela* and *amahoender* operate routes outside the township confines, providing workers with transport from township locations to work destinations in Hout Bay and Llandudno as well as operating routes to shopping malls, the clinic and other facilities. These sedan taxis collect passengers on the street and from an informal rank. If the taxi is fully loaded, individual costs are reduced so that the function of the informal rank is to enable passengers to group together to subsidise costs. Short trips cost R7 per person. Most of the informal taxi drivers live in Imizamo Yethu, and the transport service is predominantly owner-operated. Unlike minibus taxi operations, informal taxi routes change throughout the day, responding to the customer demands to access particular destinations in the surrounding suburbs (see Figure 7.10.)

Sedan taxis in Windhoek similarly benefit from route flexibility. As we demonstrate in Chapter 6, the economy of Eveline Street is influenced by sedan taxi transport. These taxis provide a means of connection and integration, moderating the tempo of

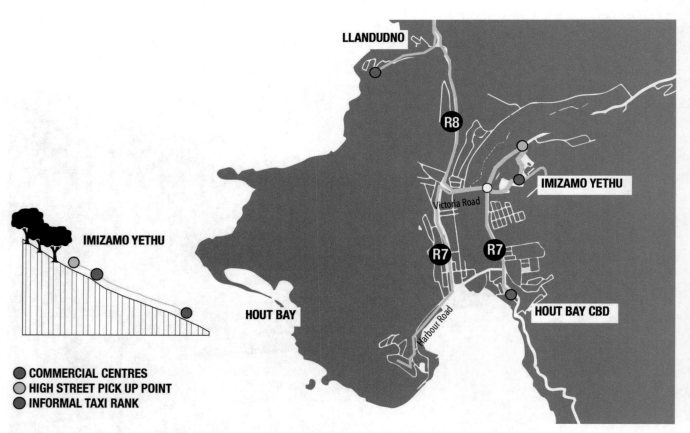

FIGURE 7.10 Taxi routes emerging from Imizamo Yethu township connecting nearby centres of employment and services
Note: The taxi plays a critical role in transporting commuters up the steep slopes of the settlement.

movement along the street through their process of operating on a drop-and-go basis and contributing towards the development of a nodal morphology in business distribution. In function, the Namibian taxis are similar to the informal taxis operating in South African townships and most are second-hand vehicles imported from Japan. In form, the main difference is that the Namibian sedan taxis are regulated and operate under strict licensing conditions. Short-distance taxi trips within the broader Katutura area cost N$10 (R10); longer trips to the CBD cost N$20 (R20); these prices are considerably cheaper than Uber taxi trips in South Africa, which cost roughly N$10 (R10) per km. Taxis ferry customers to bars on Eveline Street and home thereafter, operating late into the night with the high street a point of origin and destination. Apart from providing a transport service, sedan taxis are major customers of the car washes as well as the print shops (where taxis obtain their compulsory signs), the wheel alignment shops, the tyre repairers, and the micro-enterprises which provide mechanical servicing or panel beating. The taxi drivers are also important customers for hair salons, the bars (where non-alcoholic drinks are commonly available), and the various street food sellers.

CASE STUDY: *A sedan taxi operator*

Steve operated two Avanza taxis in the greater Philippi (Browns Farm) area. (See Figure 7.11).

He drove one and employed a driver to operate the second. His first job in Cape Town was in the construction industry, although he reported that the wages were so poor that he left this employment and started driving an 'old' Cressida, working on a commission basis for another person. In 2008, after two years of driving he saved R25 000 and purchased his own Cressida from a woman in Bellville.

FIGURE 7.11 An Avanza taxi driver, Browns Farm

He recalled: '*My aim was to own my own pela and once I had it, I went to the [minibus] terminus to talk to the taxi owners to register my Cressida.*' The registration fee was R2 500. One of the taxi bosses set out the rules: '*You do not go to Cape Town. You only operate here in Nyanga, Philippi, Gugulethu and areas around. Do not go outside. You can go to Delft but don't pick commuters from there.*' Steve's taxi business was highly profitable. By 2010, he had succeeded in saving R250 000 in cash, including '*a five-litre container full of coins*', and he went to Toyota to purchase an Avanza. This plan was not straightforward as Steve did not have a driver's licence or a bank account and, according to him, the Toyota dealer would not sell him a vehicle without these documents. It took Steve six months to convince his brother, who possessed both of these institutional relationships, to purchase the vehicle on his behalf.

Steve had remained in business since then. He said: '*I like the Avanza because you make quick money; every day you make money.*' He started work at 5 a.m. and finished at 9 p.m. The standard fee per passenger within the catchment was R8. At the end of the month and into the first week of the new month, Steve was able to make between R800 to R1 500 per day from the car he drove. He expected the driver of his other Avanza to return earnings of between R400–R600 and to purchase petrol. In order to operate his Avanza, Steve had to pay the Nyanga taxi association a fee of R200–R300, although the collection of this fee was haphazard and Steve embarked on a strategy of cat and mouse to avoid the tax. He explained that the association '*just collects anywhere. Every driver knows who the collector is. If the collector sees me, he stops me and asks me to pay. I try as much as I can to evade the collector. If I see him collecting in one street, I change direction. We do not get receipts. There are so many drivers and the collector sometimes forgets who has paid and who has not. He cannot issue a receipt because he has no time to write down details.*'

Steve planned to exit the sector in the future. Though the business was profitable, the hours were long and drivers were constantly getting traffic infringement fines and were subject to informal taxes and the dictates of taxi bosses. According to Steve, some of these individuals operated 10 to 15 vehicles, though in Steve's words '*most of the owners are not staying here.*' Then there were the challenges of crime and vehicle accidents. He explained that there was an informal rule to manage this risk: '*If I crash into someone, I have to pay that person there and then. We go to the [local] panel beaters and get quotes, then the guy you crashed into takes you to the bank to withdraw the money to pay the panel beater, not any other time. Now.*' His long-term plan was to purchase a house as he lived in a shack. He reflected: '*I want to sell the two cars and build flats for rental... It's a better business because you don't pay petrol, you don't pay electricity, you don't pay fines or [the] association fee. I will sell the two cars once I buy a house.*' Still he reminisced about the old Cressida business: '*We made a lot of money that time. The fare was only R3 but then we made R500 per day.*' He felt that there were now '*too many players*' in the market.

Thugocracy and violent entrepreneurship

Public and private road transport services fall within overarching provisions of the National Land Transport Act (No. 5 of 2009). The aims of the Act are overseen by the National Department of Transport (NDoT). The Act clarifies the concurrent roles and responsibilities of the three spheres of government in public transport regulation: National government oversees transversal alignment with national transport policies, whereas the licensing and hence regulation of taxis falls under the jurisdiction of provincial authorities. Municipal government, the base of the governmental system, has jurisdiction of all road users within its domain (since most roads are municipal property) and is primarily responsible for the provision of supporting infrastructure (such as taxi ranks) and wholly responsible for the monitoring of taxis in transit in terms of municipal road traffic by-laws and public transport operating licence conditions. Despite the demarcation of specific roles, transport regulation is complicated by the inclusion of non-state actors who represent select interests, one of which is to sustain the regulatory system in spite of its faults. Apart from (most) minibuses, township sedan taxis are excluded from institutional regulation and hence operate informally. The partial formalisation of the minibus sector provides a sharp insight into the intermeshing of money and the power which is derived from wealth, political allegiances, organisational magnitude and violence.

Minibuses maintain their inclusion in the formal economy with the aid of a powerful financial-industrial complex. In the regulatory process, a degree of power has been afforded to groups representing taxi owners or associations which today control route use rights, access to ranks and other opportunities. These associations consider themselves as de facto rights holders of demarcated routes (Boudreaux 2006) and wield influence in the issuance of operating licences through the statutory requirement that applicants register with an association (Mhlanga 2017). From a purely operational perspective, the association fulfils a coordinating function and simplifies the task of regulation through their roles such as communication between the regulator and taxi operators, supposedly adjusting (upwards or downwards) the number of taxis in response to route demand and in the resolution of disputes; roles which Lomme (2008) has described as 'effective if discreet and inconspicuous' (p. 4).

To strengthen their operational power, the several hundred associations have consolidated into local and sub-regional political alliances or 'mother bodies'. These structures have succeeded in enhancing the power for their membership through mobilising against competing associations in the struggle over routes, challenging state actions that impact on the profitability of the sector and dominating individual taxi operators. At present mother bodies are allied to one of two overarching structures: South African National Taxi Council (SANTACO, established in 2001 with state funding) and the National Taxi Alliance (NTA). SANTACO was intended as an umbrella body to represent the minibus sector on behalf of its constituents, organised by provincial bodies, regional structures and local associations. In operational terms, SANTACO has no control over the mother bodies, some of which are accused of carrying out 'route invasions and hostile takeovers' (Boqwana 2018, p.10). The exercise of power by the mother bodies is akin to the conduct of organised criminal networks that engage in 'violent entrepreneurship' (Volkov 2002, p. 25) to enforce contractual agreements, maintain compliance with informal rules, and extract fees to finance their 'discreet and inconspicuous' market interventions. Volkov argues that violent entrepreneurs fulfil a role as suppliers of 'protection' (pp. 28, 53) in a context in which the state is weak and/or unable to respond to the complexity of informality. In such a context, he argues, violent entrepreneurs substitute and complement state roles in terms of instituting (institutionalised) systems of measurement, rules and means of enforcement to ensure an 'orderly exchange' of goods or services. In the context of a crisis of mobility, whose roots lie in the peripheral situation of townships and under-provision of rail and bus services, the taxi associations potentially facilitate a relatively orderly provision of transport services. The analogy with violent entrepreneurs stems from the control of mother bodies by 'big men' who institute a thugocracy of governance in their organisations wherein rules are underpinned by violence. In the operation of minibuses in Johannesburg, for example, taxi routes from the South (Soweto) and Northern settlements such as Ivory Park converge in the CBD whereupon passengers seeking to transit either southwards or northwards are compelled to change taxis as they enter routes of a different power bloc. The relevant licensing authorities are unwilling to grant operating licences to enable minibuses to traverse across these routes out of fear that this would result in violent conflict.

The 2005 Commission of Enquiry into the causes of taxi violence in the Western Cape (Ntsebeza 2005) provides a rare insight into the strategies of mother bodies, particularly their systematic use of violence to defend and advance business interests. In the townships of Cape Town, the mother bodies include the Cape Organisation for Democratic Taxi Association (CODETA), whose powerbase is spatially situated in Khayelitsha, and the Cape Amalgamated Taxi Association (CATA), which broke away from CODETA and has its powerbase spatially situated in the older township of Nyanga. CODETA and CATA have been the main protagonists in a two-decades long taxi war whose battles centre around disputed taxi routes, including rights to ply trade along the routes in Delft South. The so-named Ntsebeza Commission heard that respective association leaders have worked their way upwards through the minibus sector through roles as vehicle drivers, rank managers and fleet owners. In climbing the leadership ranks, these emergent 'big men' have had to engage in struggles within and outside of their respective associations, thus acquiring experience in the use of violence to exert strategic control over an association and to advance the business interests of its members. The Commission's report described the leaders as 'warlords' whose authority is 'feared' and decisions obeyed.

Drawing their revenue from levies on members, protection fees on township businesses and fines issued to the drivers, mother bodies enforce their system rules through violence and intimidation, with their core focus to control routes and ranks (Dugard 2001). State weakness has allowed mother bodies to facilitate market dominance using methods that include arson, murder and intimidation to enforce silence and sustain a 'culture of lawlessness' (Ntsebeza 2005, p. 82). As Dugard (2001) notes, hit squads are a 'vital component' of a mother body's system of control (p. 18), while the Ntsebeza Commission found that hit men are 'paid up to R12 000 for a single contract killing' (Ntsebeza 2005, p. 53). Although thousands of people have been killed in taxi wars, so great is the public fear of retribution that the state has struggled to take action against the leadership and perpetrators of violence. During the period 1991–1999, 2 007 persons were killed as a direct consequence of taxi violence (cited in Dugard 2001, p. 13). The 'wars' and killings continue to the present. In the struggle for the Delft South route, a 'low intensity war' has raged since about 2015. In May 2018, with respect to a single battle in this 'war', 10 people were killed, including the Chairperson of the Delft Taxi Association (Isaacs, 2018). In times of 'war', the 'mother bodies' hire professional assassins, some of whom are said to be former freedom fighters, to murder taxi drivers, the leaders of rival associations or simply to carry out revenge killings. The political connectedness and power of senior taxi leaders was demonstrated during the 2005 Ntsebeza inquiry when a number of subpoenaed respondents were murdered despite participating in a state witness protection scheme. In addition to their turf struggles, mother bodies have also been implicated in challenging alternative forms of public transport, including bus and rail services and other forms of sedan taxi competition. In recent times taxi associations have challenged the state to disband the BRT systems which are being established in metropolitan areas and major towns, to reform the taxi recapitalisation programme (Boudreaux 2006), to oppose the pricing of new vehicles and to obtain direct control over state subsidies.

At the heart of the township minibus taxi economy is a financial-industrial complex, based on a relationship between vehicle finance organisations (eg Transaction Capital, a Johannesburg Stock Exchange [JSE] listed financial holding company, owns the SA Taxi Finance Company) and taxi vehicle manufacturers. SA Taxi Finance Company is the market leader in providing finance to entrepreneurs to purchase new minibuses. Large business has a vested interest in sustaining the dominance of minibuses as the sole provider of inter-suburban taxi services. The financial-industrial complex enables large businesses (who provide financial services, new vehicles and after-sales support) and taxi federations such as SANTACO and NTA to control the minibus transport system. Their collective influence shapes the terms of finance, insurance, maintenance services and resales. The idea of a 'complex' refers to the informal collaborations of financial and industrial interests which coalesce around the need to influence or maintain public policy, often through aligning their strategic interests with government needs or political pressures. In the minibus sector, the political pressure derives from the goal of the taxi associations and their leadership to sustain the minibus role as a public transport service and ownership structure in which most of the leaders possess large fleets of vehicles. Their self-interest neatly aligns with the corporate objectives to sell costly new minibus vehicles (recommended retail prices for the Toyota Quantum ranging from R486 300 to R525 600 cash price in 2018) and to contractually tie the purchasers into a raft of services provided by subsidiary businesses and other large businesses. To these objectives, big business and corporates have aligned moral, psychological and material interests, deemed to be central characteristics of an industrial-financial complex. These interests are symbiotic with government objectives to sustain the manufacturing of minibus vehicles, nurture black entrepreneurship and appease a powerful grassroots organisation. In this context, taxi formalisation is not used to facilitate inclusive opportunities for township entrepreneurs and investors, but as a mechanism to safeguard established operators and accommodate corporate business interests. As we learnt in Steve's story, most of the 'big-men' beneficiaries of this business arrangement who operate fleets of minibuses do not live in the township.

In support of an agenda to modernise and formalise the minibus industry (and under pressure of the vested interest groupings), the NDoT instituted a taxi recapitalisation programme to remove 'older' vehicles from the public transport system (using a 'scrapping allowance' as an incentive), reduce the total number of taxis, and introduce new vehicle fleets. The programme aimed to formalise taxi operations through transforming vehicle operators into registered businesses and instituting sectoral labour regulation. Had the recapitalisation programme been fully implemented, the minibus system would have limited opportunities for (new) entrants, while externalising all allied services to formal businesses situated outside the township. Instead, the watered-down version of recapitalisation that has emerged thus far has merely reinforced the political power of the taxi associations and strengthened the interests of the industrial-financial complex. It is important to note that apart from the washing of cars, township micro-enterprises gain almost no direct benefit from the recapitalised minibus taxis. The new vehicles which enter the system (some of which have benefited from recapitalisation subsidies) are symbolic of the outflow of value from places like the Delft South high street to corporate capital and the 'big men' who dominate the sector and wield influence over the mother bodies.

Outlook

The post-apartheid state recognised the need to reduce the costs and efficiency of public transport services for township residents. Under the influence of World Bank thinking, the NDoT adopted policies to develop 'Integrated Mass Rapid Public Transport

Networks'. In this vision, the transport networks would integrate rail, bus and minibus systems (intermodal integration), though the state would prioritise and enhance the economic viability of business services (including BRT and conventional business) through the provision of operational subsidies (Figure 7.12).

In addition, the buses would directly compete with minibuses through new routes at the point of origin within the township, thus resulting in bus routes that 'meander excessively…to prevent minibus taxis from feeding or distributing' route demand (Lomme 2008, p. 8). These ideas found fertile ground among metropolitan municipal planners who had come to embrace Transit Oriented Development (ToD) as a planning strategy to redress spatial injustice.

ToD thinking first arose in North American cities in the 1980s as a response to the effect that high use of private vehicles was having on transport, spatial development and sustainability (Bickford & Behrens 2015). ToD is premised on a 'utopian' set of ideas with respect to the reorientation of land use in strategic points (such as transport corridors and nodes) towards high density settlement and public transit rather than urban sprawl and private transport, with the objective to achieve more spatially inclusive, liveable and sustainable cities (Harber 2018; The South African Property Owners' Association and the South African Cities Network 2016). As Harber (2018) has argued, the ToD vision rests on achieving increased density, pedestrian walkability and mixed-use landforms, which in turn, enables the provision of mass rapid public transport. Instead, city politicians have embraced ToD thinking to justify investment in BRT transport with the singular aim of replacing the minibus taxi system, a move applauded by non-minibus commuters who have become impatient with what is perceived as the state's failure to control lawlessness

FIGURE 7.12 Buses, minibuses, and a horse and cart
Note: There are three different orders of public transport – of which public buses receive the bulk of state subsidies. Some municipalities have aimed to integrate bus and minibus services.

of taxi drivers and associations. The introduction of BRT routes into the townships and establishment of related infrastructure has profound development implications for local transport services and organic spatial transformations.

Our analysis of Eveline Street (Chapter 6) shows that urban characteristics are transforming towards greater density, walkability and mix-uses without specific ToD interventions. In this case, sedan taxi services fulfil an enabling mechanism, providing a fluid, flexible and highly responsive transport system which not only transports clients to high-street businesses but is a major customer of township based micro-enterprises. Sedan taxis travel in both directions along the streets, offering a multiplicity of pick-up and drop-off stages and providing a truly door-to-door service. Despite the investment to establish BRT infrastructure within the township, the insecure environment in many settlements decreases the scope of walkability, with only sedan taxis able to provide a safe and relatively efficient mode of transport between township homes and the high street. The comparative advantages of sedan taxis (over minibuses and buses) are particularly evident at night when these taxis enable a diverse night-time leisure economy in Eveline Street which is contingent on the safe and efficient passage of participants. With significantly lower societal externalities than South African minibuses, the sedan taxis in Namibia illustrate the gains from a reduction in scale (smaller vehicles), formalisation and thus state control, owner operation and route flexibility. The collective benefit of the regulated Namibian sedans far outweighs the informal *amaphela* taxi system which, while flexible (and relatively affordable) within the confines of neighbourhoods, operates under the patronage of minibus associations and embraces lawlessness, partly in pursuit of profit and partly due to state weaknesses.

Due to its efficiencies, potential to contribute to the development of the township economy, and its status as a black-owned business sector, there is a strong imperative for broadening and deepening the inclusion of township transport services within ToD and intermodal transport plans. Taking a different approach to formalisation, the objectives should be twofold: first, to widen benefits to include informal taxis; and second, to shift the minibus system towards a township base where a wider range of micro-enterprises could provide services. These changes would require government to reconsider the minibus concept or at least think about how a range of taxi services can collectively participate in intra-area transport. To enhance public safety and redress the governance challenges, the state needs to persist in seeking to reform the employment models under which drivers currently work. At present, these are weighted against the drivers and are largely non-compliant with the sector determination (such as working conditions, hours and rates of remuneration). A system of owner-operators and a more affordable range of vehicles (applied to both minibus taxis and sedan taxis) would shift economic power away from the current fleet owners while simultaneously redirecting profits away from the financiers and manufacturers towards the owner-drivers and township-based support services. If the power of the associations could be significantly mitigated, the potential efficiencies and comparative advantages of minibuses could be better harnessed to improve access to mobility in ways that are safer and more affordable than subsidy-dependent BRT and rail services.

8

WINNERS AND LOSERS IN THE GROCERY TERRITORIAL BATTLE

In this chapter we argue that informality has produced an opportunity for non-resident investors to capture the retail grocery market and together with corporate supermarkets has wrested the spaza sector away from indigenous entrepreneurs.

CHAPTER 8

Winners and losers in the grocery territorial battle

Spaza shops are the iconic township home-based business. These small grocery retail shops provide affordable and localised access to groceries and other daily necessities, selling items such as bread, milk, flour, cool drinks, soap, cigarettes, paraffin and liquor (see Figure 8.1. and Figure 8.2).

Spaza shops were one of the first township businesses to emerge during the apartheid era, operating from people's home as an organic response to the overwhelming demand for convenient access to retail goods which residents otherwise had to purchase from formal-sector businesses outside of the neighbourhood. In general, spaza shops are unregistered cash-based businesses which do not adhere, in the strict sense, to municipal land-use

FIGURE 8.1 The spaza shop is a conspicuous and often branded structure that is easily accessible to the public

FIGURE 8.2 Spaza shops carry a diverse range of products, including cosmetics, fruit and vegetables, sweets and cigarettes and liquor products

and regulatory requirements for selling perishable foods. Spaza shops are situated within residential properties in a variety of spatial situations, occupying garages and repurposed bedrooms, or working out of shipping containers and corrugated iron structures. The size of the spaza market is unclear although market researcher Neilsen (2016) reported that the sector comprises some 134 000 shops with collective trade amounting to R46 billion per annum.

The name spaza derives from township slang and denotes a 'hidden activity', with the name itself derived from the isiZulu verb '*isiphazamisa*' meaning a 'hindrance, impediment or disturbance' towards the formal economy from which black entrepreneurship was excluded (Spiegel 2005, p. 194). As a statement of resistance, the significance of spaza shops in the nascent township economy grew in importance during the shop boycotts of the 1980s. Through surreptitiously 'hindering' opportunities for formal business, spaza shops provided an indispensable retail service to the adjacent community as well as an economic livelihood (freedom) to the shopkeepers. From its origins, the spaza sector was typically operated by middle-aged female entrepreneurs who ran these micro-enterprises from their homes, combining household roles such as childcare with shop activities. The spaza shop was akin to the community pantry, with the shopkeeper commonly a community figure who knew her/his customers personally and who provided the social functions of information, surveillance and help in times of food crisis. The early generation of spaza micro-enterprises was service-oriented in that they were primarily responsive to needs within the neighbourhood rather than solely focused on the profits to be derived from the grocery market, selling items of high demand at prices that were sustainable to the micro-entrepreneur though respectful of the community's economic situation.

Bheki's story of the establishment of their spaza is indicative of the process through which South Africans entered into business (2/1347/F/40). The business started from his aunt's house, selling *'small items such as airtime, chips, sweets and other basic items such as bread.'* The business was started by Bheki's father and was a sustainable concern providing family employment. Over the years the business grew steadily. As Bheki recalled: *'there wasn't any other shops in the area and the community was eager to support their shop as it meant people did not have to travel far to get these goods.'* With the profits from the business, they purchased a shipping container which was positioned on the street opposite where the shop operated. They operated a public pay-phone which helped to generate good profits (at a point in time when such phones were in high demand, see Chapter 3). Through the business, Bheki's father was able to purchase two vehicles to operate as informal taxis. Although the informal taxi business did not succeed because the vehicles regularly broke down, the shop continues to operate and has survived the subsequent increase in competition by selling liquor.

In the post-apartheid period, the spaza sector has undergone dramatic change and disruption. We have noted four major changes. First, along with liquor traders, spaza shops have established supply-chain linkages with product manufacturers and distributors from whom they have obtained signs, coolers and regular product deliveries. Second, from the 1990s onwards formal supermarkets have emerged on the fringes and in some cases, inside the township, and thus provide residents with closer access to groceries at prices cheaper than most spazas could sustain. Though spazas retained their geographic advantage over supermarkets, further competition came from the third major change; since around 2010, a new class of immigrant shopkeeper has opened shops deep within the township neighbourhoods. These immigrant entrepreneurs have since come to dominate the market as the South African shops were unable to compete with reduced prices and the more diverse product range in these bigger (and better) shops (Charman, Petersen, & Piper, 2012). Alcock (2018) refers to these entrepreneurs as 'guerrillas' and refers to their businesses as 'spazarettes', an acknowledgement of the notable difference in the business size from traditional spaza outlets (p. 215). Fourth, the change in nature of South African violence from political to societal (Barolsky 2005) has heightened the risks to cash-based micro-enterprises, with spaza shops emerging as a central target for theft of cash and merchandise. The female micro-entrepreneurs who pioneered the spaza market have subsequently largely gone out of business, either closing their shops or leasing them out. Today, township spaza shopkeepers comprise mainly male, immigrant, informal employees employees who report to a 'boss' who, in most cases, does not work in the shop itself. As a result, the relationship between the shopkeeper and the neighbourhood community has become depersonalised, while the shop itself has transformed into a profit-oriented business more closely resembling the retail model of the mini-market supermarkets than the community stores that previously characterised the township.

In this chapter, we will argue that the informality of the spaza business model (bound to its tradition as a 'hidden' business) has produced an opportunity for non-resident township investors to capture the retail grocery market and together with corporate supermarkets has wrested this sector away from indigenous entrepreneurs. This chapter addresses this transition and reflects on the implications. Our analysis is spatially informed, at three gradients: one, we examine the ownership changes at the small-area level through the Delft case study; two, at the micro-context level we detail the layout of shops and the spatial strategies of shopkeepers in response to crime and violence; and three, we describe the expansion of shopping malls on adjacent neighbourhoods.

In terms of our analysis of power, we show how economic advantage (including power derived from ethnic networks) has enabled immigrant entrepreneurs to capture a market where, previously, existing businesses were comparatively weak and disconnected.

Spaza shops in Delft South

The case of Delft South in Cape Town provides a sharp insight into the dynamics of township grocery retail markets. We initially studied spaza shops in 2010 and 2011 within our broader investigation of township businesses. We separated the grocery traders into two categories – spaza shops and house shops – with spazas considered to be micro-enterprises that operated as stand-alone, signposted, dedicated retailers, with assets including a commercial glass-doored fridge, selling at least six of eight grocery products (bread, milk, cigarettes, soft drinks, rice, maize, sugar and cooking oil) and operating for five days per week or longer. In line with the results across other sites, grocery retailing via spaza shops and smaller house shops accounted for one third of all the 880 identified micro-enterprises in Delft South. In 2010/11, a total of 177 spaza shops were identified and interviewed. In spatial terms, these businesses were remarkably evenly spaced and distributed throughout the site, with each spaza shop serving a specific neighbourhood consumer base determined by the proximity and walkability to the shop. These characteristics were found in all other sites. We encountered shops operating in a range of spatial situations, both in residential properties and on public land (streets) within residential areas. Our research sought to understand competitiveness within the spaza sector through examining business models, product pricing as well as external influences on the business, including crime and violence.

One aspect of the research investigated the subject of proprietorship and found that the ownership and operations of the then shops was evenly split between South Africans and immigrants (see Figure 8.3.).

The new spaza entrepreneurs had either established new shops in residential homes or taken over faltering businesses, renting the premises for R2 000 pm on average. In our interviews, the South African shopkeepers discussed the challenges of crime, followed by competition from the new spaza shops (especially price discounting), while the immigrant shopkeepers spoke mainly about crime, though many where hesitant to exchange information without permission of the 'boss'. We noted that some of the informants had only worked in Delft for a few months, a subject which Liedeman (2013) investigated and found evidence of the operation of ethnic networks through which the new spaza investors accessed finance and low-cost labour.

The research was undertaken at a time of mounting tension towards immigrant entrepreneurs, which in certain townships saw xenophobic attacks on shops, resulting in burning, looting and killings (International Organization for Migration 2009). We found high risks of crime to all spaza shopkeepers. Although the immigrants were more sorely affected, the data showed that both South Africans and immigrants, respectively, were subject to robbery (23% vs 39%) and theft (37% vs 16%), with cases of murder (2% vs 5%) and attempted murder (9% vs 5%) reported by both groups (Charman & Piper 2012). A spaza shop employee (2/2122/M/nd) told us that he experienced harassment on a regular basis, giving the examples of '*constant stone throwing, death threats and threats of robbery.*' He told us about a particular incident in which a customer accused him of selling a fake lighter and in the resulting quarrel he was stabbed – yet no one came to his assistance. Among South African shopkeepers, we heard numerous complaints of what was considered to be '*unfair*' competition.

0   0.50   kilometres

● Immigrant (90)

● Local (89)

FIGURE 8.3 Map showing the distribution of spaza shops in Delft South by nationality of ownership, 2011

In one such case, the informant (2/2124/M/nd) complained about a new shop, operated by Bangladeshis, which opened spatially opposite his shop and then *'tried to undercut his prices.'* He said that *'the law is that [new shops] must be 100m away, but the Bangladeshis do not adhere to this rule.'* At a focus group workshop to discuss these developments, a shopkeeper recalled her experiences of business decline: *'There was a time when I sold 100 loaves of bread a day. Do you know how much bread I sell now? I take ten bread, seven white and three brown, and yesterday I only sold two of them. And today I did not even take bread. That just shows you how much down the business came.'* Another participant reflected on the mood among the South African shopkeepers, saying:

'The government don't know where xenophobia really starts. Its starts with animosity that been built up inside of the people's spirit in the area.' (SLF 2015).

In 2015, we revisited Delft South to conduct a follow-up study to assess change in the Delft township economy over time. While many new micro-enterprises were evident, particularly women survivalist sellers of fruit, vegetables and snacks, the total number of spaza shops had declined in number by 14% from 177 to 152. The spaza sector was one of only two business categories that registered a decline in business numbers in the period 2011-2015, the other being phone shops (See Charman & Petersen, 2017). Of the 177 spaza shops originally identified, a staggering 126 (70%) had ceased trading by 2015 (see Figure 8.4).

- Closed (126)
- New (85)
- Established (68)

FIGURE 8.4 Map showing the distribution of spaza shops in Delft South, indicating spatial changes and business closure over the period between 2011 and 2015

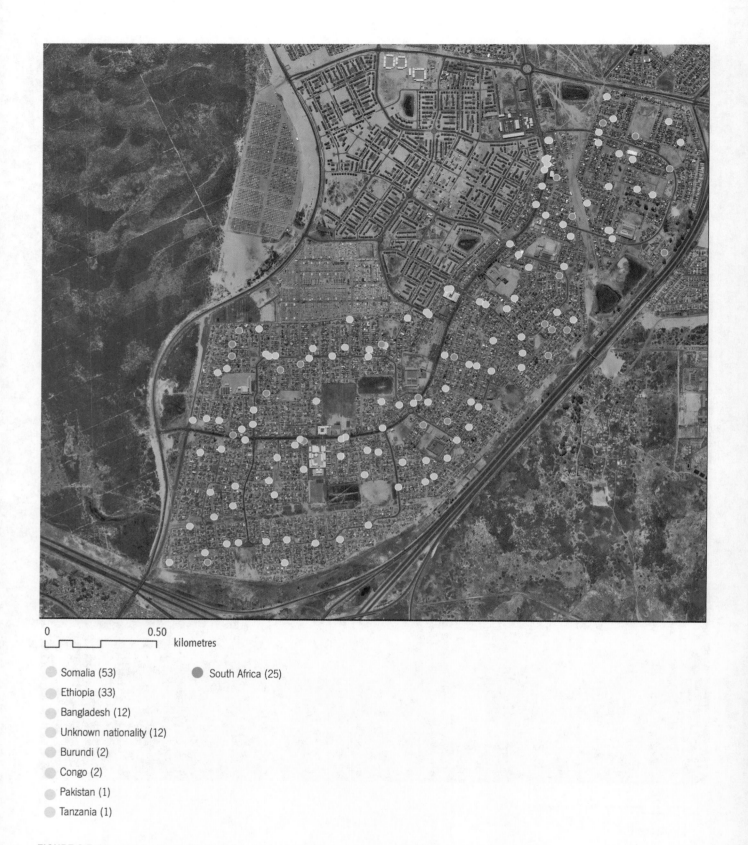

0   0.50

kilometres

- Somalia (53)
- Ethiopia (33)
- Bangladesh (12)
- Unknown nationality (12)
- Burundi (2)
- Congo (2)
- Pakistan (1)
- Tanzania (1)

- South Africa (25)

FIGURE 8.5 Map showing the distribution of spaza shops in Delft South by nationality of ownership, 2015

Furthermore, merely 53 shops continued to operate from precisely the same physical locality, in other words the same residential property or site on public land. In addition, even in those cases where the shop was still operating from the same property, we discovered in many cases that the business ownership had changed hands, with the business sold onto new investors. A mere 12 shopkeepers from the population of 152 recalled participating in the 2011 survey. Local residents confirmed that spaza shops were frequently bought and sold within the immigrant business networks that had come to control the spaza market in Delft. The shift in the spatial location of the spaza shops was indeed a consequence of lessor dissatisfaction with the rental arrangements, with shop owners repeatedly signing landlords into complex, multi-year, legal lease agreements and in many cases selling on the leased shops to new investors, with the outlets also being used as both commercial and residential home for commonly two to three shop employees.

By 2015 the spaza sector was in a state of flux. Shops were opening, closing down, shifting trading sites to different localities and changing ownership. There was also evidence of consolidation in ownership with businessmen now owning a series of shops either outright or in partnership arrangements. Of the 152 spaza shops, 82% were now owned by immigrant entrepreneurs from Somalia, Ethiopia and Bangladesh (the spatial distribution is shown in Figure 8.5).

Through interviews with the shopkeepers and residents, we found that the great majority of the outlet retailers were employees, with the actual owners rarely encountered in the shop (Charman, Petersen, & Piper 2012; Liedeman 2013). Our 2010/2011 research into the prices of select items found that the immigrant-run businesses were retailing at a discount and this was indeed outcompeting the smaller South African shops. In a parallel research undertaking, Hartnack and Liedeman (2016) interviewed the shopkeepers who had recently ceased trading; this was Mavis's story:

> I helped South African people to start shops, by linking them up to my Coca-Cola deliveries, but the Somalians, we could not stand up to them. After 2010 my business was already going down. There were now two Somali shops in the area. Something told me to go to their shops and buy coffee. I did this and saw that they were selling it for R4.50, but [the cost] price was R4.80, and I charged R5 to make a profit! I saw that this was also happening with milk, cigarettes, bread and Omo as well…I felt they were undercutting our prices so that we could close shop, and then they would be able to raise their prices once they had captured the market. (p. 21)

From survivalist to entrepreneurs

The trend in Delft South of immigrants dominating informal retail grocery markets has been reported in a number of studies (Basardien, Parker, Bayat, Friedrich & Appoles 2014), including a national survey of spaza shops (Petersen, Thorogood, Charman & du Toit 2019). In reflecting on this change, we focus on two questions: one, what has enabled this transition to happen?; and two, why have South African survivalists not adopted more competitive business strategies?

Historic legacy

Early studies of South Africans in the spaza sector found that the typical business was financially vulnerable and weak in competitiveness (Ligthelm 2005). Most spazas were deemed 'survivalist' in character rather than entrepreneurial, with one commentator finding that the sector had little growth potential (Ligthelm 2008). South African shopkeepers typically operated on an autonomous basis, reliant on immediate family members for labour. The business was small in size, stocking only the most essential grocery items while operating hours were dictated by the rhythms of family life, for example, closing for trade if the shopkeeper had to fetch stock or collect school children. Few shops traded continuously from early morning to late night. The shopkeeper would purchase items from formal wholesalers, only restocking once shelves were thoroughly depleted. Business operations were not networked, and as with many township micro-enterprise entrepreneurs, spaza shopkeepers tended to view neighbouring shops as competitors whom they could not trust in matters of procurement (a topic we explore in Chapter 12).

Importantly, competition between shops was weak. Most shops tended to sell their products at informally agreed floor prices, keeping profits low on staples such as bread, flour and rice but seeking to gain a higher mark-up on non-essentials. The traditional South African spaza business approach tended to avoid price competition on core items, with competition mediated through geographic market advantages (being the closest shop within the neighbourhood) and support for the business underpinned by social relations and kinship networks. Shopkeepers would supply goods on credit, though modest in amount and confined to persons deemed trustworthy (such as the heads of households, rather than young persons) and rarely was credit offered on discretionary items such as cool-drink or biscuits. Although these shops were able to survive for long periods through selling staples to the neighbours, the business model was systemically weak and highly vulnerable to competition from new business approaches.

Informality as a strategy

As shown in the Delft South case, most shops are situated in residential areas and serve small geographic niche markets whose catchment extends no further than one or two streets. In order to compete with the traditional shops, new businesses needed to be established within residential areas, positioned in close proximity to existing shops and serving the same client base. To create a competitive market segment would require the establishment of thousands of competing shops, bearing in mind that in the mid-2000s when the transition commenced there were at least 83 348 spaza shopkeepers, according to the StatsSA QLFS data (Wills 2009). Yet this task was rapidly achieved. Today, entrepreneurs from African countries (notably Somalia and Ethiopia) and Asian countries (notably Bangladesh), among others, control around 89% of the (urban) township spaza market in Cape Town and Johannesburg, and 72% of all spaza outlets sampled from all provinces nationwide (Petersen et al. 2019).

The market dominance of immigrant-owned spaza shops has been achieved through both specific business and operational strategies that include shareholder ownership models, the use of collective purchasing, price discounting on core products, and the vertical integration of the shops with wholesalers and suppliers. These strategies have benefited from informality partially in consequence of municipalities having neither the law enforcement capacity nor the political will to enforce the myriad of by-laws on home-based grocery retailing. The spaza sector is poorly regulated in comparison to the liquor sector. All home-based businesses are subject to land-use system controls (including zoning schemes), whereas businesses engaged in the sale of perishable foods are required to comply with regulations to ensure food safety as well as environmental health standards (both regulatory competencies of municipal government).

Under-regulation weighs to the advantage of what Petersen et al. (2019) describe as 'informalist' entrepreneurs. Informalists respond to the inability of the state to systematically regulate informal business per se, thus enabling such entrepreneurs (in the township and elsewhere) to largely avoid compliance with the law on immigration, labour employment, the requirements for business registration, product specific restrictions (such as tobacco control legislation) and intellectual property rights. Informalists also tend to disregard informal institutions, such as the 100 m exclusion 'rule' quoted above, where these conditions limit the scope for profit maximisation. We need to emphasise that the business strategies and opportunities from informality which have enabled immigrants to dominate spaza markets vary from business to business, with approaches differing in geographic contexts and between different nationalities. It is also important to recognise that immigrants and refugees to South Africa are constitutionally entitled to work and conduct businesses (Socio-Economic Rights Institute of South Africa & South African Local Government Association 2018), including operating spaza shops, though this right is not 'unlimited' with respect to the infringement of other laws. Furthermore, we recognise that many immigrant shopkeepers are not informalists and operate their businesses within the same framework of disadvantages as South African survivalists.

Ethnic and interrelated business networks increasingly featured heavily in the rapidly evolving spaza sector. Somali spaza operators in Delft and Browns Farm referred to their geographic areas of business footprint as a 'stronghold' in which members of this community had established a network of shops (Liedeman 2013) and sought to control the market, even paying competitors to cease trading (Figure 8.6).

Similar ethnic networks were identified in Ivory Park (among Ethiopians) and in Thabong (among Bangladeshis). This was achieved through purchasing existing shops, opening new shops, driving competitors out of business through aggressive price competition, forming agreements to restrict market competition, threats and actualised violence. We came across the influence of violent entrepreneurship in two respects: first, where

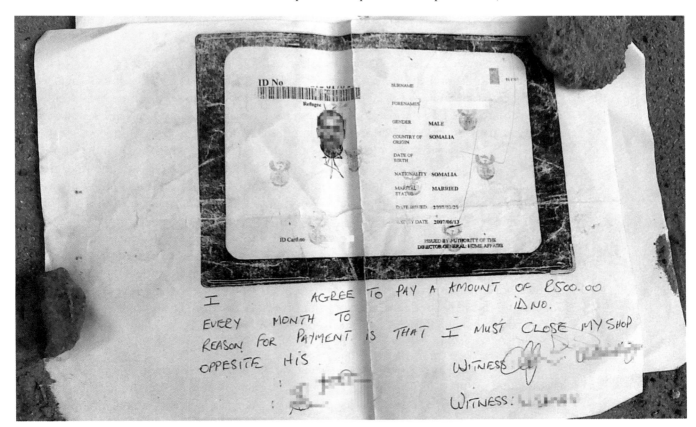

FIGURE 8.6 An informal agreement between shopkeepers, requiring one to cease trading in return for a monthly payment

violence is used to force a competing business to close through threats, robbery or murder; second, where 'protection services' are provided, enabling a business to operate within a hostile environment. Whereas in the first respect, the violent entrepreneurs are engaged in operating spaza shops themselves (either directly or indirectly), in the second respect, the violent entrepreneurs are usually 'big men' within the community who afford protection to the immigrant investors.

In all of the nine South African sites, informalist-run spaza outlets were usually staffed by male employees, with the business managed on a day-to-day basis by a junior partner who is usually from the same country as the investor. Some businesses employ vulnerable South African Development Community migrants, Malawians in particular. Our research dispels the claim that immigrant spaza businesses in the township extend work opportunities for South Africans (Gastrow & Amit 2013). Through in-depth interviews with those shopkeepers willing to talk openly, we learnt that spaza employees were bound to the business via informal and illegal labour practices. These practices range from beneficial share-ownership schemes to highly exploitative conditions. Poor working conditions include the requirement that employees surrender their passports; that they reside inside the shop – sometimes in the retail space; that they operate the business for seven days per week working up to 16 hours per day (opening around 6 a.m. and closing the shop around 10 p.m.); and that they work for rates of remuneration below the statutory minimum wage. These terms of employment are plainly illegal. Such an exploitative labour system enables the informalist entrepreneur to control and commodify their workers, with the system often overseen by clan and community elders who uphold and enforce informal contractual agreements. Situating the power of oversight within community structures effectively prevents disgruntled workers from seeking more favourable working conditions with other countrymen, while their precarious status as immigrants prevents them from exiting the sector altogether or pursuing state intervention.

The employee model of immigrant shops differs from the owner-operator model in smaller (and survivalist) South African spazas. In situations where these small spaza businesses are reliant on labour, it is usually supplied by family members who work on a part-time basis and are remunerated on an in-kind basis or paid an allowance. Wages are low and below the statutory minimum. In the survivalist model, the business has to be responsive to the changing household demands which frequently require the reallocation of labour away from the shop to other functions, including childcare and social obligations. The contrasting situation of South African and immigrant businesses is underpinned in our survey data. We interviewed 1 051 spaza businesses of which 48.5% were South African shopkeepers. Among the South Africans, the average age of the business owner was 40 years, 49% of the shopkeepers were women and the shops had, on average, been in operation for 8.4 years. In contrast, among immigrants, the average age of the shopkeeper was 28 years, 6% of the shopkeepers were women and the shops had, on average, been in operation for 2.9 years. In the employment of labour, the two business models contrasted sharply: whereas around one-third of South African shops employed labour, mostly household members, 71% of immigrant shops employed at least one additional worker.

While we were unable to investigate at depth the issue of multiple store ownership due to the difficulty in finding the business owners and/or their reluctance to share information, we recorded 46 cases in which the shopkeeper owned multiple shops. In these situations, the shops are usually run by junior partners (still employees), with the owner responsible for stock procurement and distribution, financial control and the management of labour, including the recruitment of workers from the home country. There is evidence that informalist entrepreneurs who succeeded in accumulating multiple shops have progressed to open upstream wholesalers with integrated transportation networks to serve multiple spaza outlets within a network. These networked shops are then able to trade for longer hours and stock a wider range of goods, with transport costs reduced as a result of centralised procurement and delivery. Such commercial networks and economic power enable the spaza shop to offer price discounts on core staple food items, a strategy used to attract customers and amplify pressure on competing businesses and survivalists, including persons now operating house shops. In price comparisons, immigrant spaza shops were generally cheaper, with the exception of the very small shops run by Zimbabweans and Mozambicans in Ivory Park (Piper & Yu, 2016).

It has been argued that the South African shopkeepers could replicate the immigrant approach to running spaza businesses, if they had a better 'basic business knowledge' (Gastrow & Amit 2013, p 30). As we point out with respect to supply chains and networks, business financing and labour, this is not simply a case of inadequate knowledge. A further disadvantage pertains to grey market products, notably (untaxed) cigarettes. In an investigation of 1 100 spaza and house shop outlets, Petersen et al. (2019) found that 52% of all cigarettes retailed in the township were untaxed on the basis of the retail price being insufficient to include the mandatory taxes and duties. In some sites this prevalence was upwards of 70% of all tobacco retailed. Spaza shops sell most cigarettes on a loose basis, as single sticks (in contravention of the Tobacco Products Control Act No. 83 of 1993), with a diverse range of grey market (under-taxed) and contraband (including fake brands and cigarettes that are wholly untaxed) cigarettes retailed for between 50c and R1 (Figure 8.7). These products are illegal in terms of the Act, though not greatly opposed within communities where they are seen simply as a low-cost substitute.

FIGURE 8.7 A range of township retailed cigarette brands, in this case predominately grey market and contraband items
Credit: Justin Patrick

FIGURE 8.8 A field research map of Delft South, including cheap cigarette samples purchased at every local spaza shop
Credit: Justin Patrick

A trend we first identified in Delft South was that immigrant spaza shops were the primary source of cheap cigarettes and thus held a market advantage over South African spaza and house shops. In our 2010/11 survey of spaza shops in Delft South, we found that 82% of shops sold contraband cigarettes; four years later, the number of retail outlets of grey market and contraband cigarettes increased to 93% of shops. The data shows that as early as 2011, 90% of immigrant-run shops had access to these products and although South African shopkeepers were also selling grey market and contraband cigarettes, the proportion of these shops was considerably fewer. Four years later, 65% of South African spaza shops in Delft sold grey market and contraband cigarettes (Liedeman & Mackay 2016) (Figure 8.8), whereas Petersen et al. (2019) found that only 36% of South African shops sold such cigarettes.

Because grey market and contraband cigarettes are supplied through secretive networks which are controlled by organised criminal groupings (see Pauw 2017, who considered the contraband tobacco trade as an aspect of state capture), supply is restricted to those entrepreneurs who themselves operate broad distribution networks, can manage bulk cash purchases and avoid state detection. The structure of the supply chain precludes the smaller shopkeepers from accessing grey market and contraband products, which in turn enables competing stores to attract customers away from the small shops. Our observations suggest that consumers are highly price sensitive, enabling the cigarette trade to consolidate around those spaza shops integrated into illegal supply networks.

Apart from the trade in illegal cigarettes, spaza shops provide a market for the sale of counterfeit groceries which impersonate legitimate brands and products (Africa News Agency 2018). With support from an industry counterfeit specialist, the researchers identified counterfeit items, including sanitary pads, cigarette papers, matches, over-the-counter medications, spices and food grains. While some of these products offer cheaper substitutes with low to moderate risks to the user, the food and pharmaceutical products present unknown risks in respect to product quality and safety. Taking a broader perspective, counterfeit products pose reputational damage to both the legitimate producers and retailers, while potentially bolstering criminal networks. As in the case of cigarettes, access to cheap counterfeits relies on linkages to wholesalers who themselves are connected to illegal supply chains. It is therefore unsurprising that spaza shops who have capitalised on their informal status have greater access to such items. The trends in counterfeit markets are unknown although such goods have the potential to become ubiquitous in years to come.

In May 2017, we interviewed an Ethiopian shopkeeper in KwaMashu. He was an employee in a 'Robot Shop' and had no shareholding in the business. We asked him about his experience of working in the business. He recalled:

> *I have been in South Africa for two years, I started in a spaza shop in Umlazi with a different boss where I was paid R400 per month. Six months ago, I came here, as this job pays R300 per month plus my boss sends another R300 to back my family in Ethiopia. When the R300 is taken to Ethiopia it is a lot of money. He also gives me food and I live in this [shipping] container [that houses the spaza outlet] with no costs. I can eat anything from the container. But next month I plan to leave as there is another boss who is offering me R400 + R400, and I will soon tell my current boss who will give me back my passport and saved money…I get my money when this contract is over…I can get the money from the boss when I need it, but I do not carry cash as if he finds money in my pocket, he will be suspicious of me.*

We asked him why 'the boss' holds onto his passport. He replied, '*the boss keeps my passport so that I do not run away…He keeps passports for security as I sit in the shop with lots of cash…The boss always tells the truth. I trust the boss.*' We sought to enquire about the ownership of the business, to which the respondent replied: '*There are so many [bosses]. Some come to deliver, but I do not know if they are bosses or not, [while] some bosses come to collect R800–R1 000 every day.*' His dream is to save money and return to Ethiopia where he plans to pursue an education. For now, he was focused on surviving and completing his contract. '*I have a friend on the outside who connects me…I give him a little money; he is my agent. While I am here in the container, he is out there networking for me – you have to get connections outside. When you are working in a shop that is air-conditioned, you are a free man.*'

Shifts in business spatial dynamics

The rise of informalist entrepreneurs and resulting transitions within the spaza business model are echoed in changing spatial dynamics. As spaza shops lost their social connection to the neighbourhood and the relationships between shopkeepers and customers depersonalised (see chapter cover photograph), so the spatiality of shops has transformed. Fewer and fewer shops permit in-store browsing, while outlets are increasingly becoming heavily fortified as a response to the threat of crime.

We examined the layout of one such spaza operating in Ivory Park. The business is owned by an Ethiopian and operates from a room rented from a South African landlord. Photos from our 2012 micro-enterprise survey records show that the shop space was formerly used as a hair salon. The landlord built the house (and extensions) from personal savings while working as a shop-steward in a manufacturing business. The shop occupies the corner position, oriented towards both a high street and a quieter neighbourhood setting, which affords the business a high degree of visibility to vehicle and pedestrian traffic. The shop was established through converting an outbuilding into a business venue with serving hatches opening onto the two respective streets. The hatch facing onto the high street is no longer used for security reasons. The shop has security bars on the serving hatches and the façade has been painted and branded by Cell C, a local telecoms company (Figure 8.9).

Internally, the shop has been partitioned by the shopkeeper into a trading and sleeping area. Two employees are permanently based in the shop: the setup enables one of the shopkeepers to rest while the other person operates the shop. The shop is open from 6 a.m. to 10 p.m. The employees have access to satellite television and are networked to other Ethiopian shops and a supply chain through which goods are delivered on a daily basis and shop takings are received. The shop is well-stocked. Our research found that the number of Ethiopian shops in Ivory Park increased from 53 to 81 in the period 2012–2017; over the same period, the number of South African shops fell from 33% to 11% of the total.

Like many township businesses, from a land-use perspective, the shop is in contravention with municipal laws. Although the business sells perishable foods, it does not have the mandatory municipal licences. Furthermore, the separation between shop and sleeping place is unplanned and illegal. In terms of the CoJ Draft Land Use Scheme (2017), the rights to operate a spaza shop are restricted to the owner/occupier of the house; the shop must be conducted from a structure for which building plans have been approved; the shop size may not exceed 36 m²; and provision should be made for off-street parking, of which there is none. Had the business sold liquor, it would have been compelled to cease trading or operate covertly. Instead, the main business challenges as reported by shopkeepers are crime and xenophobic attitudes. According to the property owner, the shopkeepers get harassed on a regular basis by children and drunk men; whereas the children are attracted to the wide range of sweets available in the shop (and then haggle with the shopkeepers over the price or number of sweets), drunks go to the shop to purchase cheap cigarettes and after lighting-up claim that they had purchased an alternative (and more expensive) brand. The property owner is called to intercede in these conflicts. The shopkeepers have been confronted by thieves on several occasions. There is a security company's (ADT) sign on the shop, which indicates that the business owners have sought to contract private security services.

The state of criminality within the spaza sector has prompted the securitisation of these businesses. In places such as Delft South, few shops permit customers to enter the premises and browse the goods. In response to the high crime levels, a number of architectural modifications are evident. Doors have been securely protected by burglar bars and windows are concealed with steel mesh, with the serving hatch constructed as an extruding, downward sloping 'trunk' cage through which transactions are conducted. These serving trunks resemble a peephole with the opening approximately the size of a loaf of bread. The trunk and its downward architecture are intended to prevent robbers from pointing a gun at the shopkeeper, simultaneously allowing him an opportunity to take refuge by crouching below the counter (Figure 8.10).

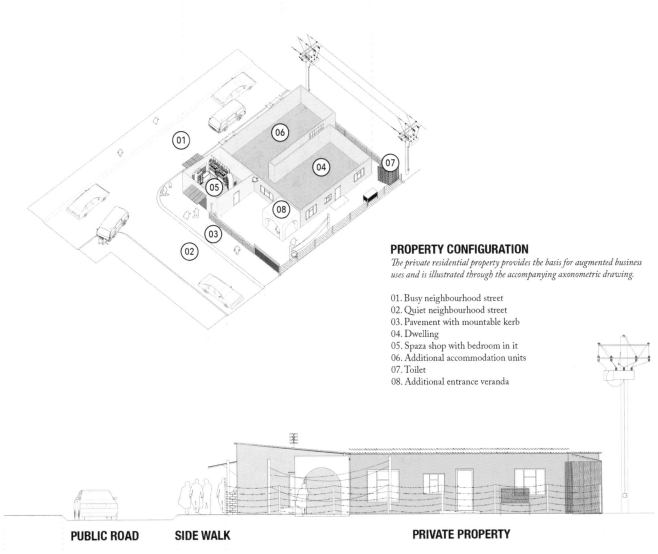

PROPERTY CONFIGURATION

The private residential property provides the basis for augmented business uses and is illustrated through the accompanying axonometric drawing.

01. Busy neighbourhood street
02. Quiet neighbourhood street
03. Pavement with mountable kerb
04. Dwelling
05. Spaza shop with bedroom in it
06. Additional accommodation units
07. Toilet
08. Additional entrance veranda

PUBLIC ROAD   **SIDE WALK**   **PRIVATE PROPERTY**

FIGURE 8.9 Photograph analysis and axonometric drawings illustrating the spatial components of the spaza shop and its relationship to the trading environment and residential property

FIGURE 8.10 Spaza shop with 'trunk' security feature protecting the shopkeeper from armed robberies, creating conditions of minimal social interaction between shopkeeper and customer

In addition, the trunk helps to minimise shop-theft by customers. Sadly, these adaptations underline the trend of depersonalisation of the relationship between shopkeeper and customer. No longer can customers see the face of the store attendant and engage in face-to-face conversation. Interpersonal communication is minimised, while the terms of trade are reduced to a crude exchange: money for goods.

Shopping malls, supermarkets and wholesalers

There are no historical precedents to shopping malls in townships. As we have noted in Chapter 4, the urban spatial design was informed by the objective to separate residential areas (townships) from business and commercial areas to be situated outside townships. From the early 1990s and advancing on the success of the Maponya Mall in Soweto, property investors (including JSE-listed entities) began to acquire land to establish shopping malls within townships on the periphery of settlements where land was available (Battersby & Peyton 2014). Prior to these investments, township residents were compelled to 'out-shop'; in other words, to purchase from shops situated outside of one's immediate residential area (Strydom 2011). In our nine South African sites, shopping malls and their accompanying supermarkets have been established in Browns Farm (Philippi), Delft South, Ivory Park, KwaMashu, Tembisa and Vrygrond. Malls provide township consumers with access to a range of products and services previously unavailable in the townships, through widening opportunities for corporatised consumption in fast-food, clothing, grocery items and leisure activities.

Mall expansion has been rapid, especially in townships where there is undeniable consumer demand for supermarkets and formal retailers. Over the period 1994 to 2012,

Battersby (2017) identified a 264% increase in the number of supermarkets in Cape Town against a population increase of 146%. In the period 2012 to 2017, the trend has continued, with 20 new supermarkets established by Pick n Pay and Shoprite alone in Cape Town, with 13 situated in malls located in townships. This expansion of malls, in particular, provides a mechanism for corporate businesses to establish a foothold in the township market. It is important to note that few corporate retailers have ventured onto the township high street. The shopping mall concept derives from the North American model of a retail island and its application in the township contexts spatially isolates micro-enterprises through the privatised control of public space within the mall. None of the malls in our sites accommodated township businesses.

South Africa's corporate retailers (Shoprite, Pick n Pay, SPAR and Massmart) in collaboration with property developers have each sought to expand their retail presence in the townships, offering many foods and beverages that were once adequately supplied by township micro-enterprises, including fresh meat, fruit and vegetables, bread and baked goods, and liquor. Most township malls contain a carefully configured suite of retailer lessees, usually with a single supermarket as the anchor tenant. Within the mix of tenants, there is commonly a liquor store (owned by the anchor supermarket chain), banks, clothes retailers and various fast-food outlets. The malls themselves as well as the majority of the retailer tenants are owned by JSE-listed corporates, with the supermarkets dominating the retail opportunities. To appease these powerful tenants, property developers have been complicit in permitting supermarket monopolisation (over food and liquor) within the mall, providing rental units at a minimum size affordable to established businesses only and imposing onerous lease conditions on tenants. These strategies prevent all but the most prosperous (or politically connected) township entrepreneurs from operating a business within a mall. As such, the profits generated within township malls get extracted from the township in a process which equates to a transfer of wealth from micro-enterprises to corporate shareholders.

The shopping mall impact on the township economy is poorly understood. It is claimed that malls significantly undermine business opportunities for informal micro-enterprises (Crush & Frayne 2011b), although other scholars point out the scale of impact is uneven and may benefit township businesses positioned to gain from increased foot traffic (Madlala 2015; Strydom 2015). The research on this subject has flagged food security concerns, including the 'food desertification' of impacted neighbourhoods through the elimination of informal food retailers (Pulker 2016). Our own investigations indicate that while shopping malls spatially exclude informal traders, their development does not necessarily eradicate opportunities for street traders situated outside the malls or residential businesses in adjacent neighbourhoods (Charman, Bacq & Brown 2019). On public land outside malls, including pavements and street verges, traders are marginalised in the sense that their land-use rights are insecure and business activities are in contravention of municipal by-laws. Some informal micro-enterprises in the high street adjacent to malls and neighbourhood localities are nevertheless able to sustain operations through providing services that are spatially more accessible and convenient in terms of the time of trade or speed of transaction, with product offerings and scale responsive to demands. Shoppers are unlikely to enter a shopping mall to purchase a single item for immediate use, such as a cellular airtime voucher, a piece of fruit or a cigarette. In weighing up the effect of supermarkets on township businesses, it is important to note that survivalist businesses have been differently impacted. Informalist businesses and larger spaza shops have been less affected, but in our field interviews, survivalists spoke of the amplified competition of supermarkets and bigger spaza shops. When asked about the main barrier to growing his business, one such shopkeeper replied: '*foreign run spazas and the malls that government placed in townships'* (2/1279/M/nd). His business was situated in close walking distance to a newly opened mall within our KwaMashu site. Nineteen other similarly situated shopkeepers bemoaned the impact of this mall and the anchor supermarket on their business. A female shopkeeper spoke pessimistically about the prospects for micro-enterprises such as hers: *'the Pick 'n Pay nearby will kill small shops as they have huge purchasing power to sell at lower prices'* (2/1681/F/nd). Even immigrant shopkeepers complained of the heightened competition, saying: *'Pick n Pay is giving us a problem, selling bread at R5. People are just running away to buy there. After just one day we are feeling bad. Pick n Pay also sells 2l Coke for R10'* (2/1811/M/nd).

The inequality between supermarkets and micro-enterprises is heightened by policies which effectively informalise township businesses. Township entrepreneurs face a distinct disadvantage in seeking to formalise their business as a result of their weak financial position, the complexities of regulatory barriers and profound land-use obstacles. In the next chapter, we will describe the predicament of liquor traders who are excluded from obtaining licences due to the strictures of land use. These strictures are no obstacle to mall developers who have the financial resources (and political influence) to navigate swiftly through municipal planning processes and obtain, for example, commercial land use in residential sites. Once land is rezoned, notes Battersby (2017), mall developers are not required to engage in processes of public participation and are usually able to obtain planning approval without undertaking a socio-economic impact assessment.

To illustrate this inequality of opportunity, consider the case of the Capricorn Square Shopping Mall (see Figure 8.11).

FIGURE 8.11 The Capricorn shopping mall
Note: The mall adheres to common spatial format: corporate fast food is situated at the entrances, whilst a single supermarket dominates the mall, targeting the low LSM market for the grocery trade, and also retailing liquor via a separate outlet.

The Capricorn mall, which is situated adjacent to Vrygrond in Cape Town, has a Pick n Pay supermarket as its anchor tenant; also within the mall, Pick n Pay also operates the exclusive liquor store (in addition to having an in-store wine retail licence) and a clothing store. The mall hosts a range of corporate and national chain stores that compete with township food services; these include McDonalds, Kentucky Fried Chicken, Pie City, Romans Pizza and Zebros. In the neighbouring Vrygrond site, we conducted interviews with 89 liquor retailers of whom the great majority operate informally and illegally. Although 33 of the businesses had endeavoured to regularise their business, only one had successfully obtained a liquor licence. The unsuccessful applicants, having revealed themselves to the authorities in the licensing process, reported subsequent high incidences of police raids, resulting in businesses downsizing and operating covertly. In this environment of police harassment, the mall liquor outlet has (unwittingly) ended up as a major supplier to the small shebeens in Vrygrond, with runners sent to the store to ferry the liquor back to the shebeen via shopping trolleys and wheelie bins. Had township liquor retailers been permitted to formalise, these businesses might have been able to secure upstream supply agreements and thus retain a greater share of the circulation of profits within the Vrygrond economy. As a further possible mall impact, it is worth noting that of our nine South African sites, Vrygrond recorded the least number of township takeaway businesses per 100 households (0.71 versus an average of 1.97).

Wholesalers and marketers have initiated strategies to capture shelf space in the spaza market, especially the food segment in which shoppers have strong brand loyalties. One of the main approaches has been to support spaza shopkeepers to obtain bulk discounts, using direct marketing and/or digital platforms. Using direct marketing, wholesalers have sought to supply shops with monthly specials and food hampers, usually comprising five products: refined white maize meal, refined wheat bread flour, white rice, white sugar and cooking oil. Hampers are usually sold at month end and vary in product size and brands. Charman et al. (2019) have argued that in order to access this competitive advantage, the shopkeepers have to enter into a partnership arrangement with the suppliers. In terms of these partnership 'agreements', the wholesaler produces a flyer each month of the product/price specials obtainable from the shop, while the shop must commit to retail the products at the price and sizes advertised. In Philippi, all the shopkeepers who had entered into these agreements were South Africans, whereas the immigrant shops sold their own hampers. As Charman et al. (2019) point out, the wholesalers wield power in these supplier agreements as these large businesses determine the brands, the composition of the hampers, set the prices and specify other products to be promoted, pressurising the shopkeeper to maintain stock that he/she would otherwise not purchase. In the cases which these researchers studied, the wholesaler's name is absent on all of the flyers.

Supply partnership such as the one described above permits spaza shops to remain competitive against supermarkets, though the profits to be made in selling food are comparatively lower than with non-food items. The benefit of these agreements accrues disproportionally to the wholesalers and JSE-listed food producers, including the major role-players of Pioneer Foods and Tiger Brands. By engaging in these strategies, corporates have sought to utilise informality in stealth as an effective 'route to market' with minimal investments. In concealing their name from flyers, for example, formal businesses knowingly supply products as well as dispensing equipment (such as coolers) and marketing services to shops that operate informally, and in many instances, illegally. Spaza shops provide a supply pipeline for selling cheap goods into the township, both those produced legally within the corporate sector and those supplied illegally by informalists. Both corporate and informalist suppliers gain from informality, with the informal relationship shielding them from the risks arising from a retail model wherein the business is non-compliant with the law, where customers receive no proof of purchase, where product sell-by dates are less monitored by the state, and where grey market, contraband and counterfeit items are more prevalent.

Outlook

Because of their origins as a pioneering black businesses, akin to incubators of township entrepreneurship, the state has adopted a light-touch approach to the regulation of the spazas. In terms of the Businesses Act (No. 71 of 1991),, shopkeepers are required to adhere to municipal land-use restrictions and comply with food safety and environmental hygiene regulations where the business stocks and trades perishable products. Yet these regulatory stipulations are rarely enforced. In the context of weak state control, the sector has undergone a profound transition resulting in the near disappearance of family-run small shops.

At the neighbourhood level, the transformation of the spaza sector has been engineered by a new class of informalist entrepreneurs who have profited from informality and capitalised on weak regulatory enforcement. In addition, the competitiveness of these businesses differs from the traditional spaza shops in three respects: first, the business operates through ethnic (commonly immigrant) networks to achieve scale in procurement and thus reduce wholesale prices; second, the business has access to subservient and hardworking labour; and third, these businesses have comparatively greater access to cheap products which, apart from groceries, include grey market and contraband cigarettes and counterfeit goods. Such cheap goods are in high demand.

Weak competitors, in particular most of the survivalists, have withered under the combined competition of spaza informalists and supermarkets. Unable to compete on price, service or scale of operations, survivalists have nevertheless continued in business by shifting to less competitive activities, including the preparation and sale of takeaway food and selling liquor (invariably on an informal and illegal basis). The closure of so great a number of South African-run spaza shops was (initially) disruptive for local communities and especially the women shopkeepers that once characterised this sector and personalised trade. The changing of ownership has brought about a decline in personal ties between store-keepers and communities as shop ownership changed and store employees are regularly rotated between the different retail outlets. It is true that xenophobic tensions amplified in response to the establishment of the first immigrant shops. To the present time, there are regular media reports of attacks on immigrant businesses and spaza shops in particular, though in some cases this use of violence relates to entrepreneurial struggles (forms of violent entrepreneurship) between shops competing over neighbourhood markets. Residents have largely come to accept the place of immigrant shops and certainly value their service (as they are usually open for trade, mainly well stocked and offer competitive pricing).

Spaza retailing is now dominated by larger businesses (or 'spazarettes'). In terms of food supply, however, the lion's share of the market in sites with close access to malls has been captured by supermarkets which control around three-quarters of township household food purchases (Battersby 2017; Charman et al. 2019). Now supermarkets are facing increasing competition from spaza informalist businesses, whose scale of operations has increased in size, with 'mini-market' type retailers emerging (Alcock 2018). Other corporates, and wholesalers in particular are developing routes to market through directly supplying spazas, particularly in the provision of month-end hampers and product specials. Digital supply platforms may bring greater efficiencies to these business relationships, though it is premature to make a judgement. Having fought so hard to capture the township spaza market, it is unlikely that informalist entrepreneurs will surrender their gains to corporates. Instead, we predict a strengthening of ethnic supply networks with informalist wholesalers taking the competition upstream. Proponents of the transformation to the spaza sector point to the diverse range of grocery products now available at the neighbourhood level as well as the price reductions arising from intensified competition. These are indeed important benefits to economically marginalised communities.

From a developmental perspective, the transformation in grocery retailing has not resulted in wider economic gains. The profits from supermarkets, wholesalers and immigrant-run spazas are repatriated away from the township. Informalist spaza shops provide no employment to local residents. As spaza shops are able to operate informally, there has been no need to invest in new business infrastructure in the manner witnessed in Eveline Street. Instead, many of these businesses operate from single-room shops, with the business relocating at short notice. Of the 304 spaza shops in our dataset that rent their business premises (for which we have data), the average rental income was R1 300 pm. This represents an insubstantial benefit to the property owners, given that most of these shops were able to generate in excess of R20 000 in profit pm. The original spaza shopkeepers recognised the need to share opportunities with other businesses, particularly house shops and street traders. The new spaza shops directly compete with these micro-enterprises, selling fruit and vegetables, frozen meat, and takeaway foods, three products in which survivalists are (were) active. Informalist spaza shops along with supermarkets and wholesalers have redirected profits away from the township economy, substantially lessening the availability of capital for reinvestment in local business that may otherwise further contribute towards growth and employment generation.

9

DRINKING VENUES AND THE LEISURE ECONOMY

In this chapter, we illuminate the contrasting outcome of South Africa's township shebeens in relation to the transformation engendered in Namibia's Eveline Street bars.

CHAPTER 9

Drinking venues and the leisure economy

Taverns and shebeens are businesses that sell liquor and provide drinking venues; whereas the former are legally licensed, the latter are not. The word 'shebeen' is of Irish origin which, presumably through its application in early industrial settings in places such as the Witwatersrand, became a colloquial term for an unlicensed and unregulated business that sells liquor and provides a social space for its consumption. In scale terms, the liquor sector is a prominent component of the township economy, second only to food retailing in terms of number and accessibility of retail outlets. We identified 2 402 micro-enterprises over the nine South African sites which sold liquor products – 23.7% of the entire census. Liquor retailers comprise home sellers, spaza outlets, restaurants, shebeens and taverns. These businesses serve as an anchor for a wider 'leisure economy' comprising bars, restaurants, street food establishments, entertainers and musicians, sex workers and businesses providing allied services such as car guards, car washers and hair salons.

The role of liquor and drinking venues in townships is a subject of policy controversy and political concern. Under apartheid, liquor laws and policies adhered to racialised objectives which included the intentional exclusion of black persons from legitimate rights to sell liquor and operate drinking venues (for historical perspectives, see Ambler & Crush 1992; La Hausse 1988; Mager 1999, 2004). With the demise of apartheid, the past injustice of preventing black South Africans from trading liquor was recognised and although the state has sought to institute norms and standards to enable micro-enterprises to trade legally, the regulatory mechanisms still effectively preclude the vast majority of participants. This can be attributed to an enduring moral panic around liquor, labour and morality. Post 1994, the constitution allocated the responsibility for regulating liquor retailing to provincial governments, while affirming the role of national government in the setting of norms and standards and the regulation of large-scale manufacturing and distribution. Each of the nine provincial administrations are now responsible for instituting liquor laws. While there are differences in the policies and laws between the nine provinces, the dominant policy narrative with respect to the township leisure economy has been on restricting informal retailers through imposing stringent conditions for the allocation of licences, a subject widely researched (see Charman, Herrick & Petersen 2014; Herrick 2014; Petersen & Charman 2010; Smit 2014). Since township liquor traders have practical incentives to regularise their business, including gaining access to formal supply chains and credit, and a reduction in the risks of law enforcement, and because many businesses have unsuccessfully sought to acquire licences, we have argued that their informality is involuntary or 'enforced' (Charman, Petersen, & Piper 2013).

The subject of township liquor regulation provides a sharp insight into the limits of state control over informality. In most conventional theories of business practice, informality is attributable to the non-enforcement of regulations on enterprises that are non-compliant, evade the law or operate illegally. The enforcement of regulation would then either compel enterprises to become compliant or, as Kanbur (2009; 2012) describes in the case of informal micro-enterprises in India, to adjust operations (in this case reducing the number of employees) so as to avoid regulatory control. The idea that more enforcement will compel liquor traders to either become compliant or adjust their operations (moving out of selling liquor) sits at the heart of state efforts to control informal liquor trading. Yet the theory falters against lived reality. Our research clearly shows that enforcement does not produce compliance and instead compels businesses to adjust their operations in order to minimise the risks of detection. As we have argued (Charman, Petersen & Piper 2013), since compliance is practically impossible, most shebeeners have chosen to 'manage intensified law enforcement impacts' (p. 4) rather than surrender their business and livelihood; put succinctly (1/229/M/65); '*I no longer want to sell liquor… [but] it's just a way of survival.*' Instead of seeking to formalise township liquor trade and institute regulatory control, state action has perpetuated the 'informalisation' of the sector, keeping micro-enterprises small and under-capitalised. In this chapter, we will illuminate the contrasting outcome of South Africa's township shebeens in relation to the transformation engendered in Namibia's Eveline Street through the application of the Business Corridors initiative.

Our analysis is set at four spatial gradients: one, the city-wide level in which we contrast the policy implications of township micro-enterprises with the leisure economy of the CBD; two, the small-area level at which we examine the varieties of liquor retailers and discuss their spatial distribution; three, the level of particular venues where our analysis shows how purposeful interventions, including the arrangement of objects and architecture, respond to risks and influence the social orientation of the venue; and four, the interpersonal relationships which constitute an infrastructure of social support and resistance. In focusing on the situation of shebeens, our analysis juxtaposes the regulatory power of the state against the collective power of shebeen owners to resist policies that perpetuate their economic exclusion. The context in which these opposing powers engage in struggle is framed by spatial legacy of apartheid, a moral panic on the role of liquor consumption in fuelling social unruliness, and the dominance of formal business in the manufacturing and distribution of products, such that a disproportional share of profits flow from township consumers to corporate investors.

Liquor regulation and moral panic

Shebeens are an iconic component of township life and culture, having had an influence which has long made their governance particularly fraught with contradictions. It is argued that shebeens have their roots in the emergence of a 'proletarianised' urban working class, first in the industrial economies on the Witwatersrand where some of the first shebeeners were white immigrants. The emergence of these micro-enterprises in the township economy is largely due to the endeavours of unemployed women (Rogerson & Hart 1986). Spatially restricted to residential ghettos, women were compelled into generating a livelihood within the home environment, with liquor trading providing an accessible point of entry into business. Until the late 1980s when the apartheid system began to crumble, township residents were forbidden from socialising outside the township, while within the township the only legal drinking venues were municipal beer halls that initially brewed and sold sorghum beer (La Hausse 1988). Beer halls were designed to provide municipalities with a source of revenue and simultaneously control township drinking practices. Figure 9.1. is of a disused beer hall in KwaMashu, spatially situated within a cluster of municipal buildings, located on a ridge within a township away from residential homes.

The emergence of shebeens in defiance of spatial and social objectives to control drinking offered township residents important sites for fomenting opposition to exclusion while nurturing cultural and social bonds. Just as drinking venues provided solace to the European working class from the hardship and drudgery of industrial labour (Jayne, Holloway & Valentine 2006), shebeens provided township residents with a space for socialisation freed of the constraints of the hyper-regulated and racialised working environment. As a space of struggle against exclusion, discrimination and hierarchy, shebeens engendered the production of culture and political debates away from the institutionalised control of the state, the church and the patriarchal family. In his study of indigenous music, Coplan (2008) notes the contribution of public drinking venues towards the development, refinement and translation of dance, theatre and music into modern expressions. As public places in which residents could meet after hours, exchange ideas and plot strategy, shebeens fulfilled an important role in the intellectual formulation of resistance towards apartheid.

From the late 1950s, as the pace of urbanisation intensified, micro-enterprises selling liquor grew in scale and sophistication to provide residents with not simply alternative social spaces to the municipal beer halls, but access to commercially produced liquor, including bottled beer. The role of shebeens in providing commercial liquor constituted

FIGURE 9.1 A defunct municipal beer hall, KwaMashu

a defeat of apartheid policies which had sought to prescribe the kind of liquor that black citizens could consume. This defeat was achieved in consort with (large scale) formal liquor producers and distributors who saw shebeens as a gateway in their pursuit of a 'route to market'. An important role player in this respect was the SAB, whose willingness to supply the township with bottled beer opened up a market of immense size (taking profits from the state brewers of sorghum beer) and enabled SAB, via the shebeen distribution channel, to monopolise the township beer market (Mager 2010; Tsoeu 2009).

As spaces of socialisation and resistance, shebeens have engendered new forms of drinking culture, which, in turn evoked societal concerns towards drunkenness in general and the hyper-masculinity of male drinkers in particular (Mager 1999; 2004). As in European working-class communities, excessive drinking became ingrained in everyday township life from the earliest days of urban settlements. To their critics, shebeens were responsible for producing drunkenness and disorderliness, outcomes which were said to impact on the drinker and residents in equal measure. The association of liquor with violence and crime sit at the heart of moral criticism towards shebeens and continue to inform much of the advocacy for spatial prohibition as a means to reduce liquor supply. At the vanguard of the prohibitionist campaign, public health scholars (in what Jane, Valentine and Holloway, 2012, describe as an epistemology of 'surveillance medicine' [p. 5]) have sought to characterise township liquor-serving venues (taverns and shebeens) as risk-laden spaces, indeed 'sex venues' where 'back rooms, corners and adjacent buildings, shacks or lots afford locations for sex' (Kalichman, Simbayi, Vermaak, Jooste & Cain 2008, p. 59). While certain shebeens and aspects of socialisation may heighten sexual activities, promote hyper-masculinity and foster conflict, literature whose objectives are to vilify shebeens oversimplify their complex (and contradictory) role in both drinking and socialisation. In an investigation of shebeens as sites of risk for violence against women, researchers found that those women who patronised the smaller, least formal micro-enterprises, regarded these venues as having lower risks, with the close-knit environment offering 'potential protection' (Watt et al. 2012, p. 1276). In support of this notion, our research found that taverns and shebeens do enhance risks to both drinkers and the broader neighbourhood, but simultaneously fulfil important roles in building connections between people, process and places that can minimise these risks. As Rogerson and Hart (1986) stressed in their research on shebeens in Soweto, undertaken in the mid-1980s at the height of the anti-apartheid struggle, 'to regard the shebeen merely as an institution for the supply of illicit liquor is to eschew [their] vital social and cultural role' (p. 156).

Political, social and academic concerns on the excessiveness of drinking in township life has engendered a 'moral panic' which has justified apartheid-era thinking on the need to control the supply of liquor into the township. These ideas have been translated into a regulatory framework which through the use of licensing as a political-legal tool (Valverde 2003) effectively disables liquor traders from being able to formalise and regularise. Although each province has taken different roads to develop their policies, most have converged on the path set by the Western Cape Provincial Government under the leadership of Helen Zille. In her ascent to power, first as the Mayor of CoCT and then as Provincial Premier, Zille and her party, the Democratic Alliance (DA), mobilised populist resentment against crime. Through problematising drugs and liquor as an interconnected root cause, Zille focused on shebeens as a low-hanging target of her administration's 'war on drugs'. One of the first steps in this 'war' was the revision of the CoCT's integrated land-use management scheme so as to disallow township residents the right to operate a shebeen from their residential house as a 'right of use'. The next major step in this 'war' was the passage into law of the Western Cape Liquor Act 2010 (WCLA).

The WCLA did away with a previous concession to township liquor traders, now requiring all liquor traders (regardless of size or spatial situation) to obtain a liquor licence via a highly bureaucratic process which entailed compliance with municipal regulations. To acquire a liquor licence, applicants had to overcome an array of complex hurdles, which includes acquiring land title, having an approved building plan, obtaining appropriate zoning (in other words rezoning their land to business use), gaining 'community' and police consent to operate the business, and adhering to operating times specified by the CoCT. The great majority of township entrepreneurs have neither the financial means nor the legal skills to navigate through this web of legislation and would, as the Zille administration planned, either be forced to stop trading or adjust their business away from selling liquor products. The complexity of the land-use system hurdles to convert residential land to business land are near insurmountable. In addition, the WCLA in concert with the CoCT restricted the operating hours for township businesses, such that off-licence retailers had to close their doors at 6:00 p.m. and on-licence venues at 11:00 p.m. These represent peak times for business, taking into account that public transport reliant wage earners spend most daylight hours out of the township at their places of work. For these reasons alone, most township liquor retailers opted to trade informally, thus embracing the risks of an illegal activity.

At the time that the WCLA was enacted into law, there were just over 8 000 liquor licences throughout the Western Cape Province, yet merely 1 169 (14.5%) had been awarded to black entrepreneurs. In spatial terms, the discrepancy was extreme. While the Cape Town CBD had 1 232 licence holders for a residential population of 206 805 in 2011, there were a paltry 177 licences awarded to businesses in the district of Mitchells Plain which encompasses the City main townships and a population of 1 112 650 (Charman & Govender, in press). Soon after the passage of the WCLA, supporting legislation would amend trading times for businesses in the CBD and historic white neighbourhoods to permit extended trading hours, concessions that would not be afforded to the township. Though framed as a measure to address moral outrage towards drinking, the WCLA would solidify spatial inequality and racial exclusion, disadvantaging micro-enterprises while privileging opportunities for those large businesses such as supermarkets to overcome the hurdles. Far from reducing the supply of liquor, Zille's war on drugs would simply shift opportunities from the informal to the formal sector, with a significant part of the 'flow' (following Lawhon's 2013 use of the idea) of liquor into the township now via supermarket liquor stores.

In thinking through the implications of 'enforced informalisation', it should be recognised that most of the liquor sold in the township is manufactured by formal businesses, the bulk by the global corporates Anheuser-Busch (ABInBev) (having acquired ownership of SAB), Distell Group Holdings (DGH), Heineken South Africa (an emerging role player) and Diageo South Africa, and legally purchased through wholesalers and distributors. The 'flow' within the supply chain thus entails a movement from the formal economy to the informal. Because retail outlets are widely available at the neighbourhood level, competitiveness necessitates a low mark-up on liquor products, except in credit sales where risks are included in the price. Hence the bulk of the profits from township drinking accumulate to corporates (who manufacture the products) and distributors, who include larger taverns. Furthermore, since the licensing system focuses on the retailer who alone bears responsibility if trading illegally or in contravention of the regulations, manufacturers and distributors are able to go about their business uncommitted to supporting township businesses to achieve formalisation, freeing them of responsibility for the consequences of informalisation or harmful drinking.

Scope and scale of retailers

Our research identified five distinct forms of liquor retailers: i. taverns (licensed businesses, the majority of which are limited to sell liquor for on-site consumption) (Figure 9.2), ii. shebeens (unlicensed businesses, which sell liquor for consumption both off and on site), iii. spaza-shebeens (unlicensed small shops that sell basic provisions and liquor for off-site consumption); iv. micro-enterprises that manufacture traditional beer/concoctions for on site-consumption, and v. occasional home-based sellers (Figure 9.3).

FIGURE 9.2 Warehoused stock highlights the role of taverns in onward supply to shebeens

FIGURE 9.3 A residential house which openly operates as a small shebeen

Of the 2 402 micro-enterprises we identified that trade liquor, the most ubiquitous are the home-sellers' category; these are not micro-enterprises in the strict sense, but should best be thought of as 'livelihoods' strategies that are largely pursued by middle-aged women and female pensioners to supplement household income. Their businesses provide an accessible source of cold beer in a social context in which (unlike middle-class suburbs) drinkers are unwilling to store liquor at home, in part out of concern that the liquor will be consumed by household members in their absence. In the site of Tembisa, we identified 577 liquor-selling outlets of which 402 fell into the home-seller sub-category. The spatial distribution is shown in Figure 9.4. Such a myriad of beer sellers enables residents to purchase 'on demand' for home consumption, avoiding altogether the public drinking environment.

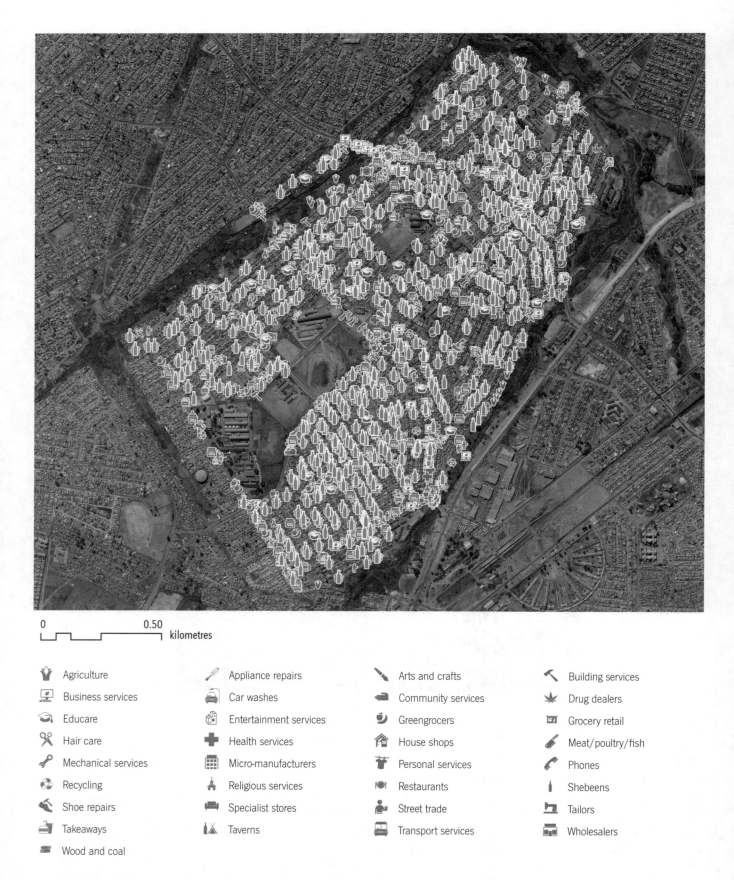

0   0.50
⌐_⌐_⌐_⌐ kilometres

Ⱳ	Agriculture	🖊	Appliance repairs	➘	Arts and crafts	⟍	Building services
🖳	Business services	🚗	Car washes	◗	Community services	🌿	Drug dealers
◔	Educare	🎨	Entertainment services	♨	Greengrocers	▭	Grocery retail
✂	Hair care	✚	Health services	👕	House shops	✎	Meat/poultry/fish
🔑	Mechanical services	🏢	Micro-manufacturers	👔	Personal services	📞	Phones
♻	Recycling	⛪	Religious services	🍴	Restaurants	⚊	Shebeens
👟	Shoe repairs	🛋	Specialist stores	👤	Street trade	⬏	Tailors
🥘	Takeaways	⛺	Taverns	🚌	Transport services	🏬	Wholesalers
🪵	Wood and coal						

FIGURE 9.4 The spatial distribution of liquor outlets is pervasive in Tembisa

Home sellers acquire their liquor products from taverns, while in informal settlements supply is obtained from larger shebeens. In our dataset, we interviewed 1 088 taverns and shebeens, of which only 163 (13%) had liquor licences. At the national scale, it is reported that there are about 25 000 taverns, whereas the number of shebeens are estimated at around 250 000 (see Charman, Petersen & Piper 2013). Tavern businesses are jealously targeted by the liquor corporates, notably ABInBev in South Africa and Namibian Breweries in Namibia, who provide material support in the process of obtaining a licence with the objective of securing long-term supply relationships. When a business obtains a liquor licence, corporate liquor manufacturers supply them with coolers (fridges) and branding (including painting the interior and exterior to align with product colours), provide a modicum of equipment and most importantly, extend the opportunity to obtain a direct supply and a line of credit. The business model, developed by SAB, is 'volume'-oriented, centred on the objective to maximise the sale of 750 ml bottles of beer (known as quarts) in cases of twelve bottles, wherein the bottles and crates are supplied on a returnable deposit. Supply agreements are usually subject to a minimum volume threshold and credit is tied to weekly sales targets. The business owner has little scope to influence the terms of trade and is subject to dictates on the price at which beer can be sold, the mixture of brands supplied, the presentation of liquor products and advertising in the venues. Taverns thus fulfil a role in the preservation of beer brands which gave credence to the idea of consumer choice in contrast to the near monopolisation of SAB in the township beer market. Throughout our interviews, criticisms of SAB were often aired. As put by one informant in KwaMashu: *'we are basically slaves for SAB because they don't help us as people who are pushing their brand'* (1/28/M/56), contrasting the township situation to liquor retailers in the suburbs who, in the eye of the informant, receive much support from SAB and are neither raided nor compelled to operate restrictive hours of trade. A common complaint was that SAB was active in building the supply network, but when the retailers get in trouble *'it's like they forget us'* (1/46/F/41).

The business model to supply taverns has been challenged in recent times as a consequence of consumers shifting their taste preferences towards premium beers, ready to drink liquor and spirit drinks. These products are accessible through supermarkets and in those taverns which target higher LSM consumers, whose number have undoubtedly grown but are still a minority. The working-class thirst for bulk, cheap beer continues to align with corporate interest, with ABInBev recently introducing 1 litre beer bottles to replace the 750 ml quarts and sustain the competitiveness of beer in price per unit terms. Industrial scale producers of cheap liquor, much of which is sold as 'flavoured alcohol beverages' under crude brands such as 'The Best' (Figure 9.5), have replicated the route-to-market model.

These liquor products (made under a legal technicality, though distributed illegally) are produced outside the township, but delivered directly to retailers. Their market entry has sought to beat the cheap wine and beer producers at their own game, selling large volume units of high strength liquor and cheap unit volume price. Producers of concoctions are another example of informalists; in this instance, these businesses operate outside the township and are mainly white South Africans with access to industrial-scale production facilities. They embrace informality as a strategy to produce and market liquor products of dubious quality (concoctions). Whereas the informalists make no pretence to support micro-enterprises, so too have corporates made minimal investment into the township economy. Apart from measures to sustain the supply chain or defend brands, corporates like ABInBev, DGH, Diageo and Namibian Breweries have (historically) made little or no investments into businesses to influence the drinking environment so as to minimise harms. Taking into consideration the 1 251 in-depth interviews we undertook, there was

FIGURE 9.5 Illegally distributed liquor concoctions are widely available from survivalist shebeens
Credit: Justin Patrick

scant evidence of brand-owner support, either within venues in terms of their infrastructure (such as improved toilets) or outside taverns in terms of street lighting, parking, facilities to manage litter and measures to reduce crime or disorderliness. Instead, corporate profit motives, through volume-driven sales, are aligned to the attainment of drunkenness.

The distribution of liquor retailers in townships indicates geographies of 'convenience and familiarity' (Charman, Herrick & Petersen 2014, p. 632), characteristics which reflect the localisation of demand and diversity of supply in terms of the uniqueness of venues as social spaces. The distribution of liquor retailers in Tembisa shows that liquor retailers are fairly evenly situated across the site; there is no agglomeration along high streets. Supply is determined by highly localised market dynamics, similar to the spaza sector, whereby outlets are positioned to serve a client base resident within a short walking distance, typically no longer than 10 minutes. Outlet density decreases in middle-class suburbs where public venues are virtually absent. In these neighbourhoods, many residents have vehicles by which they can access liquor outlets elsewhere, private recreational space within the property and greater freedom to store and consume liquor within the home setting. Such factors reduce the need for the kind of publicly accessible space afforded by shebeens. At the same time, the dormancy of a leisure economy within township high streets is an outcome of historical legacy (as a result of the tradition of socialising in local neighbourhood venues) and the policy barriers which have hindered business growth in these spatial localities.

From our dataset, we can discern the broad contours of township liquor retailers. Across both licenced and unlicensed categories, we learnt that the average age of entrepreneurs is 39, with the median length of time in business being four years. The longevity of liquor trading is significant given the perilousness of informal trade (with 86% of outlets being unlicensed). Around 42% of retailers sell only for off-site consumption. Just over half of taverns and shebeens (51%) are male-owned (in contrast to the mainly female home-sellers). Liquor trading in the nine South African sites is dominated by South African

FIGURE 9.6 Shebeen operated by African migrants, serving those cultural groups

entrepreneurs (92% of respondents), though immigrants also trade liquor in certain communities such as Imizamo Yethu and Ivory Park. A small number of immigrants have begun to operate legal taverns, though the licensing requirements technically limit this development to legal citizens; still, licences are sold informally (Figure 9.6).

About half of the persons we interviewed in liquor retail businesses reported that they employ at least one other person, in addition to casual labour services, for tasks such as cleaning, collecting stock and providing security. Using the volume of beer sold on a weekly basis as a proxy indicator of enterprise size, we differentiate the sector into three classes of business: micro-businesses selling less than five crates per week (33%), predominantly survivalists; small businesses selling more than five and less than 20 crates per week (46%); and medium-sized businesses selling more than 20 crates per week (21%). The 221 enterprises in the medium business category account for the bulk of volume sales, though, even in this segment, only around one third of businesses have liquor licences. It is mainly these larger businesses which corporate liquor companies have sought to incorporate within their supply chains. The small and micro-businesses often operate from shacks (54% of unlicensed outlets) with few assets. We identified a further 93 businesses (8% of total) that sold traditional (home-brewed) beer, the majority of which accommodate on-site consumption (Figure 9.7) and are run by women. Despite its indigenous roots, the state has never sought to nurture this artisanal industry to advantage the township brewers and their economic beneficiation.

On-consumption drinking venues are grounded in socialisation. Yet the investment in leisure facilities in venues is modest on the whole, especially in contrast to the leisure economy of Eveline Street. In our dataset, 27% of outlets have pool tables, 18% have juke boxes and 17% show satellite TV (DSTV). For licensed venues, the figures for pool tables increase modestly to 35% of venues, though the proportion of businesses with juke boxes and DSTV increases more substantially to 31% and 46% respectively. Taverns are important spaces for township residents to watch live sporting events which

FIGURE 9.7 Traditional beer being produced in barrels

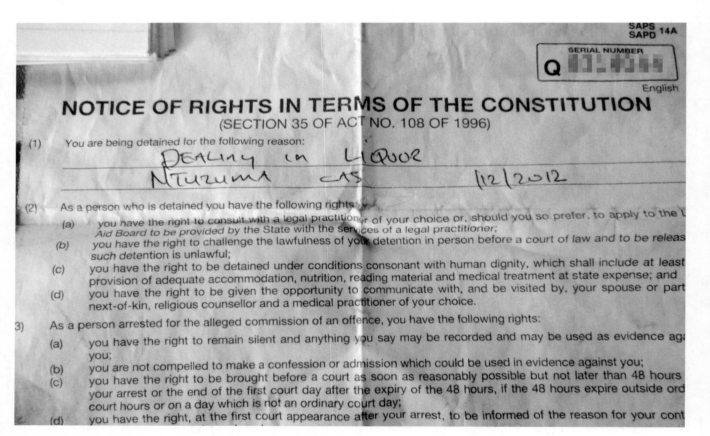

FIGURE 9.8 Notice of detention handed to a shebeener in KwaMashu

are only broadcast via subscription TV. Weekends are when most of the business (and socialisation) takes place with on-site consumption venues reporting less than 15% of their business Monday through to Thursday, after which sales intensify on Friday night, Saturday throughout the day and on Sunday afternoon.

The weekend period of heightened bar drinking is when taverns and shebeens contribute most to external impacts, including harms resulting from violence and drunken disorderliness. A high proportion of these impacts occur not in the venue, but in the street outside. For justifiable reasons and during the weekend periods, venues are heavily policed. Just over 42% of taverns and 49% of shebeens reported having been subjected to police raids in the past year with roughly one third of shebeen owners reporting that their business was closed through police action. Police action is commonly not directed at reducing risks such as fights, but at closing businesses that trade illegally or are non-compliant with the licence conditions (see Figure 9.8).

As a consequence of the legal mandate of the police to monitor the sector from a licensing perspective, shebeens and their owners are systematically subject to harassment, stock confiscation, detention and prosecution, which includes fines and imprisonment. Selling liquor without a licence is illegal and the prosecuted shebeen owners receive a criminal record which in turn renders them ineligible to apply for or possess a liquor licence. As most shebeen owners are permitted the option of paying an admission of guilt fine in terms of the 1977 Criminal Procedures Act, thus avoiding detention in a police cell, thousands have accepted their guilt without knowing the implications or their constitutional rights. Throughout our research, liquor traders complained about the police. A tavern owner in Ivory Park bemoaned: '*I cannot understand why the police apply rules impartially. I have been fined for not having an entertainment licence, fined for not complying with health standards, fined based on new laws. I won't pay these fines because they are not reasonable and even the policemen who drink here (his tavern) support me*' (1/142/M/42). A shebeen owner in Vrygrond, who had been in business for over 17 years at the time of our interview, argued that while her shebeen had not been affected, most shebeens were systematically targeted, in contrast to the drug dens: '*the police don't bother us and they call us the old age home…[because] mainly women without husbands and some men come here to drink and keep each other company… we close early and don't sell illegal things like drugs…[whereas] these people [merchants] operate all hours of the day and are busy killing our children with what they are selling but they do not close the drug house*' (1/740/F/nd).

To minimise the risks of police raids, shebeen owners use age-old tactics such as hiding the liquor stocks off site, configuring the venues to avoid detection, and bribing the police. As one respondent acknowledged: '*I was raided three times, but I bribed them [the police] on all occasions…they just closed me down and no arrests were made*' (1/1196/F/nd). Importantly, our research also taught us that owners undertake a range of strategies of social and spatial control to mitigate harms among drinkers and prevent conflict with the community. In their most simple form, these strategies involve crude policing, as reported by a long-operating shebeen owner: '*though there is crime here [in the community] I have never experienced it myself because we use street justice in this place*' (1/58/F/52).

Sweet Home Farm

Our research found that the distribution of shebeen venues is considerably higher in informal settlements (slums) than formal settlements. For this reason, we turned to the informal settlement of Sweet Home Farm where we sought to understand the productive as well as contradictory and risk-related implications of drinking venues. Our micro-enterprise census in 2011 identified 109 shebeens in the site, reflecting the highest density of all the research sites. In the course of our interviews, we noted that different shebeens were configured to pursue very different business strategies, a differentiation which could be loosely categorised based on their interior spatial arrangement, relationship to place, service offering, client base and ecosystem of interdependent micro-enterprises such as bottle recyclers and fast-food sellers. We therefore undertook a closer examination of the interaction between objects, spaces, persons and practices in five different venues (see Charman, Petersen, & Govender 2014; Govender 2015). Our interest in the micro-context builds upon a foundation of social research which shows how context influences not simply the practice of drinking but the impacts of drinking, which in certain contexts can 'create social relationships and solidarities' in productive ways (Latham 2003, p. 1713) (see also Jayne, Valentine & Holloway, 2008).

Venue differentiation

We found that each shebeen caters to a unique market segment. An inventory audit revealed that satellite TVs, pool tables, juke boxes, type of liquor, variety and quantity of seating, size of establishment and the proprietor's business objectives all influence the nature of the shebeen and differentiate their service within the market.

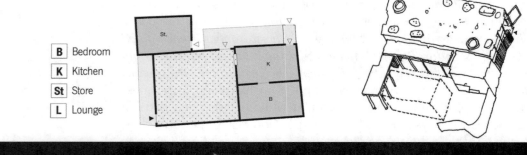

B	Bedroom
K	Kitchen
St	Store
L	Lounge

FIGURE 9.9 Image showing the veranda scene at night in a Drinkatainment shebeen

Note: The diagrams illustrate the architecture of the venue and the relationship between domestic and public spaces.

Across the spectrum, we focused on five characteristic types. The spatial layout of the five cases studies is analysed below.

The first type we described as 'drinkatainment' venues (Figure 9.9), borrowing from the term used to highlight the centrality of liquor in the night-time leisure economy in northern cities (Bell 2007). These venues targeted young patrons, both men and women, providing a range of entertainment including loud music, satellite TV and juke boxes, while selling a range of liquor products, enabling heavy drinking and hyper-sexualised socialisation.

The second type we characterised as conversational venues (Figure 9.10). These venues target elderly patrons but provide no entertainment apart from the opportunity to socialise, with socialisation grounded in conversation and singing (religious songs), selling beer and cheap wine or concoctions.

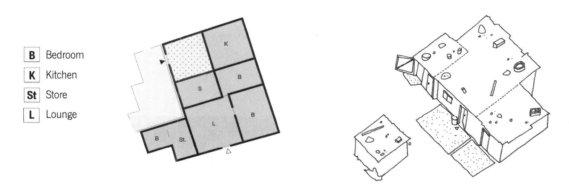

B	Bedroom
K	Kitchen
St	Store
L	Lounge

FIGURE 9.10 Image showing socialisation in a courtyard of a conversational shebeen

Note: The diagrams illustrate the architecture of the venue and the relationship between domestic and public spaces.

Our third type is neighbourhood venues (Figure 9.11). These shebeens are similar to the 'drinkatainment' venues but are differentiated in terms of their relationship with clients. The business targets a more gendered diversity of clients with most patrons known personally to the owner. The venue is accessible to users throughout the day; during the daytime, for example, it provides a public space and entertainment venue (with equipment such as pool tables and jukeboxes) around which socialisation occurs and in which drinking fulfils a relatively minor function.

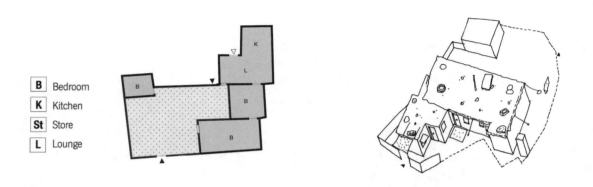

B Bedroom
K Kitchen
St Store
L Lounge

FIGURE 9.11 Image showing the house interior of a neighbourhood shebeen and its serving hatch to the clients
Note: The diagrams illustrate the architecture of the venue and the relationship between domestic and public spaces.

Our fourth type is *iSloti* (slang, meaning to 'slot' a pool ball) venues (Figure 9.12). These shebeens target mature male patrons (and exclude women), with the aim of providing an intimate space of socialisation for men around a game of pool and modest consumption of liquor and where the pursuit of drunkenness is discouraged.

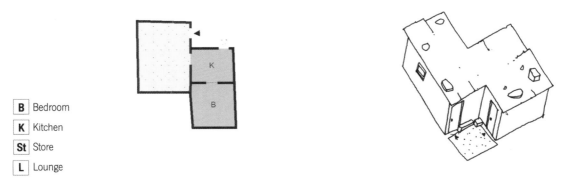

B Bedroom
K Kitchen
St Store
L Lounge

FIGURE 9.12 Image showing the interior of an *iSloti* shebeen centred around the pool table
Note: The diagrams illustrate the architecture of the venue and the relationship between domestic and public spaces.

We identify a fifth type which we describe as traditional venues (Figure 9.13). These businesses target elderly men (and women), serving traditional beer (*uMqombothi*) and bottled beer (but no other liquor). These venues are configured to facilitate the reproduction of traditional culture while the practices of drinking seek to reinforce solidarity/sharing, the connection with ancestors and rural roots and practices.

The people-centred architecture of the shebeen plays an important role in its sustainability. Through its construction technique and assemblage of commonly salvaged metal sheeting and timber planks, venues are structurally adaptable. The technology and materials afford dexterity to the construction process which can be altered at short notice by one or two persons. This enables the proprietor to adjust physical spaces to respond to any threat or opportunity, thus enhancing resilience. Some of the examples of these responses include the removal of a room to make way for more entertainment space; the

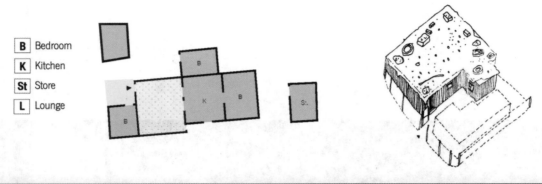

B	Bedroom
K	Kitchen
St	Store
L	Lounge

FIGURE 9.13 Image showing the interior of a traditional shebeen and the socialisation around the fireplace

Note: The diagrams illustrate the architecture of the venue and the relationship between domestic (private) and public spaces.

installation of security gates to prevent robberies; the construction of makeshift urinals and toilets; and the installation of ledges for drinks to prevent them from being spilt (which can result in conflict) or serving hatches which connect the venue to private rooms and thus permit the owner to maintain a rigid divide between public and private spaces.

Programmatic usage

These five types of liquor outlets demonstrate the complex and diverse range of drinking venues and challenge imagined stereotypes. While all shebeens enable liquor consumption and socialisation and harbour potential risks of violence and deviance, the shebeen owners actively manage these spaces to minimise risks.

CASE STUDY: *Louise's shebeen*

Louise, who operated a neighbourhood venue in Sweet Home Farm, maintained a constant vigil over activities within her venue and used management techniques as well as spatial devices to minimise conflict. Her business model was grounded on three strategies: first, she was able to draw members of her family into the business on a flexible basis, as need required; secondly, she had built informal networks with other businesses, including other shebeens from whom she obtained stock; and third, she had managed to create and sustain a social space where neighbours, friends and acquaintances could coalesce in social solidarity outside of the intensity of an informal settlement. If she senses a potential conflict situation within her venue, Louise immediately turns off the music and ceases serving customers. She often amended the architecture of the venue to re-influence social dynamics through altering the seating arrangement, adding shelves and windows, and changing internal partitions.

CASE STUDY: *Rosline's shebeen*

In a different example of shebeen management, Rosline, who operated a conversational venue, restricted her patrons to older men and permitted customers to purchase beer on credit so long as their wives gave authorisation, which she obtained by phoning them. This strategy ensured that she maintained a good relationship amongst a segment of the community.

While shebeens are a place of gathering, entertainment and business, they are simultaneously a private home. These seemingly opposing functions co-exist through the imposition of sophisticated control mechanisms, thresholds and unwritten rules for users to manage the interplay between public and private. In the case of Louise's venue, the carefully orchestrated arrangement of entrance, bedroom, kitchen, lounge, shebeen venue and courtyard establishes spatial rules and hierarchies. The kitchen serves both the shebeen and house. Through a hatch related to this space, Louise is able to regulate the atmosphere of the environment, controlling music and lighting, and serving patrons while having clear surveillance sightlines to entrances and the main shebeen space.

Depending on time of day, use and accessibility, the shebeen space and its related courtyards can be accessed by the greater public. Some spaces easily transition into a meeting space, made possible as a consequence of their facilitation of movement paths into the greater neighbourhood and from having open entranceways and seating (Figure 9.14). The space of the shebeen is permeable and connected to adjacent yards allowing children to run through the space or meet and play when desirable. With surveillance from operators, it is a safe and protected space.

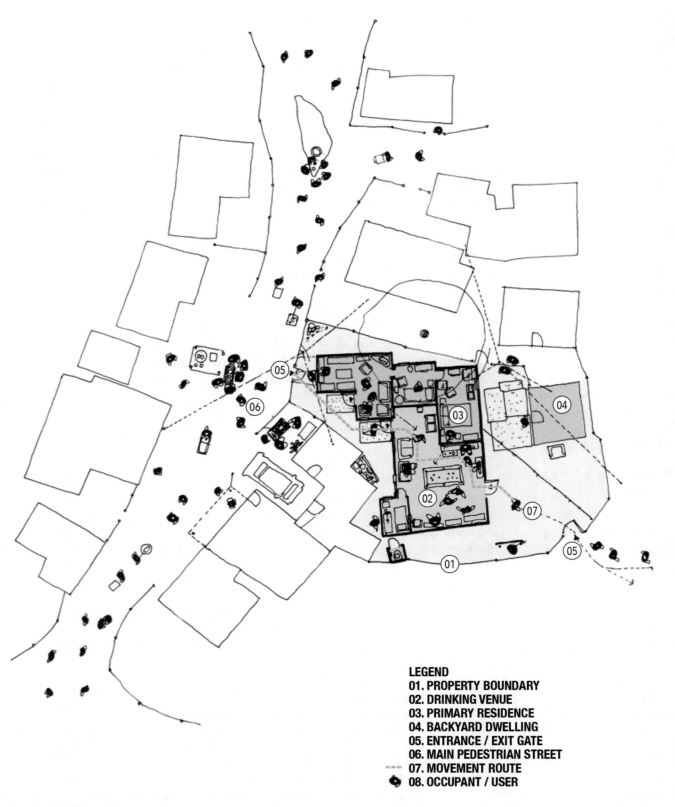

LEGEND
01. PROPERTY BOUNDARY
02. DRINKING VENUE
03. PRIMARY RESIDENCE
04. BACKYARD DWELLING
05. ENTRANCE / EXIT GATE
06. MAIN PEDESTRIAN STREET
07. MOVEMENT ROUTE
08. OCCUPANT / USER

FIGURE 9.14 Diagram illustrating the spatial connections of a shebeen to the interior yard and adjacent streets with the venue creating a pathway between different parts of the settlement

Resistance

Most shebeeners are able to resist and subvert the authority of the police through pre-emptive strategies such as buying small quantities of stock (thus reducing losses when the police raid), maintaining constant surveillance so as to allow the owner sufficient time to close the venue and hide, paying bribes to the police, hiding liquor stocks off site, situating the venue separate from their place of residence, locking the customers inside and forging agreements with neighbours around trading times. Yet the mandate for the police to raid shebeens has not simply shut down businesses but resulted in police brutality and fuelled corruption (Herrick & Charman 2013). In our survey, we documented numerous accounts of police having demanded bribes and owners paying them. The intensification of policing which accompanied the WCLA has had little to no impact on reducing public access to liquor through shebeen outlets. Most shebeen owners have no alternative to pursuing their business, while others persist in resistance to policies which are seen as unjust, discriminatory and residual aspects of apartheid. As a woman who sold traditional beer exclaimed, '*I cannot stop [running the shebeen] because there is no other business that I know!*' (1/1236/F/nd). Mama Duma, who has run a conversational shebeen for at least three decades, refuses to stop trading, saying: '*I have run from the police all my life…[and] I will never stop selling liquor, not until I die.*' Her business is not simply a livelihood, but a means through which she has acquired a formal house, educated her children and begun to uplift her family out of poverty (interview cited in Charman 2016). In the course of our research, we came across a small shebeen with a public sign posted above the entrance; it read: *I am selling beer, please don't tell the police.* (Figure 9.15).

FIGURE 9.15 Hand-painted sign on a shebeen announcing: "I am selling beer, please don't tell the police"

This provides a sharp example of the absurdity of the prohibitionist approach in social contexts where shebeens represent symbols of struggle against exclusion, even if they also bring about a range of complex and contradictory outcomes.

Outlook: transformative possibilities

In the CBDs of South African metros, leisure activities are fulfilling an important role in stimulating economic growth while simultaneously eroding old orders of spatial exclusion. Sites such as Long Street in the Cape Town CBD provide opportunities for participants from diverse social classes, ethnicities, nationalities and gender identities to mingle in an environment with the potential to foster progressive social relationships and solidarities. Yet the scope of this policy-enabled development has been narrowly restricted to the town centres and commercial nodes in middle-class suburbs and denied in the township context. Given the significance of the township leisure economy in scope, scale and social implications, the developmental outcomes of current regulatory policy require careful consideration. In Sweet Home Farm and other sites, the collective resistance of shebeen owners has rendered the policing on informal outlets unworkable. As in the apartheid era, the operation of shebeens undermines the objectives of regulation and formalisation. Through their business networks and the role of micro-distributors who transport liquor supplies from the licensed outlets using cars, shopping trolleys, wheelbarrows and wheelie bins, and in their business practices such as the provision of credit sales and late-night trading, township shebeens ensure that the supply of liquor meets demand. At the macro-level, the business model of corporate producers as well as the concoction informalists rely on retail outlets shifting large volumes at low unit price points, hence encouraging taverns and shebeens to drive sales which, in turn, results in harmful consumption. Yet prohibitionist-leaning policies are still championed. We have argued that this policy logic has been advanced through the moral panic around drinking and the particular role of shebeens as sites that are 'unruly and unpredictable' and which result in disproportionate levels of harm, undermining efforts to regiment the working class. As Pieterse and Simone (2013) observe, within all such spaces in the emerging and informal city, unruly and unpredictable sites are also 'pregnant with possibility' (p. 12).

While 'pregnant with possibility', the township leisure economy has distributed a low dividend. As a whole, the great majority of shebeens and even licensed taverns can be described as under-capitalised, with little investment into the property, business assets and operational systems. It is rare to find liquor-drinking venues that provide food services, offer a range of non-alcoholic beverages and have separate toilets for male and female customers. It is even rarer to find venues with outdoor seating, either in the manner of some Eveline Street bars which place tables and chairs on the sidewalk or in the guise of beer gardens. Through steep institutional hurdles, the state actively prevents entrepreneurs from regularising their businesses. Instead of eradicating informal liquor trading, policy compels businesses to operate informally and illegally, stimulating a multitude of micro-enterprises whose logic requires that they operate in a covert, risk-averse and survivalist manner set deep in residential areas. The progressive business outcomes we identified in the case of Eveline Street are rarely witnessed in the South African township. Furthermore, state investments to reduce risks within the night-time and weekend recreational environment through, for example, the installation of CCTV surveillance, streetlights and regular patrols have been rarely undertaken.

Can shebeens have a role in unpicking apartheid spatial regimentation and contributing towards authentic and liveable neighbourhoods? As spaces of shared social interaction, venues can enable relationship-building between the operator, patrons and the wider community. Where shebeens generate social conflict, these relationships between business and communities must support strategies to reduce risk and minimise conflict. Building relationships between opposing interests to achieve a safer environment is not always possible. But this should not obscure the possibilities to influence and indeed alter socialisation around drinking so as to reduce risks to the participants and the broader community. We responded to this challenge through developing a 'safe shebeen' concept that utilises signs, symbols and house rules to specify do's and don'ts when socialising, through clearly stating actions that constitute universally unacceptable behaviour (see Chapter cover) (SLF 2014). The 'safe shebeen' strategy was developed through a participatory engagement with shebeen owners and community members in Sweet Home Farm. Sixteen shebeeners ended up adopting a collectively devised system of house rules within their own venues, aiming to introduce subtle patron-centred behavioural changes. Some venues installed toilets for their patrons; some businesses turned down music volumes; and customers were visibly cautioned on risky, inappropriate and anti-social behaviour, including sexual harassment. While strategies which empower shebeeners should not be seen as a panacea to harm liquor reduction, informal control systems (based on institutional rules; see the analysis in Chapter 12) need to be recognised as part of an appropriate approach to regulation. If more shebeens could obtain licences and if formalisation were matched to greater incentives, then far greater possibilities could be unlocked, encouraging owners to make the kinds of investments in infrastructure, assets and systems that enable more productive and less conflictual social outcomes. State power could then be used in an enabling rather than purely repressive manner.

KOTA MENU

Pup n BEEF

ACHAAR·POLONY·CHiPS — R 5.00   R 10

ACHAAR·POLONY·CHiPS·Eggs — R 6.00

ACHAAR·POLONY·CHiPS·CHiesse — R 7.50 VieNA

ACHAAR·POLONY·CHiPS·CHiess·ViANA·Eggs — R 9·00   half RACIEN

ACHAAR·POLONY·CHiPS·CHiess·Eggs·RACHIEN· R10

ACHAAR·POLON·EggS·CHiess·RACHIEN·VieNA — R 12

KOTA CHiCiN — R 20·00

AMBURG — R 15.00

CHiPS — R 10.00

RiCE & CHiCiN

10
THE CULTURE AND CONVENIENCE OF FOODSERVICE

In this chapter, we focus on informal food retailers, especially street businesses and micro-enterprises selling takeaways, anaylsing the spatial, enterprise and cultural considerations that shape their business strategies.

CHAPTER 10

The culture and convenience of food service

South Africa's formal food economy is highly industrialised throughout the farming and processing components, with ownership concentrated among corporates that include Tiger Brands, Pioneer Foods and RCL Foods. This characteristic of restricted ownership extends along the value chain. As with processing, food retailing is dominated by JSE-listed corporates, with four companies – Shoprite Holdings, Pick n Pay Group, Spar Group and Massmart-Walmart – wielding enormous market power through controlling around two thirds of the total South African retail market, which was valued in 2016 at about R485 billion (Trade Intelligence 2017). Through their economic power, corporate supermarkets dominate grocery retail opportunities in the township shopping malls, operating either through flagship brands or subsidiaries that include discount retailers. Shoprite Holdings, for example, operates the USave brand, OK Foods, Liquor Shop and Hungry Lion, all targeting LSMs 1–7 segments (lower-income households). Independent retailers, including spaza shops, have a 23% share of the grocery market by value (Trade Intelligence 2017), though are nevertheless reliant on supplies from corporate controlled 'cash-and-carry' wholesalers. Spaza shops, street traders and informal food service businesses are thought to provide up to 45% of South Africa's entire demand for food (Greenberg 2015).

Informal food sellers fulfil an important role in providing residents with better access to food and hence greater convenience to shopping; offering food on more affordable terms; and selling foods which meet cultural preferences (Petersen & Charman 2017). Scholars argue that informal businesses offer sales on credit (Battersby & Peyton 2014), thereby extending a safety net to the poor whose income is often tied to the monthly grant cycle. While some entrepreneurs do permit credit purchases, it is likely that the scale is overstated, with the practice restricted to specific instances where traders and customers have long-established relationships (see Neves & Du Toit 2012). Apart from improving food accessibility, the informal township food system is recognised as an important means of livelihood for survivalists (Crush & Frayne 2011a; Petersen & Charman 2018). In addition, informal retailers are said to lessen urban food insecurity (Skinner & Haysom 2016) through providing access to food on terms that are both flexible and favourable. Our research, which we detail in this chapter, confirms that these micro-enterprises support local buying habits and provide residents with accessibility to a range of foods. It should be noted, notwithstanding, that the food system implications of informal businesses have not been extensively studied. This point has been made (for example, in Even-Zahav 2016) to temper claims that these businesses are more sustainable and beneficial than the formal, corporate-controlled system. While informal micro-enterprises may improve food availability within neighbourhoods, there is evidence that the informal systems are not necessarily more flexible, more affordable, or offer better quality food products, and when it comes to groceries, most residents prefer shopping at supermarkets (Charman, Bacq & Brown 2019).

In this chapter, we focus on informal food retailers, especially street businesses and micro-enterprises selling takeaways. We analyse the spatial, enterprise and cultural considerations that shape their business strategies. Micro-enterprises which provide food service (in other words, prepared meals) constitute an important sub-set within the township economy, providing a service that differs qualitatively from the corporate fast foods which have begun to enter the township market through a foothold in shopping malls. We will show that while informal businesses are diverse in range and size, the sub-sector accommodates a large number of survivalists – virtually all of which are interconnected to formal businesses. As a result of their reliance on formal suppliers, when a shock occurs within the corporate food system, such as the 2018 Listeriosis crisis, the shockwaves travel down the chain from the formal to the informal where the impact can be severe. We first describe the informal food system and examine the business dynamics before considering the implications of this supply dependency. In spatial terms, our analysis builds on the comparative research results across our nine South African sites and then focuses at the neighbourhood level and micro-context levels, where we show how the spatial positioning of micro-enterprises helps to enhance the resilience of survivalists within the system.

The food system

In its dual contribution to business opportunities and food security, the informal food system is a major component of the township economy. Grocery retailing and specialist trading of fresh meat/poultry/fish, fruit and vegetables (greengrocers), food service, including takeaway food, and (non-rural) agricultural production account for 39% of all micro-enterprises (Petersen & Charman 2017). The figure would be higher still if we were to include street traders and liquor retailers who often include food items within their product range. The number of micro-enterprises in related enterprise categories for each of the nine South African sites is shown in Table 10.1.

TABLE 10.1 The number of micro-enterprises in related enterprise categories for each of the nine sites

	Brown Farm	Delft South	Imizamo Yethu	Ivory Park	KwaMashu	Sweet Home Farm	Tembisa	Thabong	Vrygrond	Total
Restaurants	3	5	6	2	1	2	10	2	1	**32**
Tuck shops	0	0	1	62	21	0	0	19	0	**103**
Agriculture	10	7	0	8	57	5	23	6	10	**126**
Meat, poultry and fish retail	56	17	4	29	3	9	11	22	14	**157**
Greengrocer	72	21	0	143	3	13	98	39	13	**402**
Grocery retail (spaza)	185	181	77	181	127	56	153	80	140	**1 180**
House shop	229	131	47	429	156	37	449	85	49	**1 612**
Total	**680**	**398**	**190**	**990**	**469**	**141**	**821**	**275**	**245**	**4 209**

As the data reveals, there are notable geographic differences in the composition of the micro-enterprise response to food system business opportunities. In assessing these differences, we do not focus on spaza shops or other grocery retailers which we analysed in Chapter 8, apart from mentioning that these businesses sell frozen and luncheon meat, fruit and vegetables and dairy products. Similarly, we acknowledge but do not include a discussion of community food security projects, including soup kitchens, as these are largely non-commercial.

Unlike urban settlements elsewhere on the African continent, there are very limited spatial opportunities for urban agricultural production in South African townships. Of our research sites, only in KwaMashu did residents have surplus land available for cropping and small-scale animal husbandry. In Tembisa, a portion of open ground situated along the river system has been enclosed by community members with fences and subdivided into arable allotments. A group of pensioners cultivates these allotments, each working a separate garden with enclosed fencing, as can be seen in Figure 10.1.

Although we did not investigate the scale of productivity, we learnt through interviews that the main function of the gardens was to provide the pensioners with a pastime and hobby, with the produce grown in their gardens of secondary importance and either consumed within their household or shared among family and friends. If suitable arable land was available, it is reasonable to predict that agriculture would have a more significant role in the township food system. We encountered a number of examples of individuals raising livestock (mainly goats, pigs and chickens) in potentially unfavourable situations, wherein the livestock are left to forage on rubbish dumps, roadside verges and wetlands within settlements.

FIGURE 10.1 Pensioners cultivating allotments in Tembisa with each working a separate garden

Micro-enterprises that specialised in selling meat/fish/poultry or horticultural produce comprise a modest 13% of businesses in the food sector on average, though in Thabong, they account for just over one fifth of all micro-enterprises. These businesses tend to operate without cold-chain infrastructure and have to compete against supermarkets, formal retailers and spaza shops who sell products which are similar or substitutable, such as frozen meat. For these retailers of fresh produce, their business advantage rests on providing a service that is spatially more accessible, more convenient (in terms of the times of trading or swiftness of transaction), more affordable (in quantity) and more culturally authentic. Within the meat/fish/poultry category we included traders selling live chickens sold from cages positioned on the street verge (see Figure 10.2). The chickens are sourced from commercial egg farms, including farms within the corporate system, as 'spent hens' (in other words, no longer able to produce eggs at a desired production level).

Through this supply chain, the informal trader provides egg producers with a market outlet for their 'spent hens' that would otherwise be sold at low cost into the meat processing industry. In Delft South, we encountered mobile fish traders selling from the back of bakkies (fresh fish, including snoek) and car boots (frozen fish). In Ivory Park and Tembisa, we identified a range of ambulatory hawkers (some pushing a trolley) and retailers travelling by motor vehicle who marketed a range of meat cuts and food products (see Figure 10.3 and Figure 10.4).

An important component of the meat sub-sector is the sale of 'fifth-quarter' products (including visceral fat, alimentary tract, visceral organs, feet and heads) both as fresh meat or cooked food. Fifth-quarter meat is often more affordable than the prime cuts sold in butcheries (in both informal and formal outlets), is culturally acceptable and for some consumers is preferable to the 'cosmetically' prepared cuts sold within formal retail (see Figure 10.5 and Figure 10.6).

These meat cuts are often sold at specific street localities, usually along high streets or close to transport nodes, where traders agglomerate. Most sellers are women. The meat itself is obtained from abattoirs or wholesalers and passes through an informal supply chain before reaching the consumer. As the product enters the informal sector, the cold chain and phytosanitary controls abruptly end, which places these products at higher risk of contamination, especially in storage where refrigeration is inadequate, notably when electricity supplies are interrupted. We witnessed, on numerous occasions, the offloading of fifth-quarter products from the rear of utility vehicles by poorly equipped handlers. Petersen and Charman (2018) argue that through developing the market for fifth-quarter cuts, informal traders permit the cost-effective 'nose to tail' (p. 15) utilisation of animal products which, in some countries, would otherwise impose an environmental problem for abattoirs. Another source of fresh meat derives from the ad hoc slaughter of pigs, chickens, goats (and less frequently, cattle) in public localities in the township, with the meat then either sold immediately via on-the-spot street sales or utilised in fast-food operations.

Fruit and vegetables are retailed through grocery shops and dedicated greengrocers (such as the example in Figure 10.7).

Some street traders stock only a limited range of items, especially fruit. In those sites where we encountered few dedicated fruit and vegetable retailers, such as KwaMashu and Imizamo Yethu, residents would acquire their supplies from either spaza shops or supermarkets. Supermarkets have emerged as important suppliers of vegetables, especially stock with longer shelf-life such as potatoes, butternut, carrots and onions,

FIGURE 10.2 Spent 'hen' chicken sales in the street of Ivory Park

FIGURE 10.3 Mobile, trolley-based, door-to-door fruit and vegetable vendors

FIGURE 10.4 The "Egg Man" of Tembisa

FIGURE 10.5 Fifth-quarter meat cuts for sale by street vendor, Browns Farm

FIGURE 10.6 Full 'nose to tail' meat consumption is a characteristic of township markets

through offering competitive discounts on combinations of four or five items (known as 'combos'). Street-based greengrocers, in contrast, serve the daily need for fruit and vegetables, situating their businesses within residential areas, usually along streets with relatively high pedestrian movement. In targeting the daily consumer, traders have adapted strategies such as selling smaller units of produce (a quarter cabbage), selling single items and preparing mini-combos, comprising a few onions, tomatoes and potatoes. In Delft South, we witnessed the historic tradition of traders selling fruit and vegetables at the doorstep from a horse-drawn cart (see Figure 10.8), a marketing strategy that is replicated in both Ivory Park and Tembisa where traders push their shopping trolleys loaded with vegetables around the residential streets, calling out 'amaveggie' and selling the mini-combos required for the evening meal (refer to Figure 10.3).

Trade in fruit and vegetables is largely male-controlled. This might reflect the requirement for transport to access the main regional fresh product markets from which the bulk of supplies are obtained on a regular basis, as well as the transport requirement to shift the boxes of product from the place of storage (home) to the trading site (street stand). The male-centredness of the sector might also reflect the attendant risks with regard to selling products with high rates of spillage, bearing in mind that few traders have access to cold-chain facilities. Where women trade in fruit and vegetables, they tend to sell smaller quantities in constant demand which could, if necessary, be consumed within the household. While we found cases where informal traders source produce directly from the farm gate (and thus obtain a discounted price), these networks are limited by the logistical requirement to purchase a large consignment (a bakkie-load) of a single product which then needs to be retailed in a short-time or the trader has then to provide

FIGURE 10.7 A township greengrocer with products packaged into small value units

FIGURE 10.8 Traders selling fruit and vegetables from door to door in a horse-drawn cart, Delft South

a storage solution. Due to the logistical and labour demands, the informal trade in fruit and vegetables on a scale above the survivalist level thus favours a collective unit, such as offered by an extended family or cultural/ethnic network. In the Cape Town townships, some fresh produce traders have been operating family businesses for two or three generations, with the businesses operating from several sites. Through a similar use of networks, Rastafari traders operate the most notable fruit and vegetable stands in Delft South, Sweet Home Farm and Philippi; Basotho traders are prominent in Philippi; and Mozambicans in Ivory Park and Tembisa.

In settlements with relatively large immigrant populations, traders have introduced new dishes and food-related customs. Mozambicans in Ivory Park have introduced 'birds-eye' chillies and garlic which have since become local food staples and are widely sold in greengrocer stands and included in takeaway meals. We identified a range of products obtained through informal (and transregional) commodity networks, including mango atchar sourced from Tzaneen, chalimbana groundnuts and beans from Malawi, mopane worms and dried kapenta fish from Zimbabwe and fresh fish from the distant Mozambique coast.

Food services

Township micro-enterprises providing food service, selling food for consumption in raw, packaged or ready-to-eat forms, are diverse in scope as well as in the scale of operations. These businesses differ from those in the formal sector, which are spatially confined to shopping malls and comprise brand restaurants, corporate fast-food and franchised outlets, and supermarkets that sell takeaway meals along with an array of snacks.

FIGURE 10.9 A street trader stand selling chips, biscuits and sweets
Note: The chips are purchased wholesale and repackaged into R0.50 and R1.00 units.

The stringent health, environmental health and fire safety standards with which these formal businesses must comply, which are enforced by both municipal authorities and the property landlords (for risk purposes), precludes informal food service businesses from direct competition within the mall context. Outside the mall, informal food service ranges from street traders selling snacks such as chips and sweets (see Figure 10.9), greengrocers selling fruit, street braais selling various meats and mealies (usually as separate businesses), and businesses that offer cooked meals and fast foods.

Each form of these food service micro-enterprises uniquely responds to market opportunities, in their spatial position, operating hours, product and price range, cultural understanding and service offering. Street traders permit shoppers to pick up an item and simultaneously drop a coin for payment, minimising the time required to complete a business transaction. At the area level, the spatial distribution of informal food service broadly resembles the residential pattern noted in the case of spaza shops, though, as we show in Chapter 5, businesses benefit from agglomeration, particularly along streets with high pedestrian traffic. The spatial distribution of takeaways in comparison to other micro-enterprises selling food and beverages in the KwaMashu case is shown in Figure 10.10.

| Grocery retail | House shops | Meat/poultry/fish | Restaurants | Shebeens | Taverns | Takeaways |

FIGURE 10.10 The spatial distribution of takeaways in KwaMashu (2015)
Note: The figures shows the position of takeaways in relation to other food-selling businesses, including shebeens, restaurants, spaza shops, house shops and retailers of meat, poultry and fish.

The businesses are dispersed, operating within neighbourhood niche markets where the business strategy focuses on proximity rather than differentiation of product.

In monetary terms, the most important sub-component of the food service sector are micro-enterprises that sell prepared foods, which in our business census were classified as takeaways and restaurants. In a recent investigation of household spending on food, Charman, Bacq and Brown (2019) found that on average households in Philippi spend R1 482 (65% of total spend) pm on food from supermarkets, R410 in spaza shops (18% of total spend) and R392 (17% of total spend) in street-food businesses, the bulk of which is spent on takeaways. While these figures might be influenced as a result of the proximity of the study site to three supermarkets, they provide an indication of the relative expenditure on food service. Figure 10.11 shows the number of restaurants and takeaway businesses per 1 000 population in the nine South African sites, which demonstrates the extent of takeaway businesses and relative scarcity of restaurants.

The main exceptions are 'shisa nyama' (meaning to braai meat) restaurants, the most successful of which combine the facilities of a butchery (where customers can select specific cuts) and a tavern and provide customers with a seated environment. Though shisa nyama businesses are few in number, some of those we identified have developed a successful (highly profitable) business concept and where the business has succeeded in formalising (and thus obtaining a liquor licence), these entrepreneurs have been able to attract corporate investment via branding, furniture, business assets and the installation of banking facilities.

In relative terms, takeaway micro-enterprises are more prevalent in sites of informal settlements, than sites of formal residential housing. There are three times as many takeaways per unit of population in Imizamo Yethu, Ivory Park and Browns Farm, for example, than in the sites of Thabong, Delft South and Vrygrond. This finding may indicate that poorer households are more reliant on takeaways than non-poor households, which might relate to the challenge of storing food and preparing meals in informal dwellings, though it also reflects 'out-shopping' on takeaways from formal businesses in sites situated close to malls. Most informal takeaways sell braaied, deep fried or stewed dishes. In the Western Cape, a renowned takeaway is the 'Gatsby', a foot-long submarine sandwich with a meat filling and fried chips; in Gauteng, the 'kota'

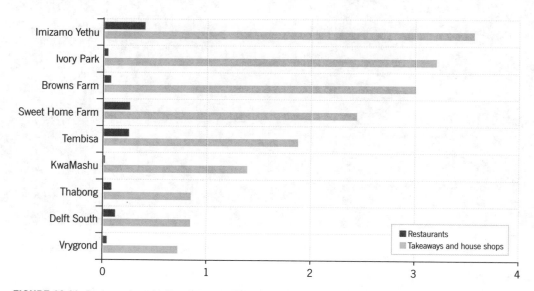

FIGURE 10.11 Restaurants and takeaways per 1 000 population across all sites

is a variation of this dish, though made from a quarter loaf of bread; while in KwaZulu-Natal, the equivalent is the 'bunny chow', but with a spicier filling. In Katutura, Namibia, the most iconic dish is kapana meat, thinly sliced and grilled on a braai, served with a dip of salt and hot chillies. Takeaways which sell products such as Gatsbys/kota/bunny chows tend to operate from permanent structures, within buildings, shipping containers or purpose-built shacks, since the businesses require access to electricity and make use of fridges for storing stock, hotplates to heat fillings and deep-fryers for cooking potato chips. Although these businesses are often situated within private landholdings, they tend to be oriented towards the public space as shown in Figure 10.12.

As seen in this image, there is no seating for customers within the street space; instead, the food is either consumed standing, taken home, or taken to a tavern/shebeen where seating is provided. The absence of seating and tables is an almost universal feature of township takeaway outlets. While this might seem counter-intuitive for business, this reflects the precariousness of the street as a space for leisure and socialisation, especially around the consumption of food (and liquor). Another feature of these micro-enterprises is the flexibility within the menu, with options to enhance the filling, such as extra meat, a cheese slice, or a fried egg. These menu options are responsive to variable consumer spending power: when money is in short supply, customers will purchase an entry-level meal option whereas at month end, the same customers might spend significantly more to upscale the meal.

Braai-meat businesses are predominantly street based. Some agglomerate in particular spatial locations, or destinations known for a specific product, such as chicken, beef or offal. In these localities, competition enhances businesses opportunities through attracting customers who might not otherwise visit the street. Their infrastructure requirements are minimal, often comprising a simple tented stand with a tarpaulin roof, a table and braai stand (see Figure 10.13).

FIGURE 10.12 Street-facing takeaway businesses
Note: These businesses are positioned within residential properties and serve passing trade, but many of these businesses provide few amenities to consume food at the premises.

Some cook on open fires over 210-litre steel drums cut in half. These businesses will usually sell a single product – such as chicken feet or giblets, beef chops, or pork chops – or two products at most, one of which tends to be sausage (boerewors). Once purchased, the braaied meat is either eaten on the spot or wrapped in newspaper to take away. Through the range of product offerings and their pricing, the takeaway sector is differentiated with businesses catering to different socio-economic and demographic consumer segments. The sellers of chicken feet and heads (known as 'walkie-talkies'), sell mainly to school children (and some women), whereas the sellers of pork or beef chops predominantly sell to men (and older women) and will deliberately exclude products such as feet and heads so as to discourage children from coming to their stand. Within the sub-category of braaied meals, traders prepare and sell 'fifth-quarter' specialties, such as cow or sheep heads (known as 'smilies'), with their clients attracted to the particular business or cluster to satisfy their 'craving' for such a dish.

Vetkoek (*amagwinya*) is an oil-fried dough bread, sold as is or filled with meat such as polony. The trade in vetkoek is largely undertaken by women who prepare the dough in advance and then deep fry it in the early morning (either within their homes or from street localities) to provide pedestrians with a breakfast snack. As there are no major infrastructural barriers or obstacles of supply chain to restrict entry into the sub-sector, the selling of vetkoek provides an opportunity for survivalists to enter into the business. Other such products (with similar low-entry barriers) are toffee apples, ice cream and ice-lollies (known as 'bompies'), and home-baked cakes or muffins, all of which are sold from homes and are in high demand from children.

FIGURE 10.13 A kapano meat destination in Eveline Street
Note: Street braai businesses often agglomerate in particular sites, selling a signature meat product.

Micro-enterprise characteristics

Whereas the spaza sector is dominated by male immigrant entrepreneurs, 87% of food service micro-enterprises are owned by South Africans, mainly women. Although many of these businesses appear to be survivalist in character (simple micro-enterprises focused on preparing and retailing one or two products), there appear to be reasonable prospects for sustainability with the average length of time in business reported as 4.2 years (Petersen, Charman & Kroll 2018). Through a follow-up survey of 113 micro-enterprises in Browns Farm, Ivory Park and KwaMashu, we learnt that the average age of the entrepreneurs was 35 years, 71% of whom were women. Women chose to operate in the food service sector for two reasons: firstly, the favourable earnings potential, and secondly, the flexibility accordant with the low barriers to operating in times and spaces suited to their needs, thus affording these women greater scope to juggle the demands of running a business with caring for dependent children. For many of these women, the income from their business was the primary source of household income. Operating on a different scale, about 20% of the sample could be considered as entrepreneurial, utilising strategies such as bulk purchasing, sophistication and variation in menus, staff employment and investment in equipment to enhance productivity. Although growth oriented, most of these micro-enterprises are engaged in short supply chains with the business replenishing stock from wholesalers and supermarkets as required. There are few businesses with the refrigeration capacity, for example, to store their meat and other perishable products; producers will usually only deliver large-volume consignments.

Most food service micro-enterprises are configured to operate at specific times. Opening hours correlate with times of high demand for the particular meal types which vary according to food categories, business scale and location. Certain localities, such as the street space outside transport nodes, accommodate different food service sub-sectors in the same space at different times. For example, in the early morning, the main trading concerns the sale of vetkoek, eggs and fruit; in the middle of the day, the space might now be occupied by traders selling ice-lollies or snacks to school children; while in the late afternoon, sellers of braaied meat would set up their stands to target returning commuters. The roving seller of boiled eggs (Figure 10.14) has great spatial flexibility and targets both early morning and lunch-time shoppers.

While trading times vary across the week, the weekends generally require traders to work longer hours. This is particularly the case for takeaways responding to the opportunities of the weekend leisure economy, in which the business serves customers late into the evening, with some entrepreneurs hawking baskets of food from venue to venue. These businesses do not adhere to specific trading times but stop selling once all their product is sold out or when it becomes evident that there is no longer consistent demand. The survivalists ensure that they never over-prepare meals that have the risk of going unsold.

We have argued that food service businesses differentiate the market through their spatial position, operating times, infrastructure setup and meal offerings. The business owners also use price mechanisms to attract certain consumer segments, though the price of items is not an indicator of business success and some of the businesses selling the smallest unit items were deemed to be amongst the most profitable. Chicken feet braaiers retail one of the lowest-priced food items in the informal food service sector, costing 50c each, though these businesses report the highest numbers of customers and sustainable profits. Across the range of businesses, the price of meals thus ranges from a few rand (for a couple of braaied chicken feet) to around R70 for a plated meal with

FIGURE 10.14 A mobile trader selling boiled eggs

Note: Note the seasoning

CHIPS SPECIAL POLONY _____ R 8.00
CHIPS POLONY YIENNA _____ R 9.00
CHIPS POLONY SPECIL VIENNA _____ R 10.00
CHIPS POLONY SPECIL HALF RUSIAN _____ R 12.00
CHIPS POLONY SPECIAL FULL RUSIAN _____ R 13.00
CHIPS POLONY SPECIL YIENNA HALF RUSIAN _____ R 15.00
CHIPS POLONY CHESE SPECIAL YIENNA HALF RUSIA _____ R 16.00
CHIPS POLONY CHESE SPECIAL YIENNA FULL RUSIN _____ R 18.00
CHIPS R 20,
POLONY R 2
RUSIAN R 5
VIENNA R 2.50
CHESE R 3

0765602923

FIGURE 10.15 A kota shop menu, indicating the price of additional fillings

meat, a starch and vegetables. The ubiquitous kota varies in price from R7 (bread and chips only), rising with each supplementary ingredient (with polony, cheese or atchar being the most popular add-ons) priced at either R1 or R2 per addition (see Figure 10.15).

While most street braai stands sell cuts in specific unit prices (such as R15 or R10), the kapana meat sellers in Namibia permit customers to specify the value of the meat they wish to purchase, thereby accommodating both those seeking a small snack and those after a larger meal. Traders work hard at maintaining good relationships with clients, especially in businesses where taste carries a premium value as in cooked meals, kotas or braaied meat cuts.

Demand, profits and strategy

The demand for informal food service is driven by a range of factors, including the close proximity to consumers, the affordability of the options and cultural preferences. As one respondent said of her competitive advantages: *'the taste of my offal drives the customers crazy'* (2/877/F/30). In a study on household purchase decisions in Philippi (Charman et al. 2019), one respondent said that their main reason for purchasing street braai was to satisfy their 'craving'. This study found that demand for street braaied meat was an important part of the food basket for the poor and non-poor, though the poorest cohort were more frequent consumers. We interviewed 75 customers of informal takeaways, varying in age and gender (38 men and 37 women). The male respondents reported spending an average of R218,26 per week, equivalent to R31.15 per day; a figure undoubtedly influenced by the fact that most had regular sources of income. The female respondents spent significantly less, an average of R96.65 per week or R13.38 per day. Although the women spend less than men, the female respondents saw takeaways in a very different light, firstly, as providing a safety net in times of financial stress when cheaper options of takeaway foods could be purchased; and secondly, as reducing the burden of domestic work when they had neither time nor inclination to cook.

We obtained financial data from 106 respondents of survivalist-type food service businesses. Some of these entrepreneurs reported on their profits with respect to daily trade, others reported on weekly trade, which included the weekend operations, and some reported on a monthly basis, which would reflect the spike in expenditure on food service when people get paid. On average, the cohort reported profiting R171 per day, R854 per week and R1 200 per month. The reported daily earnings are probably the most representative since most food service traders do not operate on a full-time basis but run their business at times and on days with highest customer demand. Taking into consideration the low levels of capital invested in these businesses, the rudimentary infrastructure and equipment, and the limited value adding within the production process, the profitability of these micro-enterprises is modest, though this needs to be seen in the socio-economic context of otherwise limited employment alternatives.

Food service businesses are constantly refining their strategies. The resilience of participants is summed up in the name of the business in Figure 10.16: 'Life Goes On: mini kitchen'.

The need to be strategically nimble is explained by one of the respondents: '*I used to sell fast foods, then people demanded more products like groceries so I turned [the business] into a spaza that sells fast food. …I am the bread winner and a spaza allows us to have food in the house*' (2/1365/F/31). Her business also sold liquor, a strategy widely noted in similar home-based operations. For a pensioner who started out selling fast food, the transition to selling liquor was a logical progression: '*People demanded alcohol so I used my grant money to order it*', the addition making her business much more '*profitable*' (1/9/F/31). We heard numerous similar examples of the strategic engagement of entrepreneurs in food service on terms which enable them to fulfil their dual concerns

FIGURE 10.16 Hand-painted sign communicating that 'life goes on' regardless of the business and other struggles

of income and food security. A spaza shop owner in Delft explained how she diversified from groceries into selling spices and Gatsbys over the '*busy*' weekend as '*I can make food for the family at the same time*' (2/1723/F/nd). A common fallback strategy for struggling survivalists is to sell meals (takeaways) or meat. One respondent sold braaied meat on the weekends, during which time he sells about 20 trays of sausages (1/563/M/38). He once worked as a cleaner and gardener, but after losing his job, he starting selling fruit and vegetables in a small spaza shop. Then '*when the Somalian shops started spreading around*', the business went into decline and he turned to selling liquor. The change in business strategy led to '*big problems when the police come and take alcohol*', to which statement he added: '*sometimes the police don't even take the beer to the police station; they just drink it.*' The respondent subsequently turned to selling meat.

CASE STUDY: *Nancy's kota takeaway*

Nancy operated a kota takeaway in Ivory Park. She had had the business for less than a year. Her story illustrates the importance of having access to suitable infrastructure to enter into the food service market. See Figure 10.17.

The business was situated in a small shop along a high street. The layout of the business resembled the setup in Figure 10.2 (above) and Nancy served customers through a window. The menu comprised fried chips, sold in three different portions, and kotas with different filling options. The most expensive item on her menu was a kota with chips, a Russian as well as a Vienna sausage, atchar sauce, a slice of polony and a slice of Parmalat cheese costing R20, though the most popular request was for a basic kota with chips costing R9. Before starting the business, Nancy was unemployed. She was formally employed as a cleaner and built her house with this income. She decided to start the

FIGURE 10.17 A takeaway business owner in her outlet

kota business as a result of the shop becoming vacant and available for use. She explained: '*My sister had a shop where a barber was renting. He disappeared without paying rent and so I asked my sister and her boyfriend if I could make use of the space. When my sister agreed, I bought a deep-frying machine and started making fresh chips. I started with just one bag of potatoes.*' In a short timeframe, the business grew. Her sister provided an important source of support (she had a job), helping Nancy with advice on where to obtain equipment and helping her with the design of her menu. She employed two people, both women and both relatives.

In setting her menu and pricing her meals, Nancy positioned her business in line with other shops, competing through her location and service, rather than price. She said, '*We look at other shops. We compare menus and that is how we price our meals. I will not sell at R7 because that will erase my commission [profit]. Even bread starts from R8 and there are other costs. We start at R9.*' The business opened at 9 a.m. and traded until 10 p.m. Nancy said that there is '*always a steady stream of customers*' to her shop. She was able to make a 100% return on her weekly investment of food products, labour and gas, which Nancy preferred as the electric fryer '*is moving too fast*', meaning costing too much in electricity. Her vision was to accommodate sit-down meals within the shop. Nancy supported her son to sell braaied chicken feet and heads on the street corner over the weekend. In her view, this business had good potential, though she bemoaned that '*my kids are lazy*'.

Polony and listeriosis

As a result of their dependence on formal production, processing and distribution industries for supplies, food services micro-enterprises are vulnerable to supply chain disruptions. The consequence of this vulnerability was witnessed in 2017/18 during an outbreak of Listeriosis, a serious foodborne disease, in the township food system. The outbreak was allegedly caused from the contamination of polony products with Listeria bacteria in the manufacturing stage, which investigators were to identify within the production facilities of Enterprise Foods (in Polokwane), a subsidiary of Tiger Brands (National Institute for Communicable Diseases 2018). Illness caused from Listeriosis was noted in 974 cases and resulted in the known deaths of 183 persons (World Health Organization 2018) although the collective impacts will likely never be known. Polony is a mechanically manufactured sausage product, derived from meat which is industrially extracted from fifth-quarter and less profitable cuts. In the township food service sector, polony is a central ingredient in 'kota' and 'Gatsbys' and along with other forms of luncheon meats ('Vienna' and 'Russian' sausages), is purchased as a snack or sandwich filler.

With the identification of the source of the disease outbreak, the National Department of Health shut down meat production units thus disrupting supply and providing public health warnings. The media-generated panic caused customer demand for processed meats to plummet. In the months following the announcement of the source of the disease, township kota businesses in Ivory Park and Imizamo Yethu (two sites we investigated) reported that their sales had declined by up to 75%. As an immediate response, just under one third of the respondents altered their menus (to provide non-polony options) and around one quarter removed processed meats from the menu altogether. While the consumer was afforded alternative options, such as cheese or an egg, these would cost R1/unit more than polony. The price difference hindered the take-up of these options, with consumers returning, over time and once the crisis was resolved, to purchasing polony fillings. This highlights their dependence on sources of meat protein which, while comparably affordable, carry unavoidable risks. The identification of the source of the Listeriosis crisis in one of the corporate food giants gave the national government an opportunity to score a 'political' victory over big business with whom the government have long had an antagonistic relationship over matters of trade and Broad-Based Black Economic Empowerment (B-BBEE).[1] Having fingered the culprit, the authorities had no need to extend their Listeria scrutiny down the value chain and to the informal sector. Considering the variable standards of hygiene in many outlets, had township takeaways been subject to similar inspection, it is highly likely that the suspect bacterium would have been found in multiple sites (although the particular strain which accounted for the 183 deaths would unlikely be evident). Our point is that only a very small minority of informal food service micro-enterprises comply with food hygiene and environmental health and safety regulations in law or intention. We learnt, for example that businesses often turn off the refrigeration at night to save on electricity costs.

Without regulatory pressure, food service entrepreneurs rarely invest in adequate equipment and production facilities. Unwashed floors, dirty counters and decrepit equipment are common. In this business environment, the corporate food producers are able to avoid investments into township micro-enterprises to safeguard the cold chain or promote conditions which could better ensure food hygiene. As we saw in the Listeriosis case, although the outbreak was attributable to corporate food producers, the impact extended to uninsured micro-enterprises that sold their products, who, in the aftermath of the market collapse, were powerless to hold the offending supplier accountable for their losses. The case neatly summarised the skewed power relationships between the formal and informal sectors within South Africa's food system. In addition to the hygiene improvements clearly required in the manufacturing process, as made evident by the outbreak of Listeriosis, there is a paired responsibility for corporate agribusiness and food producers to lead strategy to raise standards in township food service businesses in partnership models.

Outlook

Micro-enterprises make food accessible, affordable and culturally relevant. Products are geared to diverse budgets and preferences. Many food offerings are not available (in form or quantity) in the formal economy, with corporate fast foods reflecting western notions of food. Corporate fast foods are hyper-regulated, whereas informal food service is unregulated and thus affords advantages for the township entrepreneur. This state of affairs enables informal businesses to operate in public space without paying rent, utilise open fires (which are not permitted under most municipal by-laws), slaughter animals on the spot, minimise investment in costly equipment and infrastructure (in accordance with regulations), and shift the business location in response to markets. These low-entry barriers enable the participation of survivalists. Since menus allow for ordering flexibility, there are usually items available at low cost while prices can commonly be negotiated. Informal food service provides benefits to the formal sector, directly for supplies and indirectly as in the example of fifth-quarter given earlier in the chapter, for the full 'nose to tail' utilisation of animal products that could otherwise go to waste or less lucrative markets. Most ingredients and supporting products, such as spices, bread, atchar, polony, eggs and potatoes, emanate from formal business suppliers. We identified virtually no township businesses adding value to food products for use downstream.

---

[1] B-BBEE is an official policy to promote procurement from black businesses, and small-medium and micro-enterprises in particular, with companies subject to annual assessment of their performace in meeting specified B-BBEE procurement targets.

As in the case of groceries and liquor retail, much profit from informal food services is extracted from the township, with corporate retailers and wholesalers being the main beneficiaries. There are weak linkages between informal businesses and the farms or factories that produce food products, apart from a handful of celebrated examples such as Mayo ice cream and Parmalat cheese slices used in kotas (Alcock 2018). Instead of seeing a trend of shortening supply chains and direct partnerships, corporates are advancing strategies to erode the informal food service share, competing through opening new stores and introducing products that require minimal cooking (such as recently introduced instant noodles in this economy). The availability of such ready-to-eat food products through spaza shops, thus addressing the constraint of access, may negatively impact on survivalist opportunities.

While there is strong case for greater compliance with food safety and environmental health standards by informal food businesses, the regulatory framework presents substantive obstacles for compliance. Some common activities, such as open-fire street braais, tend to be illegal. Few micro-enterprises have the capital and would be willing to invest in the infrastructure and equipment to fulfil the range of municipal compliances, which pertain to food storage, pest control and food and fire safety. It is unsurprising that only 7% of the takeaway outlets in our sub-survey had some level of municipal compliance, though rarely did we encounter businesses that were totally compliant. Yet of those that were partially compliant, the micro-enterprise usually had refrigeration, their premises were clean and presentable, and the businesses appeared to be more profitable than their entirely informal counterparts. The upside for consumers of potentially lower health risks warrants thinking about how informal food service could be coaxed into a degree of compliance with health and environmental regulations, on terms that are suitable to the context, affordable and incentivise the business operator.

Our evidence supports the claim that informal food services contribute towards livelihoods and food security in the township. In recognising these benefits, we wish to highlight two caveats. The first, as pointed out by Neves and Du Toit (2012), that while generating an income through business and achieving household food security can overlap, the two are 'subtly different objectives' (p. 134). Separating these objectives matters in micro-enterprises where the business confronts high levels of 'off-take', in other words, family consumption before retail. Depending on the context, eating the stock can present inefficiencies to both micro-enterprise and food security objectives, undermining both in circumstances of stiff business competition and when the food is of poor nutritional quality. The second caveat addresses the argument that informal food service micro-enterprises enhance food security, especially for the poor. There is no doubt that the sheer number and diversity of food service businesses (including grocery retailers) make food more easily accessible, provide affordable options, and sustain cultural cuisine. Yet informal food service is not necessarily safer or nutritionally healthier. Much of the food sold in township takeaways is calorie-dense, while in the case of meals such as Gatsby/kota/bunny chow, the nutritional value can be limited. While diets high in saturated fats, sugar and refined foods would likely result in degenerative health effects (Popkin 2003), there are few healthier alternatives in takeaways. The non-prevalence of seated venues (apart from liquor-serving outlets), means that cultural conventions around food, including the use of cutlery and crockery and the socialisation through eating, have been disabled. With an eye on the corporate fast-food industry which increasingly competes for township business, the informal sector has sought to mimic its objectives, serving food fast, serving to standing consumers who then eat from their hands, and disguising poor quality through spicing and salting. There is no room within this business model for healthier eating options.

11

SERVICES AS SOCIAL INFRASTRUCTURE

In this chapter we focus on three widely prevalent and socially important services: hair care (in the form of barbering and hair dressing), educares and traditional healing, and examine how these services contribute to building social infrastructure.

CHAPTER 11

Services as social infrastructure

There are a myriad of businesses providing services in the township economy, accounting for 26% of the micro-enterprises identified in our site census. In terms of our classification, these include micro-enterprises undertaking the repair of appliances (such as TVs and microwaves), builders and renovators, business services (including copy shops, business sign writers), car washing, community services (such as food kitchens), entertainment (DJs and musicians), mechanical repairs, personal and religious services. In this chapter, we focus on three widely prevalent and socially important services: hair care (in the form of barbering and hairdressing), educares and traditional healing. Despite the importance of the service economy in the township, there has been limited research on service businesses. Prior research has focused on specific aspects of these sectors, such as the quality of the education provided in educares or socio-psychological efficacy of traditional medicines. In contrast, our main concern is the collective contribution of these services to building social infrastructure within the township economy.

The hair-care, educare and traditional healing categories collectively comprise around 10% of all township businesses. These sectors nurture livelihoods for women. Unlike most retail sectors (apart from shebeens), customer support for various service businesses is gendered, with women supporting a particular business because the service is provided by women and vice versa. All the educares in our study were operated by women for this reason. Gender can be important in the orientation of such service businesses, creating different opportunities for men and women as is evidenced in the hair-care sector where women operate hair salons and men barber shops, with the two sub-categories providing qualitatively different services. In addition, in all three sectors, service provision is highly personalised and informed by cultural practices, with skills acquired through apprenticeship and practice. The personal connection between the provider of services and the client sustains the demand for a large number of businesses and holds in check processes of market concentration, meaning that a great number of survivalist businesses can be accommodated in the market.

Educares (childcare businesses that cater for children between the ages of 0–6 years) provide an essential service in the form of accessible and affordable childcare, allowing parents (especially mothers) to participate in the labour market. In contrast to hair care, the educare and traditional healing sectors are subject to sector-specific regulations which influence and impact the business model. We argue that the regulatory framework, while well-intended, produces enforced informalisation in that micro-enterprises which are unable to comply with the regulations are compelled to trade informally and illegally. As in the case of liquor-trading businesses, the regulations are enforced in an idiosyncratic manner through random inspections or as a consequence of ad hoc, broader 'clampdown' directives. The educare case is of particular interest because registered businesses are entitled to access state subsidies, thus providing a strong incentive (in theory) for a business to formalise. Yet this has not happened. Where educares operate informally, the business is unable to receive the subsidies paid per child attendee and takes the risk of being shut down or served with compliance notices. We will argue that this state incentive, on current terms, is inappropriate to many educares and thus does not benefit some of the most disadvantaged families. Of all township micro-enterprises, educares and traditional healers are the most akin to an indigenous social enterprise. These micro-enterprises deliver a low financial return, generally speaking, yet provide a high social value. At the community-wide level, they provide a social infrastructure which facilitates networking, information exchange, and access to social assets. Access to these unseen services fosters a collective sense of place making and helps to disrupt the dormitory nature of settlements. While a place-making role can understandably be attributed to hair salons and educares, whose social value is self-evident, so too is the role of traditional healers through addressing the personal and social obstacles of township residents.

Our analysis traverses multiple spatial gradients. At the neighbourhood level, we consider the spatial situation of these service businesses, noting (where relevant) gendered influences. Then at the micro-context we examine the internal physical architecture of businesses, focusing on the influence of objects as signifiers of specific cultural and social messages. Lastly, we discuss the invisible infrastructure – such as the skill of hairdressers, the social networks among educare operators, or the ability to communicate with ancestors and understand dreams, connecting people spatially to the lands of their ancestors – which constitute the social relationships that secure and safeguard conditions for doing business.

Hair care

Hair-care services are provided through salons, barber shops and individual braiders. The range of hair-care services has grown in tandem with expanding populations and improvements in personal incomes of township residents, and over time, micro-enterprises in the sector have shifted in spatial terms from a residential base to locations on the high street. Figure 11.1 and Figure 11.2 provide two examples of the infrastructure form.

From a business perspective, the development of hair-care services has benefited from four main influences. The first influence stems from transatlantic and transAfrican cultural diffusion. African immigrants set up businesses in both inner cities and townships, in which they have introduced styles derived from urban African and North American hip-hop culture (Weller 2011). In township salons, these styles are communicated through iconography, including signage and posters (see the posters in Figure 11.2). The diffusion of hip-hop culture has created a new lexicon of identity and fashion demand, of which hair styles are a supporting aspect. The second influence is the innovation of shipping-container infrastructure. Many of the new hairdressers and barbers have established their business in disused shipping containers, a business strategy commonly used in European and Asian informal markets (Mörtenböck & Mooshammer, 2015). These containers became accessible to the township market around the late 1990s, are relatively affordable (costing up to R15 000), robust and secure, and importantly, can be positioned along high streets. The establishment of businesses in containers had an added benefit in that it enabled the entrepreneur to sell their business (including the outlet, infrastructure and location) as a single entity. The third influence follows from

FIGURE 11.1 A container-based hair salon

FIGURE 11.2 A converted residential house used as a hair salon; the different gendered services are shown on the advertising boards

spatial shifts in business positioning, including the shift away from homes to high-street locations. The relocation of hair-care businesses to sites with high pedestrian footfall created brand-building opportunities, including signage and music, so that the business owner could align their service offering to expressions of popular culture and then target market niches, such as the supporters of particular football clubs, fans of a particular hip-hop artist or people of a shared ethnic/cultural identity. The fourth influence is the widening of availability and accessibility to industry products. The globalisation of hair-care and skin-product supply chains that accompanied the establishment of import businesses (sourcing from Asian suppliers and China in particular), opened up new sources of product supply into townships, thus reducing input costs and diversifying the product and style range (see Figure 11.3).

We conducted interviews with 207 hairdressers and barbers in the sites of KwaMashu, Ivory Park, Imizamo Yethu and Tembisa. As mentioned in Chapter 3, hair salons and barber shops are one of the few categories in which the majority of micro-enterprises operate on the high street. Hair-care businesses operate in different infrastructural situations with almost 63% operating from shacks, 17 in brick structures, 9% in containers, 6% within residential homes and 4% from diverse locations. The large number of businesses operating from shacks reflects the customer priority of reputation for service excellence, the business and facilities over the actual business form. Still, we generally observed that shack-based businesses situated in residential areas (as opposed to the high street) were more survivalist than entrepreneurial businesses.

Just over one third of the hair-care business owner respondents were South Africans (37%), a third were Zimbabweans (33%) and around 15% were Mozambicans (Figure 11.4).

African immigrants from the countries that pioneered changes in the township hair care, including the Democratic Republic of Congo (5.5%), Ghana (1.9%) and Nigeria (0.5%), are few in number, though this finding may simply reflect the particular sites in which the research was conducted. In Delft South, in contrast, only one of 27 high-street salons is operated by a South African (Charman & Petersen 2017). The sizeable proportion of immigrant hairdressers and barbers is not unique either to the township or the wider South African economy. Dihel and Goswami (2016) argue, in the context of a World-Bank-funded study, that hair-care services constitute an important tradeable service in the African context, improving the livelihoods of individuals who perform services across political borders. Whereas conventional economics regards services such as hairdressing as 'non-tradeable' because, so the theory goes, 'low'-skilled and 'low'-valued services cannot be rendered at a distance, Dihel and Goswami demonstrate that there are many examples where individuals cross borders to perform services for which their skills are highly valued (in relation to competing local services). This takes us to the important argument that the presentation of hair is highly 'political', in a gendered and social sense, especially in post-colonial contexts where hair is a signifier of identity and positionality. As Erasmus (1997) writes in her critique on 'discourses on black hair', 'hair is socially constructed, imbued with meaning and with multiple identities' (p. 16). Hairdressers and barbers therefore fulfil a central role in social processes, enabling individuals to shape or embrace identities. And because the hair salon/barber shops are an intimate social space in which the service is grounded on relationships, the nationality and ethnicity of the hairdresser or barber is insignificant to the trust between client and service provider. It is interesting to note that hair salons are less seldom targeted in the episodic waves of xenophobic violence in the township context which are directed at foreign-run spaza shops in particular. In our survey, none mentioned xenophobic threats as a constraint to

FIGURE 11.3 The availability of hair-care products and accessories has grown substantively in the township economy

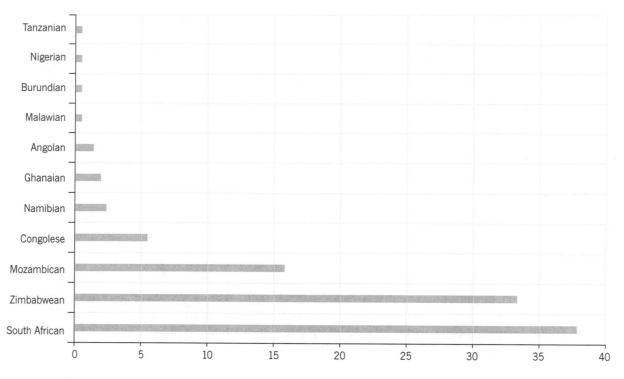

FIGURE 11.4 The nationalities of hair-care business owners across the research sites

doing business, though one individual spoke about his concern for conducting business without 'legal documentation' (4/2363/M/19).

Over half (55%) of the survey respondents were male, averaging an age of 27.4 years, whereas the average age of the females was 30 years old. Our cohort of hair-care micro-enterprises had been operating, on average, for 4.37 years. Most of the hair stylists and barbers are permanently involved in the day-to-day running of the business, and usually trade six days a week and operate from 9 a.m. to 6 p.m. Although the need to employ staff varies between different sub-sectors (barbers vs hair salons vs braiders) across the sector as a whole, merely 15% of the respondents were owner-operators, whereas 42% employed one additional person, 32% two additional persons, and 11% three additional persons. These figures confirm that the sector has high potential for job creation, though it should be noted that most employees are remunerated on a commission basis (so their income is dependent on the number of clients served). Furthermore, it is not uncommon for commission-based employees to be subject to rental fees which are paid to the owner of the micro-enterprise, landlord or whoever controls the salon or shop.

Skills are a key determinant of business success. As signifiers of identity, contemporary hair styles demand high levels of skill, gained through practice and experience, though confirmed through reputation and recognised in the market through customer demand. This process can take years, while skills alone are insufficient to ensure the viability of a start-up. In order to establish a customer base, the emerging hairdresser or barber seeks out opportunities that accompany working within a salon or barber shop (in terms of its facilities and spatial location), and access to customers who, in turn, provide an introduction to social, cultural or ethnic networks. The investment required to rent a suitable venue presents a potentially high entry barrier, so the option to work in an existing salon on a commission basis has multiple benefits, including access to a physical space and an inroad into a customer base. A different pathway into the sector is via the skills and social networks derived from hairdressing as a hobby. In the words of one respondent: 'we started at school with our other friends and at that time we did not always charge and then we realised we could make money' (4/2614/F/22); or as explained by another, 'I was unemployed after leaving school so I taught myself by plaiting my sister's hair until I got good at it and started charging others' (4/2548/F/29).

An important factor in marketing hair-care micro-enterprises is their location. The preference for high-street locations is shown in Figure 11.5 in the case of Tembisa.

Within the high street, we noted that hair-care businesses benefit from clusters that are often situated at nodal points, near transport hubs or shopping precincts. Positions on the high street afford spatial flexibility to business. This is used to place signboards, store water and provide seating on which customers can wait to be served or receive service. High-street businesses access electricity and water in buckets obtained from the residential properties situated to the rear and commonly use the space in front of the shop as storage and a seating area for customers. In one interview, when asked about his business assets, the barber respondent included 'open space' in his list as this was where he prefers to shave his clients (4/2514/M/32). In contrast to those entrepreneurs competing on the high street, some hairdressers (hair braiders in particular) preferred working from home as the rent saving outweighed the financial benefit of a high-street location. We noted that many of these home-based micro-enterprises were poorly advertised. In the view of one respondent, 'if you put the name of your business on your house then people undermine you because they believe you should only put the business name on a proper structure...like a container' (4/2502/F/26).

	Agriculture		Appliance repairs		Arts and crafts		Building services
	Business services		Car washes		Community services		Drug dealers
	Educare		Entertainment services		Greengrocers		Grocery retail
	Hair care		Health services		House shops		Meat/poultry/fish
	Mechanical services		Micro-manufacturers		Personal services		Phones
	Recycling		Religious services		Restaurants		Shebeens
	Shoe repairs		Specialist stores		Street trade		Tailors
	Takeaways		Taverns		Transport services		Wholesalers
	Wood and coal						

FIGURE 11.5 Map of Tembisa, high streets and hair-care businesses

High-street hair salons communicate a branded social message via hand-painted signage on the exterior walls of the business premises. Business names are commonly derived from the name of the (original) owner and then differentiated into gendered segments through the additions of the terms barber shop (targeting men) and salon, parlour, beauty, nail bar (targeting women). Some names target specific groups through the business name; these can be ethnic, religious or cultural, such as the name G-Unit Barber Shop, an abbreviation taken from the name Guerrilla Unit after an American hip-hop group. Corporate brands such as Dark and Lovely (L'Oreal Group) encroach on the social and business environment, competing against indigenous styles and projecting messages to reshape identities and stimulate product dependence. Salons and barber shops are fitted out, internally, with mirrors, counters, wash basins, furniture and posters showing specific cuts and styles. The external brand message is reinforced, on the internal walls, through posters of sports stars, actors and musicians who align to their sub-cultural identity. Some have television and hi-fi systems to entertain their clients and underwrite the position of the salon/shop as a social space. The sociability of the hair salon can be seen in the time-sequence photographs of a salon on Eveline Street, Figure 11.6 and Figure 11.7, where, during the day, female customers sit outside the business partaking in street life, whereas at night, activities are confined to the inside of the salon.

Hair salons require more investment than barber shops and offer a more diverse range of services, though businesses in this sub-sector are not necessarily more profitable as hairdressing treatments are very laborious and time-consuming. Among our surveyed businesses, the lowest price for a single service in either barber shops or hair salons was R10. For men, their average price was R51 and highest price was R400, whereas for women, their average price was R122 and highest R600. Across the dataset as a whole, the informants earned R1 000 for 3.6 days work on average, equivalent to about R250 per day. As with most township businesses, these micro-enterprises operate on a cash basis, obtaining income from the hairdressing service and selling certain products, which range from cosmetics and hair accessories to hardware items (such as locks), liquor and drugs. None of the hair-care businesses was formally registered.

Once a hairdresser/barber has established a good reputation (for their skills and social etiquette), their clients are easily retained. Similarly, some individuals established their business after people had recognised their skills and began to request a similar service. A hairdresser (2/2559/F/25) recalled that she learnt her skills from doing her daughter's hair and once people 'saw how she did her own child, they started coming to her'.

We encountered several incidences of hair salon clients travelling from outside the research site to a specific salon/shop to sustain their relationship with a specific hairdresser or barber. This presents opportunities for the employee but risks for the business owner. As the start-up costs of establishing a salon are comparatively modest (apart from infrastructure), an employee with an established reputation can decide to break away and set up on their own or purchase the business. Should they decide to set up a new micro-enterprise, with their own unique brand, the former employee has good prospects of retaining their clients and indeed poaching clients from their former salon/shop. We heard numerous accounts of how employees had acquired capital to operate the business, learning of a range of different strategies: 'The three of us friends used to work for someone else and we decided to pool our savings and buy this container and tools' (4/2554/M/22); 'I was working in the salon and ended up buying it piece by piece' (4/2575/M/28); 'I worked for someone 'til I acquired experience…' (4/2692/M/31). For entrepreneurs choosing to purchase the business, we learnt that a container-based hair salon or barber shop could be purchased as a 'business in a box' for between R20 000 and R30 000.

FIGURE 11.6 Spatial flexibility in and around hair salon premises and their capacity to support socialisation
Note: This Eveline Street hair salon has a distinct pattern of operation between day- and night-time uses.

FIGURE 11.7 At night, the business activities and socialisation retreats into the building
Note: Other businesses, including a takeaway and street braai, commence trading.

Educares

Micro-enterprises that provide ECD-type services, commonly known as 'educares' or sometimes 'daycares', approximate the objectives of social enterprises (which use commercial strategies to achieve business sustainability and simultaneously produce a social impact). Educares provide a child-minding service (care) as well as some educational instruction (education). Through taking care of young children, from newborn babies to pre-school learners (6 years of age), educares allow working parents to leave their children in safe hands, knowing that the child will be secure (in recognition of the dangers of the home environment and risks of abuse in this context), be fed, in the case of babies, have their nappies changed, be afforded an opportunity for social interaction with other children and receive an element of learning, though the latter is not always the overriding objective. We encountered a range of micro-enterprises as well as formally constituted social enterprises which offer ECD-type services in the township economy, as shown in Figures 11.8 and Figure 11.9.

These ranged from home-based child minders (often survivalists), to informally established educares, to religious organisations and non-governmental organisations (NGOs) operating fully-fledged ECDCs. As a collective, they differ in scale, relationship to regulation, spatial organisation and emphasis towards the objectives of education and or religious instruction, provision of nutrition and social care, to list some of the major differences. Here, we focus on educares: micro-enterprises which provide a social service and social infrastructure to the benefit of both children and their parents. Our purpose is not to critique, through a broad-brush approach, the quality of the educational service, which obviously varies from case to case. Since there is a large body of research evidence showing the carry-through effects of early childhood education on adult life (Drake & Stringer 2016), the quality of educational service provided in educares has been a subject of great concern to government and philanthropic organisations.

In recognition of the rights to education, the national government has instituted measures to intervene in the township educare sector with the objective of improving the quality of the teaching and learning. The rationale is to ensure that children receive the best possible educational stimulation within a child's first 1 000 days and thereby offer the necessary foundation for subsequent school learning. An important strategy to achieve this goal is through the provision of state subsidies from the Department of Social Development (DSD) (birth to four years of age) and through the Department of Basic Education (DBE) (five to six years of age) (Atmore, Van Niekerk, & Ashley-Cooper 2012). The provision of grants to the operators of an educare is contingent on the formalisation of the micro-enterprise in terms of a myriad of conditions as specified by the DSD and DBE (and refined by the respective provincial entities) and municipal land-use regulations. These objectives square with the policy requirements for educares to be formally registered (as required in the Children's Act No. 38 of 2005). In a review of progress towards this goal, Atmore et. al. (2012) report that despite an increase in government spending on the sector, only about 58% of the children in registered educares received the state subsidy. The authors note with concern that 'many more children are in unregistered ECD centres' (p. 138), the number of which are unknown. The prognosis of a sector operating largely outside the remit of the Children's Act and receiving no state support has promoted grant-dispensing institutions to target funding towards the training of educare staff and the provision of technical support to assist educares to formalise. As we have shown in Chapter 4, since formalisation is aligned to property (the micro-enterprise must be definable in terms of a legal relationship to land and infrastructure), one of the greatest obstacles to formalisation are land system barriers, including land-use

FIGURE 11.8 Signage for a survivalist educare facility

FIGURE 11.9 Example of an informal educare with good facilities in front yard of private house

zoning, land encroachment, non-compliance with building standards and the absence of property title. While well intended in its objectives to facilitate the registration of educares, neither the state nor NGOs are likely to deliver formalisation at scale under these constraints. The onerous requirement of registration has the consequence of limiting the number of subsidised educares to the sub-component, which are typically larger businesses, operating in non-residential properties (some outside residential areas) with stronger NGO linkages. We consider that the educare sector provides a further example of how a stringent regulatory framework gives rise to 'enforced informalisation'.

Across our nine South African sites, educares account for 2% of the micro-enterprise activities. The availability of individual businesses, using a measure per 1 000 population, varies from Vrygrond with the highest availability (3.9 per 1 000) to Ivory Park with the lowest availability (1.48 per 1 000). There are numerous factors affecting both the supply and demand for educares. On the supply side, an important influence is the role of religious organisations and external NGOs in either operating educares or providing financial and technical support. On the demand side, the level of household income and the outlook of the parents with respect to the quality of educational support and concerns around safety are important variables in shaping demand. We interviewed 197 educares which collectively accommodate 7 946 children and provide employment to 653 persons, 529 of whom work on a full-time basis.

The educares we identified are almost entirely run by South Africans (99%); all, apart from a few wife and husband teams, are women operated (94%). The average age of these women was 53.7 years old, which suggests that the women who run educares can be best characterised as 'surrogate' grandmothers rather than 'surrogate' mothers, seen from the perspective of their role as care-providers (following the use in Drake & Stringer 2016). A common characteristic of the educare owners – certainly those owner-operators – is their deep concern for the welfare of children. The desire to do something to 'protect' children was often cited as a reason for starting the business, though many commenced in business from a position of unemployment. A similar concern is shared by educare owners who established the business with the objective of transferring the skills they acquired in teaching, nursing or domestic work in the formal (non-township) economy to the home environment and their own community. These educare owners were noticeably better placed in terms of skills, investment capital and social standing to grow their businesses, though the barriers to formalisation were universal.

In accordance with the variance in settlement characteristics across the sites, it is unsurprising that 49% of educares operate within a residential house, 26% within a shack, 18% within a separate brick-building structure, 3% within a refurbished shipping container (usually linked to an NGO project) and a small number of businesses operating from structures such as prefabricated buildings. The larger educares might use a combination of several different structures to operate the business. Many of those operating from separate brick structures represent a sub-group who have made purposeful investments to their properties to provide specific facilities; this cohort includes ECDCs run by NGOs and religious organisations. But regardless of the structure from which they operate, most educares are situated in residential locations where they serve the neighbourhood demand for childcare services (and surrogate 'grandmotherhood') away from home.

In Chapter 4, we provided an example of a case in which the educare operator, Jane, made considerable investments to provide an additional classroom, a separate kitchen, a sickbay/office, and specialist toilet facilities to align her business with regulatory requirements. She was nevertheless unable to attain compliance since she did not own the property; because the buildings were non-standard; and the building footprint encroached across the cadastral boundary. As such, her efforts to enter the regulatory realm constitute what Drake and Stringer (2016) refer to as 'ceremonial compliance' (p. 181). This takes us to the point that educares which operate from a residential home benefit from using the existing infrastructure in a spatially and economically efficient manner, without imposing additional investment demands on the business owner. In this situation, the lounge may double-up as a classroom, the bedroom may double-up as a sick room, food is prepared in the home kitchen and the children access the existing bathroom or toilet. Utilising existing infrastructure, the micro-enterprise has high potential to attain sustainability, subject to the (timely) payment of fees. Should the educare proceed to attain regulatory compliance, either through compulsion in Jane's case or as a strategic move to access new resources, only then does the business need to raise capital to invest in assets and infrastructure to become formalised. Such investments are undertaken with careful consideration, for the costs can be difficult to recoup without state subsidies. Furthermore, if the business were to cease trading, the homeowner would be saddled with potentially unusable infrastructure (such as small toilets) which would need further capital to be repurposed for an alternative use.

At the time of our research, fees varied from R150–R300 per child per month (the average cost for babies was R217 and for older children it was R186). In the case of registered micro-enterprises (with the DSD), average fees were R154 for babies and R130 for children, which indicates that the investment costs from registration are not offset through increased fees. The current state subsidy ranges from R12–15 per day per child, varying between provinces. Given that a high portion of children (even in registered educares) are not subsidised, the investment required for formalisation is difficult to recover through the business (from the subsidy and fees), leaving the educare operator in a predicament between ensuring sustainability and responding to social obligations. A major complaint from owners is that because their clients are poor, many of them default on their fees. As most educare owners see themselves as caregivers, they are reluctant in general to exclude a child for reasons of non-payment, despite their frustrations with parents who might prioritise expenditure on other obligations. As a result, a number of children within educares attend at little and sometimes no cost. For example, Jane, the educare owner we featured in Chapter 4, had four non-paying learners, two of whom lost their father to a '*ritualistic killing*' (3/2399/F/nd).

Across the cohort, 71 respondents (36%) reported that they were registered with the DSD and 33 (16%) said that they were registered with the DBE. Yet merely 25 of these businesses received the state subsidy for child attendees. Educare operators do not see themselves as competing within a market, rather as persons offering a community service in a sustainable way. The relationship between educare owners is socially complex, with more interdependence, collaboration and information sharing than (for example) the relationships of mutual respect and solidarity common amongst street traders.

The educare owners in Delft South – whom we engaged in a participatory action research process to understand the challenges of formalisation – informed us that their fellow business owners had a clear understanding such that any of the educares within their network would not accept a new placement if the parents of that child had outstanding debts with another educare. Such an agreement constitutes part of what Drake and Stringer (2016) recognise as the community assets to which township educares contribute and from which they derive social capital (including stature).

Through a DST process, one of the participants, Lanie (SLF 2017b), shared an account of her struggle to formalise an educare in Eindhoven (Delft South); Figure 11.10.

Like many of the informants in our dataset, Lanie learnt her teaching skills and developed a vision for her business through working as a teachers' assistant for three years. She opened her educare in 2016, operating from a '*wendy house*' which doubled up as her home situated in the residential backyard of a formal house. Within a year, the business grew to accommodate 20 children. She reflected back on this period: '*I was excited to see the educare growing and every day I couldn't wait to see the children the next day…Some of them didn't want to go home to their parents*'. But then a competing educare emerged.

The new business was started with financial support from the church, operated from a commercial building within the church property and had, from the outset, linkages to the provincial DSWD. Since the new educare had access to state subsidies and sponsorship from philanthropic NGOs, it was able to reduce school fees and thus soon acquired learners from surrounding educares. As a result, Lanie's educare dropped in size from 20 to 8 learners. She reflects through her story: '*Losing those children from my centre was very sad. It felt like I was losing my own children. Each day it breaks my heart to see the children pass my centre. They look at me through the window and wave on their way to the other centre. And they are wearing my track suits [the school uniform she developed]. I feel like I have lost everything I worked so hard for.*'

FIGURE 11.10 An illustration by Lanie used in her DST about her educare, highlighting her strong personal relationship with the children

The story highlights the fragility of educare businesses within a competitive market environment in which price dominates, whereas their social capital (credibility) and the community assets which underpin sustainability are devalued. To compete in this market, survivalists like Lanie would need to secure land ownership, obtain municipal compliance with building standards, rezone the property and then register the business. In reflecting on these obstacles, Lanie said despondently: *'it's [these processes are] very expensive and I have no one to help me. The government needs to know how hard it is for people like us, who are so passionate about our work, to run even a small EDC [educare]'*. She ended her story with a rallying call to the community of which she and her business are assets: *'...as EDCs in the Delft community, we need to stand together and help each other to fight for our children'*.

The spatial logics of township educares underline the importance of 'safety' in shaping both the demand for educare and their supply. Parents demand safety for their children on the route to the educare in the mornings and afternoons and at the venue itself. Out of concern for safety, parents are inclined to send their children to a local educare (where proximity equates to safety), so long as it meets other criteria. Possibly the most important of these criteria is the reputation of the educare owner and their standing within the community. On the flip side, educare owners with a high standing within the community are also better placed to access community assets and resources, from networks to training to ad hoc asset transfers, which in turn results in a better business. Since the notion of safety is linked to the social reputation of the educare operator herself, it is unsurprising that 88% of the educares in our census were owner-operated. In response to safety concerns, the educare owner was expected by her client parents to invest in security-related infrastructure, such as a secure perimeter fence and lockable gate, and personally maintain vigilance over the children and their caregivers. To many parents, the investments to ensure safety are considered more important than the nature of the dwellings from which the business operates, so an educare running from a shack as in Lanie's situation, is not necessarily seen as inferior so long as safety is ensured, the children are adequately fed and have access to a toilet.

While the safety of children is paramount to the success of an educare, this should not mean that parents do not desire well-equipped facilities or educational instruction. Parents are realistic about the balance between the quality of the educational service and the cost of attending the educare given the general absence of state subsidisation. Yet, to assess the quality of education in terms of ECD facilities and infrastructure can be very misleading. In terms of playgrounds, our data shows that 42% of the educares have dedicated facilities, though in the older settlements such as KwaMashu, where settlement densities are lower than newly established townships, 88% of the educares have playgrounds. Though some educares are situated close to public parks, few owners are willing to take their children to these parks, citing their concern for safety. As such, children in educares without playgrounds are commonly housebound – although play activities still occur. Our data on playgrounds need to be seen in the context of the substantial variation in the size of business, using pupil numbers as a means of differentiation. The smallest educares accommodate merely a handful of children. The median ratios of children per educare, separated into three age groups for the entire dataset are: 5 babies per educare, 20 children of 1–5 years old per educare, and 11 children over 5 years of age per educare. To emphasise the argument that most educares are very small businesses, our data shows that 48% of educares accommodate fewer than 10 children in total. The average ratio of full-time carers/teachers to children for all educares combined is 1:15, which falls within the recommended norms and standards (Department of Social Development 2014).

An important proxy indication of quality (from the parent perspective) is that the educare provides meals. We found that 78% offer school meals. In most educares, a meal menu posted on the wall announces this service to parents. The provision of two meals is considered the norm; a breakfast of porridge and bread and a cooked lunch or sandwiches. Some educares require parents to provide an additional snack-pack if the child is to remain in 'after care' and return home in the early evening when their parents get back from work. School meals are made from low-cost ingredients, using foods that are accessible from local sources and sometimes donations from businesses or NGOs which are distributed via the community network. The state subsidy ringfences a portion of the funds for expenditure on meals, though this requirement is virtually impossible to monitor. As in the case of the 'school menu', wall posters of the English alphabet, learning charts and programme schedules are used as devices to signify service excellence (see Figure 11.11, Figure 11.12 and Figure 11.13).

The programme schedule holds a prominent place and conveys to parents and visitors the rigid structure and routine to which the children are subject. Educare programmes generally follow a similar template (acquired through the community network of educare owners) and include mealtimes, toilet times, play times, rest times and times for educational activities. To carry out the schedule, the educare businesses selectively invest in equipment and resources, prioritising tangible assets such chairs and tables, sleeping mats, and playground equipment (though neither books nor stationery) over investments in intangible resources, such as qualified carers.

FIGURE 11.11 Wall posters, learning charts and programme schedules signify messages and ceremonial compliance with registration

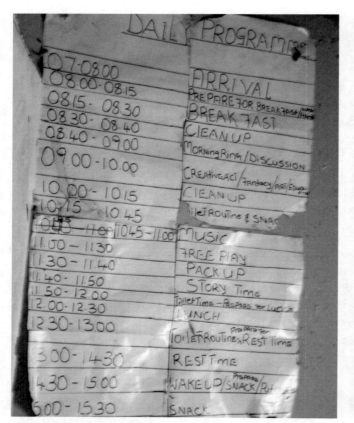

FIGURE 11.12 and FIGURE 11.13 Most educares display a wall chart of the daily programme, indicating structure and discipline

The investment strategies for township educares are constrained by three factors: first, limited and set finance which the business can mobilise through its fee structure; second, the spatial constraints of the home situation; and third, the complexity of the bureaucratic and legal processes to achieve regulation. Additionally, the majority of educare owners are subject to the psychological fear that comes from running a non-registered (and non-compliant) business. The weight of this pressure can be swiftly amplified if children come to harm, as occurred in the incidence of Listeriosis identified in educare-attending children after consuming polony on the premises (Kubheka 2018), or, in the worst case situation, die at school. This happened, as we learnt in the tragic incident told in Jerome's DST when a child who was incubating a bacterial infection died while in his care (SLF, 2017d). As he recalled in his narrative of the event: '*My wife was so traumatised, that she just collapsed. Some of the child's close relatives who were there [on the scene] blamed me for what happened. But I was too busy trying to calm my wife for them to disturb me. What broke my heart so much was to see my wife crying so uncontrollably, while I didn't know what to do…I contacted some of our ECD forum members and they were there for a short while to support us. At that moment, it felt like my whole life was changing, and we felt like giving up everything, because of all the complaints the [deceased child's] family had made against us.*' Fortunately for Jerome and his wife, the business was registered and records from past health inspections were used as evidence to show that the educare was compliant. Had the business not been registered, they would have been compelled to close and might have faced prosecution for contravening the Children's Act and a host of other regulations.

Traditional healers

Traditional healing is an important ethno-cultural service utilised by potentially 80% of Africans (World Health Organization 2002). In South Africa, traditional healing is linked to specific cultural practices, including ancestor veneration and herbalism, with practitioners respectively known as *amagqirhas* and *amaxwhele* (among the amaXhosa) (Ngubane 1977) (See Figure 11.14).

Among Rastafari groups in the Western Cape, herbal practitioners are known as 'bush doctors' (Aston Philander 2011) (see Figure 11.15).

Although there are important cultural, gendered and regional differences in traditional healing practices, knowledge has fluidly transferred across space and time and the practice remains both culturally and practically relevant today. Traditional healers work to resolve socio-physical and medical problems with specific herbal treatments and/ or ancestor-inspired medicinal blends primarily based on wild-harvested biological ingredients (Mander, Ntuli, Diederichs & Mavundla 2007). Within townships, there is high demand for traditional healing services. Petersen, Moll, Hocking and Collins (2015) found that two thirds of respondents in the settlements of Sweet Home Farm, Imizamo Yethu and Vrygrond (three of our sites) reported to have used traditional medicine (herbal preparations) in the previous twelve months. It is said that traditional healing services are not simply an alternative to western medicine, but for some people and some ailments are seen as a preferable service (Natrass 2006). Here, we focus on the role of traditional healers in two respects; first in respect to their

FIGURE 11.14 A woman healer and her apprentices, Ivory Park
Note: Traditional healers are culturally diverse, with practitioners commonly known as *amagqirhas* and *amaxwhele*

FIGURE 11.15 Rastafari-inspired "Bush Doctors", Vrygrond

role in building spatial connections, linking people to their ancestors, places of tradition, and distant physical environments, and second, in respect to their role in redressing social crises. Through these mechanisms, traditional healers enable urban residents to make sense of the rapidly changing urban landscape, while retaining their linkages to culture and community.

In contrast to much western medicine, which focuses on addressing symptoms of an illness, traditional healing responds to the question 'why am I feeling ill?' and therefore considers an ailment from the spiritual (often first) and the physical perspective (Dold & Cocks 2012). Herbalists such as *amaxwhele* (individuals referred as *ixwhele*, commonly known as *inyanga* in isiZulu) and bush doctors provide remedies to treat a range of illnesses, including gastrointestinal problems, urogenital complaints, skin ailments and cardiovascular diseases (Aston Philander 2011). Part of the skill of the healer lies in their specialist knowledge of the medicinal value of plant material and other substances (Truter 2007). Where the cause of illness is derived from personal conflict such as jealousy, hatred or revenge, or social crises such as joblessness, economic downturns, and matters such as business competition (see Hickel's 2014 contextualisation), the traditional healer practises a combination of herbalism and divination. This is to treat the affliction of *Idziso* or 'African poison' which can result in misfortune, illness and death (Ashforth 2002). Believed to be sent by a witch, *Idziso* eventually consumes its victim, with its removal requiring treatment by the *amagqirha* who practise at the interface of religion, magic and medicine (herbalism) (Cocks 1997). Through their ability to maintain contact with ancestors (and the ancestral land), *amagqirha* and *amawhele* are able to learn about the causes of misfortunes and prepare the required herbal treatments from specific biological resources on the strict advice of ancestors.

Healers are trained through apprenticeships under the direction of elders, usually upon receiving a calling. The training can take many years and entails learning about aliments, medicinal ingredients and undergoing a series of specific ceremonies. As practitioners, the healers acquire medicinal ingredients from wild-harvested sources, either collecting it themselves, purchasing at *muti* markets (after the isiZulu word for tree), or acquiring it from other healers (Figure 11.16).

Research on the sourcing of ingredients for traditional medicine in KwaZulu-Natal (Mander 1998), Eastern Cape (Dold & Cocks 2002), Mpumulanga and Limpopo Provinces (Botha, Witkowski & Shackleton 2004; Williams, Witkowski & Balkwill, 2007) and the Western Cape (Petersen, Moll, Collins, & Hockings 2012; Petersen, Charman, Moll, Collins & Hockings 2014), all point to the cultural importance of obtaining wild-harvested biological materials. In spatial terms, these materials are obtained from traditional lands which, in the current timeframe, are situated under different states of ownership and include communal land, private farms and state-protected areas. A few of the informants in our survey sourced ingredients from other countries, including Zimbabwe, Uganda and Kenya (one respondent said that he travels to Kenya to source medicine 10 times a year) (5/2798/M/23). The biological composition of the medicine is thus a symbolic device to connect the patient to their ancestral homes (see Figure 11.17).

The reliance on wild-harvested resources presents a risk to resource conservation (see Petersen et al. 2014), though this risk needs to be understood in political terms. For the Rastafarian bush doctors, the denial of their rights to access medicinal plants inconservation areas is seen as a strategy by '*the powerful [who] want our land*', whereas access '*to the herbs gives us equality*' (5/2807/M/25).

Due to its social and medicinal importance, traditional healing is subject to the Traditional Health Practitioners Act (No. 22 of 2007). The Act provides a regulatory framework to ensure the efficacy, safety and quality of traditional healthcare services, thus seeking to formalise the industry and incorporate traditional practices into the national healthcare system. The Act requires traditional headers to apply to a professional council to be registered, including in their application proof of qualifications and character references (Street & Rautenbach 2016). The Act is however largely ineffectual, for apart from stimulating membership of traditional healer associations, the sector remains largely informal and outside of any formal frameworks.

We interviewed 98 healers across the sub-groups of *sangomas* (62%), *inyangas* (13%), faith healers (1%) and Rasta-inspired bush doctors (23%). Of our respondents, 56% were men of average age 45 years, while the average time in the trade was 11 years. Traditional healers are characteristically older people and provide healing services on a 'lifelong' basis from the time of the calling. Since the business model is based on the reputation of the practitioner, the longer a traditional healer remains in practice the stronger their reputation becomes and (potentially) the better their client base. Although it is difficult to obtain accurate information on business turnover, most healers can be regarded as survivalists, though the more sustainable entrepreneurs earn around R3 500 per month (Petersen, Moll, Hockings & Collins 2015), commonly in addition to other work opportunities. We found anecdotal evidence to indicate that some practitioners have succeeded in building profitable businesses, seeing over 100 clients a month. Amongst our survey respondents, the lowest price charged for a consultation was R50, whereas the highest price was R500. The average price was R165.

FIGURE 11.16 The trade of traditional medicine occurs both on the street and in *muti* markets
Note: Wild harvested products are preferred.

FIGURE 11.17 Traditional healing combines the ancient, spiritual and modern
Note: This is reflected in medicines, practices and symbolism.

In considering traditional healers from a micro-enterprise perspective, we observed a subtle spatial divide between those healers operating from high-street localities and those operating from residential homes. Most high-street traditional healers are men; and while most women operate from their homes, this is not an uncommon practice for South African male healers as well. On the high street, the businesses have signage, the *muti* is on open display, and the healer operates as both a 'chemist' and 'physician'. Some businesses have private 'consulting rooms' within the shop, thereby enhancing micro-enterprise legitimacy. The location of the business on the high street is purposeful, affording clients a high degree of anonymity that would not be possible for a business situated in a residential situation. It is not uncommon to find 'notice boards' on display outside the shop within the shop itself, advertising the range of services provided. Often these services target personal anxieties (around sexual performance, body image and reproduction) as well inflictions of what scholars describe as the 'crisis of social reproduction' (Hickel 2014, p. 2), which include joblessness, competition, and the inability to fulfil social obligations. It is to these concerns that, in some cases, charlatans masquerading as exotic traditional healers have set up shops on the high street (see Figure 11.18 and Figure 11.19) and advertise their services (see Figure 11.20 and Figure 12.6).

Some of these herbalists claim to emanate from 'mysterious' places (to an uninformed person) such as the Island of Pemba and to be of regal status, offering *mutis*, magical trinkets and clairvoyance into the futures that await their clients.

In contrast to the high-street chemists and 'prophet healers', the majority of township traditional healers operate as a social enterprise, rather than business. These social

FIGURE 11.18 High-street healers capitalise on common public anxieties
Note: Some of these operators could be considered charlatans.

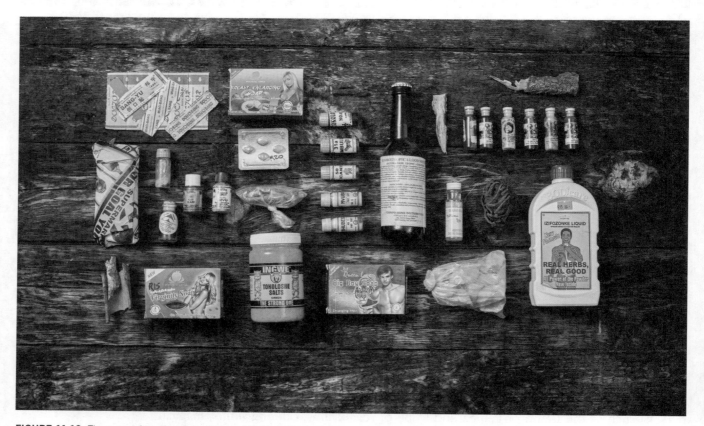

FIGURE 11.19 The range of traditional medicines available in the market includes grey market and counterfeit products
Credit: Justin Patrick

FIGURE 11.20 An informalist business, advising illegal (and potentially unsafe) health services
Notes: Informalist entrepreneurs operate via cell-phone appointments to provide a range of informal and potentially unsafe services on reproductive and sexual health needs. Their services are advertised via flyers and posters, the latter often glued to lampposts.

micro-enterprises are not commercially advertised but use tell-tale signifiers such as the presence of certain plants or animals, the colour in which a building (residential house) has been painted and/or its architectural style. Within the cohort of *sangomas*, 45% of our respondents consulted with one or fewer clients per week; similarly, 46% of the bush doctors consulted with one or fewer clients per week. In the words of one of the respondents: '*I do not see practising in traditional medicine as a business…I am only providing a service to the people*' and she chose to maintain her service as '*a private issue*' rather than one that is advertised (5/2715/F/nd).

In understanding the role of traditional healers as part of a community social institution, it should be recognised that 'true' healers (as opposed to others who can be seen as charlatans) do not select this career path, but are 'called' to fulfil this role by the ancestors. One respondent explained that she had a calling in 2002 while worshipping at her church, the ZCC (Zionist Christian Church). As she preferred the church to the role of healer, she at first resisted but since accepting her calling has been able to help people find employment (5/2714/F/54). Another respondent explained that he used to work in Johannesburg but struggled to concentrate on the job because the calling gave him no rest. He then quit his job and accepted the calling. As a practising healer, he does not need to promote his services for his patients '*dream about him and are then directed to his place*' (5/2723/M/55). It was recalled on numerous occasions that those who reject the calling may experience severe illness and psychosocial trauma. As a consequence of the close relationship between the healer and their ancestors, many insisted on not marketing their service, instead relying on the news of their powers to spread through the ancestors themselves or via word of mouth. In consequence of their sense of responsibility towards the community – to appease the ancestors, drive away evil spirits, counteract witchcraft, and assist people to obtain spiritual support for their economic endeavours – traditional headers usually provide their services on credit terms. Some customers pay their debts, but many abscond or 'run away'. This challenge threatens any business sustainability; as one respondent summed up: '*some clients come and they are bankrupt so I need to treat for free to fix their problem and this is a problem*' (1/2788/F/65). Despite their best efforts, when their business downturns, the traditional healer is saddled with the double burden of financial ruin and the 'wrath of the ancestors', or in the words of a respondent: '*the ancestors are angry – they have made me lose my customers, lose my money, and then lose my life*' (5/2795/F/65). Traditional healers have undergone an extensive internship. In this respect, some provide education and counselling as much as a specific health service.

Outlook

In this chapter, we have examined three important business sectors which, though different, collectively contribute towards place making. The significance of their respective roles lies in the reshaping of the township away from its historical design, as a residential dormitory, to a settlement where people feel secure (if not safe) in their sense of belonging and are able to forge individual and collective strategies to pursue their dreams and fulfil their social obligations. All three sectors facilitate spatial connections, either to the ancestral past of cultural cohesion or a modern future of cultural fluidity. In different ways, the three sectors provide a response to the 'crisis of social reproduction' which many township residents confront. Hair-care services enable individuals to either differentiate themselves or conform to cultural norms and labour market expectations; educare services enable parents (especially mothers) to exit the township for employment or education, in the knowledge that their children are secure and learning to adapt within a structured environment; and traditional-healer services address social, psychological and physical 'barriers' that inhibit progress in the urban environment. We have also shown how these sectors differentially provide business opportunities for women.

The three sectors fulfil a role in building a social structure which supports networking and information exchange. In this social function, hair salons and educares are spatial sites which facilitate meetings, conversation and gestures that enable individuals to increase their social capital within the community. We saw in the case of educares how the core strength of the sector, in other words its resilience, lies in the collective assets such as peer support to which the owner has access, something that neither state not grant-dispensing NGOs (adequately) recognise in their focus on formalisation. Traditional healers help to realise the potential of this social capital through redressing the causes of crises which undermine networking and information exchange, and spell discord, while securing the support of the ancestors.

Through focusing on their social role, we have treated these sectors as fulfilling a function of building social infrastructure, which in business terms is equivalent to operating an enterprise with dual social and business objectives. The notion of social enterprise squares with a considerable proportion of the educares that we identified and interviewed and, though less obvious, applies to some of the traditional healers. Our recognition of the social function of such service-oriented businesses should not detract from the profit logic which accounts for most hair-salon businesses and also the high-street chemists and 'prophet healers'. For educare owners and traditional healers, the tension between the social and business motives are cast in relief through the efforts of the state to regulate, which requires the entrepreneur to make compliance investments. For those micro-enterprises that choose to become formalised, the compliance investments can potentially improve the 'quality' of the service, as we have seen in the case of educares, but can also undermine sustainability and the social value of the business.

Jelous Down Coca-Cola

12
SUSTAINING BUSINESS AND COPING WITH RISK

In this chapter we analyse some of the strategies and informal institutions that township business persons utilise to grow their business, invest profits in new endeavours and cope with risks.

CHAPTER 12

Sustaining business and coping with risk

In the formal economy, the strategies that businesses pursue are influenced by the regulatory framework and the role of formal institutions. In business studies, formal institutions are understood as laws, regulations and the relevant supporting state agencies (Webb, Tihanyi, Ireland & Sirmon 2009). The regulatory framework, as one example of a formal institution, influences what activities a business may legitimately pursue and specifies conditions under which the business is required to operate in compliance with the law. These might require investments to comply with matters such as environmental health, safety standards and labour conditions. Similarly, regulations might specify minimum standards, traceability and transparency, which are widely applied, for example, to food products and their supply chains. As we have argued in earlier chapters, formal regulatory frameworks have considerably less influence in the township economy where informality is widespread, apart from a few sectors such as liquor retail, undertaking and the provision of educational services where businesses have strong incentives to formalise. Yet even in these sectors where regulatory compliance is best enforced, the existence of legal-institutional frameworks does little to prevent individuals from operating businesses illegally, as is the case for the majority of liquor retailers and educare operators. In these and other sectors where adherence to rules is often enforced, trading informally necessitates gearing the business to avoid what scholars describe as 'the undesired attention' of regulatory authorities as well as the 'unwanted attention' of criminals and enemies (Kistruck, Webb, Sutter & Bailey 2014, p 4). From the perspective of institutional theory, such informality is described as the consequence of the incongruence between formal and informal institutions (Webb et al. 2009; Williams & Shahid 2016). Informal institutions, in this sense, refer to the set of norms, practices, values and beliefs that are widely shared across a population and embodied in culture. Selling beer and providing childminding services, to return to the examples above, might be illegal under formal laws, but are accepted as morally legitimate and culturally acceptable under informal institutions, certainly amongst a sufficiently large segment of the township population to be regarded as 'legitimate' informal business.

Institutions fulfil an especially important role in the formal economy. Financial institutions enable formal businesses to raise capital and manage risk through purchasing services such as insurance. Additionally, legal institutions safeguard intellectual property, maintain brand and product integrity and enable entrepreneurs to securely transact and manage the risks of capital investments. Although these institutional products and services can benefit the township economy, such as with respect to property rights and in providing licences to minibus taxis and taverns, their penetration in informal markets is relatively shallow. The truncated reach of formal institutions can be attributed, in part, to the existence of alternative, organically-emergent, informal institutional services and organisational rules that influence business practice in terms of providing alternative strategies of investment and risk control. Steven, the Avanza taxi operator whose story is told Chapter 7, said that if someone causes a motor accident then in accordance with practice they are required, there and then, to settle the repair costs in cash. In this chapter, we argue that these informal institutions and practices exist alongside, complement and contest state regulation and formal institutions. Furthermore, community and social relations influence the 'ways of doing business', and in certain contexts this influence supersedes formal regulating institutions. An important point is that these influences are not simply 'informal' alternatives, embraced to avoid regulatory capture or evade taxation or resist state authority, but mechanisms that can enable entrepreneurs to protect and grow their business (and secure the value of their investment) even in times of operational challenges.

In this chapter, we analyse some of the strategies and informal institutions that township business persons use to grow their businesses, invest profits in new endeavours and cope with risks. We argue that for many (micro-) entrepreneurs, informal institutions and practices provide more effective benefits to the business than formal institutions. Although the benefits of informal institutions might equate to a sub-optimal outcome, such as the comparative advantages of taverns (formal institutions) versus shebeens (informal institutions) in respect to access to supply chains and risks of non-compliance, their elevated importance reflects the pervasiveness of informality in the township context. This is attributable to a combination of the centrality of cash in transactions, the ineffectiveness of regulatory authorities, the power of 'big men' who use informality as a business strategy and socio-cultural influences. The influence of social context on decision-making is central to our understanding of informal institutions. In *KasiNomics*, Alcock (2015) writes: 'the belief system which says "take care of the past and the future will take care of itself" is deep seated. ...This belief system can influence things like planning and investment. If you can choose only one, what is more important? A burial plan or an education plan?' (p. 101). There are, as a result, a diverse range of micro-enterprises that service funeral events and unveiling ceremonies, including informal financial services which aim to minimise the cost-burden on a bereaved household (Figure 12.1 and Figure 12.2).

Our spatial analysis on this topic centres on the level of invisible infrastructure, for which symbolic and anecdotal evidence is required as shown in the example of the ceremonial investments to sustain cultural practice and connections to ancestors. Additionally, we examine spatial influences at the micro-context level where the consequences of certain practices are evidenced in the arrangement of infrastructure, the vernacular architecture and strategies to minimise an appearance of wealth. Just as informal institutions are difficult to conceptualise, being invisible to outsiders, so too are the power responses which are embodied in rules, practices and norms. These responses range from 'self-levelling' pressures, to reciprocal understandings which underpin cooperative and mutual support in savings societies, to actions that use violence to enforce contractual agreements.

FIGURE 12.1 A township funeral service where large investments are made for honouring the dead

FIGURE 12.2 'Taking care of the past': a ceremonial post with sacrificial horns

Business strategies

Fronting

The township economy exerts a 'self-levelling' pressure on most entrepreneurs. From a community perspective, successful entrepreneurs can be scorned by their communities, with their success attributed to power of the entrepreneur to mobilise social, spiritual (including magic), economic and/or political resources rather than recognition of entrepreneurial drive (Ashforth 2005; Hickel 2014). In the township context, overtly successful businesses can be the subject of community suspicion and jealousy, occasionally even witchcraft accusations, or simply 'pulled down' through network withdrawal and sabotage (Koens & Thomas 2015). When asked about the main challenges that impacted on the family business, one KwaMashu informant responded: *'my mother was bewitched by neighbours because she runs a spaza shop and that also she bought a house'* (2/1302/F/37). Whereas the particular spaza shop was deliberately shabby in appearance, thus signalling a message that the business was survivalist, neighbours perceived the link between the spaza shop and the residential house as a sign of entrepreneurial success. The perception of entrepreneurship as something alien to social norms aligns with African nationalist ideology which holds the state, not private individuals, responsible for economic growth and wealth distribution (Anciano & Piper 2019). This constitutes a paradox in African nationalism. On the one hand, individual wealth accumulation through small business is seen (from the African National Congress [ANC] Party perspective) in suspicious terms (prompting the question: how can it be possible?); on the other hand, wealth accumulation through state and corporate B-BBEE measures is seen conversely as politically acceptable (see Figure 12.3).

FIGURE 12.3 Flagrant display of political wealth, *shisa nyama* Ivory Park

Note: Unlike township entrepreneurs who tend to conceal their incomes, earning considerable wealth from the state is celebrated with conspicuous consumption among the political elite and 'big men'. Photograph taken in Ivory Park.

The latter has given rise to the 'capture' of state procurement processes through strategies commonly known as 'tenderpreneurship' (Piper & Charman 2018). In Zukisani's DST (SLF 2017c) about his land struggles (see Figure 12.4), he retells how the local ANC ward councillor sought to oppose the operation of his container-based barber shop on the grounds of its spatial situation within the road reserve (public land), because, in his view, the business was seen to be successful rather than because the business spatial situation was unlawful. As he recalled: '*Why am I the only one being singled out, among so many? [other businesses also on public land]. I realised that they were jealous that my business was growing and the officials wanted to be bribed… [Yet in doing this business] I was simply acting on the words of the former president – Thabo Mbeki: 'Vuka uzenzele (do it yourself).'*

In some contexts, the distrust of entrepreneurs towards the state (and politicians) as a consequence of corruption and misuse of resources has influenced people's decisions to disengage with formal institutions (Littlewood, Rogers & Williams 2018). Similar concerns might inform the actions of businesses that operate in township markets, though our evidence indicates that those entrepreneurs who strategically embrace informality do so as a consequence of state weakness rather than as an action of political dissatisfaction.

From the early days of our field research, we learnt to avoid questioning business owners on their apparent entrepreneurial 'success', since the notion of success necessitated an unwelcome confession. It is for this reason that many 'successful' business persons seek patronage from political leadership and forge links to industry and influential bureaucrats. Relations of patronage fulfil an important role in helping these individuals to navigate

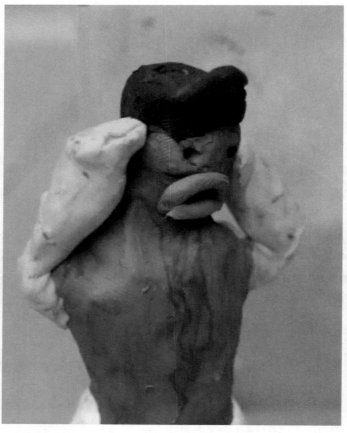

FIGURE 12.4 A scene from Zukisani's digital story where he, as a micro-entrepreneur, details his challenges with local politicians hostile to his success

state procedures and reduce the hurdles of red tape that impact on formalisation, to obtain favourable industry supply chain agreements, and to pacify common community jealousy (and thus opposition) towards individual success. Yet even with strong patrons, 'successful' entrepreneurs are acutely aware of the risks of operating their business within the township. The owner of the popular *shisa nyama* restaurant whose parking lot features in Figure 12.3 above situated her business on the settlement periphery (relocated away from its original location), with the owner intentionally residing outside the area.

To avoid criticism and resentment from the accumulation of wealth, often entrepreneurs adopt a strategy of 'downwardly mobile' fronting to give an impression of shabbiness in order to appear as economic survivalists (Figure 12.5).

Strategies of fronting align with the notion of Ubuntu which, from an epistemological viewpoint, holds that competition and inequality are un-African virtues which undermine traditional values of community and reciprocity. Ubuntu derives from the root for a 'person' (-*ntu*). The notion of Ubuntu has been employed in the post-apartheid nationalist project to promote African humanism, wherein the idea is based on the set of values and norms that historically governed extended family and village relationships, with an emphasis on consensus, mutual respect and selflessness. As an idea which has been 'reified' and given 'quasi-magical properties', the use of Ubuntu as a developmental paradigm has been justifiably criticised, not least because it overlooks the centrality of reciprocity at the base of all village relationships (McAllister 2009). The notion of Ubuntu contradicts the often-expressed view that neighbours would rather support the 'outsider' than see an 'insider prosper'. In one account, a shopkeeper bemoaned: '*[even if I have*

FIGURE 12.5 Visible business investments are minimal, but this does not mean the enterprise is unsuccessful
Note: A well-known (and well patronised) business within a destination of chicken braai outlets, Browns Farm.
Credit: Justin Patrick

all the [right] products in my shop…they [customers] will still go to the Somalians out of spite…because they do not want to see my business grow…even if I have the same prices as the Somalis' (2/1640/F/nd).

We have sought to argue throughout this book that entrepreneurial behaviour is informed by culturally specific and locally pertinent social rules, norms and relationships, some of which are indeed rooted in historical village life. Street traders who sell comparable items, for example, do not compete on price, but sell their goods at the same price per unit as all other traders. Instead, acceptable forms of competition in this situation are based on location (the position at the micro-context level within the market), product range and marketing approach, such as compiling a unique combination of vegetable products. While price competition is seen as unacceptable, pre-capital notions of discounting such as the offer of a *pasella* (from the isiXhosa verb root to give a present; whereas in isiZulu, the word *basela* derives from the verb root to beg), for example, when a grocery trader gives the customer an extra banana as 'a present' if a whole bunch is purchased, are deemed as acceptable (as a request) and reasonable (as a reward). In this sense, Kinyanjui (2019) refers to the *utu-ubuntu* business model, drawing on her experiences of informal markets in Nairobi. She argues that the *utu-ubuntu* model 'operates on the basis of humanity and solidarity […which helps traders…] harness their own agency through the sharing of experience and through self-regulation' (p. 2). We see evidence of these informal institutions in the practices of street traders in Chapter 5, though when taking into consideration the power responses which frame opportunities, not least the violent taxi entrepreneurs and spaza informalists, there are limits to the scope of collective self-regulation with respect to 'surplus deployment' for communal benefit. We see business practices as more capitalist than communalist, in general, though undertaken in ways that embrace cultural norms, symbols and belief systems.

The strategy of fronting generally applies to both the business and individual. Township entrepreneurs do not, in general, project a body image that could be associated with wealth. Instead, most dress down (both themselves and their businesses) to promote the message that their business is survivalist and profit-shy. Exuberant displays of personal wealth are almost never witnessed amongst township business persons, apart from the small group of (powerful) entrepreneurs who operate businesses in the township under the patronage of political leadership and powerful organised groupings, such as the leaders of taxi mother bodies discussed earlier. On one occasion, while conducting research in Ivory Park, we witnessed an exclusive sedan vehicle 'cruising' the neighbourhood. On enquiring from locals about this car and its occupants, we were told: *'they are drug dealers; they don't live around here'*. This said, outside of the micro-enterprise business sector, even among the poorest township residents, citizens take pride in their physical appearance and signifiers of status, justifying investment in fashionable branded clothing, footwear, apparel, hair styles and cell phones (see Alcock 2015). Ownership of a vehicle is both a measure of achievement and signifier of sophistication, taste and social attitudes via vehicle selection. While the township might be a space in which outsiders visit to parade their wealth and status (as in Figure 12.3), for insiders, wealth is subject to informal taxation (and sometimes resentment and jealousy), thus expressed more modestly.

'Luck'

We were often told that the success of an entrepreneur could be enhanced by 'luck'. This can occur in ways that are positive, to their benefit, or negative, to the disadvantage of competitors. In his research on the causes of xenophobic violence in a Durban township, Hickel (2014) argues that people (and young men especially) attributed the success of foreign-run spaza shops to witchcraft. We found that such thinking was more broadly applied, whereby people view 'luck' not as a consequence of entrepreneurial behaviour, but rather the influence of supernatural forces obtained through secret means. In the Cape Town township of Imizamo Yethu, Petersen, Moll, Hockings and Collins (2015) found that some 62% of 228 local households utilised traditional medicines in the previous 12 months, of which 17 of the top 19 medicines were used for 'cultural ailments, including luck enhancement' (p. 1051). In this respect, it is common to find advertisements on street poles and flyers throughout the township advertising the services of spirit mediums, herbalists and fortune tellers. In addition to providing medicines to enhance sexual performance and enable fertility, these healers offer to improve 'luck' and spiritual protection. Dr Kahima and Mama Surea, who once operated in Tembisa (along with other locations in Gauteng) in promoting their services as a palm reader and psychic, ask potential clients: 'Is everything becoming bad to your side?', to which they offer 'lucky charms', 'protection charms' and magic rings (see Figure 12.6).

This decidedly traditionalist conceptualisation of luck as a supernatural force has an important role in the establishment and operations of township businesses, and though difficult to interpret in conventional business studies and economics, is clearly reflected in the words of one traditional healer in Imizamo Yethu who simply stated: '*[a]bove this township is a gigantic cloud of black magic, and it controls absolutely everything that we do!*'

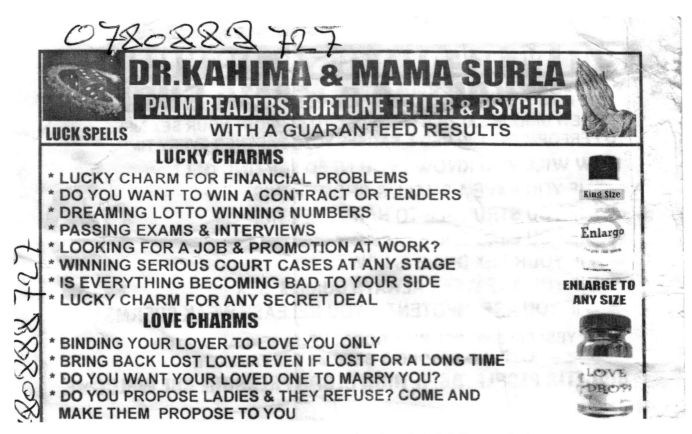

FIGURE 12.6 'Guaranteed results' from local palm readers, fortune tellers and psychics reflect a belief in supernatural influences in business and social lives

Reciprocity and favours

Social reciprocity is an important non-material resource for informal businesses. There are different aspects to reciprocal relationships, which collectively constitute an 'economy of favours' through which people seek opportunity and manage risks (for the original use of this term, see Ledeneva 1998). One such aspect of these favours is the relationships between the business owner, their competitors and their customers. Where an informal business is highly personalised, for example, in the hair-care, educare or liquor retailing sectors, the business relies on social relationships to establish its customer base. This necessitates that the entrepreneur makes a significant investment of social capital to establish personal ties through getting to know their clients and providing them with the occasional 'favour'. In some instances, the intention of granting favours might be altruistic, where for example, an individual perceives the primary function of the business to provide a social product or service, rather than achieve a profit outcome. Such business practices are undertaken to secure reciprocal support at a point in the future. A small house shop that provides bread on credit, without charging interest on this particular product (hence the favour), is an example of such practice. But it also means that many township business models are reliant on a continuous investment in social reciprocity, which in turn limits the pursuit of profit. As Neves and Du Toit (2012) argue: '[t]he neo-classical economic logic of maximising profit and minimising costs inadequately captures the potentially multiple objectives of economic informality… which include socially embedded considerations' (p. 135).

Social investment can take diverse forms, such as favourable customer terms, provision of credit or short-term loans, and other less obvious economic and social favours. We came across several examples in the tavern sector where the tavern owner had made their venue accessible to non-customers during the daytime for community meetings, to children so as to watch television or videos during the daytime, or to people seeking shelter from the weather. Such social investments are not only good for businesses but enable the entrepreneur to secure community support and create goodwill among customers. Fostering a good relationship with neighbours builds the social capital required to defend the entrepreneur against potential community threats to her/his business. Shebeen owners in sites like Sweet Home Farm where police raids constantly target illegal outlets would not be able to operate without community acceptance and reciprocal support. The incongruence between the formal institution (liquor policy) and informal institution (general acceptance of beer selling) was demonstrated in Chapter 9. Immigrant spaza shop entrepreneurs have also recognised the need to invest in reciprocity to protect their businesses from competitors and xenophobic thugs. These investments range from extending credit to loyal customers to providing cigarettes to street gangsters and in some sites like Delft South, providing monthly subsidies to gang leaders who provide 'protection' services.

Investments in social reciprocity also apply in relationships between businesses. These investments are spatially evident, for example, along the high street or in nodes where entrepreneurs share responsibility for controlling the space. In Chapter 5, we showed how micro-enterprises operating on a high street in Ivory Park accommodate diverse activities within the street through permitting flexible and fluid use of space and infrastructure resources. In one such micro-context, shopkeepers afford trading space outside the shop to micro-enterprises with limited spatial requirements, permitting them to set up their operations within the building overhang. In a similar logic, street-based businesses secure agreements with adjacent residential property owners to access utilities (such as water, electricity and the use of toilets); to repurpose boundary walls contingent with the sidewalk to display sale items; and to store trading goods at night. These agreements sometimes entail cash payments, but often include reciprocal 'favours' where the business owner compensates the homeowner with in-kind offerings, including providing surveillance over the property while the owner is away from home. The need to build social reciprocity is especially important for street traders who face insecure tenure, are vulnerable to eviction or dispossession, and endure petty crime and police harassment. For most street traders, the business requires working long hours at their stand or stall, reducing the amount of non-trading time during which the trader is able to engage in home-based activities. The high labour demand is especially burdensome on women who have to juggle business and social responsibilities, such as looking after children. Through investing in social relationships with other traders, individuals are able to make reciprocal demands on each other to 'mind their stalls' if attending to home matters and prevent encroachments onto their stands. This might entail surveillance (watching over each other's stock), conducting trading on behalf of an absent business owner, and upholding a land-use claim (in other words, to prevent site encroachment) when the owner is temporarily absent. These reciprocal exchanges are strongly informed by gender to the extent that women and men operate in different sectors within reciprocities of sisterhood and brotherhood, within which there might be secondary subdivisions of ethnicity, race and religion.

Entrepreneurs may form alliances with stronger networks as part of a strategy of 'defiance', to actively confront 'institutional pressures' (Sutter, Webb, Kistruck & Bailey, 2013). The term has been used to refer to responses by socially legitimate informal businesses against socially illegitimate actors, such as gangsters or thugs. Such power responses can be (and are) mobilised in xenophobic actions to defend or capture markets. In the township context, the most powerful networks are the taxi associations and political grouping such as the South African National Civic Organisation (SANCO) or the *Abahlali baseMjondolo*, the shack dwellers' movement. These networks provide a 'latent power' (Sutter et al. 2013, p. 753) which can then be activated in response for which more subtle strategies such as coordination, compromise or negotiation might be ineffective. Taxi drivers are known as 'enforcers' of informal institutions, especially outside and surrounding the transport hubs which serve as their operational base. Accessibility to latent power is especially important in sites where gangs control much of the territory, such as Delft South, whereas the high-street territory falls under the hegemonic authority of taxi associations. Political networks like SANCO offer protection to specific groups of entrepreneurs and can intervene to resolve disputes between business owners or other parties. In Sweet Home Farm, the first immigrant spaza shopkeepers to operate businesses in the settlement rented premises from leadership of *Abahlali* and SANCO respectively, with the two leaders affording the new businesses with protection from crime and a buttress against community opposition.

Social institutions

Social and human capital

Human and social capital are important to all businesses. In formal and established businesses, human and social capital are strengthened through, inter alia, investment in the skills development of employees, improvements to the working environment and investments in durable networks, such as membership of formal associations. In simple terms, human capital is understood as knowledge and technical skills, whereas social capital refers to the social resources that can be drawn upon through a network of relationships. Investments in social and human capital are also important for informal micro-enterprises, though the 'interplay' of human and social investments (Rooks, Szirmai, & Sserwanga 2009) does not necessarily result in the growth of the business in ways that can be anticipated. Rooks et al. (2009) argue that benefits to be derived from social investments can be influenced by size of the network and its resources. Large networks with weak resources, such as clan membership, can be less beneficial than small networks with strong resources, such as access to the suppliers of a product in high demand (for example, contraband tobacco or certain traditional medicines).

Most township micro-enterprises are sole proprietorships where network investments are made in consideration of the household, rather than the business per se. This means that members of the household are usually the primary recipients of human capital investments, though the boundaries between the micro-enterprise and household are fluid and generally overlap. Investing in the household is sensible for multiple reasons, though two factors are especially important: first, the household (and extended) family functions as a social safety-net in times of crisis, with survival often dependent on remittances (Du Toit & Neves 2009); and second, the family provides a mechanism for expanding and sustaining business activities over long periods without compromising centralised control or 'entrepreneurial orientation' (Zellweger, Nason & Nordqvist 2012, p. 143). The latter is important, as we show below, in strategies of divestment. It was common to hear business owners refer to the main legacy of their business in terms of financially enabling their children to attend school, college or university to obtain a formal qualification. The business itself had little to show in terms of investment in assets, equipment or systems. The reallocation of resources from business investment to household members shows that micro-enterprises do pursue long-term strategies, though these decisions tend to prioritise reducing the dependence of the family on the business through, for example, investing in the capacity of one's children to obtain formal employment. We did not encounter widespread evidence of where human capital investments had resulted in a specific benefit to the enterprise, though this reflects the fact that most township micro-enterprises are of young age. Over time, we would anticipate greater evidence of intergenerational businesses where the investments in human capital translate into productivity enhancement for the family business.

That said, Jack's business, a tavern and spaza shop situated in Ivory Park, provides an insight into how such an investment of human capital might ultimately benefit township business.

CASE STUDY: *Jack's business*

Jack, the business owner, sponsored both of his sons, via the profits of his business, to complete university degrees. Although the sons had other career ambitions, one having studied drama at the University of the Witwatersrand, both returned 'home' to work in the business where they applied their skills to introduce modernisation within the business, including instituting electronic stock control and a CCTV surveillance system. In this case, Jack's human capital investment resulted in financial investment into the property from which the business operated, thus transforming the original RDP-style house into a double-story building which accommodated the sons' families, while spatially separating the retail premises for the tavern and spaza shop. The spatial and social complexity of Jack's business can be seen in Figure 12.7 and Figure 12.8, where the residential development connects what would otherwise appear as two separate businesses.

In Chapter 8, we provided an example of how social capital is mobilised amongst immigrant shopkeepers to enable supply chain efficiencies and access low-cost labour, and strategically concentrate investment in shops within specific neighbourhood

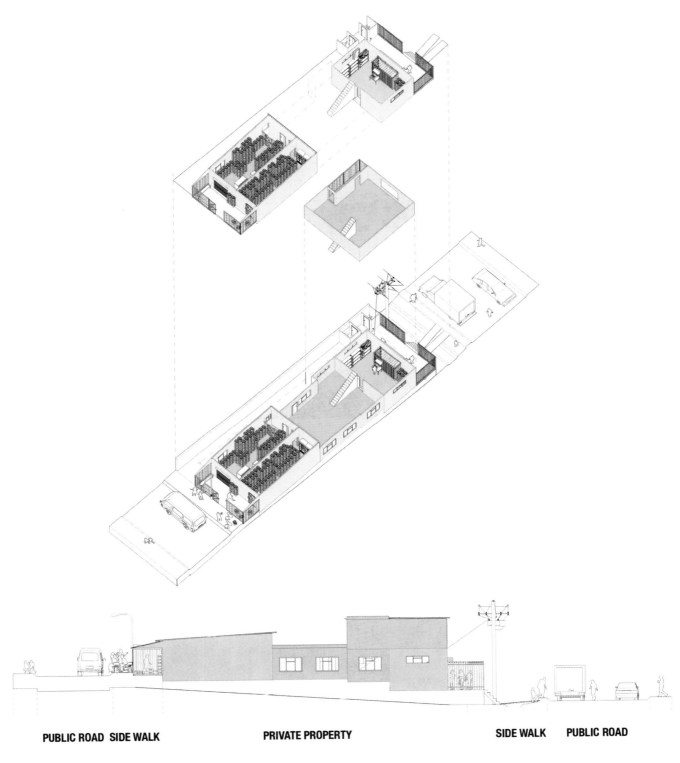

PUBLIC ROAD SIDE WALK   **PRIVATE PROPERTY**   **SIDE WALK**   **PUBLIC ROAD**

FIGURE 12.7 An illustration of how a residential property supports (and is organised into) two linked, but spatially separate businesses on neighbouring streets

FIGURE 12.8 Photographs of the two separate businesses, set-out to limit perceptions of business success

geographies. In the liquor sector, traders have organised into associations with the strategic objective of mobilising collective action against the liquor laws (and their enforced informalisation from formal institutional protection), another form of 'defiance'. While these associations have had limited influence on policy, their value lies in providing mutual support, sharing practical and strategic knowledge, and in linking the traders to liquor manufacturers. In Chapter 11, we highlighted the importance of social capital for township educare owners who, through their networks, institute norms of minimalising competitiveness among one another and good practice, dispense information and provide a platform linking individual educares to the state and industry or NGO sponsors. The relationship between micro-enterprises and networks can be formally constituted, based on membership, or informally and thus varies in strength. Strong networks, such as the taxi driver associations, have the power to impose impermeable barriers on entry into the sector, micro-manage the spaces in which the micro-enterprise can operate, and influence the modalities of the business such as the cost of service. While less controlling, weak networks can offer indispensable information, such as those amongst the Rastafari bush doctors who utilise their networks to access far-flung sites for wild harvesting, often on farms and private reserves, about which knowledge and logistical support is given. Apart from helping with the harvest, the bush doctors reported marketing their stock of traditional medicine through Rastafari-inspired religious groupings who provide access to an important customer base.

The church

Religious institutions fulfil a psychological and material role in managing risks. As part of this role, religious institutions enable access to a social network, provide solace and offer spiritual as well as moral guidance for attendees. For micro-enterprise entrepreneurs who believe that their business success can be impacted by supernatural intervention, either good or bad, religious institutions are guarantors against unforeseen risks and threats.

The institution of the church is widely supported in township communities. Most residents claim to be religious, whereas secularists are in the great minority. The high levels of religious devotion sustain a diversity of churches that are broadly aligned to the orthodox Anglican, Methodist and Catholic faiths, Jehovah's Witness, African Zionist, Pentecostal, and independent churches. Across the nine South African sites, the research identified 293 religious institutions (roughly one per 300 households), with the majority falling into the categories of African Zionist and independent churches (see Figure 12.9).

Apart from those churches which fulfil a missioning function, the majority of small churches operate on a financially independent basis, providing the pastor or church leader with an income stream. As micro-enterprises in their own right, these township churches derive income from tithes, providing services to officiate in marriages, funerals and unveiling ceremonies, and selling commodities such as 'holy' oil, water or salts. There were incidences where some of these religious institutions were directly linked to micro-enterprises (including educares, traditional healers and occasionally a house shop or even a shebeen) with the business and church often run from the same premises. Some of these businesses arose as a philanthropic service for members of the congregation and subsequently evolved to become financially autonomous micro-enterprises. The principal of an educare in Ivory Park which emerged through this development trajectory explained: 'The church members volunteered to take care of some kids for free. They brought the kids food and drinks. After a while they needed to get some income and so charged R50 until 2010. Then they hired qualified teachers and charged R100 from 2010' (3/2323/F/n.d.).

FIGURE 12.9 The great majority of township churches are independent of mainstream services and are best seen as business opportunities for the church leader

The use of religion as a business strategy is an old phenomenon. Some of the townships' fastest growing churches include the Brazilian-originated Universal Kingdom of the Church of Christ, which openly promotes a doctrine of prosperity in which wealth accumulation and personal enrichment are deemed rewards of devotion. Churches provide an important social network for marketing and business opportunities. In one such instance, an entrepreneur sold Avon products through small-group church interactions, including at weekly prayer meetings. In another example, a spaza shop owner explained that the business mainly served members of the ZCC and thus specialised in commodities that are particularly required by devotees of the church, including '*Excella cooking oil, skimmed milk, Trekker coffee and the like*' (2/1901/F/25). Formal businesses have recognised the potential of the church to provide access to difficult to reach segments of the market. Cell-phone companies, banks and insurance brokerages, amongst others, have established exclusive retail agreements with, for example, the ZCC to sell their products to its members, in terms of which a portion of the service fee goes to the church.

In the traditional healing sector, a number of healers gave examples of the linkage between 'business' and church, participating as both a member of the church while simultaneously assisting congregants with their 'cultural problems' (for which the orthodox doctrine was deemed inadequate) such as helping people to protect their businesses, accessing work opportunities and protecting people's homes from housebreaking and other forms of evil intent.

Capital

Stokvels

Stokvels are one of the most important informal institutions through which township entrepreneurs seek to manage risk and strengthen social capital. The term *'stokvel'* originated in the 19th century in the Eastern Cape and makes reference to the cattle auctions (stock fairs) at which people would pool resources to make a purchase (Lukhele 2018; Verhoef 2001). The term has since become synonymous with small-size groups which enable savings, minimise risks and build social bonds between members. It is thought that there are more than 800 000 *stokvel* groups in South Africa representing 11 million persons (Lukhele 2018), which could be true if one includes the diverse range of *stokvel*-like informal institutions within this number. There are a number of derivatives of the term *stokvel* as well as regional terms, including *mogodisô* (after the Sotho word *gogodisô*, meaning 'to grow') and *gooi-gooi* (after the Afrikaans word *oorgooi* 'to throw over'). The term is also applied to informal insurance products and food-banking groups. In her history of the *stokvel* movement, Verhoef (2001) argues that the main driving force was small networks of women who embraced *stokvels* as a saving mechanism because these institutions were independent of patriarchal control. Saving was one strategy to safeguard against their marginalised position within their husband's extended family to which his relatives held traditional rights. Verhoef discerns four main types of *stokvels*: burial societies, savings clubs, investment groups and 'high-budget' *stokvels*. The latter consists of a large membership of persons with higher income and social standing, whose purpose is to provide opportunities to their members to make 'a lot of money' through a process of wealth acquisition with extravagant rituals and celebrants (Verhoef 2001, p. 13).

Stokvels have a diverse set of member rules and operational procedures, in accordance with the group rules on governance. Unlike cooperative societies (which incidentally have a much smaller influence on the township economy), *stokvel* membership is through invitation alone and the member's continued participation in the group is subject to strict adherence to rules and commitments. For this reason, *stokvels* are usually restricted in member numbers and further limited by their operating mechanisms (such as instances where members receive cyclical benefits). The *stokvel* rules are defined in a constitution or written agreement. While the function of *stokvels* varies as saving or credit institutions, they provide enforceable mechanisms (through expulsion for non-compliance) for mobilising regular financial deposits. The member contributions are managed by a treasurer or chairperson and held in cash, banked, invested or used for procurement of specific goods for future disbursement. While their function might be to enable savings or provide credit, *stokvels* operate through social mechanisms and thus require of the members to socially invest into the network through participating in meetings, attending funerals and weddings, for example. This function is overlooked by the formal financial institutions which, in seeking to capture the *stokvel* market, have developed a number of savings products that rationalise the savings rules and procedures and thus separate the financial aspect from its social roots. These initiatives have had limited success (Mulaudzi 2017). As Alcock (2015) explains:

> the power and allure [of *stokvels*] to their members is the social connectedness it gives to each member. The protection of group assistance, the social fun of the *stokvel* meeting where members gossip and feast and laugh together. They fulfil a social benefit first, a financial one second. (p. 94)

For entrepreneurs, *stokvels* provide a savings opportunity and a mechanism to manage and minimise risk such as cushioning the impact of social obligations on the household (rather than insurable business-specific risks such as theft or vandalism). We learnt that entrepreneurs tend to mitigate financial 'shocks' of social obligation through proactive measures, such as supporting neighbourhood watches, patronising local political leadership and enhancing investment in security systems. Social obligations within the household, extended family or networks are non-negotiable and require ongoing financial and social commitments. In this respect, critical social events that require financial investment include deaths, marriages, family home-coming events, and cultural celebrations such as rites of passage into adulthood or unveiling ceremonies. In anticipation of high-risk events such as deaths in the family, some *stokvel* arrangements are constituted to allocate resources to each member on an as-needed basis in specified tranches, while providing all members with a lump-sum payout on an annual basis. Annual savings payouts enable the members to undertake substantial investments in property or to purchase assets.

Groups of business owners utilise *stokvel* principles to enhance resource capacity and thus boost business performance on a rotational basis. Such groups tend to be less discerning towards membership, accommodating members out of solidarity (rather than on strict terms) and to strengthen social reciprocity. An example is a tavern-owner *stokvel* whose members make regular financial contributions for disbursements on a rotational basis. When a member receives payment, they host an event at which all members provide support, hence enabling the beneficiary to monetise the advantage. MaLinde (1/128/F/32), a shebeen owner in Tembisa, explained how her stokvel operated: '*Twelve people make up the stokvel and they each contribute towards the running of the business. Every two weeks, we pool money together and purchase beer to the value of what is in the kitty. Each person usually pays R100 per week. Together we make regular purchases of up to 20 cases every 2 weeks.*' While entrepreneurs utilise *stokvels* to mobilise savings and the social network in support of their business, direct forms of cooperation in business are rarely embraced, such as group purchasing.

In contrast to the social underpinning of *stokvels*, the national government has driven entrepreneurs to form legally constituted cooperatives to benefit from development support programmes, providing direct and indirect incentives. Yet the weight of evidence indicates that such cooperatives have a high failure rate, mainly due to people's unwillingness to share liability amongst strangers and low levels of interpersonal trust where the social network is weak. Of the 22 619 cooperatives which the Department of Trade and Industry (DTI) had helped to register, only 2 644 were still operational in 2012 – an 88% failure rate (DTI 2012). The great majority of individuals whom we interviewed said that they would be unwilling to enter a cooperative and preferred doing business alone or with close family members (spouses, siblings, children, relatives), with the business firmly under their 'entrepreneurial orientation'. The steadfast reluctance to pool financial resources was cited as one explanation for the inability of South African spaza shops to withstand the competition of immigrant entrepreneurs.

Money lending

Shortage of capital was commonly listed in our enterprise survey as one of the main constraints affecting the growth of the business. While capital availability does present a major challenge, this should not be understood as the lack of access to finance. Most entrepreneurs do not access credit from formal financial institutions, for a myriad of reasons, including a lack of formal banking history, the absence of non-tradeable or legally protected assets, and the complexity of the finance application requirements such as those for business plans, registration certifications, and approved municipal building plans for the business premises. While township entrepreneurs are unable to secure micro-finance, institutional lenders actively promote borrowing to formal sector employees with work contracts, providing them with unsecured loans on evidence of employment. These low-skill and often low-paid formal sector employees have greater access to formal institutional micro-finance than entrepreneurs, many of whom run stable and profitable businesses. As a result of their de facto financial exclusion, entrepreneurs tend to obtain business finance through five mechanisms: i) arranging with a family member (usually) in formal employment to access an unsecured loan; ii) drawing on household or family savings, including obtaining capital through the sale of non-core assets; iii) borrowing from an informal money lender known as a 'mahodisana' (Verhoef 2001) (from the Sotho *hoda*, meaning to pay back) or colloquially as *mashionisa*; iv) acquiring a loan from a formally registered micro-lender; and v) the use of cash windfalls, including redundancy or pension pay-outs, either to establish the business or enhance enterprise capacity.

Across the spectrum of businesses we examined, there were three distinct perspectives towards business finance: one cohort had no desire to obtain loan finance and aimed to avoid debt-dependency altogether; the second cohort desired finance, but either could not access formal institutional loans or preferred to access finance via social mechanisms, such as family, due to the comparative advantages of flexible repayment terms; the third cohort desired financial access from available sources, including informal money lenders. While collecting data on business finances, our evidence suggests that most entrepreneurs utilise family savings as investment capital. Where family savings are unobtainable, the individual may seek to access institutional finance, either via the strategy of family loans or directly through (the relatively few) micro-finance organisations targeting small, medium and micro-enterprises (SMMEs). Additionally, SMME micro-finance organisations often pursue strategies of group lending, via organisational structures such as cooperatives (formal or informal), a strategy which is unappealing to independently-minded entrepreneurs. Seldom do entrepreneurs borrow from *mashionisas* for capital investments.

Mashionisas typically offer short-term loans to fulfil unmet household consumption needs, mitigate risk events, or settle urgent debts which could pose a serious risk. We learnt that entrepreneurs who operate profitable businesses are an important source of informal lending. In some instances, money-lending is the core generator of income, the business providing the institutional framework and social relationships to establish a client base. But we also learnt that micro-lending is highly risky, and several informants spoke of their experiences of loan defaulting as the reason why they would no longer engage in micro-lending.

CASE STUDY: *Nonkuthula's money-lending business*

Nonkuthula is a *mashionisa* in Delft South. She has been lending out money since 2002, providing loans at 50% interest per month (See Figure 12.10 and Figure 12.11).

She had about 10 customers per month, most of whom she knows, though, in her words, '*some are referred to me by friends, for example when people are drinking beers they would say go to sister Nonkuthula, you gonna get the money there.*' The size of the loan varied and was based on lender's income. She restricted the loan amount for old-age pensioners to R500 but would consider larger sums (up to R2 500) if a person had a stable income or if the loan was for a social need, such as a funeral. If she has doubts about the trustworthiness of the lender, Nonkuthula will insist on holding onto their

FIGURE 12.10 A money lender or *mashionisa* in Delft South holding the bank cards of the 'runaways', clients that have not repaid their loans

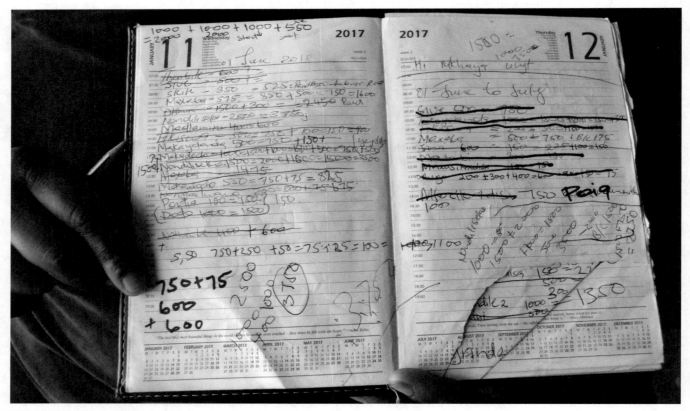

FIGURE 12.11 The *mashionisa*'s ledger

Note: Loans are issued at 50% interest per month. Lenders are not required to sign for the loan but based on an interpersonal agreement between the lender and the *mashionisa*.

card (bank or SASSA cards) as well as the personal identification number (PIN) and official identification documents. Most <u>lenders</u> repay the loans within the month, but some abscond. She complained: '*When they want money, they come to me but when it's paying back its me who goes to them to look for them. I knock on their doors and tell them I want my money…They know they don't mess with me. Some hide in their hoodies to conceal identity when they see me…Some even threaten to go to the police, and I tell them they would go there to report assault after I deal with them.*' The loan agreement was simply based on a mutual understanding between Nonkuthula and her customers. There was no documentation and Nonkuthula maintained the ledger simply '*to calculate how much money was paid out and how much was paid back. I know I gave so-and-so a certain amount. Some people come back and undervalue what they took, and I go to the book and show them.*' In spite of her fierce reputation, some loans are never repaid; Nonkuthula calls these '*the runaways*'. She refuses to lend to backyarders because they '*leave early in the morning [and] deep in the night.*'

Divestment

Township informal businesses are cautious to reinvest profits into infrastructure, branding and social capital development (or other business strategies). With some exceptions, most limit investment in business premises and infrastructure to achieve basic functionality, without (what is seen as unnecessary) expenditure to enhance the design for the sake of service excellence or aesthetic appearances. Dressing down the external projection of a township business can be a strategy to conceal business success in order to avoid the risks of theft, public criticism and jealousy. The strategy of presenting a survivalist front is akin to the practice in traditional farming societies of hiding the cattle (or 'cattle loaning') (Shackleton, Shackleton & Cousins 2001, p. 586) whereby the owners of large herds distribute cattle among family and patrons and so reduce resource demands against their wealth. In the township context, divestment strategies make it difficult to assess the true profitability of micro-enterprises. For example, street traders who operate with minimal functional infrastructure and sell items such as clothing, cooked food and fruit and vegetables can, despite appearances, be highly successful entrepreneurs with substantial cash incomes. Similarly, taverns in poor condition with broken windows amidst piles of empty liquor bottles or spaza shops that sell goods through a small window/hatch can be turning over thousands of rand per day. An important aspect of this strategy to manage and downplay entrepreneurial success is the tactic of divestment. In this strategy, entrepreneurs seek to divest resources away from a successful micro-enterprise into alternative business ventures, rather than reinvestment in the primary business by enhancing infrastructure or improving facilities. A successful township entrepreneur might own a tavern, operate a taxi, run or rent out a spaza shop and may have a number of residential property investments, particularly those providing accommodation units. Often divestments to other businesses are made in different geographical localities and business sectors, reinforcing a disconnection between entrepreneurial achievement and visual evidence.

Another strategy which micro-entrepreneurs utilise to minimise the risks associated with wealth accumulation is to spatially separate the site of business from their home residence. In some instances, the entrepreneur might elect to shift their home to a different locality, in a different township or suburban neighbourhood, again to reduce the association between their home lifestyle (and property investments) and business activities. In the course of our research, we encountered numerous examples of this strategy, especially among successful tavern operators who, in addition to seeking to present a survivalist front, had a valid reason for relocating their home life away from the business premise since trade is conducted late into the evenings, with the environment of drinking venues potentially generating inconvenience for residential life. As part of this strategy, one such individual told how he operated an old model Toyota Cressida as his 'township' car to be used for business purposes, using his Mercedes Benz for residential use where his status as a financially successful individual would attract less of the 'wrong kind' of attention.

Outlook

Informal institutions fulfil an important role for township business, creating and simultaneously maintaining social networks, systems of rules and practices. Since these institutions are poorly understood by 'outsiders', the forays of financial services, for example, have not penetrated far into the township cash economy. In earlier chapters, we highlighted the successes (and implications for micro-enterprises) of corporate business which developed pathways into this market through supply chain expansion and the establishment of retail outlets, to list some of the core strategies. With respect to the financial services sector, corporates have sought to extend formal financial services to micro-enterprises with limited success. Inroads have been advanced in the provision of insurance products, like personal funeral plans, or cellular phone money transfer services, which have enabled informalist entrepreneurs to repatriate profits out of South Africa through a channel which avoids the stringent exchange controls on formal businesses via conventional banking services. Otherwise, the role of formal and regulated financial services in micro-enterprise operations remains shallow. Few township micro-enterprises have accessed bank finance. Where entrepreneurs have succeeded in acquiring small loans, these are usually accessed via informal lenders who do not evaluate the business but lend on the basis of social relationships and network resources. For similar reasons, few township businesses have taken out insurance policies on their business premises, vehicles, stock or assets. Yet township business persons are acutely aware of risks of doing business as a result of endogenous and exogenous 'shocks' to their intertwined investments in the household and business. Shocks include crime and violence, police raids and other forms of regulatory action by the state to halt business activities, business competition, and demands on the household arising from events such as unemployment, death and socio-cultural pressures. To offset risks, individuals commonly set aside cash savings with the money either held in the bank or stashed at home. When a business activity is deemed to cause damage or physical harm, either directly or indirectly, the owner is required to recompense the third party on the spot, paid out in cash. Louise, a shebeen owner featured in Chapter 9, was required to pay a sum of R20 000 to the family of a customer who had died in her venue, even though she had had no role in the killing. As in cases such as this, micro-enterprises require unhindered access to informal insurance finance for which savings rather than loans is the primary strategy.

In this chapter, we have focused on some of the main strategies through which entrepreneurs seek to mitigate risks. These strategies provide two lessons. First, township entrepreneurs recognise the need to embrace both short-term and long-term strategies. The argument in business literature that informal entrepreneurs are guided by short-term priorities, which then shape the nature of the business and investments, overlooks the various unseen investments in long-term needs which include taking 'care' of the past (see Kelliher & Reinl 2009). This leads to our second lesson. Business in the township economy is undertaken within a framework of informal institutions of social norms, values and practices. One such framework includes the simple 'rules' within the market to safeguard rights and maintain 'fair' competition. These are informal, and constitute what Hiebert et al. (2015) describe as based less on 'dos and don'ts' but on a 'multitude of incentives and disincentives, and measures of a more persuasive nature' (p. 10).

Such 'persuasive' measures can include violence (as we learn from the *mashionisa*), intimidation and witchcraft. In some instances, organised bodies such as taxi associations and civic associations as well as local street committees and neighbourhood gangs, can be mobilised to intervene in enforcing contractual business agreements, through violence or intimidation. On the 'incentive' side of the spectrum, an important form of institutional order derives from mutual reliance and hence reciprocal exchange. These social institutions are important in enabling entrepreneurs to call for 'favours', whether these relate to acquiring a place to store stock, keeping an 'eye' on the business, or providing assistance in running a business while the entrepreneur is absent. Informal institutions fulfil an important role in solidifying group actions. In this respect, *stokvels* enable individuals to voluntarily associate for the purposes of saving, managing risks and providing mutual support. A key element in their institutional effectiveness is the exclusivity of membership, constituted as a small network with valuable resources, in contrast to formal cooperative institutions which are constitutionally more inclusive but weak in resources once external incentives have been depleted. *Stokvels* illustrate that collaboration is undertaken as a strategy rather than objective.

We have argued that informal institutions enable economic investment and business growth. Our research brings into question the base assumptions in conventional business studies which hold that markets are inefficient and cannot improve social welfare in the absence of formal institutions. We are doubtful, for this reason, about the role of technology in the form of cell-phone 'apps' to change the way micro-enterprises conduct business in respect to supply chains, introduce digital banking and modernise business practices. The strategies utilised and institutions engaged by township entrepreneurs are not simply informal alternatives but provide a qualitatively different and indeed sometimes superior set of economic arrangements for undertaking business and reducing risks. While noting their benefits, we recognise that economic power is unevenly distributed and informal institutions can, through their mobilisation, particularly in terms of power responses, serve to reinforce inequality, while undermining social and cultural practices which might otherwise enable opportunities and distribute surplus for wider benefit. Although many businesses project a survivalist front, this does not mean that the businesses are survivalist or that market opportunities are equally accessible.

WE APOLOGISE FOR
ANY INCONVENIENCE
CAUSED DURING
ILDING OPERATIONS

13
CONCLUSIONS: PROTECT, CONSTRAIN AND DISRUPT

In this book we demonstrate that within the township economy the trajectory of business development is influenced by the extraction of surplus value to benefit companies and individuals who reside outside of these settlements.

CHAPTER 13

Conclusions: protect, contain and disrupt

Overview

In this book, we have sought to provide a new understanding of the township economy, through the prism of its informal micro-enterprises and their entrepreneurs. From a macro-perspective, we have sought to demonstrate that the township economy is an entity of particular spatial characteristics in which the trajectory of business development is influenced by the accumulation of wealth to benefit companies and individuals who reside outside of these settlements. In this process, we have argued that the state has enabled and afforded these extractive businesses with the institutional room to manoeuvre. This has been done, in one part, through apartheid-inspired restrictions on micro-enterprises and, in another part, through state inability (even reluctance) to intervene in markets and against dominant business practices. From a political economy perspective, the constraints on township micro-enterprises resemble a situation of colonialism, with micro-enterprises subject to enforced informalisation and large businesses (including corporates) able to extend their control over markets into these marginalised geographies. While we highlight the overriding logic of profit extraction, we simultaneously recognise, taking a more fine-grained and closer perspective, the 'insurgence' of micro-enterprises responding to opportunities in spite of the state, both independently and in consort with external businesses. We are particularly sensitive to what we describe as 'people-centred' responses and the strategies and innovations employed to enter into markets. We have sought to illustrate how, in different contexts and for different actors, the ability of individuals to establish or grow business is either advanced or restrained through the influence of power. For many township entrepreneurs, such power influences severely limit economic opportunities; in contrast, for much fewer, power enables networks, groupings and 'big men' to dominate local markets and participate alongside (and sometimes in competition with) bigger businesses in extractive accumulation. We have characterised these outcomes in binary terms, as survivalist and entrepreneur responses, though we recognise that there is also a middle-ground position.

In reaching our overarching conclusions, we restate our three principal objectives. One, we sought to contribute towards a theoretical framing for assessing qualitative and quantitative evidence (our own and that from secondary sources) of the constraints that hinder the growth of township micro-enterprises. Two, we sought to identify actions that currently (as well as in the future) unlock opportunities to grow informal businesses in size, sustainability and sophistication, including legal status, while accommodating new

292

entrants from within township communities. Three, we sought to investigate the ways in which micro-enterprises contribute towards the place making of townships in ways that either reinforce or erode apartheid legacies and the implications thereof for social inclusivity.

The research that informs our analysis was undertaken by collecting primary evidence from 10 sites in South African and Namibian settlements. Our evidence comprises quantitative data from sources including a business census and firm surveys, and qualitative insights from interviews, observations, measurement, diagrams and photography, and participatory, co-produced visual outputs. Considerations of space and time were afforded a central influence in our theoretical framing. We differentiated between six levels of spatiality: one, the comparative level wherein we contrasted data across geographic sites; two, the city level at which we considered specific settlements and their relationship to the urban geography; three, the small-area level at which we provided detailed evidence on the variation and distribution of different categories of micro-enterprise, including cases of sites which change over time; four, the neighbourhood level where we focused on the spatial dynamics of localised markets; five, the micro-context level wherein we discerned intimate spatial and relational influences, including the role of objects; and six, the level of invisible infrastructure of norms, practices, values and beliefs that provided the bedrock of the social relationships which secure and safeguard conditions for doing business. Thinking through the subject of township entrepreneurship in space and time enabled us to shift our focus across multiple spatial terrains and timeframes. On the downside, this weighting towards space/time framing has meant that our findings are not necessarily universal to all townships settings at all times over the past decade. There are no doubt settlements to which our findings are less applicable, such as those located on the peri-urban areas or on tribal trust land where agricultural activities might fulfil a greater role, or in the urban context on municipal, established housing estates or within historically migrant hostels. Furthermore, we make no claim that our results are applicable in developing countries with different urban geographies, socio-political characteristics, economic structures and unfamiliar variables of power such as paramilitary or military control over markets.

The broad consistency of the different kinds of evidence across the research sites implies that our findings have wider resonance. We identified similarities in the scope and proportional scale of enterprises. The evidence shows the dominance of retail activities selling groceries, food and beverages, with the majority of businesses operating from residential settings. Many of these activities can been regarded as 'survivalist', though this does not imply an absence of business strategy or a profit-generating function. We found high streets accommodated roughly a quarter of total business activities, notably of service-related enterprises such as hairdressing. In the high-street context, we recorded patterns of spatial layering, clustering and ordering in each site, with the street space itself constituting a fluid, informal land-use system accessible to multiple users and controls. Though complex in social structure, high-street markets enable greater productivity than residential areas through densification, synergies between businesses, and the fluidity of land use, to name some of the key devices. Where markets have been formally established, such as those around transport nodes, the evidence indicates that urban planners are unable to replicate a similar environment of entrepreneurship. Though 'pregnant with possibilities', to borrow the term of the Africanist urban scholars, Pieterse and Simone (2013, p. 12), we found, nevertheless, that most South African township high streets are in an early phase of development in comparison to Eveline Street in Namibia. In Eveline Street, we saw how formal institutions (including titling, land-use zoning and business licensing, and state enforcement agencies) are (more closely) aligned to the informal institutions (values, norms and unwritten rules), allowing for purposeful investments in both the private and public realms to enhance business (optimising the commercial outcome) while improving the quality of the social environment.

It is from the high street that township residents connect to inner-city and commercial areas. The minibus transport system arose in response to the inability of the state to provide adequate (affordable, efficient and reliable) spatial connectivity. While the minibus system has beneficial aspects, it generates a concentration of political-industrial-financial power and, as an agency of economic development has weak transformative possibilities for micro-enterprises and does not incubate disruptive spatial outcomes required to undo the apartheid legacy. A contrasting outcome was identified in the role of (informal) sedan taxis which operate within a notably more responsive, adaptive and decentralised system, creating routes on consumer demand and linking residents to micro-nodes and high-street clusters. Yet these taxis are excluded from the benefits of formal institutions, including operating licences, access to finance and routes out of the township. The asymmetry in power relationships is a theme and influence, similarly, in the major retail segments, notably in the case of spaza retailers and the case of taverns and shebeens. In the spaza sector, our research documents the transformation in ownership and business strategies which has accompanied the establishment of shops by immigrant entrepreneurs. The new shops operate on a larger scale with evidence of horizontal and vertical integration and provide a more competitive service and stock a wider range of products. As a result of the incapacity of the state to enforce laws with respect to household grocery retailing, these shops are able to operate in non-compliance with formal requirements. Informality thus provides a competitive advantage against both survivalist micro-enterprises within localised markets and supermarkets situated on township periphery. The financial success of the new shopkeepers has resulted in the closing of most survivalist businesses, many of whom were South African women in a transition noted nationwide. At the area level, shopping malls operated by stock-market listed companies encroach into the township spatial environment, providing a secluded architecture for corporate businesses while simultaneously disqualifying micro-enterprises from setting up shops within the mall compound. From a perspective of opportunity, the sole beneficiaries of these shopping malls are the street traders who precariously trade on the perimeter fence and entrance sidewalks situated on the outside.

In the case of the liquor trade, the incongruence between formal institutions (regulation, law enforcement) and informal institutions (norms, values, cultural practices) is greatest of all enterprise sectors. Here the majority of micro-enterprises trade illegally and are consequently subject to intensive law enforcement with the result that the businesses have stock confiscated and the operators are frequently arrested, given fines, prosecuted and imprisoned either within the judicial process upon their arrest or as a final sanction. Yet these businesses mainly sell products that are both legal and obtained through legal transactions. Despite the intensity of state violence, most shebeen owners elect to continue in business. We have argued that their situation should be understood as one of enforced informalisation since the majority of operators would want to obtain a licence to conduct business (to reduce police raids), if only the institution was accessible. Since the issue of a licence is contingent on compliance with the formal institutions of land use, the applicant needs to secure ownership (title), rezone the property for business use, and ensure that their buildings are compliant with land-use stipulations and building standards. Additionally, the prospective applicant would still need to comply with a raft of other compliance criteria, which entail police inspections and community oversight.

In no other sector, possibly with the exception of educares, does the path to formal institutional inclusion demand such high levels of financial, human and social capital investment.

The reward for formalisation can be muted. Although there is a high demand for liquor in neighbourhood localities (with the shebeen fulfilling the equivalent function of home storage), the market is subject to monopolistic control. The dominant corporate beer producer built its 'route to market' business model through supplying taverns with high-volume orders to be on-sold at low margins, which in turn helps to maintain demand for low prices per volume products. This supply model 'straitjackets' retail outlets to sell products at low profit, with licensed taverns functioning as a conduit of onward supply to the unlicensed shebeen. The model has allowed liquor producers to remain an arms length away from having to take responsibility for the consequence of illegal trade or the sustained culture of heavy drinking, with its associated social and economic costs. The context of micro-enterprise informality thus provides formal businesses an efficient and profitable 'route to market'. In this extractive business process, minimal accountability or investment is required of the supplied businesses. The same situation has also emerged in the relationship between (corporate) wholesalers and spaza shops, as well as those who supply products to micro-enterprises selling takeaway food.

Township micro-enterprises derive their legitimacy, regardless of the business's legal status, by providing services that are culturally acceptable within communities. This notion is reinforced through the respectability afforded to entrepreneurship as a means to sustain livelihoods in a context of high unemployment, spatial marginalisation and resource constraints. Throughout our engagements in the field, over and over we heard the same message: '*I am not committing a crime*'. Such terms of legitimacy apply to most of the business sectors we analyse in this book, with the (possible) exception of some of the informalist-run spaza shops which are seen as businesses originating from outside the community and adhering to different norms and values. We have argued that micro-enterprises have an important role in the process of place making, particularly in the residential context, a function similarly fulfilled by a range of businesses including, less obviously, hair salons, educares, religious institutions and traditional healers. In providing much needed public space where residents can meet to socialise and recreate, to exchange information, to connect with social networks, and to invest in human and social capital, these micro-enterprises collectively contribute to the disruption of the urban fabric that once constituted planned dormitory settlements. We have argued that the micro-enterprises which produce a socio-economic outcome in this respect should be seen as 'pioneers', who through their operation set out spatial landmarks (and nodes) for future economic growth and diversification, including creating opportunities for new entrants. The case of Eveline Street provides a microcosm of insight for the future possibilities for business growth, diversification and place-making transformation in ways that begin to narrow the gap between the city and the township. As a collective, place-influencing micro-enterprises make the townships liveable, authentic and culturally visible in the sense of enabling residents to identify transformative opportunities within the urban landscape. It is largely due to these businesses that the township retains an enduring hold on its residents, including those whose income affords them an opportunity to relocate to wealthier neighbourhoods but who often choose not to.

We end our narrative overview with an examination of the informal institutions which underpin enterprise strategies, enable informal markets to function in reliable and predicable ways, and provide mechanisms to manage risks. These institutions are often illegible to conventional scholarship in business management and economic development studies and therefore have not been systematically researched and are, consequently, omitted from most of the economic prognoses on informal economy development (see, for example, Fourie 2018c). Yet the township economy supports a repository of 'social technologies', including traditions, beliefs and practices that guide business activities (Du Toit & Neves 2014). We show how a set of informal institutions function to enable opportunities for new entrants to start-up businesses, including survivalists, to trade in public spaces such as street pavements. Informal institutions help to ensure that businesses compete on terms considered to be 'fair', which in turn puts pressure on comparatively more successful entrepreneurs to downplay their financial achievements. In order to avoid looking 'rich', successful township business persons might adopt strategies of fronting (keeping their businesses shabby in appearance), divesting earnings into different businesses in different settings, or investing in human and social capital detached from the business, to list some common strategies. We argue that reciprocal exchanges (rather than notions of a selfless Ubuntu) are a foundational aspect of social etiquette in an economy in which survivalists in particular frequently request and return favours. All such exchanges are grounded in social relationships, constituted on trust. Often, they are founded on kinship, patronage, friendship, though for immigrants both ethnicity and nationality can offer a proximal basis for social networking and coordination of business investment strategies. For this reason, social networks fulfil an important role for township informal businesses, with strong networks providing access to capital, effective risk management institutions, marketing opportunities and hard to obtain goods and services such as contraband tobacco. To analyse micro-enterprises without their underpinning in relationships of reciprocity and complex social networks is to miss the infrastructure that can ensure not simply the survival of the business but the opportunities for future growth. It is for these reasons that township micro-enterprises should be seen as strategic, a feature of even survivalist business endeavours that persist not necessarily to grow the business but to find a pathway to re-enter the (formal) labour market as opportunities arise.

Themes

This book set out to provide a different perspective on Southern Africa's township economy through taking readers on a journey across space and time. Our objective was to reconcile two divergent narratives; one that characterises informal businesses as 'necessity'- rather than 'opportunity'-driven and locked into a traditional sector with structural deficiencies (Mahajan 2014), in contrast to one that characterises informal micro-enterprises as strategic, responsive and innovative, whose social technologies are potentially sophisticated (Alcock 2015; Du Toit & Neves 2014). We accept that there is truth in both narratives. Looking across the 10 sites, it is easy to conclude that the informal micro-enterprise component of the township economy is under-performing. Township residents need to travel outside their settlements in order to access an array of services and products that are (only) obtainable in either the commercial districts of the city or in shopping malls. The list includes household furniture, new clothing and footwear, motor vehicles, service contracts for phones, financial institutions such as banking and insurance brokerage, and western medical care. Micro-enterprises cannot compete with supermarkets (or large retailers) whose scale of operation and vertical integration affords these businesses a competitive advantage and it is understandable why residents express a demand for shopping malls in the township, not simply for access to commodities and services, but as safe social spaces (Chevalier, 2015). But this is not the most important message.

We are in agreement with scholars who argue that there are structural impediments hindering growth opportunities, but we counter that it is not these impediments per se that 'prevent a modernising component from growing' (Fourie, 2018c, p. 457). Instead, informal micro-enterprises ought to be seen as following a completely different development trajectory. Most businesses operate in a non-western context, with the form, appearance and operations reflecting both pragmatic decisions and socio-cultural considerations. Though different, micro-enterprises can be sustainable, do grow in financial scale and can enable the entrepreneur to generate wealth. Some businesses also create employment (though this is not necessarily their aim) and are capable of technological innovation, though they prioritise social strategies to minimise risks over reinvestment within the business. Often the direction of development is not towards larger units of production or mechanisation, hallmarks of 'modernisation', but towards divestment into multiple different businesses and investment in property. The latter strategy is evident in neighbourhood development, the establishment of rural homes far from the source of income, investments to establish low-cost residential units or, where suitable conditions permit, to develop multi-purpose buildings with both commercial and residential functions.

The township economy represents a valuable platform for the acquisition of entrepreneurial skills, a means to obtain investment capital, and access to the social networks that connect to informal institutions. These resources have enabled many thousands of individuals to uplift themselves from poverty and secure intergenerational benefits for their immediate family and kinship. The precise scale of this upward elevation is difficult to quantify for the benefits are continually dispersed through investments in human and social capital development as much as in physical assets and savings. The economic contribution of micro-enterprises can be seen, notwithstanding, in the changing township landscape. Older settlements like Tembisa, Thabong and KwaMashu are unrecognisably different from their initial form. New settlements like Ivory Park and Delft South are fast undergoing a process of rebuilding and economic reordering. And in informal settlements, such as Sweet Home Farm and parts of Vrygrond, where the state has only provided a cursory infrastructure of roads and public utilities through communal service points, a process of development through construction is underway with micro-enterprises fulfilling an important role in the provision of a service infrastructure and the creation of public spaces. In all these sites, much of the changing economic landscape aligns to the spaces in which entrepreneurs undertake businesses, with the spaces and places of greatest change correlating to sites of highest business intensity. Furthermore, the imprint of micro-enterprises can be seen in the township lifestyles, in the fusion of the traditional with the modern and the ritualisation of business activities within social events, such as stokvel meetings.

In assessing the economic achievement of township micro-enterprises, we draw attention to five themes that weave through the book. These themes are: i) differentiated opportunities; ii) space matters; iii) institutions are incongruent; iv) corporate power stifles transformative potential; and v) informality nurtures economic resistance.

Differentiated opportunities

We differentiate township business between survivalists and entrepreneurs. Survivalists are in the great majority. Survivalist businesses respond to economic opportunities in the logic of supplementing household income, drawing on existing resources of financial, human and social capital. Most are engaged in selling food, grocery items and beverages, including liquor products. While many survivalists are able to sustain their business through spatially nimble strategies, including a minimal investment in infrastructure, and through making products relatively more affordable and accessible than competitors, most are not entrepreneurial and will abandon the business if alternative income-generating opportunities emerge. Entrepreneurs have a different propensity for financial risks. These individuals have characteristically invested in physical infrastructure and equipment, employed workers on a full-time or casual basis and sourced products competitively, in some cases from importers or manufacturers operating upstream of the wholesale outlets upon whom their survival is reliant. To differentiate the business and signify its credibility, most entrepreneurially oriented businesses are named, with the name displayed on signage, business cards or websites. Entrepreneurs draw on human and social capital to advance and amplify their businesses, prioritising their own financial gains. We have shown how immigrants have mobilised finance and access to products through ethnic networks, as another example of utilising these resources, to enter into and dominate markets over survivalist businesses.

An important difference between survivalists and entrepreneurs, notwithstanding, is their respective power responses to structural constraints. For survivalists, their core power responses lie, first, in maintaining social infrastructure through reciprocal investments and, second, in securing continued patronage and exemptions from more powerful actors, such as property owners. Such patrons provide access to trading sites (or indeed the right to trade in direct spatial competition), storage for their goods, electricity and water connectivity, for instance. For entrepreneurs, one of the core power responses for residentially based retail businesses lies in developing or maintaining their business as the dominant outlet within a niche market and then defending their position through overt and covert strategies to restrict competition. In the transport sector, taxi entrepreneurs mobilise through constituted organisational structures to control the market and exclude sedan taxis from competition for routes. On the high street, in one particular case, business persons have utilised the power embodied within formal state institutions to unlock legally protected land rights, which in turn has enabled these entrepreneurs to obtain business licences while safeguarding their development investment in property. We have described three notable power responses within the array of entrepreneurial strategies: i) the violent entrepreneurs; ii) the informalists; and iii) the business pioneers. We illustrate the role of these entrepreneurial power responses in different spatial and sectoral contexts; respectively, the minibus taxi sector, the spaza-shop sector and the high-street tavern owners. It must be stressed that these power responses are not mutually exclusive. Successful township entrepreneurs may use modes of violence (including magic) along with subversions of informality in efforts to dominate their market niche and/or protect business interests, while nevertheless affording spatial, economic and social benefits to non-competing survivalists and others.

Gender relations bisect our differentiation of micro-enterprises. Survivalists are predominantly (not exclusively) women, whereas the violent entrepreneurs and informalists of our case studies are predominantly men. Through our spatial lens, we find that women are spatially compelled to operate businesses from either their home or within the adjacent neighbourhood to accommodate their gendered social responsibilities within the family. The predominance of men and women in particular sectors reflects contrasting gendered influences on social capital, including skills training, cultural expectations and enabling support structures. Men predominate in sectors providing mechanical and repair services as well as taxi transport. Women predominate in educares and food takeaways and have an equal shareholding of liquor retail (especially shebeens), hair care and traditional healing markets. In the hair-care sector, the businesses are gendered in orientation and client base, so that hair salons and barber shops operate within separate market segments. Female-operated educares and businesses which provide traditional healing characteristically operate as social enterprises, providing a social benefit as a core business objective and tapering profits to base levels of affordability. Service provision is not only gendered, but highly personalised and informed with cultural practices and norms.

Space matters

Our second theme is that space matters in informal markets and business strategies. The geospatial census identified broadly uniform patterns in business distribution. These revealed a separation between the high street and residential localities. High streets present a more diverse range of spatial opportunities in which to conduct business; these are influenced by, among other things, the intensity and direction of pedestrian movements, the configuration of transport infrastructure, the street morphology and the availability of space within the sidewalk or on open ground to accommodate different infrastructural propositions. Although residential localities accommodate a narrower range of business categories, similar spatial opportunities are replicated across the terrain, with each neighbourhood presenting a geographic micro-market to serve the demand for (top-up) groceries, fast food and beverages. The range of businesses in these niche markets is remarkably similar in all our sites. Neighbourhood markets were stable and therefore non-dynamic in the past, permitting home-based micro-entrepreneurs to operate their business with little threat of competition, resting on their locational advantage to secure business from neighbours. We have shown how this spatial opportunity has been disrupted in recent times, in part through the emergence of new spaza shops willing to compete on service and price, and in part through the establishment of supermarkets on the township periphery.

Our socio-spatial research showed that space also matters in the micro-context, within the micro-enterprise itself. We provided examples of street traders who optimise the use of space to benefit from the high-street opportunities of marketing and access to customers. Far from being the passive actors that characterise the notion of 'necessity' entrepreneurship, the traders make strategic decisions with respect to the use of infrastructure (and in its architecture), their position on the street environment, and in respect to their precise location within the street market space, with some choosing to agglomerate with others selling similar products or services. In the residential context, we show how entrepreneurs have sought to optimise the use of their property to fulfil both residential and commercial objectives. In some cases, optimisation requires the strategic encroachment of buildings beyond building lines and boundary lines, onto neighbours' land and state property. Additionally, we provide evidence of the repurposing of residences into commercial space, a development that sometimes includes investment in security systems or the construction of dedicated infrastructure such as children's playgrounds or toilets. In the case of shebeens in informal settlements, the research highlights the configuration of space to maintain internal boundaries between public (bar) and private (home) use, separating different users while still enabling the entrepreneur to fulfil the important role of spatial control (from surveillance to action). The architecture of the internal drinking venue includes features whose purposeful objective is to minimise risk (to themselves and participants), afford surveillance from the serving counter, control movement into and within the venue, and facilitate spatial connections into neighbouring parts of the settlement.

Our case studies highlighted the myriad ways people adapt and innovate the use of space. Yet space can also present a major constraint to doing business. A limitation of space can foreclose on entrepreneurial ambitions to make the kinds of investments required to formalise the business, such as in the educare case study where the owner was required to build a separate kitchen, a sick room, an additional classroom and specialised toilets. To unlock future business opportunity from such investments, the investor would need to comply with land-use system criteria that are generally unattainable for most township entrepreneurs. Space limitation also impacts on opportunities for street traders, in situations where the use of public space is subject to the control of more powerful entities, for example. The exclusion of micro-enterprises (and street traders) from shopping mall precincts presents one situation of this scenario. In the taxi sector, we advanced an argument on the spatial exclusion of informal taxis from the formally constituted taxi routes which connect the township to commercial centres. Access to these routes, we demonstrate with evidence, would benefit both township commuters and allied micro-enterprises. The former would derive route flexibility (and potentially greater efficiency), while the latter would gain from providing vehicle services and the spatial-nodal effect which sedan taxis enable. We found that time has an important bearing on the use of space. Businesses in the leisure economy, for example, operate into the night and on weekends. For street traders, trading space faces premium demand at month end when people receive income. There is also a diversity of users trading in the same spaces across different times of the day as trading cycles track commuter movement.

Institutions are incongruent

Our third theme is that formal and informal institutions are mostly incongruent, in other words, misaligned and counteractive in certain situations. For micro-enterprises that require compliance with institutions of land use, the incongruence of their actual land-use situation with formal land-use institutions such as operating on land without appropriate zoning, means that these businesses are rendered illegal. Non-compliance can in turn impede access to business licensing, thus closing off access to benefits from formalisation which include the rights to trade, access to state subsidies and inclusion in government as well as industry SMME development support programmes. Yet these businesses are able to operate illegally and attract informal institutional support because township residents regard most micro-enterprise endeavours as a legitimate means to earn a livelihood. Furthermore, state agencies are generally sympathetic towards their situation, except where they have been specifically mandated into action (such as in the case of liquor trading) or where the opportunities for corruption warrant action. In response to community legitimisation of informal land use, arguments have been made against formalisation, certainly where it entails measures which would significantly constrain or hamstring operations (Charman, Petersen, & Piper 2012; Crush, Chikanda & Skinner 2015; Fourie 2018a). We agree that current terms of formalisation are largely unsuitable and unattainable for all but the largest township businesses.

Formalisation can provide a means to enhance business operations, reduce externalities and achieve socially desirable objectives. In pursuit of formalisation, we have shown how entrepreneurs have purposefully adjusted their businesses practices or made investments to substantially alter the business environment. These reactions include 'ceremonial' (non-approved) actions undertaken to align the business with institutional compliance. In these responses, the entrepreneur has undertaken a careful assessment of the risks of informality versus the benefits of formality, weighing their decision between the objectives of keeping the state away from interference (through seeming to be compliant) and obtaining legal approval. Where the pressure of formalisation is strong, such as on educares, liquor outlets and minibus taxis, entrepreneurs have taken action to reduce business risks so as to avoid state confrontation that might arise therefrom. The provision of separate toilets for male and female patrons in taverns is one such example. In contrast, where the pressure of formalisation is weak and where law enforcement is ineffective, as in the spaza sector, amongst fast-food outlets, in shebeens, amongst traditional healers and informal sedan taxis, we saw less evidence of readjustments to the business. This is not to suggest that the businesses within these segments of the township economy are less attentive to social concerns, but to argue that unconstrained informality provides greater scope for subterfuge to entrepreneurs who seek to profit by any means necessary.

The Eveline Street case revealed how an alignment of land institutions helped to reduce the risks of trading illegally, thus contributing towards an enabling environment into which both state and entrepreneurs have made investments. We have argued that the outcome has had a measurable impact on the local economy in terms of property development, enhancements to the social space within bars and in the public domain, technological investments within businesses, and improvements to public space through street lighting, paving, outdoor seating, the installation of traffic-calming measures and the provision of police surveillance, to name some of the main interventions.

Corporate power stifles

Our fourth theme is that corporate power in general stifles the transformative potential of micro-enterprises to stimulate economic growth and reshape the urban environment. This influence is seen in the minibus taxi system wherein a complex of financial-industrial-political interests conspire to preserve a mode of public transport to the exclusion of diverse elements with broader transformative possibilities. In critiquing the power within this complex, we acknowledge that minibuses do have positive aspects, such as providing a comparatively efficient means of public transport (relative to state-operated rail and bus services) or in terms of its comparatively low subsidisation requirement. Our criticism focuses on the value chain wherein a substantial portion of the profits is extracted out of the township economy and accrues to powerful individuals who own fleets of taxis and the JSE investors whose businesses control the financing, insurance and servicing of minibuses. Taxi owners collaborate through organised bodies to protect the system from internal and external threats. These bodies utilise formal institutions (including taxi routes) and informal mechanisms (including organisation) to regulate the system, in particular to control competition. The repertoire of informal strategies of regulation constitute rule by thugocracy, based on the systematic use of violence, in direct and latent forms. This informal mode of regulation shields the vehicle owners and their corporate partners from sharing responsibility for the consequences of violence, which include the death of drivers, association leaders and ordinary commuters, extortion and harassment. The power of interest groups which sustain the minibus system truncates formal institutions (licensing, routes, state subsidies and access to institutional finance and so forth) from extending similar benefits to informal sedan taxis. We have argued that these taxis are more suitable to micro-enterprises, providing an alternative transport system that is better adapted to local economic conditions, requires less start-up capital and affords greater opportunities for owner-operator control.

Corporate influence can be seen in various levels in the township economy. In this book, we have restricted our analysis of corporate power to those sectors where corporate strategies directly influence the sale of products and the organisation of business. In spatial terms, the scope of corporate influence extends from billboards, to shop-signage, to shelf-products, to delivery vehicles, to pop-up marketing campaigns, to wholesale depots and retail enclaves, and to financial services for purchasing digital products and transferring money. We found no evidence of corporate investment to create a physical presence outside of shopping malls, saving these companies from establishing a presence on the high street and investing directly into township property. Some of the corporate businesses in malls compete directly with micro-enterprises, selling products that could be obtained through these existing township businesses. Apart from their price competitiveness, the mall liquor outlets provide little significant benefit over taverns, for example. In pointing to this market encroachment, we are not advocating a Schumpeterian 'small is beautiful' philosophy, but simply drawing attention to the power of corporate investors to overcome the institutional barriers such as land-use rights which inhibit micro-enterprises from formalising, accessing institutions and growing in scale. Corporatised fast-food makes use of the mall anchorage and position at the entrance/exit to disseminate western notions of food that glorify refined, salty and fatty products, thus setting expectations to which micro-enterprises are pressured to imitate. Alternative township fast foods with greater possibilities for challenging corporatised foods are rarely accommodated within malls, a result which is partly due to the strategic objective of the mall owners to preserve the integrity of the mall as a bastion of corporate brands and franchise retailers.

Corporate producers have long sought to develop 'routes to market'. In most sectors, the main barriers to compete in the township market were the small size of micro-enterprises, their sheer number and the 'necessity' orientation of the operator, rather than regulatory obstacles. This has meant that corporates have been able to supply micro-enterprises, regardless of whether the business was informal and illegal in some or all of its practices. Tobacco companies supply cartons of cigarettes in full knowledge that the cigarettes would be on-sold as loose sticks in contravention of the law. Beverage and grocery companies supply shopkeepers with signage and fridges (and in turn demand exclusive trading terms), and many corporates have supported businesses irrespective of their compliance with municipal by-laws, land and building regulations or other regulatory conditions such as labour rights applicable in the formal economy. While utilising the opportunity of informality to trade outside of the regulatory framework, corporates have simultaneously absolved themselves from risk to their brands and reputation in the event of product failure or business externalities. In an age where contraband products have entered into the township market, corporates whose products are sold through micro-enterprises have concealed any risks to their brands because brand loyalty is regarded as more important than product integrity or consumer safety, commonly leaving consumers uninformed of the presence of counterfeit versions of their own products.

We conducted a detailed analysis of the liquor sector, wherein the role of dominant corporates is especially problematic. Liquor producers have made scant investment into township businesses, apart from supporting the formalisation of a minority of taverns, content to rely on the informal supply chains and unlicensed shebeens to transfer their products into the market. By channelling supply through a business model based on high-volume product turnover, in which the margins for the retailer are squeezed, the largest share of the profits from liquor sales is extracted for the producer and their shareholders. The high profitability of the system rests, in large part, on the ability of the corporate liquor producer to distance their companies from negative social and health consequences attendant on drinking in general and the business externalities of the township liquor retailers in particular (who sell the bulk of their product). We have argued that the corporate dominance is safeguarded within government policies, one aspect of which seeks to prevent the formalisation of micro-enterprises. Yet within the township liquor sector, there are possibilities for an alternative outcome, one in which micro-enterprises could shift from selling corporate brands to local products. In imagining a different outcome, we should note that brewing and distillation are indigenous skills, controlled by women; hence, the failure of the state to nurture the production of liquor products in micro-enterprises should be viewed as constituting an acceptance and endorsement of the corporate system and its profit-extraction effects on the township economy.

Informality nurtures economic resistance

Our final theme is that informality nurtures economic resistance to the benefit of entrepreneurs willing to operate illegally and, for some, illegitimately as well. The fluid and flexible use of land and infrastructure is an example of how micro-enterprises optimise their use of resources, working around the institutional constraints. Such dexterity occurs at multiple levels. At the micro-context, we showed how entrepreneurs construct 'infrastructure' from social relationships and utilise spatial situations, objects and practices to react with speed and precision to market impulses. The traders hawking vegetables in (stolen) shopping trolleys and calling out to potential customers is one of numerous examples. We also noted deftness in micro-enterprises with physical infrastructure. Since such businesses are not locked into long-lease agreements, the entrepreneur can easily shift from one location to another, as we noted in the case of the spaza shops in Delft South. Such practices of spatial adjustment enable street traders to test different localities at different times before establishing a permanent site. Within businesses, the flexibility afforded by informality permits the entrepreneur to pivot towards different income streams, shifting the focus of the business away from high risk to more profitable activities. Some South African shopkeepers are able to survive through reorienting the business towards selling liquor and fast food, though retaining the semblance of a spaza shop. We identified a similar process amongst shebeen owners who, when the threat of police raids intensifies, refocused the business towards activities such as selling fresh meat or fast foods, or converting their venue into an arcade games shop.

Throughout this book we have sought to highlight the evidence of how informality can create a market opportunity, which in turn affords benefit to micro-enterprises, their suppliers and the customers. Some opportunities arise from the incongruence between formal and informal institutions. Informal taxis, unlicensed shebeens and unregistered educares are examples. Micro-enterprises can provide products and services which are widely seen as legitimate, even though they are illegal. Retailing cheap cigarettes, contraband clothing and various traditional and non-licensed medicines, and Fafi gambling, fulfil the criteria of legitimate, yet illegal, activities. Informality also affords opportunities for some entrepreneurs to exploit others and customers through dubious business practices and products. The industrialists who produce and sell concoctions, the healers who sell magic wallets or 'snake oil' remedies, international church syndicates who extract tribute for unverifiable services, the spaza networks that exploit migrant workers and sell counterfeit goods to unsuspecting customers, the vehicle thieves who operate 'chop-shops' selling spare parts and the drug dealers who sell heroin and crystal methamphetamine fall into this category. In these sectors, the weakness of governability advantages individuals with economic power, who can, if required, mobilise capital, legal means, network support and/or violence to defend their position within the market.

Outlook

We end this book by reflecting on actions which could influence the trajectory of micro-enterprises in the township economy. This final outlook is not intended as a manifesto for policy-making. Rather we seek to highlight aspects that deserve nurturing, not least to unlock the 'possibilities' for intensification, diversification and transformation. We have intentionally focused on a narrow range of state policies, pointing to instances in the respective chapters where laws and their implementation (or equally their weak application) directly impact on entrepreneurship, positively and negatively. Our choice in limiting the focus to a narrow range of government policies is a reflection of the complete disconnection between the actual situation of micro-enterprises and the imaginary township economy that politicians desire. We have sought to recognise people-centred responses even in sectors and strategies which may unsettle western ideas or Ubuntu sentimentalism about how township micro-entrepreneurs ought to run businesses. It is fanciful for policy-makers to think that entrepreneurs will simply not respond to market demand, and (for example) withdraw from selling products like liquor and contraband tobacco, or from trading in sites of dense pedestrian footfall, if law enforcement is intensified. An important lesson is that enforcing informality does not alter the entrepreneurial pursuit of opportunity, but merely changes the trajectory of businesses development and growth. Since our research has found no evidence to indicate possibilities for leveraging micro-enterprises towards industrialisation, technological modernisation, or the formation of cooperatives, as well as stimulating youth entrepreneurship – important policy concerns in the current age – we conclude that government prospects of achieving these objectives are low.

We organise our suggested actions under three headings: protect, constrain and disrupt. These headings benefit from the differentiation of strategies which Chen, Jhabvala & Lund (2002) propose, though our orientation is not solely towards government policies and agencies, but actions which could be undertaken by state, non-state and private actors, including civil society organisations and businesses. The latter include informal township micro-enterprises.

Protect

There is wide consensus that the most vulnerable and financially marginal entrepreneurs, who we have characterised as survivalists, need protection (Chen, 2018). This begins with accepting that these individuals are working legitimately, in other words, in alignment with community-centred norms, values and cultural practices, though the products they trade might be illegal and they might not have institutional land rights to operate from a particular site. These entrepreneurs operate at the end of the supply chain and have little influence on the process of production or distribution wherein economic power lies. They operate from spatial locations which are affordable, accessible and practical. These spaces include streets and pavements, open fields, backyard structures and rooms within a house. Their businesses utilise infrastructure in an incremental manner, probing and experimenting to reduce risks. Many of these survivalists are women, while men too were found conducting the most precarious activities, with gender having a shaping, not discriminatory, influence. Furthermore, even survivalists engage in strategic arrangements, which include utilising the social networks of kinship, friendships and tightly constituted groups. Our point is that even though survivalists embrace agency through networking, incremental or silent encroachment, and selling illegal goods (or legal goods illegally), their endeavours are vulnerable to individuals and businesses with greater power.

These more powerful entities range from thugs and criminals who rob traders; to the violent entrepreneurs in the taxi sector; to the informalist spaza-shop entrepreneurs who use price competition and illegitimate practices to dominate neighbourhood niche segments and control all grocery retailing; to the shopping mall developers who spatially restrict opportunities for micro-enterprises; and to the state law enforcement agencies who individually or institutionally seek to control when, where and how survivalists conduct businesses. Survivalists need protection from these groups. One form of protection could entail regulation, to convey institutional rights onto their businesses, though the entry barriers would need to be sufficiently low to recognise their resource constraints. If we consider the restrictive scope of municipal street-trader plans, the inflexibility of physical trading structures outside transport hubs, the impracticality of municipal by-laws, or the hostility of the state towards survivalists operating in regulated sectors, we see little prospect for a regulatory solution. It is unlikely that the mindset of politicians is amenable to change, not least because the evidence for and against regulation remains a contested domain. From an administrative perspective, there is little point in formalising survivalist micro-enterprises as their income is too low to raise tax revenue and their businesses per se pose little direct social threat to society or other businesses. Another means of protection is through organisation in bodies with collective decision-making power. It is important to recognise that collective organisation is not a panacea, as advocated in some sectors and spatial situations (Bénit-Gbaffou 2016; Chen 2018). Our experience in the township is that these organisations can (and are) dominated by the self-interest of their leadership and there is a tendency with informal trader organisations to 'privatise' space with the objective to control access to markets and extract tributes (Stillerman 2006). A further path towards securing protection is through patronising violent entrepreneurs and interlopers. As much as the minibus sector warrants our critique, we concede that taxi drivers can and do protect informal traders at the ranks. In another example, we have also found evidence of survivalists working with street committees or even gangs to enforce legal contracts against clients in a comparatively stronger position, such as shop tenants who withhold rent or refuse to vacate the building after the expiry of an agreement, and to enforce 'justice' in crime situations. We see that this pathway of protection is likely to remain important in survivalist strategies, not least so long as the state remains hostile towards what township communities often see as legitimate informal micro-enterprises (run by individuals who would be otherwise unemployed) and state agents are motivated by corruption.

Constrain

Not all informal micro-enterprise activities are deserving of protection. Some threaten other businesses and weaken opportunities for new market entrants. Some entrepreneurs seek to dominate markets and profit from unsuspecting, ill-informed and simply poor consumers. The embracing of opportunities of informality by informalists in the spaza sector, where businesses engage in exploitative labour practices, peddle contraband and counterfeit products and aim to dominate geographic market niches in a way that precludes opportunities for survivalists is one such situation. Liquor businesses that trade in an illegitimate manner, operating in disrespect of community norms through opening until late at night, generating noise, failing to provide adequate toilet facilities and stimulating public disturbances is another situation. In the minibus taxi sector, the unrestrained use of violence under the direction of organised structures has direct consequences for drivers, commuters and alternative forms of transport which remain subservient. Across each sector we found examples of practices that ought to be constrained. These include charlatan healers, sham churches, unqualified (and unsafe) medical services and educares which place children at risk of harm. The use of infrastructure and buildings in ways that are harmful or unsafe also falls within the catalogue of informal business activities with detrimental consequences.

The prospect of addressing such problematic strategies of business through 'engagement' are minimal, we would argue, our scepticism being based on the failure of various engagement-type interventions such as public meetings to discuss the problem, awareness messaging and self-monitoring. State pressure also needs to be applied through tools such as regulation, though institutional controls are only effective when the regulatory bar is placed at a level that is attainable and where recognition is afforded to legitimate practices. Our examination of the regulation of the liquor trade provides a case of how inappropriate policies serve to exclude and marginalise rather than include and transform and thus meaningfully reduce potential harm caused by liquor usage. There is little evidence to support the idea that regulation can be made effective through intensifying securitisation strategies alone; top-down measures (such as policing) require some bottom-up compliance (a realignment of informal rules and norms). Action to increase the policing of minibuses has had little impact on the lawless behaviour which characterises business operations in the sector. There must be pressure within supply chains, targeting manufacturers, wholesalers and distributors who maintain routes to market through working with informal micro-enterprises that knowingly operate on an illegal and illegitimate basis. Township entrepreneurs who, on a regular basis, spend huge amounts of money purchasing stock from formal businesses are simply too large in size to be afforded the right to operate informally. Similarly, informalists who transfer substantial sums of money via cell-phone banking platforms outside South Africa should be made to account for the funds acquired. These individuals (or networks) have the means to operate within the law, but voluntarily choose informal strategies so as to avoid institutional compliance and income-tax obligations. So, the point of pressure should be directed towards formal businesses which embrace opportunities to partner with cash-generating informal businesses, permitting them to limit their exposure and risks. But such is the power of corporates in the South African economy that it is unlikely that the state will have the confidence or capacity to effectively 'disrupt' this business. Thus, it is probable that extractive business practices will continue as usual, until such time as informal businesses challenge the corporates through creating alternative sources of supply and distribution. Only then, we suspect, the state will be pressurised to react.

The modes of constraining informality that are most likely to intensify are those constituted at the micro-context. These actions will entail various scales of social mobilisation and the actual or threatened use of violence. We have seen this in the case of the spaza sector through targeted (and indiscriminate) attacks on immigrant-owned shops. At a different level, we have also seen how community groups have compelled trading time restrictions on shebeens or compelled businesses to adhere to floor prices on select products. In the minibus sector, the associations can enforce adherence to 'rules' and impose penalties on drivers which range from fines to dismissals to the enforcement of a dress code, as happens in Ivory Park where drivers have to be dressed in a collar and tie when they work on Mondays. In the educare sector, power is exercised in more subtle ways through networks where access to resources, information and opportunities can be denied to individuals who operate in ways that may bring about collective risk.

Disrupt

If the many 'possibilities' that we highlight in this book are to be unlocked or amplified, it will be necessary to disrupt systems. These include land use, building standards, principles of planning and design, production, supply chains, business regulation and government support programmes. The Eveline Street case provides an insight into the transformative possibilities arising from relaxing land-use zoning and enabling businesses to operate legally and thus attract investment. The resulting supportive spatial and economic disruption to what was historically a homogenous residential settlement was established upon an evolving high-street model. Through means such as broadening the width of the sidewalk, introducing soft kerbing and environmental improvements such as street lighting, traffic calming and CCTV, the local economy has organically diversified and grown. Looking from the outside, such disruptive change might provide a sense of discomfort for policy-makers and investors who perceive micro-enterprises as 'unruly'. Yet where we have seen evidence of disruption to systems and business practices, the pace of change happens quickly. Sector business characteristics are constantly evolving and will look different in the future, but exactly what changes occur will depend on the appropriateness or otherwise of the mechanisms applied through which activities are protected or constrained.

In our analysis of specific topics, we have sought to highlight some of the major opportunities for disruption. Illustratively, the following state actions could, through 'disruptive' changes to policies and practices, enhance economic responses. One, inflexible land-use systems could be revised. Two, settlement layout could prioritise spatial opportunities for business, particularly on high streets though also in residential situations. Three, overly restrictive by-laws could be overhauled. Four, dominance over markets ought to be restricted, as larger businesses tend to retard the emergence of alternative opportunities which might be more adaptable and suitable to micro-enterprise growth and enhanced social outcomes. Five, the design and function of shopping malls which exclude micro-enterprises presents a further opportunity for disruption whereby the state could proactively legislate for inclusion. A sixth target is the supply chains which provide routes to market, perpetuating surplus extraction and informal business practices. B-BBEE codes could be reformulated to necessitate investment at the end of the value chain. Lastly, development programmes could be calibrated to reflect the differentiation within micro-enterprises and take cognisance of our findings that most survivalists are unlikely to develop into competitive businesses, let alone follow a modernising trajectory, and therefore strategies must be low-geared.

Such disruption will require confronting powerful interest groups. Some of these groups operate within political parties; some hold bureaucratic positions in the state and manage institutions across the three tiers of government; some are positioned with educational institutions and think-tanks where research aims to shape and defend policy; some manage corporate entities; and some are business investors. With the balance of this power falling across these stakeholders and allied with current political and corporate interests, the most likely outcome is the current inertia when it comes to supporting the township economy in transformative ways. The bureaucrats who oversee state institutions are quick to formulate policies in subservience to their political leaders, but slow to implement and cautious of disruption. Against all the evidence we present in this book, there are (and will be) new findings which suggest different ideas and analysis, some of which will be utilised, no doubt, to justify state inertia and sustain policies to satisfy political audiences rather than embrace a path along which people-centred economic responses can be nurtured. As we have sought to demonstrate through this book, township entrepreneurs have sufficient resolve, capital and social technologies to navigate their own paths towards economic growth, though reshaping policies and reducing the scale of extractive business would enable swifter growth and deliver more inclusive benefits.

References

Africa News Agency. (2018). Northern Cape police bust R77m Hartswater counterfeit factory. *The Citizen*. Retrieved from https://citizen.co.za/news/south-africa/1976653/northern-cape-police-bust-r77m-hartswater-counterfeit-factory/

Alcock, G. G. (2018). *Kasinomic revolution: The rise of African informal economies.* Johannesburg, RSA: Tracey McDonald

Alcock, G. G. (2015). *KasiNomics: African informal economies and the people who inhabit them.* Johannesburg, RSA: Tracey McDonald

Ambler, C., & Crush, J. (1992). Alcohol in Southern African labor history. In J. Crush & C. Ambler (Eds.), *Liquor and labor in Southern Africa* (pp. 1–55). Athens, OH: Ohio University Press

Anciano, F., & Piper, L. (2019). *Democracy disconnected: Participation and governance in a city of the south.* London, England: Routledge

Arrive Alive. (2018). *Minibus taxis and road safety.* Retrieved from https://www.arrivealive.co.za/Minibus-Taxis-and-Road-Safety

Artefacts. (n.d.). Calderwood, Douglas McGavin. Retrieved from https://www.artefacts.co.za/main/Buildings/archframes.php?archid=2679

Ashforth, A. (2002). An epidemic of witchcraft? The implications of AIDS for the post-apartheid state. *African Studies, 61*(1), 121–143. http://doi.org/10.1080/00020180220140109

Ashforth, A. (2005). *Witchcraft, violence, and democracy in South Africa.* Chicago, IL: University of Chicago Press

Aston Philander, L. (2011). An ethnobotany of Western Cape Rasta bush medicine. *Journal of Ethnopharmacology, 138*(2), 578–594. http://doi.org/10.1016/j.jep.2011.10.004

Atmore, E., Van Niekerk, L., & Ashley-Cooper, M. (2012). Challenges facing the early childhood development sector in South Africa. *South African Journal of Childhood Education, 2*(1), 120–139. Retrieved from http://www.nda.org.za/home/43/files/Research Reports/Challenges-facing-ECD-Sector-in-SA-Prof-Atmore.pdf

Barolsky, V. (2005). *Transitioning out of violence: Snapshots from Kathorus.* Johannesburg, RSA: Centre for the Study of Violence and Reconciliation

Basardien, F., Parker, H., Bayat, M. S., Friedrich, C., & Appoles, S. (2014). Entrepreneurial orientation of spaza shop entrepreneurs: Evidence from a study of South African and Somali-owned spaza shop entrepreneurs in Khayelitsha. *Singaporean Journal of Business Economics and Management Studies, 2*(10), 45–61

Battersby, J. (2017). Food system transformation in the absence of food system planning: the case of supermarket and shopping mall retail expansion in Cape Town, South Africa. *Built Environment, 43*(3), 417–430

Battersby, J., & Peyton, S. (2014). The geography of supermarkets in Cape Town: Supermarket expansion and food access. *Urban Forum, 25*(2), 153–164. http://doi.org/10.1007/s12132-014-9217-5

Bell, D. (2007). The hospitable city: social relations in commercial spaces. Progress in Human Geography, 31(1), 7–22. DOI: 10.1177/0309132507073526 Bayat, A. (1997). Un-civil society: The politics of the 'informal people'. *Third World Quarterly, 18*(1), 53–72. https://doi.org/10.1080/01436599715055

Bénit-Gbaffou, C. (2016). Do street traders have the 'right to the city'? The politics of street trader organisations in inner city Johannesburg, post-operation clean sweep. *Third World Quarterly, 37*(6), 1102–1129. http://doi.org/10.1080/01436597.2016.1141660

Berrisford, S. (2011). Unravelling apartheid spatial planning legislation in South Africa. *Urban Forum, 22*(3), 247–263. http://doi.org/10.1007/s12132-011-9119-8

Bickford, G. & Behrens, R. (2015, July). What does transit-oriented development mean in a South African context? A multiple stakeholder perspective from Johannesburg. *Proceedings of the 34th Southern African Transport Conference.* Retrieved from http://repository.up.ac.za/handle/2263/57751

Black, G. F., Davies, A., Iskander, D., & Chambers, M. (2018). Reflections on the ethics of participatory visual methods to engage communities in global health research. *Global Bioethics, 29*(1). http://doi.org/10.1080/1 1287462.2017.1415722

Botha, J., Witkowski, E. T. F., & Shackleton, C. M. (2004). Market profiles and trade in medicinal plants in the Lowveld, South Africa. *Environmental Conservation, 31*(1), 38–46. http://doi.org/10.1017/S0376892904001067

Boudreaux, K. (2006). Taxing alternatives: Poverty alleviation and the South African taxi/minibus industry. *Mercatus Policy Series, Policy Comment No. 3.* Arlington, VA: Mercatus Centre, George Mason University

Centre for Affordable Housing Finance in Africa. (2016). *Residential property market processes as found in Delft, Western Cape.* Johannesburg, RSA, Retrieved from http://housingfinanceafrica.org/app/uploads/Delft-Research-Report-FINAL_2016sm.pdf

Charman, A. (2016). Illegal drinking venues in a South African township: Sites of struggle in the informal city. In T. Thurnell-Read (Ed.), *Drinking dilemmas: Space, culture and identity* (pp. 62–80). Milton, England: Routledge

Charman, A., Bacq, S., & Brown, K. (2019). *Supermarkets, street traders and spaza shops: Spatial determinants of formal retailers' impact on informal micro-enterprises in Philippi, Cape Town (Research Report Series No. 2).* Pretoria, RSA: DST-NRF Centre of Excellence in Food Security. https://foodsecurity.ac.za/wp-content/uploads/2019/02/FINAL_CoE-RR-002_SLF-Feb-2019.pdf

Charman, A., & Govender, T. (2016). The relational economy of informality: Spatial dimensions of street trading in Ivory Park, South Africa. *Urban Forum, 27*(3), 311–328. http://doi.org/10.1007/s12132-016-9290-z

Charman, A., & Govender, T. (in press). The creative night-time leisure economy of informal drinking venues. *International Journal of Urban and Regional Research*, (forthcoming)

Charman, A., Govender, T., & de Villiers, S. (2017). *The impact of land systems on micro-economic investments: Ivory Park case studies.* Cape Town, South Africa: Sustainable Livelihoods Foundation. Retrieved from http://livelihoods.org.za/wp-content/uploads/2017/12/Impact-of-Land-Systems-of-Micro-Economic-Investments.pdf

Charman, A., Herrick, C., & Petersen, L. (2014). Formalising urban informality: Micro-enterprise and the regulation of liquor in Cape Town. *The Journal of Modern African Studies, 52*(04), 623–646. http://doi.org/10.1017/S0022278X14000615

Charman, A., & Kotzen, B. (n.d.). *Photovoice: Street life in Ivory Park.* Cape Town, RSA: Sustainable Livelihoods Foundation

Charman, A. J. E., & Petersen, L. M. (2015). A transnational space of business: The informal economy of Ivory Park, Johannesburg. In J. Crush, A. Chikanda, & C. Skinner (Eds.), *Mean streets: Migration, xenophobia and informality in South Africa.* Cape Town, RSA: Southern African Migration Programme, the African Centre for Cities and the International Development Research Centre

Charman, A., & Petersen, L. (2017). Temporal and spatial enterprise change in a township informal economy: A resurvey of micro-enterprises in Delft South. *REDI3x3 Working Paper 26.* Retrieved from http://www.redi3x3.org/paper/temporal-and-spatial-enterprise-change-township-informal-economy-resurvey-micro-enterprises

Charman, A. J. E., Petersen, L. M., & Govender, T. (2014). Shebeens as spaces and places of informality, enterprise, drinking and sociability. *South African Geographical Journal, 96*(1), 31–49. http://doi.org/10.1080/03736245.2014.896281

Charman, A., Petersen, L., & Piper, L. (2012). From local survivalism to foreign entrepreneurship: the transformation of the spaza sector in Delft, Cape Town. *Transformation: Critical Perspectives on Southern Africa, 78*(1), 47–73

Charman, A. J., Petersen, L. M., & Piper, L. (2013). Enforced informalisation: The case of liquor retailers in South Africa. *Development Southern Africa, 30*(4-05), 580–595. http://doi.org/10.1080/0376835X.2013.817306

Charman, A. J. E., Petersen, L. M., Piper, L. E., Liedeman, R., & Legg, T. (2015). Small area census approach to measure the township informal economy in South Africa. *Journal of Mixed Methods Research, 11*(1), 36–58. http://doi.org/10.1177/1558689815572024

Charman, A., & Piper, L. (2012). Xenophobia, criminality and violent entrepreneurship: Violence against Somali Shopkeepers in Delft South, Cape Town, South Africa. *South African Review of Sociology, 43*(February 2013), 81–105

Charman, A., Tonkin, C., Denoon-Stevens, S., & Demeestére, R. (2017). Post-apartheid spatial inequality: Obstacles of land use management on township micro-enterprise formalisation. Cape Town, RSA: Sustainable Livelihoods Foundation

Chen, M. (2018). The South African informal sector in international comparative perspective: Theories, data and policies. In F. Fourie (Ed.), *The South African informal sector: Creating jobs, reducing poverty.* (pp. 26–47). Cape Town, RSA: HSRC Press

Chen, M., Jhabvala, R., & Lund, F. (2002). Supporting workers in the informal economy: A policy framework. *ILO Working Paper on the Informal Economy, Employment Sector,* (November), 603–610. Geneva, Switzerland: ILO

Chevalier, S. (2015). Food, malls and the politics of consumption: South Africa's new middle class, 32(1), 118–129. *Development Southern Africa.* https://doi.org/https://doi.org/10.1080/0376835X.2014.965388

Cichello, P., & Rogan, M. (2018). Informal-sector employment and poverty reduction in South Africa: The contribution of 'informal' sources of income. In F. Fourie (Ed.), *The South African informal sector: Creating jobs, reducing poverty.* (pp. 226–247). Cape Town, RSA: HSRC Press

City of Windhoek. (2012). *Industrial survey.* Windhoek, Namibia: City of Windhoek

Cocks, M. L. (1977). *Towards an understanding of Amayeza esiXhosa stores (African chemists).* Unpublished master's dissertation. Rhodes University, Grahamstown, RSA

Coplan, A. (2008). *In Township Tonight! – South Africa's black city music and theatre.* (2nd ed.). Chicago, IL: University of Chicago Press

Creswell, J. W. (2014). *Research design: Qualitative, quantitative and mixed methods approaches* (4th ed.). Thousand Oaks, CA: SAGE

Crush, J. S., & Frayne, G. B. (2011a). Urban food insecurity and the new international food security agenda. *Development Southern Africa, 28*(4), 527–544. http://doi.org/10.1080/0376835X.2011.605571

Crush, J. S., & Frayne, G. B. (2011b). Supermarket expansion and the informal food economy in Southern African cities: Implications for urban food security. *Journal of Southern African Studies, 37*(4), 781–802. http://doi.org/10.1080/03057070.2011.617532

Crush, J., Chikanda, A., & Skinner, C. (2015). Introduction. In J. Crush, A. Chikanda, & C. Skinner (Eds.), *Mean streets: Migration, xenophobia and informality in South Africa.* Cape Town, RSA: Southern African Migration Project

DataFirst. 2016. *South Africa – SLF Township micro-enterprise survey 2010-2013* (zaf-slf-tms-2010-2013-v1). Retrieved from: https://www.datafirst.uct.ac.za/dataportal/index.php/catalog/596

Department of Social Development. (2014). *Audit of early childhood development (ECD) centres.* Retrieved from http://www.dsd.gov.za/index2.php?option=com_docman&task=doc_view&gid=608&Itemid=39

Dihel, N., & Goswami, A. G. (2016). Informal trade in services in Sub-Saharan Africa – unchartered territory. In N. Dihel & A. G. Goswami (Eds.), *The unexplored potential of trade in services in Africa: From hair stylists and teachers to accountants and doctors.* (pp. 31–45). Retrieved from http://documents.worldbank.org/curated/en/477321469182630728/The-unexplored-potential-of-trade-in-services-in-Africa-from-hair-stylists-and-teachers-to-accountants-and-doctors

Dold, A. P., & Cocks, M. L. (2002). The trade in medicinal plants in the Eastern Cape Province, South Africa. *South African Journal of Science, 98*(December), 589–597

Dold, T., & Cocks, M. (2012). *Voices from the forest. Celebrating nature and culture in Xhosaland.* Johannesburg, RSA: Jacana Media

Drake, L., & Stringer, L. (2016, September). Social innovation within the South African early childhood development sector. In M. M. Dichaba & A. A. Sotayo (Eds.), *South African international conference on education.* (pp. 173–198). s.l.: African Academic Research Forum

DTI (Department of Trade and Industry). (2012). *Integrated strategy on the development and promotion of co-operatives.* Pretoria, RSA: Department of Trade and Industry

Dugard, J. (2001). From low intensity war to Mafia war: Taxi violence in South Africa (1987–2000). *Violence and transition series, 4 (May).* Johannesburg, RSA: Centre for the Study of Violence and Reconciliation

Du Toit, A., & Neves, D. (2009). *Informal social protection in post-apartheid migrant networks: Vulnerability, social networks and reciprocal exchange in the Eastern and Western Cape, South Africa (No. 74).* Washington, D.C.: Brooks World Poverty Institute

Du Toit, A., & Neves, D. (2014). The government of poverty and the arts of survival: Mobile and recombinant strategies at the margins of the South African economy. *Journal of Peasant Studies, 41*(5), 833–853. http://doi.org/10.1080/03066150.2014.894910

Erasmus, Z. (1997). 'Oe! My hare gaan huistoe': Hair-styling as black cultural practice. *Agenda: Empowering Women for Gender Equity, 32*(1997), 11–16. http://doi.org/10.1080/10130950.1997.9675579

Even-Zahav, E. (2016). *Food security and the urban informal economy: The state of knowledge and perspectives from street-food traders in Khayelitsha.* Unpublished master's thesis. University of Stellenbosch, Stellenbosch, RSA

Fatoki, O. (2014). The causes of the failure of new small and medium enterprises in South Africa. *Mediterranean Journal of Social Sciences, 5*(20), 922–927. http://doi.org/10.5901/mjss.2014.v5n20p922

Fourie, F. (2018a). Analysing the informal sector in South Africa: Knowledge and policy gaps, conceptual and data challenges. In F. Fourie (Ed.), *The South African informal sector: Creating jobs, reducing poverty* (pp. 3–25). Cape Town, RSA: HSRC Press

Fourie, F. (2018b). Informal-sector employment in South Africa: An enterprise analysis using the SESE survey. In F. Fourie (Ed.), *The South African informal sector: Creating jobs, reducing poverty* (pp. 103–151). Cape Town, RSA: HSRC Press

Fourie, F. (2018c). Enagling the forgotten sector: Informal-sector realities, policy approaches and formalisation in South Africa. In F. Fourie (Ed.), *The South African informal sector: Creating jobs, reducing poverty.* (pp. 439–476). Cape Town, RSA: HSRC Press

Fourie, L. J. (2003). *Rethinking the formalisation of the minibus-taxi industry in South Africa.* Unpublished master's thesis. Retrieved from https://repository.up.ac.za/bitstream/handle/2263/26930/00dissertation.pdf?sequence=1

Friedman, F. (2000). *Deconstructing Windhoek: The urban morphology of a post-apartheid city (The Bartlett Development Planning Unit).* Retrieved from https://www.ucl.ac.uk/bartlett/development/case-studies/2000/aug/111-deconstructing-windhoek-urban-morphology-post-apartheid-city

Gastrow, V., & Amit, R. (2013). *Somalinomics: A case study on the economics of Somali informal trade in the Western Cape.* Johannesburg, RSA: African Centre for Migration & Society, University of the Witwatersrand

Gibbs, T. (2014). Becoming a 'big man' in neo-liberal South Africa: Migrant masculinities in the minibus-taxi industry. *African Affairs, 113*(452), 431–448. http://doi.org/https://doi.org/10.1093/afraf/adu044

Gordon, R., Nell, M., & Di Lollo, A. (2011). *An investigation into the delays in issuing title deeds to beneficiaries of housing projects funded by the capital subsidy.* Pretoria, RSA: Urban LandMark

Govender, T. (2015). Home Sweet resilience: Lessons from shebeens. *SLUM Lab, 9,* 106–111

Greenberg, S. (2015). *Corporate concentration and food security in South Africa: Is the commercial agro-food system delivering?* Retrieved from http://www.plaas.org.za/sites/default/files/publications-pdf/PLAASRuralReportBook1-Stephen-Web.pdf

Gulyani, S., & Talukdar, D. (2010). Inside informality: The links between poverty, microenterprises, and living conditions in Nairobi's slums. *World Development, 38*(12), 1710–1726. http://doi.org/10.1016/j.worlddev.2010.06.013

Harber, A. (2011). *Diepsloot.* Johannesburg, RSA: Jonathan Ball

Harber, J. (2018). The transformation of Eveline Street, Windhoek. *Journal of the South African Institute of Architects, 91,* 10–19

Hart, K. (1973). Informal income opportunities and urban employment in Ghana. *The Journal of Modern African Studies, 11*(1), 61–89. http://doi.org/10.1017/S0022278X00008089

Hartnack, A., & Liedeman, R. (2016). *Factors that contribute towards informal micro-enterprises going out of business in Delft South, 2010-2015: A qualitative investigation (No. REDI3x3 Working paper 20).* Retrieved from http://www.redi3x3.org/papers-results?field_paper_all_value=&field_summary_value=&title=&field_author_value=hartnack&field_project_type_tid=All&field_research_nid=All

Herrick, C. (2014). Stakeholder narratives on alcohol governance in the Western Cape: The socio-spatial 'nuisance' of drink. *South African Geographical Journal, 96*(1), 81–96. http://doi.org/10.1080/03736245.2014.896278

Herrick, C., & Charman, A. (2013). Shebeens and crime: The multiple criminalities of South African liquor and its regulation. *SA Crime Quarterly, 45,* 25–33

Hickel, J. (2014). "Xenophobia" in South Africa: Order, chaos, and the moral economy of witchcraft. *Cultural Anthropology, 29*(1), 103–127. http://doi.org/10.14506/ca29.1.07

Hiebert, D., Rath, J., & Vertovec, S. (2015). Urban markets and diversity: towards a research agenda. *Ethnic and Racial Studies, 38*(1), 5–21. http://doi.org/10.1080/01419870.2014.953969

Hirt, S. (2007). The devil is in the definition: Contrasting American and German approaches to zoning. *Journal of the American Planning Association, 73*(4), 436–450

International Organization for Migration. (2009). *Towards tolerance, law and dignity: Addressing violence against foreign nationals in South Africa*. Retrieved from https://www.atlanticphilanthropies.org/wp-content/uploads/2015/09/IOM_Addressing_Violence_Against_Foreign_Nationals.pdf

Isaacs, F., & M. Silverman (2018, May). Reflections on capital web through researching everyday practices in Delft. *Paper presented at the 3rd UDISA Conference*, Cape Town, 9 May 2018

Isaacs, L. (2018). *Delft Taxi Association chairperson shot dead*. Retrieved from http://ewn.co.za/2018/05/21/delft-taxi-association-chaiperson-shot-dead

Jayne, M., Holloway, S. L., & Valentine, G. (2006). Drunk and disorderly: Alcohol, urban life and public space. *Progress in Human Geography, 30*(4), 451–468. http://doi.org/10.1191/0309132506ph618oa

Jayne, M., Valentine, G., & Holloway, S. L. (2008). Geographies of alcohol, drinking and drunkenness: A review of progress. *Progress in Human Geography, 32*(2), 247–263. http://doi.org/10.1177/0309132507087649

Jayne, M., Valentine, G., & Holloway, S. L. (2012). What use are units? Critical geographies of alcohol policy. *Antipode, 44*(3), 828–846. http://doi.org/10.1111/j.1467-8330.2011.00927.x

Kalichman, S. C., Simbayi, L. C., Vermaak, R., Jooste, S., & Cain, D. (2008). HIV/AIDS risks among men and women who drink at informal alcohol serving establishments (shebeens) in Cape Town, South Africa. *Prevention Science, 9*(1), 55–62. http://doi.org/10.1007/s11121-008-0085-x

Kanbur, R. (2009). *Conceptualising informality: Regulation and enforcement*. Retrieved from www.people.cornell.edu/pages/sk145

Kanbur, R. (2012). *A simple framework for understanding police differences on informality*. Retrieved from www.kanbur.dyson.cornell.edu

Kelliher, F., & Reinl, L. (2009). A resource-based view of micro-firm management practice. *Journal of Small Business and Enterprise Development, 16*(3), 521–532. http://doi.org/10.1108/14626000910977206

Kerr, A. (2015). Tax (i) ing the poor? Commuting costs in South African cities (Research project on employment, income distribution and inclusive growth). *REDI3x3 Working Paper No 12*. Cape Town, RSA: Research Project on Employment, Income Distribution and Inclusive Growth. Retrieved from http://www.redi3x3.org/sites/default/files/Kerr%202015%20REDI3x3%20Working%20paper12%20-%20Commuting%20costs.pdf

Kingdon, G. G., & Knight, J. (2004). Unemployment in South Africa: The nature of the beast. *World Development, 32*(3), 391–408. http://doi.org/10.1016/j.worlddev.2003.10.005

Kinyanjui, M. N. (2019). *African markets and the utu-ubuntu business model: A perspective on economic informality in Nairobi*. Cape Town, RSA: African Minds

Kistruck, G. M., Webb, J. W., Sutter, C. J., & Bailey, A. V. G. (2014). The double-edged sword of legitimacy in base-of-the-pyramid markets. *Journal of Business Venturing, 30*(3), 436–451. http://doi.org/10.1016/j.jbusvent.2014.06.004

Koens, K., & Thomas, R. (2015). Is small beautiful? Understanding the contribution of small businesses in township tourism to economic development. *Development Southern Africa, 32*(3), 320–332. http://doi.org/10.1080/0376835X.2015.1010715

Kubheka, T. (2018). Soweto daycare owner recounts ordeal after children ate polony. *Eyewitness News*. Retrieved from https://ewn.co.za/2018/03/13/soweto-daycare-owner-recounts-ordeal-after-children-ate-polony

La Hausse, P. (1988). *Brewers, beerhalls and boycotts: A history of liquor in South Africa*. Johannesburg, RSA: Ravan Press

Latham, A. (2003). Urbanity, lifestyle and making sense of the new urban cultural economy: Notes from Auckland, New Zealand. *Urban Studies, 40*(9), 1699–1724. http://doi.org/10.1080/0042098032000106564

Lawhon, M. (2013). Flows, friction and the sociomaterial metabolization of alcohol. *Antipode, 45*(3), 681–701. http://doi.org/10.1111/j.1467-8330.2012.01028.x

Ledeneva, A. V. (1998). *Russia's economy of favours: Blat, networking and informal exchange.* Cambridge, London: Cambridge University Press

Legassick, M. (1974). Legislation, ideology and economy in post-1948 South Africa. *Journal of Southern African Studies, 1*(1), 5–35. http://doi.org/10.1080/03057077408707921

Liedeman, R. (2013). *Understanding the internal dynamics and organisation of spaza shop operations: A case study of how social networks enable entrepreneurialism amongst Somali but not South African traders in Delft South, Cape Town.* Unpublished master's thesis. University of the Western Cape, Cape Town, RSA

Liedeman, R., & Mackay, B. (2016). *A smokescreen economy: the nature and scale of township grey market cigarette trade in Delft (2016).* Retrieved from http://livelihoods.org.za/wp-content/uploads/2018/05/A-Smokescreen-Economy-township-grey-market-cigarette-trade-in-Delft_booklet.pdf

Ligthelm, A. A. (2005). Informal retailing through home-based micro-enterprises: The role of spaza shops. *Development Southern Africa, 22*(2), 199–214. http://doi.org/10.1080/03768350500163030

Ligthelm, A. A. (2008). A targeted approach to informal business development: The entrepreneurial route. *Development Southern Africa, 25*(4), 367–382. http://doi.org/10.1080/03768350802316138

Littlewood, D., Rogers, P., & Williams, C. (2018). Experiences, causes and measures to tackle institutional incongruence and informal economic activity in South-East Europe. *Current Sociology*, 1–22. http://doi.org/10.1177/0011392118788911

Lloyd, N., & Leibbrandt, M. (2018). Entry into and exit from informal enterprise ownership in South Africa. In F. Fourie (Ed.), *The South African informal sector: Creating jobs, reducing poverty* (pp. 151–177). Cape Town, RSA: HSRC Press

Lomme, R. (2008, November). Should South African minibus taxis be scrapped? Formalizing informal urban transport in a developing country. In *Proceedings of the CODATU XIII Conference Ho Chi Minh City, 12-14 November.* (pp. 1–18). London, England: Omega Centre

Lukhele, A. (2018). *Three decades of stokvel banking.* Retrieved from http://nasasa.co.za/site/wp-content/uploads/2018/05/Three-Decades-of-Stokvel-Banking-Andrew-Lukhele-NASASA-2018.pdf

Madlala, T. (2015). *Do large retailers displace small informal retailers? The case of Pick n Pay in Kwamashu.* Retrieved from https://researchspace.ukzn.ac.za/xmlui/handle/10413/14576

Mager, A. (1999). The first decade of 'European beer' in apartheid South Africa: The state, the brewers and the drinking public, 1962-72. *Journal of African History*, 367–388. Retrieved from http://www.jstor.org/stable/10.2307/183619

Mager, A. (2004). 'White liquor hits black livers': Meanings of excessive liquor consumption in South Africa in the second half of the twentieth century. *Social Science & Medicine, 59*(4), 735–751. http://doi.org/10.1016/j.socscimed.2003.12.005

Mager, A. K. (2010). *Beer, sociability and masculinity in South Africa.* Cape Town, RSA: UCT Press

Magonya, P. (2013). 'The businessman'. In A, Charman, & B. Kotzen (n.d.). *Photovoice: Street life in Ivory Park*. Cape Town, RSA: Sustainable Livelihoods Foundation. Photograph available from: https://www.facebook.com/photo. php?fbid=445408218881161&set=o.139425629568079&type=3&theater

Mahajan, S. (2014). A conceptual framework for the township economy. In S. Mahajan (Ed.), *Economics of South African townships: Special focus on Diepsloot*. (pp. 51–62). Washington, D.C.: The World Bank

Maloney, W. F. (2004). Informality revisited. *World Development, 32*(7), 1159–1178. http://doi.org/10.1016/j.worlddev.2004.01.008

Mander, M. (1998). *Marketing of indigenous medicinal plants in South Africa: A case study in KwaZulu-Natal*. Rome, Italy: Food and Agriculture Organisation of the United Nations

Mander, M., Ntuli, L., Diederichs, N., & Mavundla, K. (2007). Economics of the traditional medicine trade in South Africa. In S. Harrison, R. Bhana, & A. Ntuli (Eds.), *South African Health Review, 2007*. (pp. 189-196). Durban, RSA: Health Systems Trust

Manhica, P. (2013). 'Women frying fish'. In A. Charman, & B. Kotzen (n.d.). *Photovoice: Street life in Ivory Park*. Cape Town, RSA: Sustainable Livelihoods Foundation. Photograph available from: https://www.facebook.com/photo. php?fbid=125297154332363&set=o.139425629568079&type=3&theater

Mbonyane, B., & Ladzani, W. (2011). Factors that hinder the growth of small businesses in South African townships. *European Business Review, 23*(6), 550–560. http://doi.org/ http://dx.doi.org/10.1108/MRR-09-2015-0216

McAllister, P. (2009). Ubuntu: Beyond belief in Southern Africa. *Sites, 6*(1), 1–10

McPherson, M. A. (1996). Growth of micro and small enterprises in southern Africa. *Journal of Development Economics, 48*(2), 253–277. http://doi.org/10.1016/0304-3878(95)00027-5

Mead, D. C., & Liedholm, C. (1988). The dynamics of micro and small enterprises in developing countries. *World Development, 26*(1), 61–74. http://doi.org//10.1016/S0305-750X(97)10010-9

Mhlanga, S. (2017). An assessment of the regulatory arrangements in the minibus taxi industry in South Africa: A primer for self-regulation. In *36th Southern African Transport Conference (SATC 2017)* 27 July. (pp. 375–387). Retrieved from: https://repository.up.ac.za/bitstream/handle/2263/62722/Mhlanga_Assessment_2017. pdf?sequence=1&isAllowed=y

Ministry of Works & City of Windhoek. (2013). Master plan of City of Windhoek including Rehoboth, Okahandja and Hosea Kutako International Airport. Windhoek, Namibia: Republic of Namibia

Monyai, D. (2013a). 'Beating all odds'. In A. Charman, & B. Kotzen (n.d.). *Photovoice: street life in Ivory Park*. Cape Town, RSA: Sustainable Livelihoods Foundation. Photograph Available from: https://www.facebook.com/photo. php?fbid=123802244482602&set=o.139425629568079&type=3&theater

Monyai, D. (2013b) 'The Trolley'. In A. Charman, & B. Kotzen (n.d.). *Photovoice: Street life in Ivory Park*. Cape Town, RSA: Sustainable Livelihoods Foundation. Photograph available from: https://www.facebook.com/photo. php?fbid=116607021868791&set=o.139425629568079&type=3&theater

Morris, M. (1976). The development of capitalism in South Africa. *Journal of Development Studies, 12*(3), 280–292. http://doi.org/10.1080/00220387608421586

Mörtenböck, P., & Mooshammer, H. (2015). *Informal market worlds atlas*. Rotterdam, The Netherlands: NAI010 Publishers

Mukhopadhyay, P. (2011). *Formality and functionality in Indian cities.* Retrieved from http://www.india-seminar.com/2011/617.htm

Mulaudzi, R. (2017). *From consumers to investors: An investigation into the character and nature of stokvels in South Africa's urban, peri-urban and rural centres using a phenomenological approach.* Unpublished master's thesis. University of Cape Town, Cape Town, RSA

National Institute for Communicable Diseases. (2018). *Statement regarding the source of the Listeriosis outbreak.* Retrieved from http://www.nicd.ac.za/index.php/statement-regarding-the-source-of-the-listeriosis-outbreak/

Natrass, N. (2006). Who consults sangomas in Khayelitsha? An exploratory quantitative analysis. *CSSR Working Paper No. 151.* Cape Town, RSA: University of Cape Town

Ndlovu, B. (2013). 'Trying'. In A. Charman, & B. Kotzen (n.d.). *Photovoice: Street life in Ivory Park.* Cape Town, RSA: Sustainable Livelihoods Foundation. Photograph available from: https://www.facebook.com/photo.php?fbid=4763135563466&set=o.139425629568079&type=3&theater

Neilsen. (2016). *Retail grocery market report.* Retrieved from http://www.nielsen.com/za/en/press-room/2016/south-africas-trade-sector-thriving-with-r46-billion-in-annual-sales.html

Nel, V. (2016). A better zoning system for South Africa? *Land Use Policy, 55,* 257–264. http://doi.org/10.1016/j.landusepol.2016.04.007

Neves, D., & du Toit, A. (2012). Money and sociality in South African informal economy. *Africa, 82*(1), 131–149. http://doi.org/10.1017/S0001972011000763

Ngubane, H. (1977). *Body and mind in Zulu medicine: An ethnography of health and disease in Nyuswa-Zulu thought and practice.* London, England: Academic Press

Ntsebeza, D. (2005). *Committee of inquiry into the underlying causes of instability in the minibus taxi industry in the Cape Town Metropolitan Area. Report to the Premier.* Cape Town, RSA: Western Cape Government

Oranje, M. (2014). Back to where it all began...? Reflections on injecting the (spiritual) ethos of the Early Town Planning Movement into Planning, Planners and Plans in post-1994 South Africa. *HTS Teologiese Studies/Theological Studies, 70*(3), 10. http://doi.org/10.4102/hts.v70i3.2781

Pauw, J. (2017). *The president's keepers: Those keeping Zuma in power and out of prison.* Cape Town, RSA: NB Publishers

Perry, G. (2007). *Informality: Exit and exclusion.* Washington, D.C.: World Bank Publications

Petersen, L., & Charman, A. (2010). Case study: Understanding the local economic impact of the closure of shebeens in the Western Cape as a consequence of the new Western Cape Liquor Act, 2008. *The Small Business Monitor, 6*(1), 102–109

Petersen, L. M., & Charman, A. J. E. (2018). The scope and scale of the informal food economy of South African urban residential townships: Results of a small-area micro-enterprise census. *Development Southern Africa, 35*(1), 1–23. http://doi.org/10.1080/0376835X.2017.1363643

Petersen, L. M., Charman, A. J. E., & Kroll, F. J. (2018). Trade dynamics in Cape Town township informal food service: A qualitative and supply chain study. *Development Southern Africa, 35*(1), 70–89. http://doi.org/10.1080/0376835X.2017.1412297

Petersen, L. M., Charman, A. J. E., Moll, E. J., Collins, R. J., & Hockings, M. T. (2014). 'Bush Doctors and Wild Medicine': The scale of trade in Cape Town's informal economy of wild-harvested medicine and traditional healing. *Society & Natural Resources, 27*(3), 315-336. http://doi.org/10.1080/08941920.2013.861558 ·

Petersen, L. M., Moll, E. J., Collins, R., & Hockings, M. T. (2012). Development of a compendium of local, wild-harvested species used in the informal economy trade, Cape Town, South Africa. *Ecology and Society, 17*(2). http://doi.org/10.5751/ES-04537-170226

Petersen, L. M., Moll, E. J., Hockings, M. T., & Collins, R. J. (2015). Implementing value chain analysis to investigate drivers and sustainability of Cape Town's informal economy of wild-harvested traditional medicine. *Local Environment, 20*(9), 1040–1061. http://doi.org/10.1080/13549839.2014.887667

Petersen, L., Thorogood, C., Charman, A., & du Toit, A. (2019). *What price cheap goods? Survivalists, informalists and competition in the township retail grocery trade.* PLAAS Working Paper (forthcoming)

Phillip, K. (2018). Limiting opportunities in the informal sector: The impact of the structure of the South African economy. In F. Fourie (Ed.), *The South African informal sector: Creating jobs, reducing poverty.* (pp. 309–327). Cape Town, RSA: HSRC Press

Pieterse, E. (2009). *Post-apartheid geographies in South Africa: Why are urban divides so persistent? Interdisciplinary debates on development and cultures: Cities in development – Spaces, conflicts and agency.* Retrieved from http://www.africancentreforcities.net/wp-content/uploads/2013/10/post-apartheid_geographies_pieterse_15dec09.pdf

Pieterse, E., & Simone, A. (2013). Introduction. In E. Pieterse & A. Simone (Eds.), *Rogue urbanism: Emergent African cities.* Johannesburg, RSA: Jacana Media

Piper, L., & Charman, A. (2018). Tenderpreneur (South Africa). In *The global informality project.* Retrieved from http://in-formality.com/wiki/index.php?title=Tenderpreneur(South_Africa)

Piper, L., & Yu, D. (2016). Deconstructing 'the foreign': The limits of citizenship for explaining price competition in the Spaza sector in South Africa. *Development Southern Africa, 33*(5), 658–676. http://doi.org/10.1080/0376835X.2016.1203758

Popkin, B. M. (2003). The nutrition transition in the developing world. *Development Policy Review, 21*, 581–597. http://doi.org/10.1111/j.1467-8659.2003.00225.x

Prahalad, C. K., & Hart, S. L. (2002). The fortune at the bottom of the pyramid. *Worldview, 26*, 1–14. Retrieved from: https://www.strategy-business.com/article/11518?pg=0

Preston-Whyte, E., & Rogerson, C. M. (1991). South Africa's informal economy. Cape Town, RSA: Oxford University Press

Pulker, A. (2016). *The relationship between urban food security, supermarket expansion and urban planning and policy in the City of Cape Town: A case of the Langa Junction mini-mall.* Unpublished master's dissertation. University of Cape Town, Cape Town, RSA

Rogan, M., & Skinner, C. (2018). The size and structure of the South African informal sector 2008-2014: A labour force analysis. In F. Fourie (Ed.), *The South African informal sector: creating jobs, reducing poverty* (pp. 77–102). Cape Town, RSA: HSRC Press

Rogerson, C. M. (1996). Urban poverty and the informal economy in South Africa's economic heartland. *Environment and Urbanization, 8*(1), 167–179. http://doi.org/10.1177/095624789600800115

Rogerson, C. M. (2016). Responding to informality in urban Africa: Street trading in Harare, Zimbabwe. *Urban Forum, 27*(2), 229–251. http://doi.org/10.1007/s12132-016-9273-0

Rogerson, C. M., & Hart, D. (1986). The survival of the 'informal sector': The shebeens of black Johannesburg. *GeoJournal, 12*(2), 153–166

Rolfe, R., Woodward, D., Ligthelm, A., & Guimarães, P. (2010). The viability of informal micro-enterprise in South Africa. *Journal of Developmental Entrepreneurship, 16*(01), 65–86

Rooks, G., Szirmai, A., & Sserwanga, A. (2009). *The interplay of human and social capital in entrepreneurship in developing countries: The case of Uganda*. Helsinki, Finland: UNU-Wider

Roy, A. (2009). Why India cannot plan its cities: Informality, insurgence and the idiom of urbanization. *Planning Theory, 8*(1), 76–87. http://doi.org/10.1177/1473095208099299

Scott, L., & Barr, G. (2013). Unregulated gambling in South African townships: A policy conundrum? *Journal of Gambling Studies, 29*(4), 719–732. http://doi.org/10.1007/s10899-012-9330-0

Sen, A. (1981). *Poverty and famines: An essay on entitlement and deprivation*. Oxford, England: Oxford University Press

Shackleton, C. M., Shackleton, S. E., & Cousins, B. (2001). The role of land-based strategies in rural livelihoods: The contribution of arable production, animal husbandry and natural resource harvesting in communal areas in South Africa. *Development Southern Africa, 18*(5), 581–604. http://doi.org/10.1080/03768350120097441

Simone, A. (2004). People as infrastructure: *Public Culture, 16*(3), 407–429. http://doi.org/10.1215/08992363-16-3-407

Sinclair-Smith, K., & Turok, I. (2012). The changing spatial economy of cities: An exploratory analysis of Cape Town. *Development Southern Africa, 29*(3), 391–417. http://doi.org/doi.org/10.1080/0376835X.2012.706037

Skinner, C. (2008). *Street trade in Africa: A review*. School of Development Studies, University of Kwazulu-Natal. Retrieved from https://wiego.org/sites/wiego.org/files/publications/files/Skinner_WIEGO_WP5.pdf

Skinner, C., & Haysom, G. (2016). *The informal sector's role in food security: A missing link in policy debates?* Working Paper 44. Retrieved from http://repository.uwc.ac.za/xmlui/handle/10566/4527

Smit, W. (2014). Discourses of alcohol: Reflections on key issues influencing the regulation of shebeens in Cape Town. *South African Geographical Journal, 96*(1), 60–80. http://doi.org/10.1080/03736245.2014.896283

Socio-Economic Rights Institute of South Africa & South African Local Government Association. (2018). *Informal trade in South Africa: Legislation, case law and recommendations for local government*. Retrieved from: http://www.seri-sa.org/images/SERI_SALGA_Informal_Trade_Jurisprudence_WEB.pdf

Spiegel, A. (2005). Refracting an elusive South African urban citizenship: Problems with tracking spaza. In S. Robins (Ed.), *Limits to liberation after Apartheid: Citizenship, governance and culture* (pp. 190–205). Cape Town, RSA: David Philip

StatsSA (Statistics South Africa). (2012). *Census 2011*. Pretoria, RSA: Statistics South Africa

StatsSA. (2019). Quarterly Labour Fource Survey. Quarter 2. Pretoria, RSA: Statistics South Africa. http://www.statssa.gov.za/publications/P0211/P02112ndQuarter2019.pdf

Stillerman, J. (2006). The politics of space and culture in Santiago, Chile's Street Markets. *Qualitative Sociology, 29*, 507–530. https://doi.org/10.1007/s11133-006-9041-x

Street, R., & Rautenbach, C. (2016, January 25). SA wants to regulate traditional healers – but it's not easy. *Sowetan Live*. Retrieved from https://www.sowetanlive.co.za/news/2016-01-25-sa-wants-to-regulate-traditional-healers--but-its-not-easy/

Strydom, J. (2015). David against Goliath: Predicting the survival of formal small businesses in Soweto. *International Business & Economics Research Journal, 14*(3), 463–476

Strydom, J. W. (2011). Retailing in disadvantaged communities: The outshopping phenomenon revisited. *Journal of Contemporary Management, 8*(1), 150–172

Sustainable Livelihoods Foundation. (2014.). *Safe shebeen project. Cape Town*. Retrieved from http://livelihoods.org.za/wp-content/uploads/2018/05/Safe-Shebeens-Narrative-Report.pdf#page=2&zoom=auto,-5,405

SLF (Sustainable Livelihoods Foundation). (2015). *Spaza shop survivalists* [Video file]. Retrieved from: https://www.youtube.com/watch?v=-sv_ZM-5or8

SLF. (2017a). Development-oriented township land use management: Learning from Eveline Street, Katutura, Windhoek. In SACN (Ed.), *The urban land paper series: A transit-oriented development lens (Vol. 2)*. Johannesburg, RSA: South African Cities Network

SLF. (2017b). *Lanie's educare*. [Video file]. Retrieved from https://www.youtube.com/watch?v=V4Qi8WB2GvE&t=0s&index=6&list=PLIWHCTyf4KVMgGIdP3kdENy6yKH57Nvr3

SLF. (2017c). *Zukisani's business challenges*. [Video file]. South Africa: Retrieved from https://www.youtube.com/watch?v=dlIVtd9TKCQ

SLF. (2017d). *Jerome ''n Donker day in my lewe'*. Retrieved from https://www.youtube.com/watch?v=eucw3WIJ_QY&list=PLIWHCTyf4KVMgGIdP3kdENy6yKH57Nvr3&index=4&t=0s

SLF & UrbanWorks. (2017). *Transformative leisure economies*. Cape Town, RSA: Sustainable Livelihoods Foundation

Sutter, C. J., Webb, J. W., Kistruck, G. M., & Bailey, A. V. G. (2013). Entrepreneurs' responses to semi-formal illegitimate institutional arrangements. Journal of Business Venturing, 28(6), 743–758. https://doi.org/10.1016/j.jbusvent.2013.03.001 The South African Property Owners' Association (SAPOA) and the South African Cities Network (SACN). (2016). *Developing a collective approach to mixed-use development in transit-oriented development*. Retrieved from http://www.sacities.net/wp-content/uploads/2016/PDF/TOD Report 2016-web version.pdf

Tivane, IDTV (2013). 'Mobile'. In A. Charman, & B. Kotzen (n.d.). *Photovoice: Street life in Ivory Park*. Cape Town, RSA: Sustainable Livelihoods Foundation. Photograph available from: https://www.facebook.com/photo.php?fbid=247172955425571&set=o.139425629568079&type=3&theater

Trade Intelligence. (2017). *Malls to markets: An introduction to South African food & grocery retail, 2016*. Durban, RSA: The Retail Workshop

Truter, I. (2007). African traditional healers: Cultural and religious beliefs intertwined in a holistic way. *South African Pharmaceutical Journal, 74*(8), 56–60

Tsele, L. (2017). *What will it take to disrupt SA's public taxi industry?* Retrieved from https://www.smesouthafrica.co.za/17264/Tech-To-Disrupt-Taxi-Industry/

Tsoeu, M. (2009). *A value chain analysis of the formal and the informal economy: A case study of South African Breweries and shebeens in Soweto*. Unpublished master's dissertation. University of the Witwatersrand, Johannesburg, RSA

Turok, I. (2001). Persistent polarisation post-apartheid? Progress towards urban integration in Cape Town. *Urban Studies, 38*(13), 2349–2377. http://doi.org/10.1080/00420980120094551

Valverde, M. (2003). Police science, British style: Pub licensing and knowledges of urban disorder. *Economy and Society, 32*(2), 234–252. Retrieved from http://www.tandfonline.com/doi/abs/10.1080/0308514032000073419

Verhoef, G. (2001). Informal financial service institutions for survival: African women and stokvels in urban South Africa 1930–1998. *Enterprise & Society, 2,* 259–296

Volkov, V. (2002). *Violent entrepreneurs: The use of force in the making of Russian capitalism*. Ithaca, NY: Cornell University Press

Walters, J. (2008). Overview of public transport policy developments in South Africa. *Research in Transport Economics, 22,* 98–108

Watson, S. (2009). The magic of the marketplace: Sociality in a neglected public space. *Urban Studies, 46*(8), 1577–1591

Watson, V. (2009). 'The planned city sweeps the poor away...': Urban planning and 21st century urbanisation. *Progress in Planning, 72*(3), 151–193. http://doi.org/10.1016/j. progress.2009.06.002

Watt, M. H., Aunon, F. M., Skinner, D., Sikkema, K. J., MacFarlane, J. C., Pieterse, D., & Kalichman, S. C. (2012). Alcohol-serving venues in South Africa as sites of risk and potential protection for violence against women. *Substance Use & Misuse, 47*(12), 1271–1280. http://doi.org/10.3109/10826084.2012.695419

Webb, J. W., Tihanyi, L., Ireland, R. D., & Sirmon, D. G. (2009). You say illegal, I say legitimate: Entrepreneurship in the informal economy. *Academy of Management Review, 34*(3), 492–510. http://doi.org/10.5465/AMR.2009.40632826

Weller, S. (2011). *South African township barbershops & salons.* New York, NY: Mark Batty

Western Cape Government. (2017). *Make sure your child is transported to school safely.* Retrieved from https://www.westerncape.gov.za/general-publication/make-sure-your-child-transported-school-safely

Williams, C. C., & Shahid, M. S. (2016). Informal entrepreneurship and institutional theory: Explaining the varying degrees of (in)formalization of entrepreneurs in Pakistan. *Entrepreneurship and Regional Development, 28*(1–2), 1–25. http://doi.org/10.1080/08985626.2014.963889

Williams, V. L., Witkowski, E.T. F., & Balkwill, K. (2007). Volume and financial value of species traded in the medicinal plant markets of Gauteng, South Africa. *International Journal of Sustainable Development and World Ecology, 14*(6), 584–603. http://doi.org/10.1080/13504500709469757

Wills, G. (2009). South Africa's informal economy: A statistical profile. *Urban Policies Research Report, No. 7 April 2009.* Retrieved from: http://library.mpib-berlin.mpg.de/toc/z2010_1353.pdf

Woodward, D., Rolfe, R., Ligthelm, A., & Guimarães, P. (2011). The viability of informal microenterprise in South Africa. *Journal of Developmental Entrepreneurship, 16*(01), 65–86. Retrieved from http://www.worldscientific.com/doi/abs/10.1142/S1084946711001719

Woolf, S. E. (2013). *South African taxi hand signs: Documenting the history and significance of taxi hand signs through anthropology and art, including the invention of a tactile shape-language for blind people.* Unpublished doctoral thesis. Johannesburg, RSA: University of the Witwatersrand

World Health Organization. (2002). *Traditional medicine strategy 2002-2005.* Geneva, Switzerland: WHO. Retrieved from http://www.wpro.who.int/health_technology/book_who_traditional_medicine_strategy_2002_2005.pdf

World Health Organization. (2018). *Emergencies preparedness, response. Listeriosis - South Africa.* Retrieved from: http://www.who.int/csr/don/28-march-2018-listeriosis-south-africa/en/

Yu, D. (2012). Defining and measuring informal employment in South Africa. *Development Southern Africa, 29*(1), 157–175. http://doi.org/10.1080/0376835X.2012.645649

Zellweger, T. M., Nason, R. S., & Nordqvist, M. (2012). From longevity of firms to transgenerational entrepreneurship of families: Introducing family entrepreneurial orientation. *Family Business Review, 25*(2), 136–155. http://doi.org/10.1177/0894486511423531

Legislation

Boqwana, J. (2018). *In the High Court of South Africa, Western Cape Division, Cape Town. Case Number: 22419/2017*. Cape Town, RSA

Businesses Act 71 of 1991. RSA. http://www2.saflii.org/za/legis/consol_act.DEL/ba1991143.pdf

Children's Act 38 of 2005, as amended by *Children's Amendment Act 41 of 2007*. RSA.

City of Cape Town. 2007. *By-law relating to streets, public places and the prevention of noise nuisances, Province of Western Cape, Provincial Gazette, 6469*. Retrieved from https://indigo.openbylaws.org.za/api/za-cpt/act/by-law/2007/streets-public-places-noise-nuisances/eng.pdf

City of Cape Town. 2015. *Municipal planning by-law*. Retrieved from: https://www.westerncape.gov.za/eadp/files/basic-page/uploads/City%20of%20Cape%20Town.pdf

City of Johannesburg. 2017. *Draft land use scheme*. Johannesburg: City of Johannesburg

National Building Regulations and Building Standards Act, 1977, RSA, as amended by, *Standards Act 30 of 1982*; *National Building Regulations and Building Standards Amendment Act 36 of 1984*; *National Building Regulations and Building Standards Amendment Act 62 of 1989*; *National Building Regulations and Building Standards Amendment Act 49 of 1995*; and *Mine Health and Safety Act 29 of 1996*

National Small Business Act 102 of 1996, as amended by *Act 26 of 2003*. RSA

National Land Transport Act 5 of 2009. RSA

Office of the Premier of the Province of Western Cape. 2008. *Western Cape Liquor Act 4 of 2008*. . Western Cape, RSA

Spatial Planning and Land Use Management Act 16 of 2013. Government Gazette, 578 (36730/559). RSA

Tobacco Products Control Act 83 of 1993. RSA

Traditional Health Practitioners Act 22 of 2007. RSA

About the authors

Andrew Charman

Andrew trained as a sociologist and development specialist, studying at the University of Cape Town and Cambridge where he obtained a PhD degree. Andrew has worked as a researcher, a project manager and development practitioner on a range of projects across diverse settings in Southern Africa, including rural areas and townships. His interest in informal markets arose from his work in Malawi supporting smallholder producers. He then worked as a researcher and consultant, advising on development strategies and policies. In 2010, Andrew co-founded the Sustainable Livelihoods Foundation (SLF) (www.livelihoods.org.za) with the aim of contributing knowledge about how people were responding to development challenges, through conducting research, enabling participatory engagement and facilitating appropriate support. At SLF, he has led a series of projects to understand the policy and regulatory barriers impacting on micro-enterprises in South Africa's townships. Andrew has wide experience of using mixed-methods research and working with researchers from across disciplines to co-produce research that speaks to people's lived realities. As a development practitioner, Andrew seeks to translate research into interventions that can better serve people's needs, challenge unfair laws and hold policy-makers to account. He has published research on a range of subjects, including food security, informal sector businesses and the politics of informality.

Leif Petersen

Leif Petersen has worked for the last 15 years in the field of South Africa's township micro-enterprises and markets. As a co-founding director of the Sustainable Livelihoods Foundation NPC (SLF), he has presented a substantive body of academic, commercial and mainstream reporting and presentations on township economy markets, in particular market intelligence for sectors including Fast Moving Consumer Goods (FMCG) retailing, supply chain development, and market dynamics of grocery trading, liquor retailing, traditional medicine, and informal manufacturing. His PhD and Post-Doctoral work has focused on qualitative understanding of businesses and consumers of traditional medicines and food in the township context. Leif has worked for a large number of corporate, public sector and international clients and has considerable experience in studies of competition in informal business, and the identification and nature of trade of items such as counterfeit goods and contraband cigarettes. In 2018, Leif concluded a nationwide inquiry into competition in grocery retailing in township informal markets – interviewing over 1 180 township FMCG businesses in all nine provinces. He has strong interests in translating SLF's insights and interconnectedness with the township economy into interventions that impact practical livelihoods of communities. Most recently this included working in collaboration with South Africa's emerging arts community in the production of a concept album and documentary promoting township music entitled the 'State of the Nation'. Leif has over 30 academic publications and numerous book chapters to his credit, but this is the first book that he has co-authored.

Thireshen Govender

Thireshen Govender is an architect practising and teaching in Johannesburg. Having graduated from the University of Cape Town as an architect, he trained in local practices in Cape Town and Johannesburg. Through the awarding of a Chevening Scholarship, he further advanced his studies in Urban Design at The University College of London (Bartlett) in the United Kingdom. He travelled extensively, widely informed by a keen interest on how post-traumatic cities define themselves socially and spatially. In 2008, he founded UrbanWorks Architecture & Urbanism, a design-research studio, to deepen knowledge on post-apartheid spatial practices in order to develop innovative and responsive design strategies towards radical transformation in South African cities. The practice works across scales and disciplines to explore how space and design can productively play a role in urban transformation through carefully curated interventions.

Thireshen leads a design-research unit at the University of Johannesburg's Graduate School of Architecture. The unit investigates and documents the spatial consequence of post-apartheid socio-economic practices in architecture and urbanism. Through his practice and research, he broadcasts his findings through writing and public talks. His practice provides an experimental means to test findings and advance architectural knowledge production.

Index

Note: Page numbers in *italics* indicate illustrations.

research sites   20–30
  Browns Farm   20–21
  Delft South   21–22
  Eveline Street   29–30
  Imizamo Yethu   22–23
  Ivory Park   23–24
  KwaMashu   24–25
  maps   *4–5*
  Sweet Home Farm   25–26
  Tembisa   26–27
  Thabong   28–29
  Vrygrond   27–28

resistance by shebeeners   213–214

right to use land
  backyard dwellings   95, 98
  Harriet's land-banking   93–95
  introduction   78–80
  investment in property   93–98
  Jane's educare (case study)   85–87, *88*
  land banking   93–95
  land transactions   92
  land-use systems   80–84
  opportunities and constraints   84–93
  outlook   99
  Steve's spaza-takeaway-tavern (case
    study)   88–92
  upgrades to property   98
  Willi's property portfolio   95–97

Rosline's shebeen (case study)   211

route to market   189–190, 197, 201, 295

S

sedan taxis   137, 151, *153,* 159–162
  Eveline Street   167
  sedan taxi operator (case study)   161–162
  see also minibus taxis

services as social infrastructure
  introduction   240–241
  outlook   264–265
  see also educares; hair care; traditional healers

shebeen interior, photograph   *39*

shebeens   47, *49*
  access to   108
  architecture   299
  availability   65
  liquor regulation   195–198
  outlook   214–215

people-centred architecture   210–211
  spatial connections   *212*
  venue differentiation   206–211

shifts in business spatial dynamics   183–186

shopping-malls   11, 74, 186–188, 218–219, 294,
    296, 305, 307

skills acquisition   70–71

small-area census method   30–35

social and human capital   277–281

social institutions   277–282

socio-spatial methods   35–37

space matters   299–300

spatial dynamics of businesses, shifts   183–186

spatial economy of township transport   154–162

spatiality, six levels   10, 293

spatial ordering
  introduction   102
  micro-spatial influences   105–108
  neighbourhood economy   102–108
  outlook   120–121
  photovoice participatory approach   116–119
  see also infrastructure and architecture

spatial patterns   55–66

spatial transformations, Eveline Street (case
    study)   133–135

spaza shops   *48*
  Bheki's spaza (case study)   172–173
  in Delft South   173–177
  immigrant owners   173–176, 178
  introduction   170–171
  outlook   190–191
  shopping malls, supermarkets and
    wholesalers   186–190
  xenophobic attacks   173–175

Steve's spaza-takeaway-tavern (case study)   88–92

stokvels   283–284

strategic financial investment   71

street exhibitions   36–37

street participants in Eveline Street (case
    study)   142–146

street traders
  and municipal by-laws   50
  products for sale   50
  and social reciprocity   277